The WebGPU !

The WebGPU Sourcebook: High-Performance Graphics and Machine Learning in the Browser explains how to code web applications that access the client's graphics processor unit, or GPU. This makes it possible to render graphics in a browser at high speed and perform computationally intensive tasks such as machine learning. By taking advantage of WebGPU, web developers can harness the same performance available to desktop developers.

The first part of the book introduces WebGPU at a high level, without graphics theory or heavy math. The chapters in the second part are focused on graphical rendering and the rest of the book focuses on compute shaders.

This book walks through several examples of WebGPU usage. It also:

- Discusses the classes and functions defined in the WebGPU API and shows how they're used in practice.
- Explains the theory of graphical rendering and shows how to implement rendering inside a web application.
- Examines the theory of neural networks (machine learning) and shows how to create a web application that trains and executes a neural network.

Matthew Scarpino is a software developer at Purdue University. He has worked on many different types of programming projects, including web applications, graphical rendering, and high-performance computing. He received his Master's in Electrical Engineering in 2002, and has been a professional programmer and author ever since.

The WebGPU Sourcebook
High-Performance Graphics and Machine Learning in the Browser

Matthew Scarpino

CRC Press
Taylor & Francis Group
Boca Raton London New York

CRC Press is an imprint of the
Taylor & Francis Group, an **informa** business

First edition published 2025
by CRC Press
2385 NW Executive Center Drive, Suite 320, Boca Raton FL 33431

and by CRC Press
4 Park Square, Milton Park, Abingdon, Oxon, OX14 4RN

CRC Press is an imprint of Taylor & Francis Group, LLC

© 2025 Matthew Scarpino

ISBN: 978-1-032-72840-7 (hbk)
ISBN: 978-1-032-72667-0 (pbk)
ISBN: 978-1-003-42283-9 (ebk)

DOI: 10.1201/9781003422839

Typeset in Times
by KnowledgeWorks Global Ltd.

Contents

Preface

When I first heard about WebGPU, I wasn't particularly impressed. There hadn't been anything wrong with WebGL or WebGL 2.0, so I didn't see the need for another API. It seemed like tech companies were creating solutions to non-existent problems.

But the more I thought about it, the more interested I became. I remember when checking email in a browser was revolutionary, and I clearly remember when the idea of watching movies in the browser seemed absurd. Today, these activities are commonplace.

With each passing year, more and more applications are moving to the browser, and it's clear why this is the case. Everyone knows how to use a browser, and web applications don't require complex installation or uninstallation. Further, applications running inside a browser (usually) can't damage your system the way that applications running outside a browser can.

As I see it, the final hurdle to running applications in the browser is *performance*. I'd be happy to play a computer game in a browser if it ran with the same performance as a regular game. I'd also be content to use a modeling tool in the browser if it executed as quickly as outside-the-browser modeling applications.

Because WebGPU enables web applications to access the GPU, it's quite possible that this final hurdle may be overcome. As I learned more about the subject, I became impressed by how simple the API was. Unlike OpenGL, WebGPU doesn't require vertex buffer objects and vertex array objects. Unlike Vulkan, WebGPU doesn't require lengthy swapchain and surface configuration.

I'm thrilled to have the opportunity to present this fascinating subject, and I've split this book's content into three parts. The first part introduces WebGPU at a high level, without graphical rendering or computation. This part consists of Chapters 1 and 2, which presents the many JavaScript objects that applications need to create in order to access the GPU.

The chapters in the second part are focused on graphical rendering. This begins in Chapter 3, which presents the overall rendering process and introduces the types of objects that need to be created in a graphical application. Chapter 4 goes further and discusses the WebGPU Shading Language (WGSL), which is needed to code vertex and fragment shaders for graphical applications.

Chapter 5 presents two topics that are vitally important when creating three-dimensional scenes. The first involves creating uniform buffers, which store data that remains constant during the rendering process. The second topic is transformations, which make it possible to move vertices within a scene. Transformations are also necessary to define the overall shape of the scene, called the *viewing region*.

While Chapter 5 focuses on setting the positions of objects, Chapter 6 focuses on setting their colors. Lighting is the process of defining how the scene is illuminated and how the illumination reflects of the objects' surfaces. In addition, textures contain image data that can be accessed to assign pixels to the objects' surfaces. Chapter 7 explores a few advanced topics related to WebGPU, including debugging, stencil maps, and accessing video.

The third part of the book focuses on compute shaders. Chapter 8 shows how to code and execute a compute application, and explains the important topic of work groups and group-local memory. Chapter 9 shows how compute shaders can be used to implement machine learning. To be specific, it shows how to code a compute application that uses neural networks to classify data.

Chapter 10 explains how WebGPU makes it possible to process images and video. Chapter 11 shows how to perform operations on large matrices, which include transposition, multiplication, and factorization. Chapter 12 explains how WebGPU applications can filter audio at high speed using the Fast Fourier Transform (FFT).

Appendices A and B present topics that aren't discussed in the WebGPU standard, but may still be of interest to readers. Appendix A explains how to code WebGPU applications with TypeScript, which adds static typing and improved error checking. Appendix B discusses the fascinating topic of Google Dawn, which makes it possible to write WebGPU programs in C/C++.

Introduction

1

One of the most extraordinary developments in the field of high-performance computing is the use of graphics processing units (GPUs). Before 2010, none of the world's top supercomputers had GPUs. But in November 2010, China's Tianhe-1A supercomputer took the top spot on the TOP500, in large part because of its 7,168 GPUs. Since then, every Number 1 supercomputer has had thousands of CPUs and GPUs. As of November 2023, the top supercomputer in the world is the Frontier system, with 561,664 CPU cores and 36,992 GPU cores.

Graphics processors are loved by gamers and performance enthusiasts alike, but they can be difficult to program. GPU architecture is so different from CPU architecture that code needs to be restructured and rewritten. Besides that, choosing a programming toolset isn't easy:

- OpenGL and OpenCL haven't significantly progressed in years.
- CUDA only runs on Nvidia devices.
- Direct3D only runs on Windows systems.
- Metal only runs on macOS systems.
- Vulkan is monstrously complicated.

Another shortcoming of these toolsets is that none of them can run in a browser. Many developers may not see this as an issue, but as browsers become more powerful, users demand greater capabilities from their applications. Web applications that can harness the power of GPUs will succeed over applications that can't.

This is where WebGPU comes in. Web applications coded in WebGPU can take full advantage of the GPU on the client's system. This means they can perform high-quality graphical rendering and general-purpose GPU (GPGPU) computing on Windows, Linux, and macOS systems.

The overall goal of this book is to explain how to code graphical and computational applications with WebGPU. The goal of this chapter is more modest—to provide a basic overview of WebGPU development. I'll start by discussing the developments that led to WebGPU's creation, and then I'll provide a top-level view of how WebGPU applications are coded.

DOI: 10.1201/9781003422839-1

THE EVOLUTION OF WebGPU

Whenever I start working with a new technology, I like to learn about its history. Why was it created? Who created it? What technological developments led to its release?

To answer these questions, this section provides a brief overview of the events and technologies that led to the creation of WebGPU. Table 1.1 summarizes the timeline.

This list may seem bewildering, but once you understand the technologies underlying WebGPU, you'll better understand why it's such a big deal. You'll also grasp the trends that will steer its future development.

IRIS GL, OpenGL, and Direct3D

In the late 1990s, I watched in fascination as a Silicon Valley salesman demonstrated an IRIS workstation. Unlike other computers, this workstation could display three-dimensional objects using lighting and shadow effects that looked breathtakingly real. I'd never seen anything like it before, and it made the Windows 95 user interface look archaic.

The IRIS was developed by a company named Silicon Graphics, Inc. (SGI), which had developed special graphics hardware called the Geometry Engine. They'd also developed a special programming language for building graphical applications called the IRIS Graphics Language, or IRIS GL.

TABLE 1.1   Milestones in the evolution of WebGPU

YEAR	EVENT
1992	Silicon Graphics, Inc. (SGI) releases the first specification for the Open Graphics Language (OpenGL 1.0)
1995	Microsoft releases DirectX to support multimedia on Windows. Includes a rendering toolset named Direct3D.
2003	First release of OpenGL for embedded systems (OpenGL ES)
2004	OpenGL 2.0 supports executing programs called *shaders* directly on the GPU—must be written in the OpenGL Shading Language (GLSL)
2011	WebGL 1.0 released, based on OpenGL ES 2.0
2014	Apple releases Metal, a toolset for 3-D development on iOS/macOS systems
2016	The Khronos Groups releases the Vulkan 1.0 specification
2017	WebGL 2.0 released, based on OpenGL ES 3.0
2017	Apple proposes WebGPU based on Metal, and Mozilla proposes API based on Vulkan
2021	First working draft (WD) of WebGPU presented by the World Wide Web Consortium (W3C)
2024	WebGPU can be accessed in nearly all major browsers, including Chrome, Firefox, and Safari

As it turned out, SGI's workstations, which cost many tens of thousands of dollars, weren't as attractive to consumers as graphics cards, which could be purchased for hundreds of dollars. Today, SGI's hardware is hard to find outside of a museum. But IRIS GL became widely popular after SGI released it as an open-source API. Their new name for the rendering API was *OpenGL*.

For many years, OpenGL was the only toolset for building applications that display 3-D graphics. The specification was free for all, and changes were managed by the OpenGL Architecture Review Board (ARB). As graphics cards became more powerful, OpenGL expanded to take advantage of the new capabilities.

In 2004, OpenGL 2.0 was released. The most important change was the ability to code special programs called *shaders*. Shaders had to be written in the OpenGL Shader Language (GLSL), and unlike regular code, they could execute on the GPU and access its resources. Shaders are a *big deal*, and a large part of this book explains how to write shaders with the WebGPU Shading Language (WGSL).

Seeking to expand its support for multimedia, Microsoft released the DirectX toolset for running games and displaying video on Windows. This included a graphics development API called Direct3D. Direct3D provided many of the same capabilities as OpenGL, including a shader language called the High Level Shading Language (HLSL).

As the years went on, Direct3D and OpenGL competed to provide developers with high-performance graphical rendering.

OpenGL ES, WebGL, and WebGL2

Taking advantage of OpenGL's popularity, the Khronos Group released a version of OpenGL called OpenGL ES (Embedded Systems). This is the most common rendering API on all Android devices and early iOS devices. OpenGL ES is essentially a subset of OpenGL, and though it provides access to most OpenGL features, including shader execution, it doesn't allow access to advanced capabilities.

In 2011, the Khronos Group released WebGL 1.0, which was based on OpenGL ES 2.0. This allowed JavaScript developers to access the same capabilities as OpenGL developers and execute shaders on the client's GPU. In 2017, the Khronos Group released WebGL 2.0, which was based on OpenGL ES 3.0.

WebGL 2.0 became moderately popular, and in 2022, it was supported by all major browsers. But once Metal and Vulkan became prominent, interest in technologies based on OpenGL waned.

Metal

Apple has a long history of following its own path, regardless of industry trends. From its proprietary software tools to its proprietary electrical connectors, Apple's leadership prefers independence over interoperability.

Therefore, it came as no surprise that Apple developed its own toolset for developing graphical applications. Apple released Metal 1.0 in 2014, and developers can access the API using Swift, Objective-C, or C++. According to its main site, Metal provides "a low-overhead API, rich shading language, tight integration between graphics and compute, and an unparalleled suite of GPU profiling and debugging tools."

Vulkan

Graphics programmers are obsessed with performance, especially when it comes to game development. While OpenGL runs well on many types of hardware, developers demanded more control over the rendering process. In particular, they wanted to control exactly how and when data objects are transferred from the CPU to the GPU. To see what I mean, run an Internet search for *AZDO*, which stands for *Approaching Zero Driver Overhead*.

To meet this demand, the Khronos Group released Vulkan 1.0 in 2016. Vulkan provides access to such low-level rendering elements as swapchains, surfaces, and descriptor sets. In addition, Vulkan applications can execute shaders written in a new language called Standard Portable Intermediate Representation, or *SPIR*. The current version is called SPIR-V.

The good news is that Vulkan met its goal of providing developers with high-efficiency, high-performance rendering. The bad news is that writing a non-trivial application with Vulkan requires a ridiculous amount of code.

I'll support this with a personal anecdote. In late 2017, I wrote a Vulkan application that performed render-to-texture operations. But when I ran the application, I got a segmentation fault. I used Vulkan's debug layer as best I could, but I couldn't figure out if the issue was with my code or the device driver. I would have posted my problem online, but my simple application had *several thousands of lines of code*, and I had no idea where the problem was.

To the best of my knowledge, the Khronos Group has never formally stated that Vulkan is OpenGL's replacement. However, the latest version of OpenGL (4.6) is seven years old, and the latest version of Vulkan (1.3.270) was released less than a month ago.

WebGPU

In 2017, the Khronos Group started to explore possibilities for the next generation of browser-based graphics, which they called WebGL Next. Apple's developers saw the potential of accessing the GPU in web applications, and they realized that creating a proprietary technology would be pointless.

With this in mind, Apple proposed an API named *WebGPU* based on their Metal language. The Mozilla Foundation, which leads the development of the free Firefox browser, proposed a similar API based on Vulkan. In time, the WebGPU API has incorporated features of Vulkan, Metal, and Direct3D 12.

Google has taken the lead with WebGPU integration, and the latest versions of Chrome (for Windows and macOS systems) enable WebGPU by default. Microsoft's

Edge browser supports WebGPU, and Firefox users can enable WebGPU by setting the dom.webgpu.enabled flag.

OVERVIEW OF WebGPU DEVELOPMENT

Now that you understand what WebGPU is, I'd like to provide a simple introduction to WebGPU development. In general, the code that makes up a WebGPU application is about 90% JavaScript and 10% WebGPU Shader Language (WGSL). To be more specific, coding a non-trivial WebGPU application requires three steps:

1. Create the JavaScript objects needed to access the GPU.
2. Create the JavaScript objects containing data and instructions to be processed by the GPU.
3. Send the data and instructions to the GPU for execution.

Steps 1 and 2 rely on JavaScript, and if you're already familiar with the language, then most of the API won't present any difficulty—you simply create objects and call their methods. But there are a *lot* of objects that need to be created, and it can be difficult to keep track of them. Thankfully, once you've coded a working application, it's straightforward to use similar code in other applications.

Step 3 is the hard part. To execute code on a GPU, you need to write special programs (*shaders*) in the WebGPU Shader Language (WGSL). WGSL is like the C programming language, but it's stripped down to focus on crunching numbers. That is, you won't need string-handling functions and you probably won't use a lot of pointers. The goal is to process numbers at high speed, and the better you understand linear algebra, the easier you'll find it to write shaders.

There are two main types of WebGPU applications:

- *graphical applications* display graphics in an HTML canvas
- *compute applications* perform a computational task, such as operating on matrices or analyzing data with machine learning

The following discussion explores the process of coding both types of applications.

Graphical Application Development

At a high level, the purpose of a graphical WebGPU application is to define the content of an HTML canvas. To be precise, the goal is to transform a three-dimensional world into a two-dimensional scene, and display the scene in the canvas. This transformation process is called *rendering*.

To implement rendering in WebGPU, an application needs to create several objects in JavaScript, including a `GPURenderPassEncoder` and a `GPURenderPipeline`. The application also needs to create special objects that contain the data needed by the GPU to define the graphical scene.

In addition to providing data, the application needs to deliver instructions to the GPU that tell it how to position the scene's objects and compute the objects' colors. These instructions must be provided in two programs:

- vertex shader—tells the GPU where to place objects in the scene
- fragment shader—tells the GPU what colors and depths to assign to the scene's fragments

These programs must be written in WGSL, and the following code shows what a simple vertex shader looks like:

```
@group(0) @binding(0) var<uniform> rotMat: mat4x4f;

@vertex
fn vertexMain(@location(0) coords: vec2f) ->
@builtin(position) vec4f {
    return rotMat * vec4f(coords, 0.0, 1.0);
}
```

This may look scary, but once you become acquainted with WGSL's data types (such as `mat4x4f` and `vec4f`) and attributes (such as `@vertex` and `@builtin`), you'll find this code to be straightforward. Chapter 4 discusses WGSL's features in glorious detail.

Compute Application Development

In addition to graphical rendering, WebGPU applications can tell the GPU to crunch numbers. Throughout this book, we'll call these applications *compute applications.* Popular uses of compute applications include machine learning, image processing, frequency analysis, and matrix operations.

Compute applications are usually simpler to code than graphical applications. There are fewer JavaScript objects to be created, and there's no need to access a canvas. Instead of being concerned with vertex buffers, an application can store its data in storage buffers, which are easier to work with.

In addition, compute applications don't require vertex shaders and fragment shaders, as graphical applications do. Only one type of shader is needed—the *compute shader.* Like vertex shaders and fragment shaders, compute shaders are written in WGSL. The following code shows what a basic compute shader looks like:

```
@binding(0) @group(0) var<storage, read_write> data :
array<f32, 32>;

@compute @workgroup_size(4)
fn computeMain(
    @builtin(global_invocation_id) id : vec3<u32>,
    @builtin(workgroup_id) wg_id : vec3<u32>,
    @builtin(local_invocation_id) local_id : vec3<u32>)
{
    data[id.x] = f32(wg_id.x) * data[id.x] + f32(local_id.x);
}
```

One major difference between compute applications and graphical applications is that a compute application can organize the GPU's processing into *work groups*. The elements of a work group, called *invocations*, can access memory specifically allocated for their group. This enables the group's invocations to work together and enables the shader to synchronize their operation.

EXAMPLE CODE

The best way to learn WebGPU is to get your hands dirty and wrestle with working code. For this reason, every chapter and appendix of this book has at least one example application. The code is freely available from my Github page at https://github.com/mattscar/webgpu_book.

Every project folder contains a file named index.html and a JavaScript file (*.js). index.html defines the structure of the web page, and the JavaScript file contains code to be executed when the page is opened. You can launch many of the applications simply by opening the HTML file (index.html) in a browser.

Unfortunately, many applications need to access external files. For these applications, you'll get an error if you open index.html in a browser. One way to get around this is to launch a local HTTP server and serve the page locally. The Node ecosystem provides the http-server package for this purpose, and Appendix A explains how to install Node and the http-server package.

SUMMARY

This chapter has introduced the topic of WebGPU, from its history to its current adoption. Simply put, WebGPU makes it possible for web applications to access the client's

GPU. By accessing the GPU, applications can render graphics and crunch numbers at high speed. Applications of the first type are called graphical applications, and applications of the second type are called compute applications.

This book explains how to code graphical and compute applications using WebGPU. The theory and practice aren't easy to grasp, but if you follow best practices, the performance gains can be extraordinary. With great power comes great complexity...

Fundamental Objects

2

The first step in WebGPU development is to create and configure the JavaScript objects needed for WebGPU operation. There are a lot of objects and methods to learn about, and it can be hard to keep track of them all. It helps to remember the overall goal of WebGPU—to send *commands* to the GPU. Some commands tell the device to render graphics, some tell the device to perform computational tasks, and some tell the device to perform memory operations.

To be precise, the goal of WebGPU is to submit objects called *command buffers* to the queue associated with the client's GPU. This requires at least six steps:

1. Access the browser's Navigator to see if WebGPU is supported.
2. If WebGPU is supported, use the Navigator to obtain a GPUAdapter.
3. Use the GPUAdapter to obtain a GPUDevice.
4. Use the GPUDevice to create a GPUCommandEncoder.
5. Configure the encoder to record commands into a buffer.
6. Submit the command buffer to the GPUQueue associated with the GPUDevice.

Most of these steps can be performed with a few lines of code. But Step 5 is more complicated than the others. This is because configuring commands requires creating multiple objects and calling their methods.

If you want to use the GPU to crunch numbers, no further steps are necessary. But if you want to render graphics, you'll need to associate the GPUDevice with a canvas. Creating the association requires three additional steps:

1. Access the Canvas element in the HTML document.
2. Obtain a GPUCanvasContext from the Canvas element.
3. Configure the GPUCanvasContext with the GPUDevice and canvas format.

Once the GPUDevice is associated with a Canvas, an application can display graphics on the canvas by calling the GPUDevice's methods. Chapter 3 will introduce the lengthy but fascinating discussion of rendering graphics with WebGPU.

This chapter explores the data structures required for these steps. The first section looks at the Navigator object, followed by the GPUAdapter, GPUDevice, Canvas, and GPUCanvasContext. Once you understand how these classes work together, you'll have a better understanding of how WebGPU operates and you'll be able to deal with any errors that arise.

DOI: 10.1201/9781003422839-2

THE NAVIGATOR

Every modern browser provides a `Navigator` object whose properties contain information about the browser's capabilities. For example, the `clipboard` property makes it possible to read the system clipboard, the `connection` property checks the network connection, and the `deviceMemory` property identifies how much memory is available.

If the browser supports WebGPU, the `Navigator` object will have another property named `gpu`. The following code shows how an application can check for this property:

```
// Check if the browser supports WebGPU
if (!navigator.gpu) {
    throw new Error("WebGPU not supported.");
}
```

If present, the `gpu` property provides two important methods:

- `requestAdapter()`—returns a `Promise` that is fulfilled with a `GPUAdapter`
- `getPreferredCanvasFormat()`—returns a string identifying the best format for graphics in the browser's canvas

These methods play important roles in WebGPU applications. I'll discuss both of them later in this chapter.

PROMISES AND GPUAdapters

Just because the client's browser supports WebGPU doesn't mean the client's hardware supports WebGPU rendering and computation. To ensure that these capabilities are available, an application needs to obtain a `GPUAdapter` by calling the `requestAdapter` method of the `Navigator`'s `gpu` property.

The `requestAdapter` method doesn't provide a `GPUAdapter` directly. Instead, it returns a `Promise`. A `Promise` is a data structure that represents an operation that hasn't been completed yet but is expected to provide a result. The `Promise` returned by `requestAdapter` represents the operation of trying to acquire a `GPUAdapter` on the client's system.

Every `Promise` is in one of three states:

- pending—The promise hasn't produced a result because the operation hasn't been completed.
- fulfillment—The operation has been completed and the promise has provided the result. When a promise enters the fulfillment state, we say that it has been fulfilled.

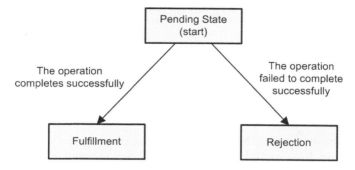

FIGURE 2.1   Execution states of a promise.

- rejection—The operation encountered an error, and no result is available. When a promise enters the rejection state, we say that it has been rejected.

Figure 2.1 illustrates how these states are related.

A `Promise` has several useful methods and properties, but in this book, we'll access `Promises` using the `await` operator. When `await` precedes a pending `Promise`, the application will wait until the `Promise` is fulfilled or rejected. The following code shows how `await` can be used with `requestAdapter`:

```
// Access the GPU adapter
const adapter = await navigator.gpu.requestAdapter();
if (!adapter) {
    throw new Error("No appropriate GPUAdapter found.");
}
```

If the `await` operator wasn't present, `adapter` would be set equal to a `Promise`. But because `await` is present, `adapter` will be set equal to a `GPUAdapter` object if the `Promise` is fulfilled. If not, the `adapter` variable will be set to null.

After an application successfully accesses a `GPUAdapter`, it can access information about the user's rendering and computational capabilities by calling the adapter's `requestAdapterInfo` method. This returns a `Promise` that provides a `GPUAdapterInfo` upon fulfillment. The `GPUAdapterInfo` has four properties, and Table 2.1 lists each of them.

The following code shows how an application can access information about the user's GPU adapter and display it in the console.

```
// Access information about the GPU adapter
const info = await adapter.requestAdapterInfo();
if(info) {
    console.log("Vendor: " + info.vendor);
    console.log("Architecture: " + info.architecture);
    console.log("Device: " + info.device);
    console.log("Description: " + info.description);
}
```

TABLE 2.1   Properties of the `GPUAdapterInfo` (read-only)

PROPERTY	TYPE	DESCRIPTION
vendor	String	Company that produced the GPU (nvidia, amd, intel)
device	String	The device's name
architecture	String	The device's architecture
description	String	Description of the device

This information can be helpful when an application needs to execute different types of code on different GPUs. The application may use workarounds if the target GPU can't execute the code properly.

For additional information, applications can access two helpful properties of a `GPUAdapter`:

- `features`—a `GPUSupportedFeatures` object that identifies the features supported by the GPU
- `limits`—a `GPUSupportedLimits` object that identifies the GPU's maximum/minimum operating parameters

The `features` property is helpful when an application needs to know about the GPU's capabilities. Table 2.2 lists the different features that can be checked and provides a description of each.

An example will demonstrate how these capabilities can be accessed. Suppose an application needs to know if the client's GPU supports control of depth clipping. It could use code like the following:

```
// Check if the client supports the depth clip control feature
if (adapter.features.has("depth-clip-control")) {
    console.log("Supported");
} else {
    console.log("Unsupported");
}
```

If you want to print all the features available on the system, you can use the following code:

```
// Display all of the supported features
adapter.features.forEach((value) => {
    console.log(value);
});
```

The `limits` property is helpful when an application needs to know the maximum parameters for a given capability. For example, the following code identifies the maximum number of vertex buffers an application can create:

```
const maxBuffers = adapter.limits.maxVertexBuffers;
```

TABLE 2.2   Device features provided by `GPUAdapter`

FEATURE ID	*DESCRIPTION*
`depth-clip-control`	Applications can use OpenGL's depth range [−1, 1] instead of the default range, [0, 1]
`depth32float-stencil8`	Elements in depth/stencil buffers can have 32-bit depth values and 8-bit stencil values
`texture-compression-bc`	Applications can use textures compressed with Block Compression (BC)
`texture-compression-etc2`	Applications can use textures compressed with Ericsson Texture Compression 2 (ETC2)
`texture-compression-astc`	Applications can use textures compressed with Adaptable Scalable Texture Compression (ASTC)
`timestamp-query`	Applications can create query sets to access timestamps
`indirect-first-instance`	Applications can set the firstInstance argument of indirect draw calls to a value greater than 0
`shader-f16`	Shaders can access half-precision (16-bit) floating-point values
`rg11b10ufloat-renderable`	Applications can use rg11b10ufloat as a texture format
`bgra8unorm-storage`	Applications can create storage buffers whose data is formatted according to bgra8unorm
`float32-filterable`	The GPU can smooth textures by filtering 32-bit floating-point values

The most important role of a `GPUAdapter` is to provide access to a `GPUDevice`. This is made possible by the `requestDevice` method, which returns a `Promise` that provides a `GPUDevice` upon fulfillment. The following code shows how this can be used:

```
// Access the GPU
const device = await adapter.requestDevice();
```

Once an application has accessed the `GPUDevice`, it can perform several operations needed for WebGPU processing. The following section discusses this in detail.

GPUDevice

The `GPUDevice` serves as a logical connection to the client's GPU, and it plays a central role in WebGPU development. Listed in Table 2.3, its methods create objects that make it possible to perform computational tasks and graphical operations.

TABLE 2.3   `GPUDevice` Methods

METHOD	*DESCRIPTION*
`createBindGroup()`	Identifies a set of resources to be bound together
`createBindGroupLayout()`	Identifies the structure and purpose of related resources
`createBuffer()`	Returns a GPUBuffer that can be used to store raw data
`createCommandEncoder()`	Creates an object that prepares and packages commands for execution
`createComputePipeline()`	Creates a pipeline for commands that perform computation
`createComputePipelineAsync()`	Asynchronously creates a pipeline for commands that perform computation
`createPipelineLayout()`	Defines the structure and purpose of each buffer created by the device
`createQuerySet()`	Creates a query set that can be used to run queries
`createRenderBundleEncoder()`	Creates a special encoder that records commands in bundles
`createRenderPipeline()`	Creates a pipeline for commands that render graphics
`createRenderPipelineAsync()`	Asynchronously creates a pipeline for commands that render graphics
`createSampler()`	Creates a sampler, which is used to extract data from textures
`createShaderModule()`	Creates an object that stores code and data related to the application's shaders
`createTexture()`	Creates a resource on the GPU to store pixel data for images
`destroy()`	Destroy the logical connection to the client's GPU
`importExternalTexture()`	Converts a video snapshot into a texture
`popErrorScope()`	Pops an error scope from the stack or is null if no error has occurred
`pushErrorScope()`	Pushes a new error scope onto the stack, which makes it possible to catch errors of a given type

These methods are important in WebGPU development, but most are too complicated to be discussed here. For this reason, I'll introduce them in later chapters as they become needed. For example, the `createTexture` and `createSampler` methods are related to textures, so a proper introduction will have to wait until Chapter 6.

GPUCommandEncoder

One of the most important methods of GPUDevice is createCommandEncoder, which returns a GPUCommandEncoder. This object is responsible for creating and storing commands that will be sent to the GPU. The following code shows how this can be created:

```
// Create a command encoder
encoder = device.createCommandEncoder();
```

Once the object has been created, the methods of GPUCommandEncoder make it possible to define operations that will be sent to the device for processing. Table 2.4 lists each of these methods.

In general, the first three methods are the most important. The first, beginRenderPass, returns a GPURenderPassEncoder that will define graphical operations for the GPU. It will take several chapters to fully explore the capabilities of a GPURenderPassEncoder.

TABLE 2.4 GPUCommandEncoder Methods

METHOD	*DESCRIPTION*
beginRenderPass()	Starts encoding a render pass to perform graphical rendering
beginComputePass()	Starts encoding a compute pass to perform computational tasks
finish()	Returns a command buffer containing the encoder's commands in sequence
clearBuffer()	Encodes a command that fills a buffer with zeros
copyBufferToBuffer()	Encodes a command that copies data from one buffer to another
copyBufferToTexture()	Encodes a command that copies data from a buffer to a texture
copyTextureToBuffer()	Encodes a command that copies data from a buffer to a texture
copyTextureToTexture()	Encodes a command that copies data from one texture to another
insertDebugMarker()	Inserts a marker into the command sequence that can be used for debugging
pushDebugGroup()	Starts a debug group with a given label
popDebugGroup()	Ends a debug group
resolveQuerySet()	Encodes a command that writes the results of a query set to a buffer
writeTimestamp()	Encodes a command that writes a timestamp to a query set

The second method in the table, `beginComputePass`, returns a `GPUComputePassEncoder`. The fields of this object store information that tells the GPU how to execute computational tasks. Starting in Chapter 8, I'll explain how this can be used to perform operations related to math, machine learning, and image processing.

The last method, `finish`, is required in every non-trivial WebGPU application. It converts the encoder's data into a `GPUCommandBuffer` containing one or more commands for the GPU. Once the application sends this buffer to the device's queue, the GPU will begin executing the commands.

GPUQueue

The `GPUDevice` has an important property named `queue`, which provides access to a `GPUQueue`. To perform GPU operations, an application needs to call the methods of the `GPUQueue`, which include the following three:

- `writeBuffer`—updates data in a buffer object on the GPU
- `writeTexture`—updates data in a texture object on the GPU
- `submit`—tells the GPU to perform one or more commands

The `submit` method is particularly important because it tells the GPU what tasks to execute (graphical rendering or general-purpose computation). To be specific, `submit` accepts the commands created by the `GPUCommandEncoder` discussed earlier. Once this is called, the GPU will start executing commands in the buffer.

After calling `submit`, an application can monitor the execution of the queue's commands by calling `onSubmittedWorkDone`. This returns a `Promise` that resolves after the queue finishes its processing tasks.

CANVAS ELEMENT

As its name implies, a canvas is a surface for displaying graphics. When WebGPU performs rendering operations, the resulting graphics are displayed inside a canvas element. Therefore, three steps are needed when using WebGPU for graphics:

1. Create a canvas element in the HTML document.
2. Access the canvas in JavaScript.
3. Obtain a context for the canvas and configure its appearance.

Canvas is one of the newer elements to be added to HTML, and it was first supported by Apple's Safari browser in 2004. It can display different kinds of graphical content, but in HTML, the <canvas> tag is rather boring. A web page can set its dimensions (width and height) and global attributes like id and hidden. But besides that, HTML doesn't provide any special attributes.

The following markup defines a 400-by-200 canvas whose ID is set to mycanvas:

```
<!-- Create a canvas in an HTML page -->
<canvas id="mycanvas" width="400" height="200"></canvas>
```

By default, a canvas appears in the web page as a blank rectangle. To set its content, an application needs to access the element in JavaScript, and this is usually accomplished by calling a method of the Document object. Canvas elements are represented by HTMLCanvasElements in JavaScript, and an application can access the corresponding element through its type (document.querySelector) or through its ID (document.getElementById).

For example, if a canvas element has been defined in HTML with an ID of mycanvas, it can be accessed in JavaScript with either of the following lines of code:

```
// Access the canvas element by type
const canvas = document.querySelector("canvas");

// Access the canvas element by ID
const canvas = document.getElementById("mycanvas");
```

In both cases, the canvas variable is set to an HTMLCanvasElement, which provides several methods that make it possible to set the canvas's content. Table 2.5 lists the five instance methods of HTMLCanvasElement.

Of these, only the first needs to be called in WebGPU graphical applications. getContext returns a context object that enables an application to define the canvas's graphics.

TABLE 2.5 Methods of HTMLCanvasElement

METHOD	DESCRIPTION
getContext(type)	Returns a drawing context for the canvas of the given type
captureStream()	Provides a real-time video capture of the canvas's surface
toDataURL()	Returns a URL containing a representation of the canvas's image
toBlob()	Returns a Blob containing the canvas's image
transferControlToOffscreen()	Transfers control to an OffscreenCanvas object

CANVAS CONTEXT

WebGPU is just one of many mechanisms for setting the content of a canvas. An application can also use WebGL, bitmap rendering, or simple two-dimensional drawing. To identify how the canvas's graphics will be set, an application needs to call getContext with the appropriate identifier.

This book focuses on WebGPU, so our applications will call getContext with the webgpu identifier. To demonstrate, the following code accesses the HTMLCanvasElement corresponding to the canvas whose ID is mycanvas. Then it calls getContext to acquire a context that can be used for WebGPU rendering:

```
// Access the canvas element by its ID
const canvas = document.getElementById("mycanvas");

// Obtain a WebGPU context for the canvas
const context = canvas.getContext("webgpu");
```

Because the context's type is set to webgpu, the object returned by getContext is a GPUCanvasContext. This provides an important method named configure, which accepts an object that controls the behavior of the rendering context. This object can define up to six properties, and Table 2.6 lists each of them.

Most of these properties relate to textures, which will be discussed at length in Chapter 6. The first two properties are the most important. The first, device, should be set to the GPUDevice discussed earlier. This is acquired through the GPUAdapter and represents the GPU on the client system.

The second property, usage, deserves more explanation. Different computers support different formats for displaying textures. The usage field tells WebGPU what texture format it should use to present the canvas's content.

You probably won't know what texture format to use in advance. Thankfully, you can use the getPreferredCanvasFormat method of the Navigator's gpu property.

TABLE 2.6   Canvas context properties

PROPERTY	DESCRIPTION
device	The GPUDevice that controls the canvas
usage	Identifies how acquired textures will be used
alphaMode	Controls transparency and opacity
colorSpace	Color format of acquired textures
format	Pixel format of acquired textures
viewFormats	Array of formats for acquired textures

This examines the user's system and returns a string identifying the optimal format of texture pixels. It returns one of two values:

- rgba8unorm—Each pixel contains four 8-bit values identifying red, green, blue, and alpha, and each value ranges from 0 to 255
- bgra8unorm—Each pixel contains four 8-bit values identifying blue, green, red, and alpha, and each value ranges from 0 to 255

The best way to understand how these objects work together is to see how they're used in practice. The following example accesses a canvas by its ID, obtains a WebGPU context for the canvas, and configures the context with the system's preferred canvas format.

```
// Obtain a canvas defined in HTML
const canvas = document.getElementById("mycanvas");

// Access a WebGPU context for the canvas
const context = canvas.getContext("webgpu");

// Get the optimal pixel format for textures
const canvasFormat = navigator.gpu.getPreferredCanvasFormat();

// Configure the context with the device and format
context.configure({
    device: device,
    format: canvasFormat,
});
```

After this code executes, rendering operations from the GPUDevice will generate graphics that are displayed in the associated context. Chapter 3 begins the discussion of creating graphics with WebGPU.

EXAMPLE APPLICATION—CREATING WebGPU OBJECTS

If you open the Ch02_ObjectCreation folder in the example code and load index.html in a browser, the GPU won't perform any graphical rendering or computation. Instead, it will execute the code in ch02_objectcreation.js, which creates five central objects needed for WebGPU rendering:

1. GPUAdapter—adapter for the client's GPU
2. GPUDevice—represents the client's GPU

WebGPU supported

GPUAdapter found

GPUDevice created

GPUCommandEncoder created

Accessed canvas in page

Obtained WebGPU context for canvas

FIGURE 2.2   The Ch02_ObjectCreation application.

3. GPUCommandEncoder—encodes operations into commands for the GPU
4. HTMLCanvasElement—represents a canvas in the page
5. GPUCanvasContext—a context for rendering graphics on the canvas

As each object is created, the code displays a message on a page. On my system, the result is illustrated in Figure 2.2.

The following code listing presents the content of index.html, which is easy to understand. The web page displays a title for the project, creates a canvas element, and loads the script from ch02_objectcreation.js.

```html
<html>
  <body>

  <h1>Ch02_ObjectCreation</h1>

  <!-- Create the canvas -->
  <canvas id="canvas_example" width="400" height="200"></canvas>

  <!-- Load JavaScript from file -->
  <script src="ch02_objectcreation.js"></script>

  </body>
</html>
```

The next code listing presents the content of ch02_objectcreation.js, which is loaded and executed by index.html. This code checks for WebGPU support and then creates the objects needed for WebGPU rendering.

```
// Create top-level asynchronous function
async function runExample() {

var msg_array = ["<h1>Ch02_ObjectCreation</h1>"];

// Check if WebGPU is supported
if (!navigator.gpu) {
    throw new Error("WebGPU not supported");
} else {
    msg_array.push("WebGPU supported");
}

// Access the GPUAdapter
const adapter = await navigator.gpu.requestAdapter();
if (!adapter) {
    throw new Error("No GPUAdapter found");
} else {
    msg_array.push("GPUAdapter found");
}

// Access the GPU
const device = await adapter.requestDevice();
if (!device) {
    throw new Error("Failed to create a GPUDevice");
} else {
    msg_array.push("GPUDevice created");
}

// Create a command encoder
encoder = device.createCommandEncoder();
if (!encoder) {
    throw new Error("Failed to create a GPUCommandEncoder");
} else {
    msg_array.push("GPUCommandEncoder created");
}

// Access the canvas
const canvas = document.getElementById("canvas_example");
if (!canvas) {
    throw new Error("Could not access canvas in page");
} else {
    msg_array.push("Accessed canvas in page");
}

// Obtain a WebGPU context for the canvas
const context = canvas.getContext("webgpu");
```

```
if (!context) {
    throw new Error("Could not obtain WebGPU context for
canvas");
} else {
    msg_array.push("Obtained WebGPU context for canvas");
}

// Get the best pixel format
const canvasFormat = navigator.gpu.
getPreferredCanvasFormat();

// Configure the context with the device and format
context.configure({
    device: device,
    format: canvasFormat,
});

// Display messages
for (var i = 0; i < msg_array.length; i++) {
    document.write(msg_array[i] + "<br /><br />");
}
}

// Run example function
runExample();
```

This code starts by creating an array of strings. As each object is created, a new string is added to the array. For example, new strings are added if GPU support is detected and if the GPUAdapter and GPUDevice are created successfully.

The code is contained in an asynchronous method named runExample. This method is necessary because JavaScript will only execute await at the top level. After the runExample method is defined, the last line of the script invokes it.

In later chapters, example applications will use similar code to create WebGPU objects. For this reason, it's a good idea to examine the code in ch02_objectcreation.js until you're comfortable with it.

SUMMARY

This chapter has presented the different objects that need to be created by WebGPU applications. The GPUAdapter serves as an adapter for the GPU, the GPUDevice serves as a logical connection to the device, and a GPUCommandEncoder packages commands into a buffer that can be submitted to a GPUQueue. Once the queue receives the commands, the GPU will start executing them.

If the application uses WebGPU for rendering, it will need to create a canvas element in HTML and then access it using JavaScript. Then the application needs to obtain a WebGPU canvas for the device and associate it with the GPUDevice. Once this association is made, WebGPU graphical rendering will be displayed on the canvas.

The next chapter further explores the process of developing graphical applications. It starts with a theoretical discussion of graphical rendering and then looks at the objects needed for WebGPU rendering. These include the render pass encoder and the render pipeline.

Rendering Graphics

3

In this chapter, we'll take our first steps into the fascinating world of graphical rendering with WebGPU. As with the preceding chapter, a large part of the coding process involves creating and configuring objects in JavaScript. In particular, most of our time will be spent exploring two objects: the `GPURenderPassEncoder` and the `GPURenderPipeline`.

But before we delve into the technical details, I'd like to provide a brief overview of the graphical rendering. The process is fundamentally similar in WebGPU, OpenGL, and Direct3D. An application executes a sequence of stages that make up the *rendering pipeline*, and this chapter begins by discussing this pipeline.

A GENTLE INTRODUCTION TO GRAPHICAL RENDERING

The goal of graphical rendering is to convert points in three-dimensional space into pixels on a two-dimensional screen. The points in space are called *vertices*, and at minimum, an application needs to specify where each vertex is located. In addition, an application can provide information such as the vertex's color, texture coordinates, and normal vector components. This per-vertex data is called *attribute data*.

Just as products are manufactured in stations of an assembly line, the steps needed to produce pixels form a *rendering pipeline*. In the early days of programming, these pipelines were always *fixed*—after the CPU sends vertex data to the GPU, the application has no control over the rendering process.

Today, we have *programmable* pipelines. In these pipelines, certain stages can be customized with special code that executes on the GPU. Figure 3.1 illustrates a basic programmable pipeline, with the programmable stages shaded in gray.

The special programs executed in the programmable stages are called *shaders*. WebGPU supports three types of shaders: vertex shaders, fragment shaders, and compute shaders. Vertex shaders and fragment shaders are used in graphical applications, while compute shaders are used in compute applications. All of these shaders must be written in the WebGPU Shading Language (WGSL), which Chapter 4 discusses in detail.

DOI: 10.1201/9781003422839-3

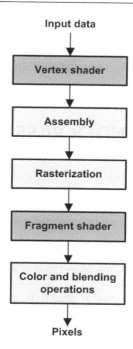

FIGURE 3.1   Programmable pipeline.

After a vertex shader processes input data, the pipeline combines vertices into basic shapes called *primitives*, such as points, lines, or triangles. The process of creating primitives is called *assembly*. Later in this chapter, I'll explain how applications can control the assembly process.

After vertices have been assembled into primitives, the next step is *rasterization*. This breaks each primitive into a two-dimensional array of elements called *fragments*. Fragments are conceptually similar to pixels, but while a pixel only has a color and a location, a fragment has a color, a location, and a *depth*.

Depth processing is a critical operation in graphical rendering. To see why, consider two primitives: Triangle A and Triangle B. If Triangle A is in the foreground and blocks Triangle B from being viewed, the fragments generated from Triangle A will have lower depth values than those generated from Triangle B. When fragments are converted to pixels, the pixels of Triangle A should be displayed on the screen instead of the pixels of Triangle B.

In the next step, a fragment shader receives the fragments produced by rasterization. It executes once for each fragment and can customize the fragment's color and depth. Many fragment shaders use lighting algorithms to set the fragment's color depending on the sources of light in the model. Chapter 4 explains how fragment shaders can be coded, and Chapter 6 shows how they can be used to implement the popular Blinn-Phong lighting model.

The last stage of the pipeline performs final operations on the processed fragments. Possible operations include depth testing, stencil testing, and blending. Depth and stencil testing will be discussed in Chapter 6. Blending refers to the process of combining the fragment's color with that of the surrounding buffer.

RENDER PASSES

When it comes to graphics, WebGPU's terminology can be confusing. The term *render pass* describes the overall environment in which rendering is performed. This structure contains all the state data that the GPU needs to produce graphics. An application provides data to a render pass by calling its methods with special data structures called *attachments*.

As the GPU executes the rendering commands, the actual display of each shape is called a *draw operation* or a *draw call*. Most rendering operations require the execution of several draw calls.

Chapter 2 introduced the objects that need to be created in a WebGPU application, and one of the most important objects is the GPUCommandEncoder. By creating and configuring this encoder, an application can define commands that will execute on the GPU.

To define a rendering operation, an application needs to perform at least five more steps:

1. Call the encoder's beginRenderPass method to create a GPURenderPassEncoder.
2. Call the device's createRenderPipeline method to create a GPURenderPipeline.
3. Provide buffers containing rendering data to the render pass encoder.
4. Define draw operations by calling one of the render pass encoder's draw methods.
5. Complete the rendering operation by calling the render pass encoder's finish method.

After the last step, the application can send the render pass to the GPU by performing two more steps. First, it needs to call the encoder's finish method to insert the render pass into the command buffer. Then it needs to call the submit method of the device's queue to send the command buffer to the GPU for processing.

The following discussion looks at the steps that define rendering operations. The first step, which creates a render pass, is particularly complicated.

Step 1: Create a Render Pass Encoder

To create a GPURenderPassEncoder, an application needs to call the command encoder's beginRenderPass method with a descriptor that identifies the rendering

TABLE 3.1 Properties of the render pass descriptor

PROPERTY	OPTIONAL?	DESCRIPTION
label	Y	Name for the render pass
colorAttachments	N	Color data needed for rendering
depthStencilAttachment	Y	Data needed for depth/stencil testing
occlusionQuerySet	Y	Data structure to store query results
timestampWrites	Y	Configuration data for timestamps
maxDrawCount	Y	Maximum number of draw calls performed in the pass

to be performed. WebGPU supports a wide range of rendering operations, so this descriptor can have several different fields. Table 3.1 lists them and provides a description of each.

Chapter 6 will discuss the depthStencilAttachment property, Chapter 7 will explain occlusionQuerySet, and Chapter 8 will look at timestampWrites. For now, the only property to know is colorAttachments, which is the only required property to create the render pass.

Before proceeding further, I'd like to present code that creates a command encoder and a render pass encoder:

```
// Create a GPUCommandEncoder
const encoder = device.createCommandEncoder();

// Create a GPURenderPassEncoder
const renderpass = encoder.beginRenderPass({
    colorAttachments: [ ... ]
});
```

This code assigns the render pass's colorAttachments property to an array. Each element of the array is an object whose properties identify a color operation. Each element can have up to five properties, and Table 3.2 lists each of them.

TABLE 3.2 Color attachment properties

PROPERTY	OPTIONAL?	DESCRIPTION
view	N	Resource accessed by the color attachment
resolveTarget	Y	Subresource affected by the color attachment if multisampling is enabled
loadOp	N	Identifies how the view's initial color should be set (load uses an existing value, clear uses the clearValue)
storeOp	N	Identifies if the view's color should be stored (store stores the color, discard discards the color)
clearValue	Y	Color to serve as the view's initial color if loadOp is set to load

In many applications, the only use of the `colorAttachments` property is to set the initial color of the canvas. In this case, the application needs to provide values for the `view`, `loadOp`, `clearValue`, and `storeOp` properties.

For example, the following code calls the encoder's `beginRenderPass` method with a `colorAttachments` array containing a single object.

```
// Set the initial color to gray
const renderpass = encoder.beginRenderPass({
    colorAttachments: [{
        view: context.getCurrentTexture().createView(),
        loadOp: "clear",
        clearValue: { r: 0.5, g: 0.5, b: 0.5, a: 1.0 },
        storeOp: "store"
    }]
});
```

In this code, the object in the `colorAttachments` array tells WebGPU that its operation affects the entire context and that the view should be cleared to the given color. This color is identified by setting components (r, g, b, and a) to values between 0.0 and 1.0. In this case, r, g, and b are set to 0.5, which means the view's initial color will be gray. The a (alpha) property is set to 1.0, which means the resulting color will be opaque.

The `loadOp` property is set to `clear`, which means WebGPU will use the value in `clearValue` to set the view's initial color. The `storeOp` property is set to `store`, so this value will be stored for later operations.

Step 2: Define the Render Pipeline

After the `GPURenderPassEncoder` is created, the next step is to define the steps of the rendering process. These steps form the rendering pipeline, which is represented by a `GPURenderPipeline` object. Working with this object requires two steps:

1. Create a `GPURenderPipeline` by calling the device's `createRender` `Pipeline` method with a suitable descriptor.
2. Associate the pipeline with the rendering process by calling the `setPipeline` method of the `GPURenderPassEncoder`.

The first step is much more complicated than the second. This is because the `createRenderPipeline` method must be called with an object that describes the rendering process. Table 3.3 lists the different properties that can be set.

Most of these properties are optional. The `depthStencil` property will be discussed in Chapter 6, so this discussion focuses on the `vertex`, `fragment`, `layout`, `primitive`, and `multisample` properties.

TABLE 3.3   Properties of the render pipeline descriptor

PROPERTY	OPTIONAL?	DESCRIPTION
label	Y	Label for the render pipeline
layout	N	Object that describes how memory resources are used
vertex	N	Vertex shader used for rendering
fragment	Y	Optional fragment shader used for rendering
depthStencil	Y	Object that describes depth/stencil testing
primitive	Y	Sets how vertices are combined into primitive shapes
multisample	Y	Optional object that configures the multisampling process

Vertex, fragment, and layout properties

The vertex and fragment properties are important because they control how the pipeline processes vertices and fragments. As discussed in the first section of this chapter, these shaders contain executable code that runs on the GPU.

The layout property identifies how the vertex and fragment shaders access data. This is a required property, and in most cases, it can be set to auto. It can also be set to a GPUPipelineLayout object, which will be discussed in Chapter 4.

The primitive property

As discussed earlier, the assembly stage of the rendering pipeline combines vertices into basic shapes called primitives. An application can customize the assembly process by setting the pipeline's primitive property. This must be set to an object that can have up to five properties, and Table 3.4 lists them all.

The topology property is particularly important. By default, WebGPU assembles vertices into a sequence of triangles—the first triangle is formed from the first-second-third vertices, the second triangle is formed from the fourth-fifth-sixth vertices,

TABLE 3.4   Primitive properties

PROPERTY	OPTIONAL?	DESCRIPTION
topology	Y	The type of primitive shapes to be created during assembly
stripIndexFormat	Y	Format of the index values used for strip topologies
frontFace	Y	Identifies which polygons are considered front-facing
cullMode	Y	Types of polygons to be culled
unclippedDepth	Y	Disables depth clipping

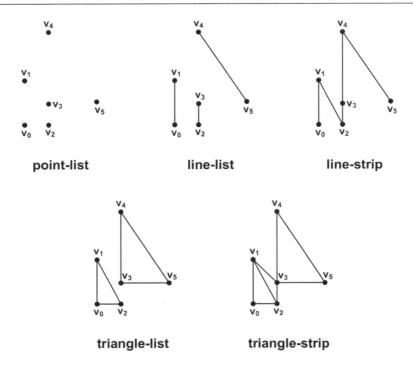

FIGURE 3.2   Primitive shapes for assembly.

and so on. Applications can tell WebGPU what type of primitives to assemble by setting the topology property to one of five values:

- point-list—Each vertex is drawn as an individual point
- line-list—Each consecutive pair of vertices forms a line
- line-strip—Each vertex forms a line connected to the preceding vertex
- triangle-list—Each consecutive triplet of vertices forms a triangle (default)
- triangle-strip—Each vertex forms a triangle connected to the preceding vertices

To clarify this, Figure 3.2 illustrates the different primitives supported in WebGPU. There are no quadrilaterals—to draw a rectangle, you'll need to draw two adjacent triangles.

By default, the assembly process combines vertices in the order in which they're provided. But as I'll explain shortly, applications can take advantage of *indexed rendering*, which tells the renderer to access vertices according to a series of index values. This can provide several advantages, including the ability to use a vertex multiple times without passing its data to the GPU multiple times.

If indexed rendering is used and the `topology` property is set to `line-strip` or `triangle-strip`, the `stripIndexFormat` property will identify the data type of each index value. If `stripIndexFormat` is set to `uint16`, the index values will be read as a series of 16-bit unsigned integers. If it's set to `uint32`, the index values will be read as a series of 32-bit unsigned integers.

Most three-dimensional graphics are constructed from connected triangles. For this reason, most of the example applications in this book set `topology` to `triangle-strip`.

Example code

Before proceeding further, it helps to see how render pipelines are used in practice. The following code creates a command encoder, a render pass encoder, and a render pipeline. Then it calls the `setPipeline` method of the render pass encoder to associate the encoder with the render pipeline.

```
// Create the command encoder
const encoder = device.createCommandEncoder();

// Create the render pass encoder
const renderPass = encoder.beginRenderPass(...);

// Create the render pipeline
const renderPipeline = device.createRenderPipeline({
    label: "Example Pipeline",
    layout: "auto",
    vertex: { ... },
    fragment: { ... },
    primitive: {
        topology: "triangle-strip",
        stripIndexFormat: "uint32",
        frontFace: "cw",
        cullMode: "back"
    }
});

// Associate the pipeline with the render pass encoder
renderPass.setPipeline(renderPipeline);
```

As shown, the pipeline tells the renderer to combine vertices into triangles, with each vertex connected to the two preceding vertices. The application will use indexed rendering, and because `stripIndexFormat` is set to `uint32`, WebGPU will read index values as 32-bit unsigned integers. The `frontFace` property is set to `cw`, so clockwise-oriented triangles will be treated as front-facing. `cullMode` is set to `back`, so back-facing triangles will be culled from the rendering.

The last line associates the render pipeline with the render pass. As a result, all drawing operations of the render pass will follow the sequence of steps defined in the render pipeline.

Step 3: Provide Rendering Data

One of the most difficult aspects of WebGPU development involves passing data to the client's device. In WebGPU parlance, a region of data storage on the device is called a *resource*, and two main types of resources are supported:

- buffers—contain general-purpose data, represented by the GPUBuffer class
- textures—contain pixel data to be displayed as a texture, represented by the GPUTexture class

Technically, the main difference between buffers and textures is that GPUs store texture data in a different type of memory than buffer data. This enables the GPU to process textures at high speed, which is a crucial capability for modern games.

The fascinating topic of textures will have to wait until Chapter 6. This chapter and the next focus on regular buffers. WebGPU supports several types of buffers, including the following four:

1. vertex buffers—store data related to vertices (coordinates, colors, normal vector components, and so on)
2. index buffers—store values that set the order in which the vertices are accessed
3. uniform buffers—store data that remains constant (uniform) between shader executions
4. storage buffers—store general-purpose data (frequently used in compute applications, rarely used in graphical applications)

Vertex buffers are required in all graphical applications, and index buffers are required in applications that perform indexed rendering. The GPURenderPassEncoder provides two methods that associate these buffers with the render pass encoder:

- setVertexBuffer(...)—associates a vertex buffer with the render pass encoder
- setIndexBuffer(...)—associates an index buffer with the render pass encoder

Both of these methods accept a GPUBuffer that contains data to be passed to the GPU. GPUBuffers are complicated to use and understand, and I'll hold off on describing them until later in the chapter.

TABLE 3.5 Draw methods of the render pass encoder

METHOD	DESCRIPTION
draw(...)	Assembles primitives by reading vertices in order
drawIndexed(...)	Assembles primitives by reading vertices by index
drawIndirect(...)	Assembles primitives using draw parameters given in a GPU buffer (reads vertices in order)
drawIndexedIndirect(...)	Assembles primitives using draw parameters given in a GPU buffer (reads vertices by index)

Step 4: Define Drawing Operations

After an application has defined the rendering process and provided the rendering data, the next step is to define the draw operations. WebGPU supports different types of draw operations, and each is represented by a method of the GPURenderPassEncoder. Table 3.5 lists each of them.

These methods can be hard to understand at first. I'll describe them here and then review their operation as they're used in later chapters.

Basic rendering

An application passes vertex data to the GPU in special buffers called *vertex buffers*. If an application calls the draw method, the renderer will access vertex data in the order provided in the vertex buffer. Put another way, the first vertex in the buffer is always the first vertex to be drawn, the second vertex is always the second vertex to be drawn, and so on.

The draw method accepts arguments that determine how vertices should be assembled into shapes. This method can be called in four ways, and Table 3.6 lists each of them.

Don't be concerned if these methods seem strange. Once you start coding, you'll appreciate why there are so many types of methods and arguments.

TABLE 3.6 Overloaded draw methods

METHOD	DESCRIPTION
draw(vertexCount)	Draw primitives using the first vertexCount vertices in the buffer
draw(vertexCount, instanceCount)	Draw primitives using the first vertexCount vertices in the buffer, create instanceCount instances of the primitives
draw(vertexCount, instanceCount, firstVertex)	Draw primitives using the first vertexCount vertices in the buffer starting from the firstVertex offset; create instanceCount instances of the primitives
draw(vertexCount, instanceCount, firstVertex, firstInstance)	Draw primitives using the first vertexCount vertices in the buffer starting from the firstVertex offset, create instanceCount instances of the primitives, set the value of the first instance to firstInstance

The first usage of `draw` tells the renderer to assemble shapes from the first `vertexCount` vertices in the buffer. The second usage of `draw` repeats the rendering process to form multiple instances of each primitive. This is called *instanced rendering*, and it's very useful when an application wants to create copies of shapes without burdening the GPU.

For example, suppose you're writing a strategy game that needs to display hundreds of soldiers. Using instanced rendering, you can define the shape of one soldier and then produce other soldiers in the scene without needing separate draw calls. Chapter 4 will show how instanced rendering is used.

If a vertex buffer will be accessed by multiple draw operations, the `firstVertex` parameter tells each draw operation where to start reading vertex data from the buffer. For example, if this is set to 100, the renderer will start assembling shapes with the hundredth vertex in the buffer.

If `instanceCount` is greater than 1, WebGPU will assign each instance a value that can be used by the vertex shader. The value of the first instance is 0 by default, but if `firstInstance` is set to a value greater than 0, that value will be used instead. Chapter 4 will explain how instance values are used in vertex shaders.

Indexed rendering

As discussed earlier, an application can define index buffers in addition to vertex buffers. An index buffer contains integers that tell the renderer how to read vertices in the vertex buffer. If the first three values in the index buffer are 2, 5, and 8, the first vertices to be drawn will be Vertex 2, Vertex 5, and Vertex 8.

One major advantage of indexed rendering is that you can repeat the drawing of a vertex without redefining the vertex in the vertex buffer. The main disadvantage is complexity—all the index values need to be stored on the GPU.

In WebGPU, an application can launch indexed rendering by calling `drawIndexed`. Like the `draw` method, this can be called in multiple ways, as listed in Table 3.7.

These methods work like the `draw` methods in Table 3.6, but the renderer selects vertices by index instead of using the order in which they're stored in the buffer. As with `draw`, the optional `instanceCount` argument identifies the number of copies to be rendered, and `firstInstance` assigns a number to the first instance.

One important difference between `draw` and `drawIndexed` is that the `drawIndexed` methods accept `firstIndex` and `baseVertex` arguments. `firstIndex` assigns an offset into the index buffer, so if this is set to 3, the renderer should start reading index values at Index 3. `baseVertex` sets a value that should be added to each index value, so if this is set to 3, the renderer should add 3 to each value it reads from the index buffer.

Indirect rendering

When an application calls `draw` or `drawIndexed`, the parameters of each rendering operation (number of vertices/index values, number of instances, and so on) need to be transferred from the CPU to the GPU. We want to avoid making small transfers to the GPU, so WebGPU makes it possible to store these parameters in a separate buffer on

TABLE 3.7   Overloaded `drawIndexed` methods

METHOD	DESCRIPTION
`drawIndexed(indexCount)`	Combine `indexCount` vertices into primitives according to index
`drawIndexed(indexCount, instanceCount)`	Combine `indexCount` vertices into primitives according to index and produce `instanceCount` instances
`drawIndexed(indexCount, instanceCount, firstIndex)`	Combine `indexCount` vertices into primitives according to index, starting with `firstIndex`, and produce `instanceCount` instances
`draw(vertexCount, instanceCount, firstVertex, firstInstance)`	Draw primitives using the first `vertexCount` vertices in the buffer starting from the firstVertex offset, create `instanceCount` instances of the primitives, set the value of the first instance to `firstInstance`
`drawIndexed(indexCount, instanceCount, firstIndex, baseVertex)`	Combine `indexCount` vertices into primitives according to index, starting with `firstIndex`, and produce `instanceCount` instances
`drawIndexed(indexCount, instanceCount, firstIndex, baseVertex, firstInstance)`	Combine `indexCount` vertices into primitives according to index, starting with `firstIndex`, and produce `instanceCount` instances, set the value of the first instance to `firstInstance`

the GPU. This is called *indirect rendering*, and for complex applications, it can dramatically improve performance.

WebGPU supports indirect rendering through the `drawIndirect` and `drawIndirectIndexed` methods of the `GPURenderPassEncoder`. Their usage is given as follows:

- `drawIndirect(indirectBuffer, indirectOffset)`—draws vertices based on parameters in `indirectBuffer` in the order in which they're stored in the vertex buffer
- `drawIndexedIndirect(indirectBuffer, indirectOffset)`— draws vertices based on parameters in `indirectBuffer` according to the index values in the index buffer

In both cases, the renderer will perform the draw operation based on the parameters stored in the `indirectBuffer`. It will start reading from the buffer from the memory address given by `indirectOffset`.

To be precise, `drawIndirect` will cause the renderer to read four values (`vertexCount`, `instanceCount`, `firstVertex`, and `firstInstance`) from the buffer. `drawIndexedIndirect` will cause the renderer to read four values (`indexCount`, `instanceCount`, `firstIndex`, `baseVertex`, and `firstInstance`) from the buffer. In both cases, the renderer will expect the values to be provided as 32-bit unsigned integers.

Step 5: Complete the Rendering Operation

The last step is the simplest. After an application has created a GPURenderPassEncoder and configured the rendering process, it can complete the recording of the rendering commands by calling the render pass encoder's end method. Once this is done, the rendering commands can't be changed further.

After an application calls end, it can call the command encoder's finish method, which returns a buffer of commands for the GPU. When the application calls the submit method with this command buffer, the commands will be sent to the GPU for execution. The following discussion presents an example of how this works.

EXAMPLE APPLICATION— CREATING A BLUE CANVAS

In Chapter 2, the example application created WebGPU objects, but didn't create a render pass encoder or submit any commands to the GPU. In contrast, the Ch03_ BlueCanvas application submits a simple rendering command that sets the canvas's initial color to blue.

As graphical rendering applications go, this isn't going to win any awards. The goal is simply to demonstrate how WebGPU's objects work together to perform a simple rendering task. Listing 3.1 presents the content of ch03_bluecanvas.js, which creates a render pass encoder that simply clears the content of the canvas created in HTML.

```
// Create top-level asynchronous function
async function runExample() {

// Check if WebGPU is supported
if (!navigator.gpu) {
    throw new Error("WebGPU not supported");
}

// Access the GPUAdapter
const adapter = await navigator.gpu.requestAdapter();
if (!adapter) {
    throw new Error("No GPUAdapter found");
}

// Access the client GPU
const device = await adapter.requestDevice();
if (!device) {
    throw new Error("Failed to create a GPUDevice");
}
```

```
// Access the canvas
const canvas = document.getElementById("canvas_example");
if (!canvas) {
    throw new Error("Could not access canvas in page");
}

// Obtain a WebGPU context for the canvas
const context = canvas.getContext("webgpu");
if (!context) {
    throw new Error("Could not obtain WebGPU context for
canvas");}

// Configure the context with the device and format
const canvasFormat = navigator.gpu.getPreferredCanvasFormat();
context.configure({
    device: device,
    format: canvasFormat,
});

// Create the command encoder
const encoder = device.createCommandEncoder();
if (!encoder) {
    throw new Error("Failed to create a GPUCommandEncoder");
}

// Create the render pass encoder
const renderPass = encoder.beginRenderPass({
    colorAttachments: [{
        view: context.getCurrentTexture().createView(),
        loadOp: "clear",
        clearValue: { r: 0.2, g: 0.2, b: 1.0, a: 1.0 },
        storeOp: "store"
    }]
});

// Complete the render pass encoding
renderPass.end();

// Submit the render commands to the GPU
device.queue.submit([encoder.finish()]);
}

// Run example function
runExample();
```

This code creates a render pass that clears the color of the view (the canvas) to a color whose RGB components are 0.2, 0.2, 1.0. These are *normalized* values, which means they lie between 0.0 and 1.0. Converting these values to unnormalized values (between 0 and 255), the color is (51, 51, 255).

This code doesn't create a render pipeline because every render pipeline needs to have a vertex shader. A proper discussion of vertex shaders will have to wait until Chapter 4, whose example project creates a render pass with a render pipeline.

Because there's no render pipeline, the code calls the render pass's end method immediately after creating it. Then it calls the finish method of the command encoder to create a buffer of commands. In this case, the commands tell the GPU to clear the color of the canvas. Once the submit method of the GPUQueue is called, these commands are sent to the GPU for execution.

BUFFERS AND LAYOUTS

Practical applications don't just fill the canvas with color. They draw *shapes*, and to draw a shape, an application needs to identify (at minimum) the coordinates of the shape's vertices. This data must be packaged in a *vertex buffer*, which will be passed to the pipeline's vertex shader.

In code, the process of creating a vertex buffer consists of five steps:

1. Create a GPUBuffer by calling the createBuffer method of the GPUDevice.
2. Associate the buffer with the device's queue by calling the queue's writeBuffer method with the GPUBuffer and its data.
3. Create a layout object that identifies the structure of the GPUBuffer.
4. Provide the layout object as part of the vertex object of the render pipeline.
5. Add the buffer as an argument of the render pass's setVertexBuffer method.

This section explores these steps and shows how they can be performed in code. Chapter 4 will show how buffers are used in real WebGPU applications.

To demonstrate how buffers are created, we'll create a buffer that contains the data needed to draw a triangle whose vertices have different colors. To be precise, the coordinates of the triangle's points are (0, 0.5), (−0.5, −0.5), and (0.5, −0.5) and the colors are green (0.0, 1.0, 0.0), red (1.0, 0.0, 0.0), and blue (0.0, 0.0, 1.0). Figure 3.3 shows what the triangle looks like.

To draw this triangle, the GPU needs to know the coordinates and colors of each vertex. Because these properties change from vertex to vertex, we refer to this data as *attribute data*. The following code shows how this data can be stored in arrays of 32-bit floating-point values:

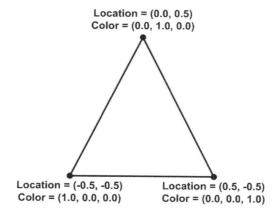

FIGURE 3.3   Attribute data for drawing a triangle.

```
const vertexCoords = new Float32Array([
   0.0,  0.5,
  -0.5, -0.5,
   0.5, -0.5
]);
```

```
const vertexColors = new Float32Array([
   0.0, 1.0, 0.0,
   1.0, 0.0, 0.0,
   0.0, 0.0, 1.0
]);
```

For the sake of efficiency, we'll combine the coordinates and colors into one large array:

```
const vertexData = new Float32Array([
   0.0,  0.5, 0.0, 1.0, 0.0,    // First vertex
  -0.5, -0.5, 1.0, 0.0, 0.0,    // Second vertex
   0.5, -0.5, 0.0, 0.0, 1.0     // Third vertex
]);
```

This array contains the coordinates of the first vertex, followed by the color of the first vertex. This is followed by attribute data for the second and third vertices. Because the data for each vertex is combined together, this data storage method is called *interleaving*. In general, this provides better performance than using separate arrays, and all the example code in this book will interleave data inside GPU buffers.

To create a GPUBuffer object to store this data, an application needs to call the createBuffer method of the GPUDevice. This accepts an object whose properties describe the buffer. This object can define a maximum of four properties, and Table 3.8 lists each of them.

TABLE 3.8   Properties of the render pipeline descriptor

PROPERTY	OPTIONAL?	DESCRIPTION
label	Y	Name to be used for the buffer
size	N	Number of bytes to be stored in the buffer
usage	N	Flags that identify how the buffer will be used
mappedAtCreation	Y	Identifies if the buffer data should be mapped to GPU memory on creation

The usage property is particularly important and must be set to a value of the GPUBufferUsage enumerated type or an OR'ed combination of multiple values. Table 3.9 lists the supported values of this type.

To demonstrate how these properties are used, the following code creates a vertex buffer intended to store the data in the vertexData array.

```
// Create a vertex buffer
const vertexBuffer = device.createBuffer({
    label: "Example vertex buffer",
    size: vertexData.byteLength,
    usage: GPUBufferUsage.VERTEX | GPUBufferUsage.COPY_DST
});
```

The buffer's size is large enough to hold the bytes of vertexData, but it doesn't hold the array elements yet. To associate data with a buffer, an application can call the writeBuffer method of the GPUQueue. This can accept five arguments, and Table 3.10 lists each of them.

TABLE 3.9   Vertex buffer usage values

PROPERTY	DESCRIPTION
GPUBufferUsage.VERTEX	The buffer can be used as a vertex buffer
GPUBufferUsage.INDEX	The buffer can be used as an index buffer
GPUBufferUsage.INDIRECT	The buffer can store draw parameters for indirect rendering
GPUBufferUsage.COPY_SRC	The buffer can be used as the source of a copy operation
GPUBufferUsage.COPY_DST	The buffer can be used as the destination of a copy operation
GPUBufferUsage.STORAGE	The buffer can be used as a storage buffer in a bind group
GPUBufferUsage.UNIFORM	The buffer can be used as a uniform buffer in a bind group
GPUBufferUsage.MAP_READ	The buffer can be mapped for reading data
GPUBufferUsage.MAP_WRITE	The buffer can be mapped for writing data
GPUBufferUsage.QUERY_RESOLVE	The buffer can be used to contain query results

TABLE 3.10   Arguments of the `writeBuffer` method

ARGUMENT	DATA TYPE	OPTIONAL?	DESCRIPTION
buffer	GPUBuffer	N	The buffer to receive the written data
bufferOffset	Integer	N	Byte offset that identifies where the write operation should begin
data	ArrayBuffer, TypedArray, or DataView	N	Source of the data to be written
dataOffset	Integer	Y	Byte offset to start accessing data from the source
size	Integer	Y	Number of bytes to be written from the source to the buffer

In this example, we want `vertexBuffer` to hold all the data in `vertexData`. The following code creates the association:

```
// Write attribute data to the vertex buffer
device.queue.writeBuffer(vertexBuffer, 0, vertexData);
```

Ideally, the GPU would automatically know which values in the array represent coordinates and which represent color components. But in WebGPU, an application needs to identify the nature of the data by associating the buffer with a layout object. This object has three properties, and Table 3.11 lists each of them.

Each element of the `attributes` array identifies an attribute type. In our example, each vertex has a location (two floating-point coordinates) and a color (three floating-point components). Therefore, the array contains two elements. This is shown in the following code:

```
// Define the layout of a vertex buffer
const bufferLayout = {
    arrayStride: 20,
    attributes: [
        { format: "float32x2", offset: 0, shaderLocation: 0 },
        { format: "float32x3", offset: 8, shaderLocation: 1 }
    ],
};
```

TABLE 3.11   Properties of the buffer layout object

ARGUMENT	OPTIONAL?	DESCRIPTION
arrayStride	N	Number of bytes between different structures
attributes	N	Array of objects defining arrangement of values for a structure
stepMode	Y	The type of structure corresponding to the layout (vertex or instance)

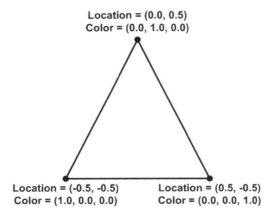

Location = (0.0, 0.5)
Color = (0.0, 1.0, 0.0)

Location = (-0.5, -0.5)
Color = (1.0, 0.0, 0.0)

Location = (0.5, -0.5)
Color = (0.0, 0.0, 1.0)

FIGURE 3.4   Layout properties of attribute data.

As shown, each element of the `attributes` array has three properties: `format`, `offset`, and `shaderLocation`. `format` must be set to a string given by *TYPExNUM*, where *TYPE* is the data type of each value (`uint8`, `unorm8`, `uint16`, `unorm16`, `uint32`, `float16`, `float32`) and *NUM* is the number of values (2, 3, or 4, depending on the type).

`offset` identifies the byte location of the attribute's data starting from the beginning of the structure. The `offset` value of the first element is 0 because it starts at the beginning of the structure. The `offset` value of the second element is 8 because it starts 8 bytes from the start of the structure.

`shaderLocation` identifies the index of the parameter received by the shader function. Chapter 4 discusses shaders, and will explain how to associate buffers with function parameters.

The `arrayStride`, `format`, and `offset` properties can be confusing, so Figure 3.4 illustrates how they relate to the triangle's attributes. Each gray rectangle corresponds to a 4-byte float, and each row of rectangles represents a vertex's attribute. Keep in mind that `arrayStride` and `offset` are given in *bytes*.

Once the layout object has been created, an application needs to provide it as an element of the `buffers` array of the `vertex` property in the `createRenderPipeline` method. To demonstrate, the following code adds `bufferLayout` to the `buffers` array.

```
// Create the render pipeline
const cellPipeline = device.createRenderPipeline({
    ...
    vertex: {
        module: ...,
        entryPoint: ...,
        buffers: [bufferLayout]
    },
    ...
});
```

TABLE 3.12   Arguments of the `setVertexBuffer` method

ARGUMENT	DATA TYPE	OPTIONAL?	DESCRIPTION
slot	Integer	N	Index for the vertex buffer
buffer	GPUBuffer	N	The buffer to be associated with the render pass encoder
offset	Integer	N	Byte offset into the buffer to be read
size	Integer	Y	Size of the vertex data to be accessed

The `module` property is set to an object that contains shader code, and `entryPoint` identifies a function in the shader. These properties will be discussed in Chapter 4.

In addition to adding the buffer layout to the render pipeline, an application needs to associate the vertex buffer with the render pass encoder. This is accomplished by calling the encoder's `setVertexBuffer` method. This requires four arguments, and Table 3.12 lists each of them.

An example will demonstrate how `setVertexBuffer` works. If the render pass encoder is named `renderPassEncoder` and the buffer is called `vertexBuffer`, the following code will create an association between the two.

```
// Associate a vertex buffer with the render pass encoder
renderPassEncoder.setVertexBuffer(0, vertexBuffer);
```

It's important to note that `setVertexBuffer` can be called multiple times with different slot values to associate multiple vertex buffers. Chapter 4 will explain how vertex shaders use these slot values to access vertex buffer data.

SUMMARY

This chapter has discussed the fundamental objects required for graphical rendering. The two most important objects are the `GPURenderPassEncoder`, which I'll refer to throughout this book as the *render pass encoder*, and the `GPURenderPipeline`, which I'll refer to as the *render pipeline*.

The render pass encoder stores all the states related to the graphical rendering process. At minimum, it must be created with color attachments that identify the rendering surface and the initial color. The example application in this chapter configures the render pass encoder to set the initial color to blue.

The render pipeline identifies the different steps of the rendering procedure. At minimum, it provides a shader module containing the special programs (shaders) that should be executed on the GPU. It also specifies what types of primitives should be formed from the vertices. Applications can create point, line, or triangle primitives, and in this book, we'll usually configure the pipeline to create triangles.

The last part of this chapter discussed the topic of buffers. You can think of a buffer as a special data structure that can be passed to the GPU. Some buffers contain vertex data, such as coordinates or colors, and other buffers contain index values that identify the order in which vertices should be rendered.

The WebGPU Shading Language (WGSL)

4

This chapter puts aside regular JavaScript code and explores the fascinating world of *shaders*, which play central roles in WebGPU operations. Graphics applications use shaders to tell the GPU how to draw shapes and assign colors. Compute applications use shaders to tell the GPU how to crunch numbers.

WebGPU supports three types of shaders, and each has a different primary role:

- **vertex shader**—sets the position of each vertex in the scene
- **fragment shader**—sets the color and depth of each fragment to be rendered
- **compute shader**—performs mathematical operations

Despite the different roles, every WebGPU shader is written in the WebGPU Shader Language, or WGSL. WGSL is based partly on JavaScript and partly on the C programming language, but unlike JavaScript and C, WGSL functions run on GPUs instead of CPUs.

This chapter presents the fundamentals of WGSL and then explains how to write vertex shaders and fragment shaders. The topic of compute shaders is discussed in Chapter 8.

FUNDAMENTALS OF WGSL

Chapter 3 introduced the graphical rendering pipeline, which behaves like an assembly line that turns vertices into primitive shapes, primitive shapes into fragments, and fragments into pixels. Two of the pipeline's stages are programmable, which means their operations are determined by *shaders*.

This section explores five fundamental aspects of WGSL development:

1. Function definitions and entry points
2. Data types

DOI: 10.1201/9781003422839-4

3. Builtin operators and functions
4. Variables and storage
5. Constants and overridden variables

This section looks at each of these topics in detail. Later in the chapter, I'll present two example applications that demonstrate how shaders can be used in graphical applications.

Function Definitions and Entry Points

At a high level, a WebGPU shader contains one or more data structure declarations followed by one or more function definitions. When defining a function, there are two essential rules to be aware of:

1. The function's name must be preceded by the `fn` keyword and must be followed by zero or more parameters in parentheses.
2. A WGSL function doesn't have to return a value. If it returns a value, its parameter list must be followed by a fat arrow (->) and the data type of the return value.

Each parameter must have an identifier followed by a colon and a data type. This is shown in the following code, which defines a function named `foo` that returns a value of type `bar`. The function accepts an argument named `arg` of type `argtype`:

```
// Example shader function
fn foo(arg: argtype) -> bar {
    return x;
}
```

A shader can have multiple function definitions, but only one function can serve as the shader's *entry point*. There are two important items to know about entry points:

1. An entry point must be preceded by an attribute specific to the shader's type (`@vertex` for vertex shaders, `@fragment` for fragment shaders, `@compute` for compute shaders).
2. The pipeline object needs to know the entry point for each type of shader that will be executed. This can be set manually by assigning the name to the `entryPoint` property. If this isn't set, WebGPU will search for the shader's attribute. If only one function has the attribute, that function will be taken as the entry point.

For example, the following code defines a vertex shader. Because it's the entry point, it must be preceded by `@vertex`.

```
// Example entry point
@vertex
fn main(arg1: argtype1, arg2: argtype2, …) -> … {
    return …
}
```

You can set a function's name to anything you like, but the parameters and return value will depend on the type of shader you're coding. I'll discuss this later in this chapter.

Data Types

One of the most difficult aspects of WGSL coding is keeping track of all the data types. This discussion divides them into five groups:

- **scalar types**—each instance has a single value
- **vector types**—each instance has multiple values
- **matrix types**—each instance has multiple rows and columns
- **array types**—containers of multiple elements with the same type
- **structure types**—named group of related data structures

There's a lot of new terminology, and don't be concerned if you don't grasp everything immediately. These types will become clearer when you start looking at practical shaders.

Scalar types

Unlike JavaScript, WGSL doesn't have data types for strings or undefined variables. There are only five basic scalar types, and Table 4.1 lists each of them.

As shown, WGSL integers have 32 bits—there are no 8-bit or 16-bit integers. However, many GPUs support 16-bit floating-point values, and these can provide performance gains for applications that need to store and process a significant number of values.

TABLE 4.1 WGSL scalar types

DATA TYPE	DESCRIPTION
bool	Boolean value (true/false)
u32	Unsigned 32-bit integer
i32	Signed 32-bit integer
f16	16-bit floating-point value
f32	32-bit floating-point value

Vector types

One advantage of using GPUs for computation is that they can process multiple values in a single clock cycle. However, the group of values must be stored in special containers called *vectors*. When a shader performs a vector operation, it operates on all the vector's values *at the same time*. For this reason, these operations are commonly called Single-Instruction, Multiple Data (SIMD) operations.

In WGSL, each vector type has the format vec*N*<type>, where *N* is the number of values in the vector and type is the type of each scalar value in the vector (see Table 4.1). For example, if a variable has type vec3<f32>, it's a vector that contains three 32-bit floating-point values. When the variable is used in an operation, all three values will be processed at once.

To simplify coding, WGSL provides aliases for common types of vectors. The first column of Table 4.2 lists these aliases, and the second column lists their full names.

For the sake of brevity, this book uses these aliases whenever possible. Keep in mind that the h refers to half-precision floats, or 16-bit floating-point values. These aren't supported by all GPUs, and you can check for half-precision support by reading the features property of the GPU adapter to see if it has an element named shader-f16. The following code shows how this can be done:

```
// Check if the client supports 16-bit floating-point values
if (adapter.features.has("shader-f16")) {
    ...
} else {
    ...
}
```

TABLE 4.2   Aliases for WGSL vector types

ALIAS TYPE	DATA TYPE	DESCRIPTION
vec2u	vec2<u32>	Contains two 32-bit unsigned integers
vec3u	vec3<u32>	Contains three 32-bit unsigned integers
vec4u	vec4<u32>	Contains four 32-bit unsigned integers
vec2i	vec2<i32>	Contains two 32-bit signed integers
vec3i	vec3<i32>	Contains three 32-bit signed integers
vec4i	vec4<i32>	Contains four 32-bit signed integers
vec2f	vec2<f32>	Contains two 32-bit floating-point values
vec3f	vec3<f32>	Contains three 32-bit floating-point values
vec4f	vec4<f32>	Contains four 32-bit floating-point values
vec2h	vec2<f16>	Contains two 16-bit floating-point values
vec3h	vec3<f16>	Contains three 16-bit floating-point values
vec4h	vec4<f16>	Contains four 16-bit floating-point values

To create a vector, you need to assign a value to each of its elements. WGSL supports variable declarations that start with `let`, `const`, and `var`, and the general syntax of declaring a vector is given as follows:

```
let var_name = vec_type(elements);
```

For example, the following code creates a vector containing four 32-bit floats:

```
let float_vec = vec4f(1.0, 2.0, 3.0, 4.0);
```

Similarly, this code creates a constant vector containing three 32-bit signed integers:

```
const int_vec: vec3i = vec3i(1, 2, 3);
```

A shader can access the elements of a vector in three main ways:

- Array notation: `float_vec[0]`, `int_vec[1]`
- Subscripts r, g, b, a: `float_vec.r`, `int_vec.b`
- Subscripts x, y, z, w: `float_vec.y`, `int_vec.w`

In addition to accessing individual elements, a shader can create subvectors of an original vector by using multiple subscripts. This is shown in the following code:

```
let my_vec = vec4f(0.0, 1.0, 2.0, 3.0);
let sub_vec = my_vec.yz;
// sub_vec contains (1.0, 2.0)
```

When accessing elements with dot notation, order is important. `my_vec.yz` is a two-element vector containing the second and third elements of `my_vec`. In contrast, `my_vec.zy` is a vector containing the third and second elements of `my_vec`.

Memory alignment is occasionally a concern in shader development, and a vector's alignment depends on its type. For vectors containing 4-byte elements, a `vec2` will be aligned on an 8-byte boundary, and a `vec3` or `vec4` will be aligned on a 16-byte boundary. If you ever get strange errors involving `vec3` data, keep in mind that these vectors are aligned on 16-byte boundaries, not 12-byte boundaries.

Matrix types

Matrix types are like vector types, but while a vector stores its values in a row, a matrix stores its values in rows and columns. Another difference is that matrices can only hold *floating-point values*, not integers or Boolean values.

Every matrix type has the format `matMxN<type>`, where *M* is the number of rows, *N* is the number of columns, and `type` is the type of each element of the matrix. The values of *M* and *N* can be 2, 3, or 4. For example, if a variable has type `mat3x4<f32>`, it's a matrix that has 12 floating point values arranged into 3 rows and 4 columns.

As with the vector types discussed earlier, WGSL simplifies programming by providing aliases for matrix types. Table 4.3 lists these aliases and their corresponding full types.

WGSL matrices are structured in *column-major order*. That is, if `mat` is a matrix, `mat[0]` is a vector containing elements in the matrix's first *column*. `mat[0][1]` is the second element of the matrix's first column.

TABLE 4.3   Aliases for WGSL matrix types

ALIAS	DATA TYPE	DESCRIPTION
mat2x2f	mat2x2<f32>	Contains four floats in two rows and two columns
mat2x3f	mat2x3<f32>	Contains six floats in two rows and three columns
mat2x4f	mat2x4<f32>	Contains eight floats in two rows and four columns
mat3x2f	mat3x2<f32>	Contains six floats in three rows and two columns
mat3x3f	mat3x3<f32>	Contains nine floats in three rows and three columns
mat3x4f	mat3x4<f32>	Contains twelve floats in three rows and four columns
mat4x2f	mat4x2<f32>	Contains eight floats in four rows and two columns
mat4x3f	mat4x3<f32>	Contains twelve floats in four rows and three columns
mat4x4f	mat4x4<f32>	Contains sixteen floats in four rows and four columns
mat2x2h	mat2x2<f16>	Contains four half-floats in two rows and two columns
mat2x3h	mat2x3<f16>	Contains six half-floats in two rows and three columns
mat2x4h	mat2x4<f16>	Contains eight half-floats in two rows and four columns
mat3x2h	mat3x2<f16>	Contains six half-floats in three rows and two columns
mat3x3h	mat3x3<f16>	Contains nine half-floats in three rows and three columns
mat3x4h	mat3x4<f16>	Contains twelve half-floats in three rows and four columns
mat4x2h	mat4x2<f16>	Contains eight half-floats in four rows and two columns
mat4x3h	mat4x3<f16>	Contains twelve half-floats in four rows and three columns
mat4x4h	mat4x4<f16>	Contains sixteen half-floats in four rows and four columns

To clarify this, consider the following code, which initializes a 3-by-2 matrix named mat_3_2:

```
// Initializes a 3-by-2 matrix with six values
let mat_3_2 = mat3x2f(0.0, 1.0, 2.0, 3.0, 4.0, 5.0);
```

The resulting matrix will have three rows and two columns. Because the elements are stored in column-major order, the first column will contain 0.0, 1.0, and 2.0, and the second column will contain 3.0, 4.0, and 5.0.

Shaders can construct matrices from vectors. For example, if vec1 and vec2 both have four elements, the following code creates a 4-by-2 matrix from the vectors:

```
// Creates a 4-by-2 matrix from two four-element vectors
const mat = mat4x2f(vec1, vec2);
```

As a result, mat[0] will contain the elements of vec1, and mat[1] will contain the elements of vec2.

Builtin Operators and Functions

WGSL provides all the operators and functions you'd expect for crunching numbers, including arithmetic and trigonometric operations (sin, cos, and tan). There are also functions for exponents (pow, exp, log), comparison (min, max, clamp), and approximation (round, floor, ceil, trunc).

This discussion looks at functions that operate specifically on vectors and matrices. These are particularly important when coding shaders, so it's a good idea to understand them clearly.

Vector operations and functions

You can perform arithmetic on vectors using the same operators that you use for scalars, and the operations are performed *component-wise*. That is, the elements in the output vector are computed simply by operating on the respective elements in the input vectors.

For example, suppose v1 contains (1.0, 1.0, 1.0) and v2 contains (2.0, 2.0, 2.0). The following operations are performed component-wise:

```
let v3 = v1 + v2;
// v3 = (3.0, 3.0, 3.0)

let v4 = v1 / v2;
// v4 = (0.5, 0.5, 0.5)
```

Operations between vectors and scalars are also performed component-wise. This is shown in the following example code:

```
let v3 = v1 + 5.0;
// v3 = (6.0, 6.0, 6.0)

let v4 = v1 / 4.0;
// v4 = (0.25, 0.25, 0.25)
```

In addition to basic operators, WGSL provides functions that operate on vectors. Table 4.4 lists five of them.

To understand these functions, it helps to think of vectors geometrically. A geometric vector has a length and direction, and is usually represented by an arrow in space, where the arrow's direction identifies the vector's direction and its length identifies the vector's length. There are three points to be aware of:

- Vectors are defined in a coordinate system. For example, three-dimensional vectors are defined in a coordinate system with three dimensions, such as (x, y, z).
- A vector can be expressed as the combination of n components, where n is the number of dimensions in the coordinate system. If v lies in the (x, y, z) coordinate system, its components are v_x, v_y, and v_z, and v can be expressed as $<v_x, v_y, v_z>$.
- The length of a vector can be obtained using the Pythagorean Theorem. That is, the square of the length equals the sum of the squares of its components.

TABLE 4.4   WGSL functions for vectors

FUNCTION	*DESCRIPTION*
`length(vec)`	Returns the length of vec
`normalize(vec)`	Returns a vector with the same direction as vec and a length of 1
`distance(vec1, vec2)`	Computes the distance between the two vectors
`dot(vec1, vec2)`	Returns the dot product of vec1 and vec2
`fma(vec1, vec2, res)`	Performs a fused multiply and add

For example, if v is a two-dimensional vector, its x-component is given by v_x and its y-component is given by v_y. The length of v, denoted by |v|, can be computed through the equation: $|v|^2 = v_x^2 + v_y^2$. In three dimensions, $|v|^2 = v_x^2 + v_y^2 + v_z^2$. This is shown in Figure 4.1.

In Table 4.4, the `length` function accepts a vector and returns its length. The `normalize` function accepts a vector and returns a vector with the same direction, but the length is set to 1. The `distance` function treats the two input vectors like points in space and uses the Pythagorean theorem to compute the distance between them.

The dot product is computed by multiplying the elements of the two input vectors and adding the products. For example, if vector v1 has components ($v1_x$, $v1_y$, $v1_z$) and vector v2 has components ($v2_x$, $v2_y$, $v2_z$), then their dot product is given as follows:

$$v1 \cdot v2 = \left(v1_x * v2_x\right) + \left(v1_y * v2_y\right) + \left(v1_z * v2_z\right)$$

In WGSL, the dot product is computed by calling the `dot` function. The resulting value tells you how closely the vectors' directions resemble one another. If the dot product is positive, they point in similar directions. If the product is zero, the vectors are perpendicular, and if the product is negative, they point in approximately opposite directions.

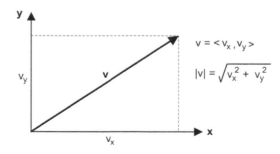

FIGURE 4.1   Vectors, components, and length.

The cross product differs from the dot product in several ways. Instead of returning a scalar, it returns a vector. The computation is more complex, and if v3 equals the cross-product of v1 and v2, then the components of v3 are obtained in the following way:

- $v3_x = v1_y * v2_z - v1_z * v2_y$
- $v3_y = v1_z * v2_x - v1_x * v2_z$
- $v3_z = v1_x * v2_y - v1_y * v2_x$

In WGSL, the cross product of two vectors can be obtained by calling the `cross` function. The resulting vector will have a direction perpendicular to the plane containing the input vectors. We say that this vector is *normal* to the plane, and we call the vector a *normal vector*. In graphics, normal vectors are frequently used to determine how light will reflect from a surface.

The last function in Table 4.4, `fma`, stands for fused multiply-and-add. This multiplies the corresponding elements of two vectors and adds the results to the elements of a third vector. If a, b, and c are the inputs, `fma` returns a * b + c. The main advantages of using this function are accuracy (reduced rounding error) and speed (it's usually performed as a single operation). `fma` can be called with scalar arguments as well as vectors.

Matrix operations and functions

As with vectors, you can add and subtract matrices in a component-wise manner using the + and – operators. But matrices can only be added and subtracted if they have the same number of rows and columns.

WGSL doesn't support matrix division, but it does support matrix multiplication. With matrices, the * operator can be used in three ways:

- matrix * scalar – multiplies every element of the matrix by the scalar
- matrix * vector – returns a vector
- matrix * matrix – returns a matrix

Chapter 5 explains how matrices represent transformations that can be used to scale, translate, or rotate points in space. For this chapter, it's important to be familiar with matrix–vector multiplication. The product of a matrix and a vector is another vector, and each element of the output vector is the dot product of one of the matrix's rows and the initial vector.

This can be confusing, so it helps to look at an example. Suppose A is a matrix whose elements are denoted a_{ij}, where i is the row containing the element and j is the column containing the element. If x is a vector, the product of A and x will produce another vector. Denoting the resulting vector as b, each element of b is computed by taking the dot product of the ith row of A and the vector x.

Figure 4.2 illustrates this graphically. The third element of the result, b_2, is obtained by taking the dot product of the third row of A and the vector x.

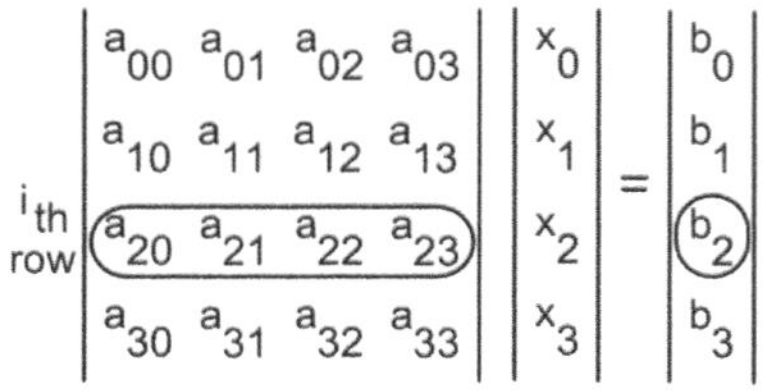

$$\underset{\substack{i\text{th}\\ \text{row}}}{\begin{vmatrix} a_{00} & a_{01} & a_{02} & a_{03} \\ a_{10} & a_{11} & a_{12} & a_{13} \\ a_{20} & a_{21} & a_{22} & a_{23} \\ a_{30} & a_{31} & a_{32} & a_{33} \end{vmatrix}} \begin{vmatrix} x_0 \\ x_1 \\ x_2 \\ x_3 \end{vmatrix} = \begin{vmatrix} b_0 \\ b_1 \\ b_2 \\ b_3 \end{vmatrix}$$

FIGURE 4.2   Matrix–Vector multiplication.

In this example, the elements of b are computed in the following way:

- $b_0 = $ (first row of A) $\cdot$ x $= a_{00} x_0 + a_{01} x_1 + a_{02} x_2 + a_{03} x_3$
- $b_1 = $ (second row of A) $\cdot$ x $= a_{10} x_0 + a_{11} x_1 + a_{12} x_2 + a_{13} x_3$
- $b_2 = $ (third row of A) $\cdot$ x $= a_{20} x_0 + a_{21} x_1 + a_{22} x_2 + a_{23} x_3$
- $b_3 = $ (fourth row of A) $\cdot$ x $= a_{30} x_0 + a_{31} x_1 + a_{32} x_2 + a_{33} x_3$

When multiplying a vector by a matrix, the number of elements in the vector must equal the number of elements in the matrix's rows. In this example, the size of x must equal the size of each row of A.

WGSL also supports matrix–matrix multiplication, which accepts two matrices and produces a third matrix. If the first matrix is m-by-n and the second matrix is n-by-p, the resulting matrix will have dimensions m-by-p.

Like matrix–vector multiplication, matrix–matrix multiplication consists of a series of dot products. Each element of the result matrix is obtained by taking the dot product of a row of the first input matrix and a column of the second input matrix. Figure 4.3 illustrates this process.

As you look at this illustration, it should be clear that switching the order of the input matrices will (probably) produce a different result. This leads to an important property of matrix–matrix multiplication: it's not commutative. If A * B = C, B * A does not necessarily equal C.

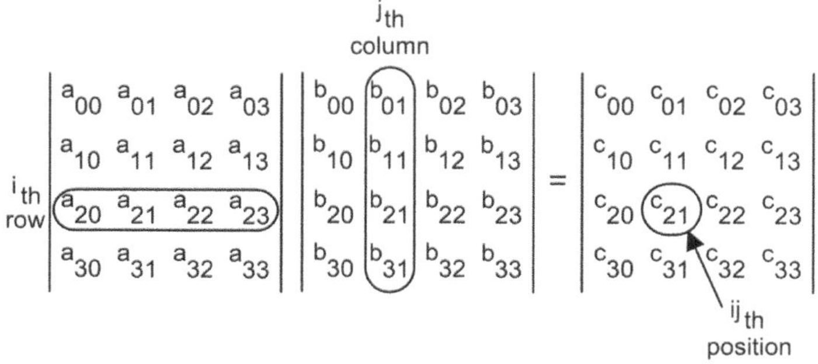

$$\underset{\substack{i\text{th}\\ \text{row}}}{\begin{vmatrix} a_{00} & a_{01} & a_{02} & a_{03} \\ a_{10} & a_{11} & a_{12} & a_{13} \\ a_{20} & a_{21} & a_{22} & a_{23} \\ a_{30} & a_{31} & a_{32} & a_{33} \end{vmatrix}} \begin{vmatrix} b_{00} & b_{01} & b_{02} & b_{03} \\ b_{10} & b_{11} & b_{12} & b_{13} \\ b_{20} & b_{21} & b_{22} & b_{23} \\ b_{30} & b_{31} & b_{32} & b_{33} \end{vmatrix} = \begin{vmatrix} c_{00} & c_{01} & c_{02} & c_{03} \\ c_{10} & c_{11} & c_{12} & c_{13} \\ c_{20} & c_{21} & c_{22} & c_{23} \\ c_{30} & c_{31} & c_{32} & c_{33} \end{vmatrix}$$

jth column — ijth position

FIGURE 4.3   Matrix–Matrix multiplication.

In addition to the arithmetic operators, WGSL provides two helpful functions that operate on matrices. The `transpose` function accepts a matrix and returns a matrix with the rows and columns switched. The `determinant` function accepts a matrix and returns a value equal to the determinant of the matrix.

Array types

Like a vector, an array contains multiple elements of the same type. But there are at least four important differences between arrays and vectors:

1. An array can store more than four elements.
2. WGSL doesn't provide operations that process every element of an array at once—a shader needs to iterate through the array to operate on its elements.
3. While a vector can only contain scalar values, an array can contain scalars, vectors, matrices, and structures. But each element must have the same type.
4. Unlike vectors, an array's alignment depends only on the type of its elements. If an array contains four-byte elements, it will be aligned on four-byte boundaries in memory.

WGSL supports two types of arrays, and the difference between them involves their number of elements, or size. Most arrays are *fixed-size*, and their size must be specified in the declaration. The size of a *runtime-sized array* can be changed at runtime. Fixed-size arrays can be defined anywhere, but runtime-sized arrays can only be used in certain situations. I've only used runtime-sized arrays in compute shaders, which will be introduced in Chapter 8.

The declaration of a fixed-size array must specify the type of its elements and the number of elements in the array. The following code creates an array named `arr`, which contains three elements:

```
// Array containing three 32-bit unsigned integers
var arr = array<u32, 3>;
```

When possible, shaders should use vectors instead of arrays. But if an object needs to store more values than a vector can hold, arrays are the only option. For this reason, when the application passes large buffers to the GPU, the underlying data is frequently accessed as an array of values.

Structure types

When a shader needs to access related data items, it's common to store them in a structure. This doesn't provide performance advantages, but it simplifies the code by organizing fields inside a named container.

As in the C programming language, a structure is declared with the `struct` keyword, followed by member declarations in curly braces. For example, the following code declares a structure named `Complex` with two floating-point members named `real` and `imag`:

```
// Example structure
struct Complex {
    real: f32,
    imag: f32
};
```

After this declaration, the shader can create structures by calling the name with member values in parentheses. The following code shows how this works:

```
const z = Complex(2.0, 4.0);
```

Structures are particularly helpful when a shader receives related data items from the application. This will become clear when we look at accessing buffer data in shaders.

Variables and Storage

WGSL supports `let`, `const`, and `var`, but there are major differences between their usage in WGSL and JavaScript. When you use `let` or `const` in a shader, you're declaring a *value*. The declaration assigns a name to a value, but the data won't be stored anywhere. In addition, `let` can only be used inside a function, while `const` can be used inside and outside of functions.

When a declaration starts with `var`, it creates a *variable* whose data will be stored in memory. This is more complicated than using `let` and `const` because a `var` declaration needs to identify the type of memory that will contain the variable's data.

To set a variable's memory type, a declaration can follow `var` with the name of an *address space* between angle brackets. For example, the following code declares a 32-bit floating-point variable to be stored in the private address space:

```
var<private> foo: f32;
```

Another way to set a variable's type is to provide a value. In the following code, it's understood that the variable will store a floating-point value:

```
var<private> foo = 1234.0;
```

In these declarations, the `private` keyword indicates that the variable should be stored in the private address space. This is available for global variables declared outside of a shader function. If a variable is intended to be used inside a function, its address space should be set to `function`. If a variable is declared inside a function

TABLE 4.5 Address spaces for variables

ADDRESS SPACE	DEFAULT ACCESS MODE	DESCRIPTION
function	read–write	Variables declared inside functions
private	read–write	Global variables
storage	read	Data in a storage buffer
uniform	read	Data in a uniform buffer
handle	read	Sampler and texture variables
workgroup	read–write	Data used by compute shaders

without an address space, it's understood that the variable will be stored in the function space. This is shown in the following code:

```
// Stored in the function address space
var foo = 1234.0;
```

Table 4.5 lists all of the address spaces available for storing variables.

Chapter 3 explained how an application can create resources that hold data intended for a shader. The two types of resources are *buffers*, which hold general-purpose data, and *textures*, which hold texture data. To access a resource, a shader needs to declare a variable in the storage, uniform, or handle address spaces. Variables that provide access to resources are called *resource variables*, and I'll discuss them throughout this chapter.

Chapter 3 also explained that attribute data (such as coordinates) changes from vertex to vertex. In contrast, uniform data remains constant (uniform) from one vertex to the next. For this reason, uniform data is stored in uniform buffers that are accessed through the uniform address space. Chapter 5 will discuss uniforms in greater depth.

The last two address spaces, handle and workgroup, will be discussed in later chapters. The handle space is only used by applications that access textures, which will be discussed in Chapter 6. The workgroup space is only used by applications creating compute shaders, which will be discussed in Chapter 8.

Constants and Overridden Variables

As we'll see, passing data from the application (JavaScript) to a shader (WGSL) is usually a complex process. You need to create special resource objects (buffers and textures) and associate these resources with specially formatted data and other objects.

If you just want to set scalar values in a shader, you can take advantage of constants (which have nothing to do with the const keyword). As mentioned in Chapter 3, the createRenderPipeline method accepts an object that includes a vertex object and a fragment object. The vertex and fragment objects have an optional property named `constants` that can be set to a sequence of name–value pairs. The following code shows how this works:

```
// Create a render pipeline that defines constants
const renderPipeline = device.createRenderPipeline({
    layout: …,
    vertex: {
        module: …,
        entryPoint: …
        constants: {
            0: false,
            22: 5.4,
            num_pixels: 256,
        }
    },
});
```

In this code, `constants` is set to an object containing three name–value pairs separated by colons. Each name can be an integer or a string. Each value can be an integer, a floating-point value, or a Boolean value.

Inside a shader, these name–value pairs can be accessed through special variables called *overridden variables*. An overridden variable can be declared in one of two ways. If the constant name is an integer, the corresponding declaration starts with the `@id` attribute containing the name in parentheses. The general form of the declaration is given as follows:

```
@id(name) override var_name: type;
```

For example, if the constants object maps 0 to false, the corresponding declaration in a shader could be coded as follows:

```
@id(0) override example: bool;
```

Even though this variable isn't set to a value in the shader, it will be set to false when the shader executes.

If the constant name is a string, the `@id` attribute isn't needed. Instead, the variable's name needs to be set to the constant's name. For example, if the `constants` object maps `num_pixels` to `256`, the corresponding declaration in the shader could be coded in the following way:

```
override num_pixels: u32;
```

The variable's value isn't set in the shader, but because of the constants object, `num_pixels` will be set to `256` when the shader executes.

Overridden variables are convenient when an application needs to pass simple scalars to a shader at compile time. They become particularly helpful when coding compute applications, which will be introduced in Chapter 8.

VERTEX SHADERS

Now that you understand the basics of WGSL, let's look at how vertex shaders are coded. The following code presents the vertex shader used in the Ch04_OrangeTriangle application:

```
@vertex
fn vertexMain(@location(0) coords: vec2f, @location(1) colors:
vec3f) -> @builtin(position) vec4f {
    return vec4f(coords, 0.0, 1.0);
}
```

This function is an entry point for a vertex shader because its name is preceded by @vertex. It accepts two parameters (a vec2f and a vec3f) and produces a vector as a return value.

There are two aspects of this code that need to be explained: the @location attribute that precedes both parameters and the @builtin attribute that precedes the return value. In my opinion, these modifiers should be called *annotations* or *decorators* because *attribute* already has a specific meaning in WebGPU. However, the WGSL standard refers to them as attributes.

The Location Attribute

The @location attribute makes it possible for shaders to access data in resources (buffers and textures). In the preceding code, this attribute precedes the shader's arguments, coords, and colors.

Chapter 3 explained how to create a vertex buffer containing the vertices of a triangle in two dimensions. Each vertex needs two attributes: the (x, y) coordinates and the RGB color of each vertex. The following code shows the vertex data is defined:

```
// Define vertex data (coordinates and colors)
const vertexData = new Float32Array([
    0.0, 0.5, 0.0, 1.0, 0.0,    // First vertex (green)
    -0.5, -0.5, 1.0, 0.0, 0.0,  // Second vertex (red)
    0.5, -0.5, 0.0, 0.0, 1.0    // Third vertex (blue)
]);
```

To make this data available to the shader, the application needs to create a vertex buffer. The following code shows how this can be done:

```
// Create a vertex buffer
const vertexBuffer = device.createBuffer({
    label: "Example vertex buffer",
    size: vertexData.byteLength,
    usage: GPUBufferUsage.VERTEX | GPUBufferUsage.COPY_DST
});
```

The application also needs to define the buffer's structure using a layout object. The following code defines a layout object for the vertex buffer, which contains coordinates and colors:

```
// Create a layout object for the vertex buffer
const bufferLayout = {
    arrayStride: 20,
    attributes: [
        { format: "float32x2", offset: 0, shaderLocation: 0 },
        { format: "float32x3", offset: 8, shaderLocation: 1 }
    ],
};
```

A vertex shader can access data in the vertex buffer through the parameters of its entry point function. Each parameter needs to have the @location(n) attribute, where n corresponds to the shaderLocation field in the layout object.

This code can be confusing, so I'll step through it carefully. The first element in the attributes array has a shaderLocation of 0. As a result, the shader can access this through a parameter preceded by @location(0). Because the element's format is float32x2, the parameter's type should be vec2f.

The second element in the attributes array has shaderLocation set to 1. The shader can access this through a parameter preceded by @location(1). Because the element's format is float32x3, the parameter's type should be vec3f.

The Builtin Attribute

A vertex shader executes once for each vertex to be processed. During each execution, a vertex shader can access three special variables called *builtin variables*. Table 4.6 lists each of them along with their direction (R for read or W for write) and data type.

The position variable is particularly important because, at minimum, a vertex shader needs to set the position of each vertex to be rendered. For this reason, WebGPU shaders either return the position variable or a structure containing the position variable as its first field.

To tell WebGPU that a variable is to be accessed as a builtin variable, you need to declare it with @builtin(*varname*), where *varname* is the variable's name. This explains why, in the preceding code, the return value is given as @builtin(position).

The vertex_index variable becomes important when a shader needs to process vertices differently depending on their order. Similarly, the instance_index

TABLE 4.6 Builtin variables for vertex shaders

BUILTIN VARIABLE	R/W	DATA TYPE	DESCRIPTION
position	W	vec4f	The location of the current vertex
vertex_index	R	u32	The index of the current vertex
instance_index	R	u32	The index of the current instance

variable is helpful for applications that render multiple copies of a shape. This is called *instanced rendering*, and I'll demonstrate how it works later in the chapter.

FRAGMENT SHADERS

Fragment shaders and vertex shaders have a lot in common—they're both coded in WGSL, and they can both access attributes like `@location` and `@builtin`. But while the fundamental role of a vertex shader is to assign locations to vertices, the fundamental role of a fragment shader is to assign color and depth to fragments.

If an application needs to associate an image's pixels with a surface, its fragment shader will be responsible for accessing the image data, which is provided in a texture. Chapter 6 explains how to create texture objects and access them in a fragment shader. Vertex shaders can't access textures, but compute shaders can.

A fragment shader executes once for each fragment to be processed. During its execution, it can access a series of builtin variables. Table 4.7 lists these variables and provides a description of each.

The first variable, `position`, can be confusing because it has the same name and type as the `position` variable used in vertex shaders. But in a fragment shader, the fragment's position is an input variable that can't be changed. In addition, its content is markedly different:

- The first two floats in `position` identify the fragment's location in 2-D space. To distinguish this space from the vertex space, the coordinates are denoted (u, v).
- The third float in `position` identifies the fragment's input depth.
- The fourth float in `position` identifies the fragment's perspective divisor, which is used in perspective transformations. Chapter 5 discusses perspective transformations in detail.

The next variable in the table, `frag_depth`, is an output value containing the fragment's depth, which ranges between 0.0 and 1.0. If the fragment shader doesn't

TABLE 4.7 Builtin variables for fragment shaders

BUILTIN VARIABLE	R/W	DATA TYPE	DESCRIPTION
position	R	vec4f	Fragment position
frag_depth	W	f32	Fragment depth
front_facing	R	bool	True if the fragment is on a front-facing primitive
sample_index	R	u32	Index of the current sample
sample_mask	R/W	u32	Indicates which samples are covered by the current primitive

assign a value to this, it will be set equal to the third float in the `position` variable. Chapter 6 discusses depth processing in detail.

Chapter 3 explained how an application can specify which primitives are front-facing using the orientation of its vertices. The `front_facing` variable is true if the current fragment lies on a front-facing primitive and false if it doesn't.

The last two variables in the table relate to sampling, which is the process by which a shader extracts data from a texture. Chapter 6 explains what samplers are and shows how these builtin variables can be used.

At minimum, a fragment shader is responsible for setting a fragment's color, so it may seem odd that none of the variables in the table refer to color. The reason is simple—every fragment shader must return a `vec4f` containing the fragment's color components (red, green, blue, and alpha). Because of this requirement, there's no need to assign a name for the return value.

An example will help make this clear. The following code presents the fragment shader used in the Ch04_OrangeTriangle application:

```
@fragment
fn fragmentMain() -> @location(0) vec4f {
    return vec4f(1.0, 0.647, 0.0, 1.0);
}
```

The return value is always (1.0, 0.647, 0.0, 1.0), which corresponds to orange. As a result of this shader, every fragment in the application will be colored orange.

SHADER MODULES

Chapter 3 introduced the render pipeline object, which is created with the `createRenderPipeline` method of the `GPUDevice`. This defines the steps used in the rendering process, and it has properties named `vertex` and `fragment` that represent the application's shaders. To configure these properties, a shader module must be created that contains the application's shader code (vertex and fragment shader code).

An application can create a shader module by calling the `createShaderModule` method of the `GPUDevice`. This accepts an object containing four properties, and Table 4.8 lists each of them.

TABLE 4.8   Properties of the shader module descriptor

PROPERTY	OPTIONAL?	DESCRIPTION
label	Y	Identifier used in debugging
code	N	String containing the shader code
hints	Y	Map that defines compiler hints for the shader
sourceMap	Y	Data used by developer tools

The only required property is code, which needs to be set to a string containing code for the vertex shader and the fragment shader. To demonstrate, the following code creates a shader module whose code is defined in a string named shaderStr:

```
// Create the shader module
const shaderModule = device.createShaderModule({
    label: "Example shader module",
    code: shaderStr
});
```

After the shader module is created, it can be used to configure the vertex and shader properties of the render pipeline. The vertex property must be set to an object that has four properties:

- module—shader module containing the vertex shader code
- entryPoint—name of the function that serves as the vertex shader's entry point
- buffers—array of buffer layouts that can be accessed by the vertex shader
- constants—optional name–value pairs that can set overridable values in the shader

The fragment property of the render pipeline must be set to an object whose properties are similar (but not identical) to those of the vertex object:

- module—shader module containing the fragment shader code
- entryPoint—name of the function that serves as the fragment shader's entry point
- targets—array of color states produced by the fragment shader
- constants—optional name–value pairs that can set overridable values in the shader

The difference between the vertex and fragment objects is that the vertex object accepts an array of buffer layout objects, and the fragment object accepts an array of color states. The Ch04_OrangeTriangle application creates a buffer layout named bufferLayout, which describes the structure of the vertex buffer. Then it creates the pipeline with the following code:

```
// Create render pipeline with vertex and fragment shader
const renderPipeline = device.createRenderPipeline({
    layout: "auto",
    vertex: {
        module: shaderModule,
        entryPoint: "vertexMain",
        buffers: [bufferLayout]
    },
```

```
fragment: {
    module: shaderModule,
    entryPoint: "fragmentMain",
    targets: [{ format: canvasFormat }]
}
});
```

Chapter 2 explained how the getPreferredCanvasFormat method identifies the desired color format of the canvas's pixels. The fragment shader needs to know how pixels should be formatted, so it's common to set the format property equal to the preferred canvas format.

The constants property of the vertex and fragment objects makes it possible for the pipeline to assign values to overridden variables in the shader. This useful capability was discussed earlier in the chapter.

EXAMPLE APPLICATION—DRAWING AN ORANGE TRIANGLE

If you look through the code in the Ch04_OrangeTriangle application, you'll see that most of the code resembles that of the Ch03_BlueCanvas application from the previous chapter. But the code in ch04_orangetriangle.js is different in at least three ways:

1. It defines a string named shaderCode that contains the code for the vertex shader and the fragment shader.
2. It creates a vertex buffer that contains attributes of the triangle's three points. It also creates a layout object that describes the buffer's structure.
3. It creates a shader module from the text in shaderCode and uses it to create a render pipeline.

To present the code in ch04_orangetriangle.js, this discussion splits it into four parts:

1. Obtaining the fundamental objects
2. Configuring the vertex buffer
3. Creating the objects needed for graphical rendering
4. Coding the vertex and fragment shaders

This sequence doesn't necessarily follow the code's organization. This is because the example code places the shader string at the top of the source file.

Fundamental Objects

Chapter 2 explained the basic objects that need to be created in every WebGPU application. These include the adapter, device, and command encoder. The following code obtains these objects and configures their behavior.

```
// Check if WebGPU is supported
if (!navigator.gpu) {
    throw new Error("WebGPU not supported");
}

// Access the GPUAdapter
const adapter = await navigator.gpu.requestAdapter();
if (!adapter) {
    throw new Error("No GPUAdapter found");
}

// Access the client GPU
const device = await adapter.requestDevice();
if (!device) {
    throw new Error("Failed to create a GPUDevice");
}

// Access the canvas
const canvas = document.getElementById("canvas_example");
if (!canvas) {
    throw new Error("Could not access canvas in page");
}

// Obtain a WebGPU context for the canvas
const context = canvas.getContext("webgpu");
if (!context) {
    throw new Error("Could not obtain WebGPU context for
    canvas");
}

// Configure the context with the device and format
const canvasFormat = navigator.gpu.getPreferredCanvasFormat();
context.configure({
    device: device,
    format: canvasFormat,
});

// Create the command encoder
const encoder = device.createCommandEncoder();
if (!encoder) {
    throw new Error("Failed to create a GPUCommandEncoder");
}
```

In addition to creating the basic objects needed for WebGPU, this code accesses the canvas element in the web page. Then it configures the canvas's context to display the result of WebGPU rendering.

The last portion of this code creates the command encoder. The application will access this encoder to create graphical rendering commands for the GPU.

The Vertex Buffer

To define the triangle to be drawn, the application needs to tell the vertex shader where the triangle's points should be placed in the scene. This requires creating a vertex buffer containing the points' coordinates. The following code creates a Float32Array containing the (x, y) coordinates and then creates a vertex buffer and its layout.

```
// Define vertex data
const vertexData = new Float32Array([
    0.0, 0.5,      // First vertex
    -0.5, -0.5,    // Second vertex
    0.5, -0.5      // Third vertex
]);

// Create vertex buffer
const vertexBuffer = device.createBuffer({
    label: "Example vertex buffer",
    size: vertexData.byteLength,
    usage:
        GPUBufferUsage.VERTEX |
        GPUBufferUsage.COPY_DST
});

// Write data to buffer
device.queue.writeBuffer(vertexBuffer, 0, vertexData);
renderPass.setVertexBuffer(0, vertexBuffer);

// Define layout of buffer data
const bufferLayout = {
    arrayStride: 8,
    attributes: [
        { format: "float32x2", offset: 0, shaderLocation: 0 }
    ],
};
```

In this code, the vertexData array contains three pairs of coordinates: (0.0, 0.5), (−0.5, −0.5), and (0.5, −0.5). These are the coordinates of the triangle's vertices, and because the coordinates change from vertex to vertex, they need to be stored in a vertex buffer.

The application creates the vertex buffer by calling `device.createBuffer`. This accepts the size of the data to be stored, which can be obtained through the `byteLength` property of the `vertexData` array. It also sets usage to an OR'ed combination of two flags:

- `GPUBufferUsage.VERTEX`—the buffer will serve as a vertex buffer
- `GPUBufferUsage.COPY_DST`—the buffer can receive data through copy operations

The second flag is needed to ensure that data can be copied into the buffer. The application performs this copy operation by calling `device.queue.writeBuffer` with the data source (`vertexData`) and the buffer (`vertexBuffer`). Then it associates the vertex buffer with the render pass encoder by calling the encoder's `setVertexBuffer` method.

The last part of this code defines the layout of the vertex buffer. In this case, the data for each vertex consists of two four-byte floating-point values, so the stride is set to $2 * 4 = 8$. There's only one attribute per vertex, so the attribute array consists of a single element with three properties:

- `format` is set to `float32x2` because the attribute contains two 32-bit values
- `offset` is set to 0 because the first value is read from the start of the buffer
- `shaderLocation` is set to 0 because the vertex shader will access the coordinates through the attribute `@location(0)`

As a result of this code, the coordinates will be stored in the vertex buffer, which will be sent to the GPU. As the GPU executes the vertex shader, it will use these coordinates to set the locations of the points to be drawn.

Graphical Rendering Objects

After creating the command encoder and the vertex buffer, the application constructs three objects needed for graphical rendering:

- render pass encoder—stores the state of the rendering operation
- shader module—provides access to the vertex shader and fragment shader code
- render pipeline—defines the rendering process

After creating these objects, the application uses the render pass encoder to send the rendering commands to the command encoder. Then it launches the draw operation to display the three points.

```
// Create the render pass encoder
const renderPass = encoder.beginRenderPass({
    colorAttachments: [{
        view: context.getCurrentTexture().createView(),
        loadOp: "clear",
        clearValue: { r: 0.9, g: 0.9, b: 0.9, a: 1.0 },
        storeOp: "store"
    }]
});

// Create the shader module
const shaderModule = device.createShaderModule({
    label: "Example shader module",
    code: shaderCode
});

// Define the rendering procedure
const renderPipeline = device.createRenderPipeline({
    layout: "auto",
    vertex: {
        module: shaderModule,
        entryPoint: "vertexMain",
        buffers: [bufferLayout]
    },
    fragment: {
        module: shaderModule,
        entryPoint: "fragmentMain",
        targets: [{
            format: canvasFormat
        }]
    }
});
renderPass.setPipeline(renderPipeline);

// Draw vertices and complete rendering
renderPass.draw(3);
renderPass.end();

// Submit the render commands to the GPU
device.queue.submit([encoder.finish()]);
```

In this code, the beginRenderPass method creates the GPURenderPassEncoder. The colorAttachments object serves two important purposes. It identifies the canvas's context as the recipient of the drawing operation, and it sets the initial color of the rendering to (0.9, 0.9, 0.9), or light gray.

After creating the render pass encoder, the application creates the shader module from the code in the shaderCode string, which will be discussed shortly. Then it creates the render pipeline, describing the vertex shader in the `vertex` property and the fragment shader in the `fragment` property. Once the pipeline is created, the application associates it with the render-pass encoder by calling the encoder's `setPipeline` method.

Once the render pass encoder is fully configured, the application encodes the draw application by calling `draw` with the argument set to 3. As a result, the GPU will execute the vertex shader and fragment shader three times. With each execution, the vertex shader will read the vertex data and set its position. The fragment shader will assign the color to the corresponding fragment.

After the encoding is finished, the application obtains the buffer of rendering commands by calling the command encoder's `finish` method. Then it sends the commands to the GPU for processing by calling the `submit` method of the device's queue.

The Vertex and Fragment Shaders

At the top of the shader, the `shaderCode` string contains the code for the vertex and fragment shaders. This is shown in the following code:

```
const shaderCode = `
@vertex
fn vertexMain(@location(0) coords: vec2f) ->
@builtin(position) vec4f {
    return vec4f(coords, 0.0, 1.0);
}

@fragment
fn fragmentMain() -> @location(0) vec4f {
    return vec4f(1.0, 0.647, 0.0, 1.0);
}
`;
```

As shown, the entry point for the vertex shader is `vertexMain`. This receives an argument named `coords`, which is a vector containing two floating-point values. Because the argument is preceded by `@location(0)`, it accesses the attribute of the vertex buffer whose `shaderLocation` is set to 0. In this case, that attribute contains the vertex's coordinates.

The primary role of a vertex shader is to define the location of the current vertex. The location must be provided as a four-element vector, so `vertexMain` creates a `vec4f` containing the content of the `coords` vector followed by 0.0 and 1.0. This `vec4f` is preceded by the `return` keyword, so it will be provided as the vertex's location.

The entry point for the fragment shader is `fragmentMain`. The primary role of this shader is to set the color of the current fragment. Like the coordinates returned by the vertex shader, the color returned by the fragment shader must be a `vec4f`. In this case, the `vec4f` contains (1.0, 0.647, 0.0, 1.0), which corresponds to orange. As a result of this shader, every fragment in the primitive will be colored orange.

PASSING DATA TO THE FRAGMENT SHADER

Suppose you want to assign different colors to each of the triangle's vertices. Because the colors change from vertex to vertex, the color components must be stored in a vertex buffer. But there's a problem. Unlike vertex shaders, fragment shaders can't access vertex buffers directly.

However, a fragment shader can access the return value of a vertex shader. In the preceding code, the vertex shader only returned the position of the vertex being processed. But we can expand this return value by creating a structure. That is, we can define a structure that contains the vertex position *and* the color data to be passed to the fragment shader.

The best way to understand this is with an example. The following code defines a structure named `DataStruct`, which contains two fields. The first contains vertex coordinates and the second field contains color data to be used by the fragment shader.

```
// Structure containing vertex coordinates and color
struct DataStruct {
    @builtin(position) pos: vec4f,
    @location(0) colors: vec3f,
}
```

To pass this to the fragment shader, the type of the vertex shader's return value must be set to `DataStruct`. Then the vertex shader needs to initialize a `DataStruct`, set its fields, and return the structure. The following code shows how this can be done:

```
// Pass a structure as the return value
@vertex
fn vertexMain(@location(0) coords: vec2f, @location(1) colors:
vec3f) -> DataStruct {
    var outData: DataStruct;
    outData.pos = vec4f(coords, 0.0, 1.0);
    outData.colors = colors;
    return outData;
}
```

Because the vertex shader returns a `DataStruct`, the fragment shader can access the structure as a parameter of its entry point function. Then it can set the fragment's color by accessing the `colors` field of the structure. The following code shows how this can be done:

```
// Receive the structure and access colors
@fragment
fn fragmentMain(fragData: DataStruct) -> @location(0) vec4f {
    return vec4f(fragData.colors, 1.0);
}
```

EXAMPLE APPLICATION—DRAWING A MULTI-COLORED TRIANGLE

Passing data from the vertex shader to the fragment shader is important to understand. To demonstrate this, the Ch04_MultiTriangle application assigns a different color to each vertex of the triangle. This color data is passed from the vertex shader to the fragment shader, which sets the fragment's color.

The code in the Ch04_MultiTriangle project is nearly identical to that in the Ch04_OrangeTriangle project, and they both create essentially the same objects. But the code in Ch04_MultiTriangle is different in three ways:

1. The vertex buffer contains color data for each vertex in addition to vertex coordinates.
2. The vertex shader returns a data structure containing the color data.
3. The fragment shader receives the data structure and uses the color data to assign colors.

This section discusses the code in ch04_multitriangle.js that performs each of these operations.

The Vertex Buffer

In the Ch04_MultiTriangle project, each point has a location (two floats) and a color (three floats). This is reflected in the following code, which creates an array containing coordinates and color components, and then writes the data to a vertex buffer.

```
// Define vertex data (coordinates and colors)
const vertexData = new Float32Array([
    0.0, 0.5, 0.0, 1.0, 0.0,      // First vertex
    -0.5, -0.5, 1.0, 0.0, 0.0,    // Second vertex
    0.5, -0.5, 0.0, 0.0, 1.0      // Third vertex
]);
```

```
// Create vertex buffer
const vertexBuffer = device.createBuffer({
    label: "Example vertex buffer",
    size: vertexData.byteLength,
    usage:
        GPUBufferUsage.VERTEX |
        GPUBufferUsage.COPY_DST
});

// Write data to buffer
device.queue.writeBuffer(vertexBuffer, 0, vertexData);
renderPass.setVertexBuffer(0, vertexBuffer);
// Define layout of buffer data
const bufferLayout = {
    arrayStride: 20,
    attributes: [
        { format: "float32x2", offset: 0, shaderLocation: 0 },
        { format: "float32x3", offset: 8, shaderLocation: 1 }
    ],
};
```

The `vertexData` array contains the coordinates and colors of the vertices. The first point, at (0.0, 0.5), has a color of green (0.0, 1.0, 0.0). The second point, at (−0.5, −0.5), has a color of red (1.0, 0.0, 0.0). The third point, at (0.5, −0.5), has a color of blue (0.0, 0.0, 1.0).

After defining the vertex data, the application creates a vertex buffer and creates a command to write the vertex data to the buffer by calling the `writeBuffer` method of the device's queue. Then it associates the buffer with the render pass encoder by calling the encoder's `setVertexBuffer` method.

The last part of the code defines the layout of the vertex buffer. In this case, each vertex has five four-byte floats, so `arrayStride` equals 5 * 4 = 20. The vertex shader needs two values per vertex, so the attributes array contains two elements. The first element identifies the coordinates (`float32x2`), and the second element identifies the color components (`float32x3`). The first attribute has a `shaderLocation` of 0, so the vertex shader can access it using `@location(0)`, and the second attribute has a `shaderLocation` of 1, so the vertex shader can access it using `@location(1)`.

The Vertex and Fragment Shaders

The shader code in the Ch04_MultiTriangle project defines a data structure named `DataStruct`, which has one field for coordinates and one field for color components. The vertex shader creates a `DataStruct` and makes it its return value. The fragment shader receives the DataStruct and uses it to set the fragment's color. The following code presents both shaders.

```
struct DataStruct {
    @builtin(position) pos: vec4f,
    @location(0) colors: vec3f,
}

@vertex
fn vertexMain(@location(0) coords: vec2f, @location(1) colors:
vec3f) -> DataStruct {
    var outData: DataStruct;
    outData.pos = vec4f(coords, 0.0, 1.0);
    outData.colors = colors;
    return outData;
}

@fragment
fn fragmentMain(fragData: DataStruct) -> @location(0) vec4f {
    return vec4f(fragData.colors, 1.0);
}
```

The operation of the vertex shader is important to understand. It creates a DataStruct variable named outData, and then sets its pos field to a vec4f containing the desired location of the current vertex. It sets the colors field to a vec3f containing the desired color of the current vertex.

The fragment shader receives the DataStruct as a function argument. It ignores the pos field and accesses the colors field, which it uses to set the color of the current fragment. This color, like the vertex's coordinates, must be provided in a vector containing four floating-point values (vec4f).

SUMMARY

This chapter has covered a great deal of ground, from the fundamentals of WGSL to coding vertex shaders and fragment shaders. WGSL may seem strange to newcomers, with odd data types like mat4x4f and odd attributes like @location(...) and @builtin(...). But the better you understand WGSL, the more efficiently your shaders will execute and the fewer errors you'll have to wrestle with.

A vertex shader executes once for each vertex in the rendering, and its primary goal is to set the vertex's location in space. To perform its operations, a vertex shader can access builtin variables, including the position of the current vertex, accessed with @builtin(position), and the index of the current vertex, accessed with @builtin(index). At minimum, it needs to return a vec4f that defines the vertex's coordinates, but it can also return a structure that contains the coordinates in addition to other data.

A fragment is essentially like a pixel, but while a pixel has a color and a location, a fragment has a color, a location, and a depth. The fragment shader executes once for each fragment, and it can access builtin variables like @builtin(frag_depth) and @builtin(front_facing). The fragment shader needs to return a vec4f containing the color to be applied to the current fragment.

To be accessible in an application, the vertex shader code and fragment shader code need to be combined into shader modules, which are then associated with a render pipeline. The pipeline can also define constants that can be accessed in shaders using overridden variables. These constants are helpful when an application needs to send scalar values to shaders outside of buffers and other resources.

If you don't have a solid grasp of all the material in this chapter, don't be concerned. Later chapters will clarify how buffers, pipelines, and shaders work together. The next chapter explains how matrices and uniform buffers make it possible to change the positions and orientations of shapes in the rendering.

Uniforms and Transformations

5

In essence, a transformation is an operation that changes the locations of a shape's vertices. This chapter looks at a specific group of transformations called linear transformations, which translate, rotate, or scale a shape. Mathematically, an application transforms a shape by multiplying the coordinates of a shape's points by a suitable matrix.

UNIFORM BUFFERS AND BIND GROUPS

As discussed in Chapter 3, a vertex buffer stores *attribute data*, which changes from vertex to vertex. A vertex shader can access data in a vertex buffer through the parameters of its entry point, and it can pass the data to the fragment shader through its return value.

Now suppose you have data that will remain constant (or *uniform*) between vertices and fragments. Storing the data in a vertex buffer is inefficient, so WebGPU provides *uniform buffers*. The process of creating, configuring, and using a uniform buffer requires five steps:

1. Create a buffer resource whose type identifies it as a uniform buffer.
2. Associate the buffer with data by calling the queue's `writeBuffer` method.
3. Access a bind group layout that describes the pipeline's bind groups.
4. Create a bind group that associates the uniform buffer with a binding value.
5. In a shader, access data in the uniform using the `@group` and `@binding` attributes.

This section discusses these steps from start to finish. To be specific, the goal is to create a uniform buffer containing the following sixteen values:

```
const uniformData = new Float32Array([
    0.866, 0.5, 0.0, 0.0,      // First column of matrix
    -0.5, 0.866, 0.0, 0.0,     // Second column of matrix
    0.0, 0.0, 1.0, 0.0,        // Third column of matrix
    0.0, 0.0, 0.0, 1.0,        // Fourth column of matrix
]);
```

DOI: 10.1201/9781003422839-5

This data represents a *rotation matrix*, and a later section will explain why these and similar matrices are important. This section explains how to create a uniform buffer that stores this data. Then we'll look at how the buffer can be accessed in a shader.

Step 1: Create a Uniform Buffer

Chapter 3 explained how to create a vertex buffer by calling the `createBuffer` method of the `GPUDevice`. This accepts the buffer's size in bytes and usage.

The process is nearly identical for uniform buffers. The only difference is that the `usage` property should be set to an OR'ed combination of `GPUBufferUsage.UNIFORM` and `GPUBufferUsage.COPY_DST`. The following code creates a uniform buffer capable of storing 64 bytes of data:

```
const uniformBuffer = device.createBuffer({
    label: "Uniform Buffer 0",
    size: uniformData.byteLength,
    usage: GPUBufferUsage.UNIFORM | GPUBufferUsage.COPY_DST
});
```

For the `usage` property, it's important to add `GPUBufferUsage.COPY_DST` when creating vertex buffers and uniform buffers. If this isn't present, the application won't be able to copy data into the buffer.

Step 2: Associate the uniform buffer with data

WebGPU provides a few ways to associate data with a buffer. The simplest method is to call the `writeBuffer` method of the device's queue. As discussed in Chapter 3, this can accept five arguments:

1. `buffer`—the `GPUBuffer` to receive data
2. `bufferOffset`—byte offset to start writing data into the buffer
3. `data`—the source of the data to be written (`ArrayBuffer`, `TypedArray`, or `DataView`)
4. `dataOffset`—byte offset to start accessing data from the source (optional)
5. `size`—number of bytes to be written from the source to the buffer (optional)

For example, suppose the device's name is `device`, the uniform buffer is `uniformBuffer`, and the data to be stored is `uniformData`. The following code tells the device to associate the data with the buffer:

```
device.queue.writeBuffer(uniformBuffer, 0, uniformData);
```

The `writeBuffer` method lets the client choose how to copy the data into the buffer. The alternative is to map the buffer to data using the methods of the `GPUBuffer`. Chapter 8 discusses this process in detail.

Step 3: Access a Bind Group Layout

In my opinion, the most annoying WebGPU objects to deal with are bind groups and bind group layouts. The goal is to reduce the number of data transfers between the CPU and GPU by combining multiple data elements into large structures.

A GPUBindGroup combines multiple resources into a single object. These resources can be uniform buffers, textures, or samplers. Each resource must be associated with an integer, and this association is called a *binding*. The object that associates resources with their binding values is called a *bind group*.

A pipeline can access multiple bind groups, and each bind group must also have its own binding values. The object that describes bind groups with binding values is called a *bind group layout*. When an application creates a render pipeline, the layout property must be associated with a pipeline layout, which manages bind group layouts.

Here's a quick summary of the relevant terminology:

1. A render pipeline has a *pipeline layout*, which contains one or more *bind group layouts*.
2. A bind group layout describes one or more *bind groups*.
3. A bind group contains one or more resources of a given type. Each resource must be associated with a binding value.

It takes a lot of code to create pipeline layouts and bind group layouts manually. But if you create the render pipeline with the layout property set to auto, WebGPU will analyze the shader code and automatically create a pipeline layout with a single-bind group layout.

An application can access a bind group layout by calling the render pipeline's getBindGroupLayout method with the layout's index. If the pipeline's layout is created automatically, its bind group layout can be accessed with the following code:

```
const bindGrouplayout = renderPipeline.getBindGroupLayout(0);
```

If your application needs several bind groups, it's a good idea to create the render pipeline's layout and bind group layouts manually. But if you don't need this level of data management, you can set layout to auto and access the bind group layout with getBindGroupLayout.

Step 4: Create a Bind Group

Even if your application only has one uniform buffer, you'll need to create a bind group that binds the buffer to a value. Bind groups are created by calling the createBindGroup of the GPUDevice. This accepts an object with the following properties:

- label—optional name for the bind group
- layout—the bind group layout that describes the bind group's resources
- entries—an array of resources and their bindings

The `layout` property can be set to the bind group layout returned by the pipeline's `getBindGroupLayout` method. The `entries` property must be set to an array of elements that identify resources and their bindings. To be specific, each element of entries must have two properties:

- `resource`—resource belonging to the bind group
- `binding`—the integer to which the resource is bound

If the resource is a buffer (specifically, a `GPUBuffer`), the `resource` property must be set to a buffer binding. This has three properties:

- `buffer`—the buffer containing data for the bind group
- `offset`—optional byte offset into the buffer for reading/writing data
- `size`—optional amount of data in the buffer to be accessed

The following code accesses the pipeline's bind group layout and creates a bind group for the uniform buffer named `uniformBuffer`:

```
// Access the bind group layout
bindGroupLayout = renderPipeline.getBindGroupLayout(0);

// Create the bind group
let bindGroup = device.createBindGroup({
    layout: bindGroupLayout,
    entries: [
        {
            binding: 0,
            resource: { buffer: uniformBuffer }
        }
    ]
});
```

The render pass encoder needs to be informed that this bind group exists. To accomplish this, the application needs to call the encoder's `setBindGroup` method, which accepts three parameters:

- the index by which the bind group should be accessed in a shader
- the `GPUBindGroup` created by `createBindGroup`
- an optional array of dynamic offset data

As an example, the following code associates `bindGroup` with the render pass encoder. The index is set to 0, so shaders can access the bind group through this value.

```
// Associate bind group with render pass encoder
renderPass.setBindGroup(0, bindGroup);
```

Once the bind group has been created and associated with the render pass encoder, shaders can access a resource's data using the index of the bind group and the binding value of the resource.

Step 5: Access the Uniform Data in Shaders

Chapter 4 explained how vertex buffer data can be accessed by preceding variable declarations with @location(n), where n is the index of the data in the vertex buffer. If a uniform buffer has been created and configured, shaders can access its data using variable declarations preceded by two attributes:

- @group(n)—identifies the bind group, where n is the index of the bind group in the render pass encoder
- @binding(n)—identifies the resource in the bind group, where n is the value bound to the resource

If an application only has one uniform buffer and one bind group, shaders can access the uniform buffer by declaring a variable with @group(0) @binding(0). As an example, the following code declares a variable that accesses the uniform buffer bound to 0 in the bind group whose index is 0:

```
// Declare variable that accesses a uniform buffer
@group(0) @binding(0) var<uniform> rotMat: mat4x4f;
```

As a result of this code, the shader will be able to access the uniform buffer's data as a 4-by-4 matrix of floating-point values. This type of variable plays an important role in graphical rendering because the matrix represents a type of transformation called a *rotation*. The following section presents code that creates and rotates a square.

EXAMPLE APPLICATION— ROTATING A SQUARE

The code in the Ch05_RotateSquare project demonstrates three new and important aspects of WebGPU development:

1. It creates a uniform buffer and a bind group.
2. The vertex shader accesses the uniform buffer as a matrix variable and multiplies the matrix by the coordinates of each vertex. Then it returns the transformed coordinates and the vertex's location.
3. It configures the pipeline to assemble vertices into a triangle strip instead of a triangle list.

FIGURE 5.1 The Ch05_RotateSquare page.

The third point is important to understand. By default, vertices are assembled into a *triangle list*, which creates one triangle from vertices v_0, v_1, and v_2 and a second triangle from vertices v_3, v_4, and v_5. But if the pipeline is configured to create a *triangle strip*, the first triangle will be created from vertices v_0, v_1, and v_2 and a second triangle from vertices v_1, v_2, and v_3. This makes it possible to draw a square (two triangles) from four vertices.

Figure 5.1 shows what the page looks like. As the project's name implies, the result of the rendering is a rotated square.

The following code listing presents the code of the Ch05_RotateSquare application. As in the preceding examples, the vertex shader and fragment shader code are combined into a string named `shaderCode`.

```
const shaderCode = `
@group(0) @binding(0) var<uniform> rotMat: mat4x4f;

@vertex
fn vertexMain(@location(0) coords: vec2f) -> @
builtin(position) vec4f {
    return rotMat * vec4f(coords, 0.0, 1.0);
}

@fragment
fn fragmentMain() -> @location(0) vec4f {
    return vec4f(0.2, 0.2, 1.0, 1.0);
}
`;

// Create top-level asynchronous function
async function runExample() {

// Check if WebGPU is supported
if (!navigator.gpu) {
    throw new Error("WebGPU not supported");
}
```

```
// Access the GPUAdapter
const adapter = await navigator.gpu.requestAdapter();
if (!adapter) {
    throw new Error("No GPUAdapter found");
}

// Access the GPU
const device = await adapter.requestDevice();
if (!device) {
    throw new Error("Failed to create a GPUDevice");
}

// Access the canvas
const canvas = document.getElementById("canvas_example");
if (!canvas) {
    throw new Error("Could not access canvas in page");
}

// Obtain a WebGPU context for the canvas
const context = canvas.getContext("webgpu");
if (!context) {
    throw new Error("Could not obtain WebGPU context for
canvas");
}

// Configure the context with the device and format
const canvasFormat = navigator.gpu.getPreferredCanvasFormat();
context.configure({
    device: device,
    format: canvasFormat,
});

// Create the command encoder
const encoder = device.createCommandEncoder();
if (!encoder) {
    throw new Error("Failed to create a GPUCommandEncoder");
}

// Create the render pass encoder
const renderPass = encoder.beginRenderPass({
    colorAttachments: [{
        view: context.getCurrentTexture().createView(),
        loadOp: "clear",
        clearValue: { r: 0.9, g: 0.9, b: 0.9, a: 1.0 },
        storeOp: "store"
    }]
});
```

```
// Define vertex data
const vertexData = new Float32Array([
    -0.5, -0.5,       // First vertex
    0.5, -0.5,        // Second vertex
    -0.5, 0.5,        // Third vertex
    0.5, 0.5,         // Fourth vertex
]);

// Create vertex buffer
const vertexBuffer = device.createBuffer({
    label: "Vertex Buffer 0",
    size: vertexData.byteLength,
    usage: GPUBufferUsage.VERTEX | GPUBufferUsage.COPY_DST
});
device.queue.writeBuffer(vertexBuffer, 0, vertexData);
renderPass.setVertexBuffer(0, vertexBuffer);

// Define layout of vertex buffer
const bufferLayout = {
    arrayStride: 8,
    attributes: [
        { format: "float32x2", offset: 0, shaderLocation: 0 }
    ],
};

// Define uniform data
const uniformData = new Float32Array([
    0.866, 0.5, 0.0, 0.0,      // First column of matrix
    -0.5, 0.866, 0.0, 0.0,     // Second column of matrix
    0.0, 0.0, 1.0, 0.0,        // Third column of matrix
    0.0, 0.0, 0.0, 1.0,        // Fourth column of matrix
]);

// Create uniform buffer
const uniformBuffer = device.createBuffer({
    label: "Uniform Buffer 0",
    size: uniformData.byteLength,
    usage: GPUBufferUsage.UNIFORM | GPUBufferUsage.COPY_DST});
device.queue.writeBuffer(uniformBuffer, 0, uniformData);

// Create the shader module
const shaderModule = device.createShaderModule({
    label: "Shader module 0",
    code: shaderCode
});
```

```
// Define the rendering procedure
const renderPipeline = device.createRenderPipeline({
    layout: "auto",
    vertex: {
        module: shaderModule,
        entryPoint: "vertexMain",
        buffers: [bufferLayout]
    },
    fragment: {
        module: shaderModule,
        entryPoint: "fragmentMain",
        targets: [{
            format: canvasFormat
        }]
    },
    primitive: {
        topology: "triangle-strip"
    }
});
renderPass.setPipeline(renderPipeline);

// Access the bind group layout
const bindGroupLayout = renderPipeline.getBindGroupLayout(0);

// Create the bind group
let bindGroup = device.createBindGroup({
    layout: bindGroupLayout,
    entries: [{
        binding: 0,
        resource: { buffer: uniformBuffer }
    }]
});

// Associate bind group with render pass encoder
renderPass.setBindGroup(0, bindGroup);

// Draw vertices and complete rendering
renderPass.draw(4);
renderPass.end();

// Submit the render commands to the GPU
device.queue.submit([encoder.finish()]);
}

// Run example function
runExample();
```

As you look through this code, it's important to see how the vertex buffer and uniform buffer work together. The vertex buffer provides different coordinates for each vertex, and the uniform buffer contains a 4-by-4 matrix that remains constant from vertex to vertex. Multiplying the matrix and the vertex coordinates produces a new set of coordinates that are rotated versions of the original.

STORAGE BUFFERS

Before we leave the topic of uniform buffers, I'd like to point out that they have one major shortcoming: they can only contain a limited amount of data. You can check this by accessing the `maxUniformBufferBindingSize` limit provided by the `GPUAdapter` object.

```
// Check the maximum size of uniforms
const maxSize = adapter.limits.maxUniformBufferBindingSize;
```

On my system, the maximum size of a uniform buffer is 65,536 bytes, so if you need to transfer more uniform data than that, you'll need to create several uniform buffers. Alternatively, you can create a *storage buffer*. On my system, the maximum size of a storage buffer is 2,147,483,644 bytes.

In code, working with storage buffers is like working with uniform buffers, but there are three main differences:

1. When creating the buffer, the `GPUBufferUsage.UNIFORM` flag must be changed to `GPUBufferUsage.STORAGE`.
2. When creating a bind group layout, the `type` property of the buffer property should be set to `storage` or `read-only-storage`.
3. When accessing the buffer in the shader, the `uniform` template should be changed to `storage`.

To clarify the third point, the following code declares a matrix variable whose data is read from a storage buffer:

```
// Declare a variable that accesses a storage buffer
@group(0) @binding(0) var<storage> mat: mat4x4f;
```

By default, storage buffers are read-only, like uniform buffers. However, storage buffers can also be created with read-write access. In this case, the shader's variable declaration should have an updated template type:

```
@group(0) @binding(0) var<storage, read_write> mat: mat4x4f;
```

The disadvantage of using storage buffers is performance. If your application needs to update data repeatedly, you're better off using uniform buffers than storage buffers.

From what I've seen, storage buffers are rarely used in graphical applications. But they're frequently used in compute applications to transfer data to and from the GPU. Starting with Chapter 8, shaders will rely primarily on storage buffers to read and write data.

LINEAR TRANSFORMATIONS

In the Ch05_RotateSquare project, the application creates a 4-by-4 matrix that can be used to transform an object's vertices. Three of the most important transformations are called *linear transformations*:

- scaling—increase or decrease an object's size
- translation—move an object a specified distance in a specified direction
- rotation—rotate an object a specified number of radians/degrees around an axis

These transformations are performed by multiplying the object's vertex coordinates by a matrix. When I first wrote the first draft of this chapter, I explained how to create these matrices manually. But in the real world, developers generate matrices by calling functions from a library.

At the time of this writing, the most popular matrix toolset for WebGPU is wgpu-matrix. This section starts by explaining how to access this package, and then shows how its functions can be used to create matrices for linear transformations.

The wgpu-matrix Library

Gregg Tavares has provided his fast 3-D math library, wgpu-matrix, under the MIT License, which allows open-source and proprietary projects to use it. The project's Github is at https://github.com/greggman/wgpu-matrix.

The wgpu-matrix library provides data structures that represent mathematical entities used in graphics. There are types that represent vectors (`vec2`, `vec3`, and `vec4`) and types that represent matrices (`mat3` and `mat4`). In this book, we're mainly interested in creating `mat4` instances, so JavaScript files start with the following statement:

```
import { mat4 } from 'https://wgpu-matrix.org/dist/2.x/wgpu-matrix.module.js';
```

If you execute this statement in most browsers, it will cause a security issue related to cross-origin resource sharing (CORS). This means you can't simply open the project's index.html in a browser and expect the code to work.

Instead, you can launch a local server that serves index.html. This can be accomplished using the `http-server` utility provided by Node.js or Python's `http.server`. Appendix A discusses the Node.js platform and explains how to install `http-server`.

TABLE 5.1   mat4 functions in `wgpu-matrix` (abridged)

METHOD	DESCRIPTION
`uniformScaling(num)`	Returns a matrix that scales vertices by the given number
`scaling(vec3)`	Returns a matrix that scales vertices by the values in the vector
`translation(vec3)`	Returns a matrix that translates vertices by the values in the vector
`rotationX(angle)`	Creates a matrix that rotates vertices around the x-axis by the given angle
`rotationY(angle)`	Creates a matrix that rotates vertices around the y-axis by the given angle
`rotationZ(angle)`	Creates a matrix that rotates vertices around the z-axis by the given angle
`mul(mat4, mat4)`	Returns the product of multiplying two matrices
`lookAt(vec3, vec3, vec3)`	Returns the matrix for the given view parameters
`ortho(left, right, bottom, top, near, far)`	Returns the matrix that performs the given orthographic projection
`frustum(left, right, bottom, top, near, far)`	Returns the matrix that transforms the viewing region into the given frustum
`perspective(fov, aspect, znear, zfar)`	Returns the perspective matrix

The `mat4` object provides several methods that create matrices and perform matrix operations. Table 5.1 lists ten of them and provides a description of each.

These methods do not generate matrices using the WGSL matrix types discussed in Chapter 4. By default, each of them returns a `Float32Array` containing sixteen floating-point values. As discussed earlier, these can be stored in a uniform buffer and accessed as matrices by shaders.

This section looks at the first seven methods in the table, which create matrices that make it possible to perform linear transformations. A later section will discuss the last three methods in the table.

Scaling

Of the three linear transformations, scaling is the simplest. When a scaling transformation is applied to an object centered at the origin, only the object's size changes: if the scaling factor is greater than one, the object grows. If the scaling factor is less than one, the object shrinks. In Figure 5.2, the scaling factor is set to 0.5, so the size of the origin-centered object reduces by half.

If an object isn't centered at the origin, scaling will change the object's location as well as its size. A shrinking object will move closer to the origin, and a growing object will move further away.

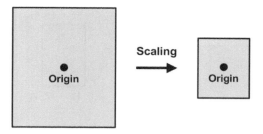

FIGURE 5.2 The scaling transformation.

The wgpu-matrix library makes it possible to scale an object uniformly in each dimension or scale each dimension differently. The `uniformScaling` method of the `mat4` object accepts a scaling factor and produces a scaling matrix that uniformly scales an object.

For example, the following code creates a `Float32Array` containing the values of a matrix that will double an object's size when multiplied by the object's vertex coordinates:

```
// Create a uniform scaling matrix
const uniformMat = mat4.uniformScaling(2.0);
```

In contrast, the `scaling` function accepts a `vec3` whose values identify how the object should be scaled in the x, y, and z directions. For example, the following code creates a `Float32Array` containing values of a matrix that will halve the object's size in the x-direction, triple the size in the y-direction, and double the size in the z-direction when multiplied by the object's vertex coordinates:

```
// Create a scaling matrix
const scaleMat = mat4.scaling([0.5, 3.0, 2.0]);
```

The `mat4` object also has a `getScaling` method that accepts a matrix and returns a vector containing the scaling factors in the x, y, and z directions.

Translation

Like scaling, translation is easy to understand. When you translate an object, you change its location but not its shape. Mathematically, translation is accomplished by adding or subtracting values from the object's coordinates: one value for the x-coordinate, one value for the y-coordinate, and one value for the z-coordinate.

For example, suppose you want to translate an object 5 units in the x-direction and 1 unit in the y-direction. You can accomplish this by adding the vector (5, 1) to the x and y coordinates of each vertex. This is shown in Figure 5.3.

In practice, graphical applications don't add values to a vector. Instead, we create a transformation matrix for translation and then multiply the matrix by the object's coordinate vectors. In wgpu-matrix, this can be done by calling the `translation` method

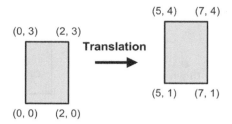

FIGURE 5.3 The translation transformation.

with a vector containing the translations in the x, y, and z directions. The following code shows how this works:

```
// Create a translation matrix
const transMat = mat4.translation([-2.0, -1.0, 2.0]);
```

When this is multiplied by an object's coordinate vectors, the object will move 2.0 units in the −x direction, 1.0 unit in the −y direction, and 2.0 units in the z direction.

Rotation

Rotation is easy to understand, but the math gets complicated. This discussion assumes that the rotation is being performed around the x, y, or z axis by an angle θ. Figure 5.4 illustrates an origin-centered shape rotated 30° clockwise around the z-axis.

The code in the Ch05_RotateSquare project demonstrates rotation by creating a matrix that rotates the object. The matrix is defined with the following code:

```
// Manually define a rotation matrix
const uniformData = new Float32Array([
    0.866, 0.5, 0.0, 0.0,      // First column of matrix
    -0.5, 0.866, 0.0, 0.0,     // Second column of matrix
    0.0, 0.0, 1.0, 0.0,        // Third column of matrix
    0.0, 0.0, 0.0, 1.0,        // Fourth column of matrix
]);
```

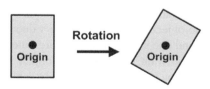

FIGURE 5.4 The rotation transformation.

Rather than setting each value manually, you can call three helpful methods of wgpu-matrix: `rotationX`, `rotationY`, and `rotationZ`. Each accepts an angle in radians and returns a `Float32Array` containing the values of the matrix capable of performing the rotation.

As an example, the following code creates a matrix that rotates an object by 45 degrees around the y-axis.

```
// Create a rotation matrix
const rotMat = mat4.rotationY(45.0 * Math.PI / 180.0);
```

Like most methods in wgpu-matrix, `rotationY` requires angle values in *radians*. If an angle's measurement in degrees is given by deg, the measurement in radians = deg * pi/180.

Combining Transformations

Many applications will need to perform several transformations on an object. Rather than store several matrices and perform several multiple matrix–vector multiplications, it's more efficient to use a single matrix that performs multiple transformations at once. Thankfully, the process of combining matrix transformations is simple—just multiply the matrices.

For example, suppose an application needs to perform Transformation A, followed by Transformation B. If Transformation A is represented by Matrix A and Transformation B is represented by Matrix B, the combination matrix C equals the product of the two matrices, B * A. When a shader multiplies C by vertex coordinates, the object will undergo Transformation A, followed by Transformation B.

Order is important. If the combination matrix C is set to A * B, Transformation B will be performed first and Transformation A will be performed second.

If matrices are stored in `Float32Arrays`, you can combine them by calling the `mul` method of the wgpu-matrix library. This accepts two arrays containing matrix values and returns a third containing the values of the product matrix. To demonstrate this, the following code creates a translation matrix and a rotation matrix and multiplies the two to produce a matrix that performs translation and rotation:

```
// Multiply two transformations
const transMat = mat4.translation([-2.0, -1.0, 2.0]);
const rotMat = mat4.rotationY(45 * Math.PI / 180);
const combinedMat = mat4.mul(transMat, rotMat);
```

If a shader multiplies `combinedMat` by an object's vertices, the object will be rotated *first* and *translated* second.

MODEL, VIEW, AND PERSPECTIVE TRANSFORMATIONS

When you code a 2-D application, the only transformations you need to know are the scaling, translation, and rotation transformations. But if you want to render objects in three dimensions, vertex transformation becomes more complex. You need to be concerned with the viewer's location and orientation, as well as the shape of the three-dimensional volume containing the model.

To take these factors into account, additional transformations are required, which means generating new transformation matrices. But before I discuss these matrices, it's important to be familiar with the different coordinate systems used in the rendering process.

Coordinate Systems

Modern 3-D applications transform an object's vertices multiple times before drawing the object. To keep track of the different transformations, developers use specific terms to refer to the coordinates at each stage. The most common terms are as follows:

1. object coordinates—initial coordinates given relative to the object's origin
2. world coordinates—the object's coordinates after being placed in the rendering volume (world), given relative to the volume's origin
3. eye coordinates—the object's coordinates after the viewer's location and orientation have been set
4. clip coordinates—the object's final coordinates after the viewing region has been defined

For example, if you download the design of a 3-D object from a web site like thingiverse.com, the object's coordinates will be given relative to a local origin, such as the object's center. Appropriately enough, these are called *object coordinates*.

To place this object into your scene, you need to perform linear transformations (scaling, translation, and rotation). The resulting coordinates of the object are its *world coordinates*.

When you play a modern 3-D game, you can adjust the point-of-view (also called the *camera*) to get a better look at the environment. To accomplish this programmatically, the application needs to transform every object based on the viewer's position. The resulting coordinates are called *eye coordinates* because they depend on how the scene is viewed.

Before any objects can be drawn, the application needs to define the overall viewing region to be displayed. Any shapes outside the region will be removed, or *clipped*, so the region is called *clip space*, and the resulting coordinates are called *clip coordinates*.

As part of the rendering process, the vertex shader needs to convert object coordinates to clip coordinates. This requires at least three transformations:

* *model transformation*—converts object coordinates to world coordinates
* *view transformation*—converts world coordinates to eye coordinates
* *projection transformation*—converts eye coordinates to clip coordinates

The rest of this discussion introduces the model, view, and projection transformations. If the viewer's position doesn't change, they can be combined into a single transformation matrix and passed to the vertex shader.

Model Transformation

Model transformations are easy to work with. These consist of the translations, rotations, and scaling operations needed to set the object's initial position and orientation. For example, if an object's new origin should be (−5.0, −4.0, −3.0), the transformation will be a simple translation that adds (−5.0, −4.0, −3.0) to each of the model's vertices. The matrix that performs the model transformation is referred to as the *model matrix*.

There is one important point to be aware of. By convention, the direction into the rendering volume is given as the *negative z-direction*. Therefore, if Object A's origin is moved to (0, 0, −5) and Object B's origin is moved to (0, 0, −10), Object B will appear further away than Object A.

View Transformation

After the objects in the model have been placed in their positions, the next step is to define how the model will be viewed. This is accomplished through the *view transformation*, which converts the world coordinates of each vertex to eye coordinates. Mathematically, this is represented by a matrix called the *view matrix*.

The wgpu-matrix library provides a special method for generating view matrices. It's called lookAt, and it accepts three required values:

* eye—vector containing coordinates of the viewer's location
* target—vector containing coordinates of where the viewer is looking
* up—vector containing components of the direction considered "up"

An example will clarify how lookAt can be used. Suppose the viewer is located at (5.0, 4.0, 3.0) and is looking at the point (0.0, 3.0, −3.0). If the viewer's up-direction is the positive y-axis (0.0, 1.0, 0.0), the following code will create an appropriate view matrix:

```
// Generate a view matrix
const lookMat = mat4.lookAt([5.0, 4.0, 3.0], [0.0, 3.0, -3.0],
[0.0, 1.0, 0.0]);
```

In many applications, the view matrix remains constant because the viewer's position and orientation don't change. But view matrices change frequently in augmented reality (AR) and virtual reality (VR) applications, where every motion of the viewer's head changes the point of view.

Projection Transformation

After positioning the object in the world and setting the viewer's position and direction, the next step is to define the volume containing the model. This is called the *viewing region*, and in most cases, it will have one of two shapes:

- A rectangular box whose opposite faces have the same dimensions
- A volume whose front face is smaller than its rear face. This is called a *frustum*.

The shape of the viewing region determines how objects will be displayed. Figure 5.5 shows what the two viewing regions look like.

The primary difference between the two regions involves the perception of depth. If objects are placed in the box-like volume, their displayed size will remain constant regardless of their position. This is a common feature of CAD programs, and the transformation that produces this result is called an *orthographic projection*.

If the viewing region is set to a frustum, near objects will be displayed larger than far objects. In other words, objects in a frustum resemble objects in the real world. This is a common feature of games and other real-world applications, and the transformation that produces this result is called a *perspective projection*.

This section looks at both types of projection transformations and presents the wgpu-matrix methods that create the corresponding matrices.

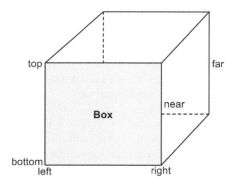
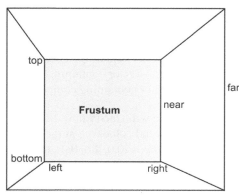

FIGURE 5.5   Viewing regions.

Orthographic projection

If a projection places an object into a box-like viewing region, it's called an *ortho-graphic projection*. These projections are simple to understand because an object's size is independent of its position in the scene.

The ortho method in wgpu-matrix returns a matrix that can be used for orthographic projections. It accepts six arguments (left, right, bottom, top, near, and far) that have the same names as the dimensions of the box on the left side of Figure 5.5. left and right set the dimensions in the x-direction, bottom and top set the dimensions in the y-direction, and near and far set the dimensions in the z-direction.

An example will clarify how ortho is used. Suppose the front face of the box should be 30 units away from the origin and the back face should be 40 units away. The horizontal and vertical boundaries should be symmetric around the viewer, and the region should occupy 50 units horizontally and 30 units vertically. The following code creates the projection matrix for this orthographic projection:

```
// Create a matrix for orthographic projection
const orthoMat =
    mat4.ortho(-25.0f, 25.0f, -15.0f, 15.0f, 30.0f, 40.0f)
```

Vertices outside this box will be removed (clipped) from the model. For example, if a vertex's x-coordinate is less than −25.0 or greater than 25.0, it will be clipped. The same goes for any vertices whose y-coordinates are less than −15.0 or greater than 15.0.

Perspective projection

In the real world, we don't view objects orthographically—they appear larger as they approach us and appear smaller as they get further away. For example, if two cubes have the same size but different positions, the one closer to the viewer will appear larger.

This phenomenon is called *perspective*. A *perspective projection* transforms objects so that they appear smaller as their positions move away from the viewer. To set this projection, an application needs to place the objects in a frustum-shaped viewing region.

An application can define the frustum's dimensions by calling the frustum method of the mat4 object. This accepts six required arguments (left, right, bottom, top, near, and far) that identify the region's boundaries. These have the same names as the boundaries displayed in the preceding figure.

Instead of setting these boundaries manually, an application can define the viewing region by calling the perspective method. This accepts four arguments:

- fov_y—the field-of-view angle in radians
- aspect—the aspect ratio (width/height)
- zNear—the depth of the near clipping plane
- zFar—the depth of the far clipping plane

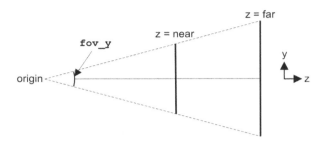

FIGURE 5.6   Field of view in the y-direction.

The first argument identifies the region's field of view in the y-direction. This measures how much of the viewer's vertical range of sight is occupied by the viewing region. Figure 5.6 shows how this angle relates to the frustum's shape.

The second argument identifies the ratio of the region's horizontal dimension to its vertical dimension. This is the region's *aspect ratio*. A common width-to-height ratio is 4/3, so this is frequently set to 1.33.

For example, suppose you want to create a viewing region with a field of view of 40° in the y-direction and an aspect ratio of 1.33. In addition, vertices should only be displayed if their z-values lie between −5.0 and −15.0. In this case, you could create the matrix for the perspective projection with the following code:

```
// Generate a matrix for perspective projection
const perspectiveMat = mat4.perspective(40.0 * Math.PI / 180.0,
1.33, 5.0, 15.0);
```

Even though the last two arguments have positive values, the coordinates of the planes are negative. That is, the near clipping plane is located at z = −5 and the far clipping plane is located at z = −15.

The product of the model matrix, view matrix, and projection matrix is commonly called the *MVP matrix*. This transforms coordinates from object coordinates to clip coordinates. The Ch05_Cubes project discussed at the end of this chapter will demonstrate how this can be computed.

INDEXED RENDERING

So far, all the drawing operations have accessed vertices in the order in which they're stored in the vertex buffer. This is fine for simple shapes, but it's inefficient when vertices need to be accessed multiple times. Rather than store multiple copies of the same vertex, it's better to use *indexed rendering*.

Indexed rendering treats the vertex buffer as an array of vertices, and uses index values to tell the renderer how the vertices should be accessed. These indexes must be provided in a buffer called an *index buffer*. For example, if the index buffer contains [0, 2, 3, 1], the rendering will access the first vertex (0), followed by the third vertex (2), followed by the fourth vertex (3), followed by the second vertex (1). If the index buffer contains [0, 1, 2, 3], the vertices will be drawn in their regular order.

Keep in mind that shaders can't access the index buffer directly. It's only used by the renderer to access data in the vertex buffer.

In general, the process of using index buffers consists of four steps:

1. Create the index buffer by calling `device.createBuffer`.
2. Write data to the index buffer by calling the queue's `writeBuffer` method.
3. Associate the render pass encoder with the index buffer by calling the encoder's `setIndexBuffer` method.
4. Perform indexed rendering by calling the `drawIndexed` or `drawIndirectIndexed` methods of the render pass encoder.

This section explores each of these steps. Then it presents *primitive restart*, which defines a special index value that restarts the assembly of primitives.

Creating an Index Buffer

The process of creating an index buffer is nearly identical to the process of creating a vertex buffer or a uniform buffer. The device's `createBuffer` creates an empty buffer of a given size and type. For index buffers, the `usage` property must be set to `GPUBufferUsage.INDEX`. The following code creates an index buffer that stores 128 bytes.

```
const indexBuffer = device.createBuffer({
    label: "Index Buffer 0",
    size: 128,
    usage: GPUBufferUsage.INDEX | GPUBufferUsage.COPY_DST
});
```

As discussed earlier, the `GPUBufferUsage.COPY_DST` flag is needed to ensure that data can be copied into the buffer.

Writing Data to the Index Buffer

Once the buffer is created, an application can fill it with data by calling the `writeBuffer` method of the device's queue. This accepts an object whose only required properties are the buffer, the data, and the offset at which data should be written.

To show how this works, the following code writes data from an array named `indexData` to a buffer named `indexBuffer`. The write operation starts at Byte 0 of the buffer.

```
device.queue.writeBuffer(indexBuffer, 0, indexData);
```

By default, all the data in `indexData` will be written to the buffer. Applications can customize this behavior by adding two arguments to `writeBuffer`: the data offset that identifies the first byte of the array to be accessed and the size of the data to be written from the array into the buffer.

Associating the Index Buffer with the Render Pass Encoder

To make sure the index buffer will be used in rendering, the application needs to notify the render pass encoder of the buffer's existence. This is accomplished by calling the `setIndexBuffer` method of the render pass encoder. This accepts four arguments:

1. `buffer`—the `GPUBuffer` to be associated with the encoder
2. `indexFormat`—the format of the index values (`uint16` or `uint32`)
3. `offset`—optional byte offset to start accessing data from the buffer
4. `size`—optional amount of data to be read from the buffer

For example, suppose `indexBuffer` is a buffer containing 16-bit index values. The following code associates it with the render pass encoder.

```
renderPass.setIndexBuffer(indexBuffer, "uint16");
```

The optional properties are omitted, so the renderer will start reading index values starting from Byte 0 in the buffer.

Perform Indexed Rendering

In preceding applications, the drawing operation was performed by calling the `draw` method of the render pass encoder. When this is called, the rendering operation accesses vertices according to the order in which they're stored in the vertex buffer.

To perform indexed rendering, the application needs to tell the renderer that vertices should be accessed using the values stored in the index buffer. This is accomplished by calling `drawIndexed` or `drawIndirectIndexed`. The `drawIndexed` method accepts an object with up to five properties:

- `indexCount`—the number of indices to be accessed in the draw operation
- `instanceCount`—(optional) the number of instances (copies) to be created
- `firstIndex`—(optional) the index of the first value to be read from the index buffer
- `baseVertex`—(optional) adds an offset to each index value
- `firstInstance`—(optional) identifies the first instance to be drawn

For example, the Ch05_Cubes project draws three copies of a cube, and each cube requires 30 index values. Therefore, the index count is 30 and the instance count is 3. The following code initiates the drawing operation.

```
renderPass.drawIndexed(30, 3);
```

By default, the three instances will all have the same location. Therefore, the vertex shader needs to transform each object's vertices differently depending on its instance index. A later section will show how this can be done.

Primitive Restart

In the Ch05_RotateSquare project, the vertices are assembled into a triangle strip, which means the first three vertices form a triangle, and each successive vertex forms a triangle with the two preceding it. Put another way, the first triangle is created from vertices v_0, v_1, and v_2 and a second triangle from vertices v_1, v_2, and v_3.

Triangle strips are popular in 3-D rendering, but when it comes to drawing cubes, there's a problem. After one face of the cube is drawn, there's no easy way to draw a triangle on a perpendicular face. One solution is to execute a separate draw operation for each face. Then the triangles on one face will always be distinct from the triangles on the other.

Another method is to insert repeated vertices so that triangles between faces will have zero area. These are called *degenerate triangles*, and this method usually provides better performance than calling draw multiple times.

WebGPU supports a third option, called *primitive restart*. This uses a special index value that tells the renderer to restart assembling primitives. When the renderer reads a primitive restart index, the next vertex will be drawn as if it was the first vertex, and it won't be connected to preceding primitives.

The special index value depends on the number of bits in each index value. For 16-bit unsigned integers, the primitive restart index is 0xffff. For 32-bit unsigned integers, the primitive restart index is 0xffffffff.

The following code creates the array of index values used in the Ch05_Cubes application. As shown, the primitive restart value is inserted after every fourth index:

```
const indexData = new Uint16Array([
   0, 1, 3, 2, 0xffff,
   7, 6, 4, 5, 0xffff,
   11, 10, 8, 9, 0xffff,
   12, 13, 15, 14, 0xffff,
   19, 18, 16, 17, 0xffff,
   20, 21, 23, 22, 0xffff
]);
```

After drawing each face, the 0xffff value tells the renderer to restart the process of assembling primitives. For example, the primitives formed from the vertices on the second line (starting with Index 7) won't be connected to the primitives formed from the vertices on the first line (starting with Index 0).

EXAMPLE APPLICATION—DRAWING CUBES

The Ch05_Cubes application demonstrates how three-dimensional rendering can be performed on WebGPU. It creates a frustum-shaped viewing region and draws three instances of a cube inside of it. Figure 5.7 shows what this looks like.

Like the Ch05_RotateSquare application discussed earlier, this application stores matrix data in a `Float32Array` and passes it to shaders using uniform buffers. But the Ch05_Cubes application has two important characteristics that make it different:

1. It creates a view matrix and a projection matrix using wgpu-matrix.
2. It creates an index buffer to store the indexes of vertexes to be drawn.
3. It draws shapes using indexed rendering and instanced rendering.

The following discussion explores these items and shows how they're implemented in the Ch05_Cubes application.

Vertex Data

Before I discuss the application's functions and shaders, I'd like to show how the vertex data is structured. The cube has six faces, and each face has four vertices. Each vertex has a location and a color. Figure 5.8 shows what this looks like.

In code, each vertex requires six floats: three for (x, y, z) coordinates and three for RGB color components. Each face has four vertices, and the cube has six faces, so the

FIGURE 5.7   The Ch05_Cubes application.

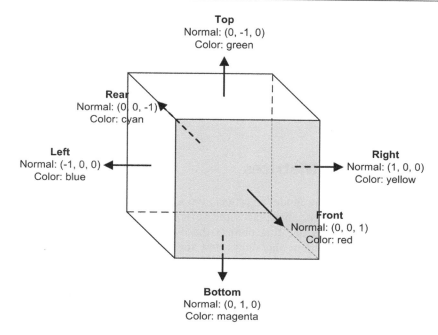

FIGURE 5.8   Coordinates and colors.

`vertexData` array contains 6 * 4 * 6 = 144 floats. To make this clear, the following code defines the coordinates and colors in the cube's left face:

```
const uniformData = new Float32Array([

    // Left face
    -1.0f, -1.0f, -1.0f,   0.0f,   0.0f,   0.8f,
    -1.0f,  1.0f, -1.0f,   0.0f,   0.0f,   0.8f,
    -1.0f,  1.0f,  1.0f,   0.0f,   0.0f,   0.8f,
    -1.0f, -1.0f,  1.0f,   0.0f,   0.0f,   0.8f,
    ...
```

Each line contains three coordinates of a vertex (12 bytes) followed by its three RGB color components (12 bytes), for a total of 24 bytes per vertex. The layout of the buffer is defined in the following way:

```
const bufferLayout = {
    arrayStride: 24,
    attributes: [
        { format: "float32x3", offset: 0, shaderLocation: 0 },
        { format: "float32x3", offset: 12, shaderLocation: 1 }
    ],
};
```

As a result of this code, the vertex shader can access the vertex coordinates (a `vec3f`) at Location 0 and the colors (another `vec3f`) at Location 1. The color data must be passed to the fragment shader through an appropriate structure.

It's important to understand that the vertices *aren't* drawn in the order in which they're stored in the `vertexData` array. The application uses instanced rendering, so the renderer will access vertices by index, and the index values are stored in the index buffer.

Transformation Matrices

To set the locations of the model's vertices, the Ch05_Cubes application performs three transformations—one that places the vertex in its desired position, one that positions the viewer, and one that defines the overall viewing region. Figure 5.9 illustrates the viewing region and shows how the cubes and viewer are positioned inside it.

To obtain this result, the application creates three matrices: the model matrix, the view matrix, and the projection matrix. An earlier section explained what these matrices are intended to accomplish. The following discussion shows how these matrices are generated in the Ch05_Cubes project.

The model matrix

The model matrix is the simplest of the three matrices. As depicted in Figure 5.9, the first cube should be positioned so that its center is located at (0, 0, −10). In object coordinates, the cube's center is (0, 0, 0), so the model matrix needs to translate its vertices ten units in the −z direction.

This can be accomplished with the `translation` method of the wgpu-matrix library. In the following code, `translation` returns a 4-by-4 matrix that translates vertices ten units in the −z direction.

```
const modelMat = mat4.translation([0.0, 0.0, -10.0]);
```

As a result of this code, the values of the translation matrix are stored in the `Float32Array` named `modelMat`.

The view matrix

As shown in Figure 5.9, the viewer is placed at (12, 4, −3) and is oriented to look at the point (0, 0, −14). The viewer's positive vertical direction should be set to (0, 1, 0).

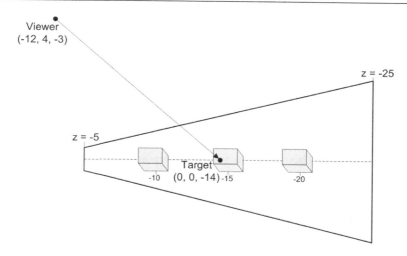

FIGURE 5.9   Cubes in the viewing region.

The view matrix sets the viewer's position and viewing direction. In the Ch05_ Cubes application, this is created with the `lookAt` method provided by wgpu-matrix:

```
const viewMat = mat4.lookAt([12.0, 4.0, -3.0], [0.0, 0.0, -14.0],
[0.0, 1.0, 0.0]);
```

The elements of this matrix are stored in `viewMat`. The vertex shader will multiply vertex coordinates by this matrix after multiplying the coordinates by the model matrix, `modelMat`.

The projection matrix

The application creates its viewing region so that objects far from the origin are displayed at a smaller size than objects located near the origin. This requires creating the frustum-shaped viewing region depicted in Figure 5.9.

The matrix that positions vertices inside this viewing region is called the projection matrix. The Ch05_Cubes application generates the elements of this matrix by calling the `perspective` method of the wgpu-matrix package.

```
const projMat =
     mat4.perspective(30.0 * Math.PI / 180.0, 1.33, 5.0, 25.0);
```

The first argument defines the field-of-view in the y-direction. In this case, the vertical field of view should be set to ±15°, so the total field of view is 30°. This is converted into radians by multiplying by pi and dividing by 180.

The second argument identifies the ratio of the region's width to its height. This aspect ratio is commonly set to 4:3, so the argument is set to 1.33.

The third and fourth arguments define the planes that bound the viewing region in the z-direction. Even though the arguments have positive values, the actual coordinates of the planes are negative. That is, the near clipping plane is located at z = −5 and the far clipping plane is located at z = −25.

Many applications multiply the model, view, and projection matrices together to obtain a single matrix that performs all three transformations. However, the Ch05_Cubes project creates multiple instances of a cube, and these instances require different view matrices. Therefore, the vertex shader needs to multiply the matrices separately.

The Vertex and Fragment Shader

After the model, view, and projection matrices are defined, the Ch05_Cubes inserts the three matrices into a uniform buffer using the method discussed earlier. That is, it calls `device.createBuffer` to create the buffer and `queue.writeBuffer` to write the matrix data into the buffer.

After the uniform buffer is created, two binding steps are needed. The application binds the buffer to a value by creating a bind group with `device.createBindGroup`. Then it associates the bind group with a value by calling `renderPass.setBindGroup`.

Once these steps are performed, shaders can access the uniform buffer through the buffer's bind value and the group's value. In the Ch05_Cubes application, the vertex shader performs six operations:

1. Access the uniform buffer through a structure of type `MVP_Matrices`. This contains the model matrix, the view matrix, and the projection matrix.
2. Multiply each vertex by the model matrix. This converts the object coordinates of each vertex to world coordinates.
3. Translate vertices in the second instance by 5 units in the −z direction and vertices in the third instance by 10 units in the −z direction.
4. Multiply each vertex by the view matrix. This converts world coordinates to eye coordinates.
5. Determine the vector from the vertex to the viewer's location. The fragment shader will use this to compute the specular component of the surrounding light.
6. Multiply each vertex by the projection matrix. This converts eye coordinates to clip coordinates.

After the last step, the vertex shader sets the fields of an output data structure. The first field identifies the vertex's clip coordinates, and the second identifies the desired color. This is shown in the following code listing, which presents the shader code of the Ch05_Cubes project.

```
struct MVP_Matrices {
    modelMatrix : mat4x4f,
    viewMatrix : mat4x4f,
    projectionMatrix : mat4x4f
}
@group(0) @binding(0) var<uniform> mats: MVP_Matrices;

struct DataStruct {
    @builtin(position) pos: vec4f,
    @location(0) colors: vec3f
}

@vertex
fn vertexMain(@location(0) coords: vec3f, @location(1)
colors: vec3f, @builtin(instance_index) instance: u32) ->
DataStruct {
    var outData: DataStruct;

    /* Apply the model transformation */
    var world_coords = mats.modelMatrix * vec4f(coords, 1.0);

    /* Translate the second and third instances */
    world_coords.z = world_coords.z - f32(instance) * 5.0;

    /* Apply the view transformation */
    var eye_coords = mats.viewMatrix * world_coords;

    /* Apply the projection transformation */
    var clip_coords = mats.projectionMatrix * eye_coords;

    /* Create output structure */
    outData.pos = clip_coords;
    outData.colors = colors;
    return outData;
}

@fragment
fn fragmentMain(fragData: DataStruct) -> @location(0) vec4f
{
    return vec4f(fragData.colors, 1.0);
}
```

In this case, the fragment shader just reads the colors field of the incoming structure and uses it to set the fragment color. In the next chapter, the fragment shader gets a lot more attention.

Creating the Render Pipeline

Aside from the shaders and the uniform/vertex buffers, most of the code in the Ch05_ Cubes project is like the code in previous projects. But there's a major difference in the code that creates the render pipeline. This is given as follows:

```
const renderPipeline = device.createRenderPipeline({
    layout: "auto",
    vertex: {
      module: shaderModule,
      entryPoint: "vertexMain",
      buffers: [bufferLayout]
    },
    fragment: {
      module: shaderModule,
      entryPoint: "fragmentMain",
      targets: [{
        format: canvasFormat
      }]
    },
    primitive: {
        topology: "triangle-strip",
        stripIndexFormat: "uint16",
        frontFace: "cw",
        cullMode: "back"
    }
});
```

In this code, the `primitive` property is different than in previous examples. The `stripIndexFormat` identifies the format of the values in the index buffer. This can be set to `uint16` for 16-bit values and `uint32` for 32-bit values.

The `frontFace` and `cullMode` properties relate to *culling*—removing triangles depending on which way they're facing. For example, if you want to display a teapot in a scene, you only want the triangles facing the viewer to be rendered. The triangles in the rear can be omitted, or *culled*, from the scene.

To configure culling, two steps must be performed:

1. Use the `frontFace` property to identify front-facing triangles. If this is set to `cw`, a triangle will be considered front-facing if its vertices are oriented clockwise. If this is set to `ccw`, a triangle will be considered front-facing if its vertices are oriented counter-clockwise.
2. Use the `cullMode` property to select triangles to be culled. If this is set to `back`, back-facing triangles will be culled. If this is set to `front`, front-facing triangles will be culled. If this is set to `none` (the default value), no triangles will be culled.

If configured correctly, culling can dramatically improve rendering performance. But it's important to make sure that the vertices used to create triangles are arranged in a consistent clockwise or counter-clockwise manner.

In the Ch05_Cubes application, `frontFace` is set to `cw`, which means clock-wise triangles will be treated as facing forward. The `cullMode` property is set to `back`, which means back-facing triangles will be culled.

Launching the Draw Operation

The Ch05_Cubes code takes advantage of indexed rendering and instanced rendering. This is accomplished with the following line of code:

```
renderPass.drawIndexed(30, 3);
```

Because the `drawIndexed` method is used, the renderer will read vertices using values in an index buffer. To be precise, it will read 30 values from the index buffer and use them to read 30 vertices from the vertex buffer.

The second argument of `drawIndexed` identifies how many copies, or *instances*, of each shape should be created. In this case, the renderer will draw three instances of the cube.

To separate the three copies, the vertex shader needs to know which instance each vertex belongs to. It accesses this information through the function's `@builtin(instance_index)` parameter, as shown in the following code:

```
fn vertexMain(
    @location(0) coords: vec3f,
    @location(1) colors: vec3f,
    @builtin(instance_index) instance: u32) -> DataStruct
```

The shader uses the `instance` parameter to update the z-values of different instances. To be specific, if the instance index is 1, the vertex coordinate's z-value is reduced by 5. If the instance index is 2, the z-value is reduced by 10. In this manner, the vertex shader separates the three copies along the z-axis.

SUMMARY

To create realistic three-dimensional scenes, developers need to be familiar with many different concepts and operations. A transformation is an operation that adjusts vertices by multiplying them by matrices. This chapter has focused on linear transformations, which include scaling, translation, and rotation.

In WebGPU applications, we can create transformation matrices by calling methods of the open-source wgpu-matrix package. In particular, the `mat4` object has several useful methods that provide matrix elements in `Float32Arrays`. The `scaling` method creates scaling matrices, the `translation` method creates translation matrices, and the `rotation` method creates rotation matrices.

During rendering, transformation is performed by vertex shaders, which multiply vertex coordinates by transformation matrices. These matrices don't change from vertex to vertex, so they shouldn't be stored in vertex buffers. Instead, they're commonly passed to the GPU using uniform buffers, whose content remains constant from vertex to vertex. Creating a uniform buffer is essentially like creating a vertex buffer, but it needs to be added to a bind group, which needs to be described in a bind group layout.

The Ch05_Cubes application created three transformation matrices with wgpu-matrix and passes them to the GPU using uniform buffers. The model matrix sets the object's position, the view matrix accounts for the viewer's location, and the projection matrix creates the viewing region that displays objects with perspective. As a result, objects farther from the viewer appear smaller.

Lighting, Textures, and Depth

6

Chapter 5 explained how transformations make it possible to position and orient objects in a viewing region. Transformations are important, but if you want to create realistic scenes in three dimensions, there are other issues to wrestle with. This chapter looks at three important topics in graphical rendering: lighting, textures, and depth.

Lighting refers to the process of changing an object's color depending on light sources in the scene. Objects far from a light source should be darker than objects near a light source, and shiny objects should reflect more light than dull objects. This chapter presents two models that mathematically determine how an object's color should be set: the Phong model and the Blinn–Phong model.

Like buffers, textures contain data that can be passed from the application to the GPU. The difference is that textures contain pixel data and are stored in special memory on the GPU. Using samplers, a fragment shader can read the pixel data and assign colors to fragments.

The last section of this chapter discusses two types of tests that fragment shaders can perform. A depth test checks a fragment's depth to see if it should be displayed in the scene or discarded. A stencil test compares values in a specially configured texture to reference values to determine how fragments should be processed.

LIGHTING

To make a two-dimensional scene appear to have three dimensions, it isn't enough to place vertices in a rendering volume. To create the illusion of depth, objects need to reflect light differently based on their orientation relative to a light source.

Many models have been developed to determine how light reflects from an object's surface. This section looks at two popular models: the Phong model and the Blinn–Phong model. In both cases, the methodology contains three steps:

1. Decide on one or more light sources. Pass this information to shaders in uniform buffers.
2. For each vertex, find the vector perpendicular to the surface. This is called the normal vector. Pass the vector data to shaders as part of the vertex buffer.

DOI: 10.1201/9781003422839-6

107

3. Using light sources and normal vectors, the fragment shader sets the color of each fragment using the lighting model.

This discussion presents the mathematics underlying both models. Then it presents the code in the Ch06_ShinySphere project, which uses Blinn–Phong shading to illuminate a sphere.

The Phong Model

In 1973, a Ph.D. dissertation by Bui Phong presented a method of simulating the reflection of light from a surface. This model treats light sources as point sources and splits each source into three components:

- ambient—background illumination present in all points
- diffuse—illumination approaches from one direction
- specular—illumination approaches from one direction and particularly affects points nearest the light source

Phong's model presents a formula for determining the illumination at a given point. The total illumination, $I = I_a + I_d + I_s$, where I_a is the ambient component of a light source, I_d is the diffuse component, and I_s is the specular component. I_a applies to every point equally, so you can think of it as the base lighting of a scene.

To compute I_d, the fragment shader needs to know the normal vector at each point and the light vector, which is the vector from the light source to the point. If these vectors have the same direction, I_d will be significant. If they're perpendicular, I_d will be zero.

Using vector math, we say that I_d is proportional to $N \cdot L$, where N is the normal vector and L is the light vector. Figure 6.1 shows what these vectors look like for a point P on the surface.

Computing the specular component, I_s, is difficult because it relates to how *shiny* the object is. To develop an expression for specular reflection, Phong made two important observations:

- The shinier a surface is, the more concentrated the brightness is around points of greatest reflectivity.
- The amount of perceived shine depends on the angle of the viewer to the reflected light.

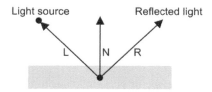

FIGURE 6.1   The light vector and normal vector.

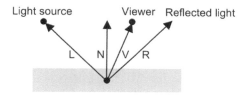

FIGURE 6.2   Vectors used to compute specular reflection (Phong model).

Taking these observations into account, Phong derived an expression for specular illumination: I_s is proportional to $(V \cdot R)^n$, where V is the vector from the point to the viewer, R is the vector of light reflected at the point, and n is the surface's reflectivity at the point.

For shiny surfaces, n will be large, and I_s will be concentrated around points where $V \cdot R$ is high. Figure 6.2 shows how these vectors are related:

The R vector in the figure is the reflection vector and has the same meaning as the R vector in Figure 6.1. Using vector projection, R can be obtained in terms of L and N:

$$R = 2(N \cdot L)N - L$$

Summing the expressions for the three light components, the Phong model presents the following equation for the total illumination of a fragment:

$$I = k_a + k_d (N \cdot L) + k_s (V \cdot R)^n$$

In this equation, k_a, k_d, and k_s are constants identifying the basic intensities of ambient, diffuse, and specular illumination. They're not mathematically derived but must be selected by the developer or artist to obtain suitable lighting properties.

The Blinn–Phong Model

The Phong model provides a good approximation to real-world lighting, but it has two significant drawbacks. First, the model produces unacceptable results when V and R are separated by 90° or more. Second, the process of computing $V \cdot R$ is unnecessarily complicated.

To resolve these issues, Jim Blinn changed how the specular component, I_s, is computed. In the Blinn–Phong model, I_s equals $(N \cdot H)^{n'}$, where H is the vector halfway between L and V and n' is a new value for the surface's reflectivity. Figure 6.3 illustrates the relationship between these vectors.

As shown, N and H are closer to one another than V and R. To make sure the specular component is close to that of the Phong model, many applications increase the exponent of $N \cdot H$. For this reason, it's common to set n' equal to four times the old exponent, n.

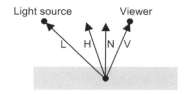

FIGURE 6.3   Vectors used to compute specular reflection (Blinn–Phong model).

Replacing $(V \cdot R)^n$ with $(N \cdot H)^{n'}$, the Blinn–Phong Model produces the following illumination equation:

$$I = k_a + k_d (N{\cdot}L) + k_s (N{\cdot}H)^{n'}$$

The following discussion presents code that demonstrates how a fragment shader can apply lighting using Blinn–Phong illumination.

EXAMPLE APPLICATION—DRAWING A SHINY SPHERE

The code in the Ch06_ShinySphere demonstrates how the Blinn–Phong lighting model can be used in WebGPU. It creates a sphere, assigns values for k_a, k_d, and k_s, and then uses Blinn–Phong lighting to illuminate the viewing region. Figure 6.4 shows what the resulting sphere looks like.

In this section, I'll explain how the fragment shader receives the lighting parameters and uses the Blinn–Phong model to set the colors of fragments. But first, I want to explain how the sphere is drawn.

Ch06_ShinySphere

FIGURE 6.4   Rendering a sphere with Blinn–Phong lighting.

Drawing the Sphere

Drawing the triangles of a sphere is not a trivial task. Of the methods that have been devised, the simplest involves splitting the sphere into sections using latitude and longitude. In the Ch06_ShinySphere project, the sphere is split vertically using 16 lines of latitude (NUM_LATITUDE) and horizontally using 32 lines of longitude (NUM_LONGITUDE). Figure 6.5 shows what this looks like.

The number of vertices in the sphere is easy to compute. There's a vertex on top, a vertex on the bottom, and a grid of NUM_LATITUDE * NUM_LONGITUDE vertices. Therefore, the code sets NUM_VERTICES to NUM_LATITUDE * NUM_LONGITUDE + 2.

To render the sphere, we need to find the (x, y, z) coordinates of the points where latitude and longitude meet. The top point is at (0, 0, R), and the bottom point is at (0, 0, −R), where R is the sphere's radius. Denoting the latitudinal angle as φ and the longitudinal angle as θ, the coordinates of the other points can be computed using five steps:

1. Use the latitude to determine the angle φ in radians.
2. Use the longitude to determine the angle θ in radians.
3. Set x equal to R cos θ sin φ.
4. Set y equal to R sin θ sin φ.
5. Set z equal to R cos φ.

To cover the sphere with triangles, the application needs to access each vertex multiple times. Rather than repeat coordinates in the vertex buffer, it's more efficient to access vertices by index. To assign indices, the example code splits the sphere into vertical regions called *slices*.

A sphere has one slice for each line of longitude, and Figure 6.6 illustrates two adjacent slices of a sphere with four lines of latitude.

As shown, each slice has a triangle at the top, one quadrangle for each line of latitude (minus 1), and a triangle at the bottom. There may be a way to draw the slices in a

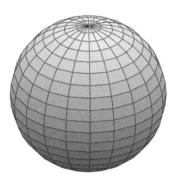

FIGURE 6.5   Dividing the sphere using latitude and longitude.

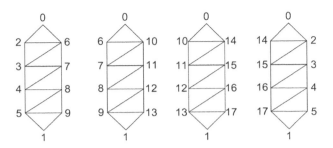

FIGURE 6.6   Triangles of adjacent slices.

connected manner, but for the sake of simplicity, we'll make each distinct. That is, once we reach the bottom vertex, we'll add a primitive restart value (0xffff) and start from the top of the next slice.

Now we can determine how many indices are needed. The first triangle requires three, each quadrangle requires two, the last triangle requires one, and the primitive restart index requires one. Taking the sum, each slice requires 2 * NUM_LATITUDE + 3 index values. The total number of required indices is NUM_LONGITUDE * (2 * NUM_LATITUDE + 3) - 1 values (the last primitive restart index is unnecessary).

We'll assign Index 0 to the top vertex and Index 1 to the bottom vertex. The remaining index values increment from top to bottom and from left to right. For example, the vertices along Longitude 0 range from 2 to NUM_LATITUDE + 2.

Listing 6.1 presents the code in the Ch06_ShinySphere application that sets the constants used to draw the sphere and iterates through the slices.

```
// Define vertex data (coordinates and colors)
const RAD = 1.5;
const NUM_LATITUDE = 16;
const NUM_LONGITUDE = 32;
const NUM_VERTICES = NUM_LATITUDE * NUM_LONGITUDE + 2;
const NUM_INDICES = NUM_LONGITUDE * (2 * NUM_LATITUDE + 3);
const THETA_CONVERSION = (2.0 * Math.PI)/NUM_LONGITUDE;
const PHI_CONVERSION = Math.PI/(NUM_LATITUDE + 1);

// Set coordinates of top and bottom points
const vData = new Float32Array(3 * NUM_VERTICES);
vData[0] = 0.0; vData[1] = 0.0; vData[2] = RAD;
vData[3] = 0.0; vData[4] = 0.0; vData[5] = -1.0 * RAD;

// Create data arrays
const iData = new Uint16Array(NUM_INDICES);
```

```
// Iterate through slices
let ptIndex = 0; let vertIndex = 2;
let theta = 0.0; let phi = 0.0;
let rad_cos_theta = 0.0; let rad_sin_theta = 0.0;

for (let lon = 0; lon < NUM_LONGITUDE; lon++) {

    theta = lon * THETA_CONVERSION;
    rad_sin_theta = RAD * Math.sin(theta);
    rad_cos_theta = RAD * Math.cos(theta);

    // Add top vertex
    iData[ptIndex++] = 0;

    for (let lat = 1; lat <= NUM_LATITUDE; lat++) {

        // Set index values
        iData[ptIndex++] = vertIndex;
        iData[ptIndex++] = (vertIndex + NUM_LATITUDE) %
(NUM_VERTICES - 2);

        // Compute phi
        phi = Math.PI/2.0 - lat * PHI_CONVERSION;

        // Set vertex values
        vData[3 * vertIndex] = rad_cos_theta * Math.cos(phi);
        vData[3 * vertIndex + 1] = rad_sin_theta *
Math.cos(phi);
        vData[3 * vertIndex++ + 2] = RAD * Math.sin(phi);
    }

    // Add bottom vertex
    iData[ptIndex++] = 1;

    // Add primitive restart
    if(lon != NUM_LONGITUDE - 1) {
        iData[ptIndex++] = 0xffff;
    }
}
```

The vertex coordinates are stored in the vData array, and the index values are stored in the iData array. The first elements in vData are the coordinates of the top point on the sphere (0, 0, R) and the coordinates of the bottom point (0, 0, −R). As a result, the index of the top point is 0 and the index of the bottom point is 1.

At the end of the loop, the index 0xffff is added to iData. This is the primitive restart value and tells the renderer that the next index will start a new shape (slice).

Uniform Data

The code in ch06_shinysphere.js creates a single uniform buffer that contains a great deal of data. The following code shows how the uniformData array is constructed and passed to the GPU for processing.

```
// Define transformation
const modelMat = mat4.translation([0.0, 0.0, -10.0]);
const projMat = mat4.perspective(30.0 * Math.PI / 180.0,
1.0, 5.0, 25.0);
const viewMat = mat4.identity();
const mvpMat = mat4.mul(mat4.mul(projMat, viewMat),
modelMat);

// Set positions
const oldCenter = new Float32Array([0.0, 0.0, 0.0, 1.0]);
const centerPos = vec4.transformMat4(oldCenter, mvpMat);
const viewerPos = new Float32Array([0.0, 0.0, 0.0, 0.0]);
const lightPos = new Float32Array([5.0, 15.0, 9.0, 0.0]);

// Set light components
const ambient = new Float32Array([0.7, 0.7, 0.7, 0.0]);
const diffuse = new Float32Array([0.9, 0.9, 0.9, 0.0]);
const specular = new Float32Array([1.0, 1.0, 1.0]);
const shininess = new Float32Array([1.5]);

// Combine data into uniform buffer
const uniformData = Float32Array.of(...mvpMat, ...centerPos,
...viewerPos, ...lightPos, ...ambient, ...diffuse,
...specular, ...shininess);

// Create uniform buffer
const uniformBuffer = device.createBuffer({
    label: "Uniform Buffer 0",
    size: uniformData.byteLength,
    usage: GPUBufferUsage.UNIFORM | GPUBufferUsage.COPY_DST
});
device.queue.writeBuffer(uniformBuffer, 0, uniformData);
```

The first element in uniformData is the matrix defining the sphere's transformation. This is obtained by multiplying the model matrix, view matrix, and projection matrix together. For this reason, the matrix is called the MVP matrix, or mvpMat.

Next, uniformData contains a series of vectors that set points in space. The centerPos vector identifies the transformed center of the sphere, which will be used by the vertex shader to determine the normal vector at each point. Next, the viewerPos vector identifies the location of the viewer, which is (0, 0, 0). Last, lightPos sets the position of the light source to (5, 15, 9). The fragment shader will use these values to determine the amount of illumination needed by the scene.

The last four elements in `uniformData` are needed by the Blinn–Phong Model:

- `ambient`—sets base lighting to light gray (0.7, 0.7, 0.7)
- `diffuse`—sets directional lighting to (0.9, 0.9, 0.9)
- `specular`—sets shiny lighting to (1.0, 1.0, 1.0)
- `shininess`—sets the exponent for the specular term to 1.5

After the `uniformData` array is constructed, the application creates a uniform buffer by calling `device.createBuffer` with the `GPUBufferUsage.UNIFORM` flag. Then it writes the data to the buffer by calling `device.queue.writeBuffer` with the uniform buffer and the `uniformData` array.

After configuring the uniform data and buffer, the application creates a bind group that binds the uniform buffer to the value 0. The following code creates the bind group and associates it with the render pass encoder (`renderPass`).

```
// Access the bind group layout
const bindGroupLayout = renderPipeline.getBindGroupLayout(0);

// Create the bind group
let bindGroup = device.createBindGroup({
    layout: bindGroupLayout,
    entries: [{
        binding: 0,
        resource: { buffer: uniformBuffer }
    }]
});

// Associate bind group with render pass encoder
renderPass.setBindGroup(0, bindGroup);
```

As a result of this code, the shaders can access the uniform buffer using its bind value (0) and the number associated with the bind group (0). The following discussion presents the code in the vertex shader.

The Vertex Shader

In the Ch06_ShinySphere application, the vertex shader performs three operations:

1. Transforms each vertex using the MVP matrix.
2. Computes the normal vector.
3. Passes data to the fragment shader.

To make this possible, the shader code defines two structures. The `InputData` struct contains the data from the uniform buffer discussed earlier. The `OutputData` struct contains data that the vertex shader passes to the fragment shader. The following code presents the definition of both structures and the code in the vertex shader.

```
/* Input to vertex shader */
struct InputData {
    mvpMatrix: mat4x4f,
    centerPos: vec4f,
    viewerPos: vec4f,
    lightPos: vec4f,
    ambient: vec4f,
    diffuse: vec4f,
    specular: vec3f,
    shininess: f32
}

/* Access the uniform buffer */
@group(0) @binding(0) var<uniform> input: InputData;

/* Output to fragment shader */
struct OutputData {
    @builtin(position) pos: vec4f,
    @location(0) normalVec: vec4f,
    @location(1) viewerVec: vec4f,
    @location(2) lightVec: vec4f,
    @location(3) ambient: vec4f,
    @location(4) diffuse: vec4f,
    @location(5) specular: vec3f,
    @location(6) shininess: f32
}

@vertex
fn vertexMain(@location(0) coords: vec3f) -> OutputData {

    var outData: OutputData;

    /* Transform coordinates */
    outData.pos = input.mvpMatrix * vec4f(coords, 1.0);

    /* Compute normal vector */
    outData.normalVec =
        normalize(outData.pos - input.centerPos);

    /* Compute direction to viewer */
    outData.viewerVec = normalize(input.viewerPos -
outData.pos);
```

```
        /* Compute direction to light source */
        outData.lightVec = normalize(input.lightPos -
    outData.pos);

        /* Set data for fragment shader */
        outData.ambient = input.ambient;
        outData.diffuse = input.diffuse;
        outData.specular = input.specular;
        outData.shininess = input.shininess;

        return outData;
    }
```

It may seem odd that most of the vectors in the `InputData` struct have type `vec4f` instead of `vec3f`. The reason for this is that WGSL aligns `vec3f` vectors on `vec4f` boundaries. This can cause shaders to access mismatched data, and a simple (though inefficient) way to deal with this is to use the `vec4f` type in place of `vec3f`.

After defining the `InputData` structure, this code creates a variable named input. Because of the `@group(0) @binding(0)` attribute, this variable accesses the uniform data as an `InputData` structure.

The vertex shader starts by declaring an `OutputData` variable and then sets its fields. The first field contains the vertex location, which is obtained by multiplying the input coordinates by the transformation matrix.

Next, the shader obtains three important vectors. It computes the normal vector by subtracting the sphere's center from the vertex's new location. It computes the vector from the vertex to the viewer by subtracting the vertex's location from the viewer's position. The light vector is obtained by subtracting the vertex's location from the position of the light source.

The last part of the vertex shader sets illumination values to be used by the fragment shader: `ambient`, `diffuse`, `specular`, and `shininess`. The following section explains how the fragment shader operates.

The Fragment Shader

Unlike the fragment shaders in previous projects, the fragment shader in the Ch06_ ShinySphere project does a lot of work. To determine the fragment's color, the shader receives several variables from the vertex shader, including vectors and lighting parameters. Then it uses the Blinn–Phong lighting model to determine how the fragment should be illuminated. This involves five steps:

1. Compute N . L, where N is the normal vector and L is the direction of light
2. Compute H, the vector halfway between L and V, the direction to the viewer
3. Compute (N . H)n', where n' is the shininess of the surface.

4. Using the results of Steps 1–3, add together the components of ambient, diffuse, and specular light.

5. Take the average of the computed light components and the original color, set to (0.5, 0.6, 0.7).

The following code shows how the fragment shader performs these tasks. In much of the computation, the possible results may exceed 1.0, which is the maximum floating-point value of a color component. For this reason, the `clamp` function is frequently employed to hold the value between 0.0 and 1.0.

```
@fragment
fn fragmentMain(fragData: OutputData) -> @location(0) vec4f
{

    /* Set minimum and maximum vectors used in clamp */
    let low_clamp = vec3f(0.0, 0.0, 0.0);
    let high_clamp = vec3f(1.0, 1.0, 1.0);

    /* Step 1: Compute N . L */
    let n_dot_l = dot(fragData.normalVec.xyz,
fragData.lightVec.xyz);

    /* Step 2: Compute H, the vector between L and V */
    let half_vector = normalize(fragData.lightVec.xyz +
fragData.viewerVec.xyz);

    /* Step 3: Compute (N . H)^n' */
    var blinn = dot(fragData.normalVec.xyz, half_vector);
    blinn = clamp(blinn, 0.0, 1.0);
    blinn = pow(blinn, fragData.shininess);

    /* Step 4: Compute sum of light components */
    var light_color = fragData.ambient.xyz +
fragData.diffuse.xyz * n_dot_l + fragData.specular * blinn;
    light_color = clamp(light_color, low_clamp, high_clamp);

    /* Step 5: Blend light color and original color */
    let orig_color = vec3f(0.5, 0.6, 0.7);
    let color_sum = clamp((light_color + orig_color)/2.0,
low_clamp, high_clamp);

    return vec4f(color_sum, 1.0);
}
```

Each of the steps is numbered in the code comments. In the second step, the shader adds the vectors representing the direction to the light source (`fragData.`

lightVec) and the direction to the viewer (fragData.viewerVec). Then it calls normalize to ensure that the vector's length will be set to 1.0. If a vector's only purpose is to identify a direction, it's a *direction vector* and its length must be normalized to 1.0.

After adding the ambient, diffuse, and specular components, the fragment shader blends the sum with the color received from the vertex shader. In this way, the shader lightens or darkens the color of the original surface.

The Shader Module and Render Pipeline

Once the vertex shader and fragment shaders are set, the application creates a shader module and uses it to initialize a render pipeline. This is shown in the following code:

```
// Create the shader module
const shaderModule = device.createShaderModule({
    label: "Shader Module 0",
    code: shaderCode
});

// Define the rendering procedure
const renderPipeline = device.createRenderPipeline({
    layout: "auto",
    vertex: {
      module: shaderModule,
      entryPoint: "vertexMain",
      buffers: [bufferLayout]
    },
    fragment: {
      module: shaderModule,
      entryPoint: "fragmentMain",
      targets: [{
        format: canvasFormat
      }]
    },
    primitive: {
        topology: "triangle-strip",
        stripIndexFormat: "uint16",
        frontFace: "cw",
        cullMode: "back"
    }
});
renderPass.setPipeline(renderPipeline);
```

As shown, the application creates a shader module by calling device.createShaderModule. Then it creates the render pipeline by calling device.

`createRenderPipeline`. The `layout` property is set to `auto`, so a `GPUPipelineLayout` object will be automatically created based on the variables in the shader code.

The `primitive` property is important because it defines how vertices are combined into shapes. The `topology` property tells the renderer to create connected triangles, and the `stripIndexFormat` property specifies that index values will be provided as 16-bit integers. Because of the `frontFace` and `cullMode` properties, the renderer will consider clockwise-oriented triangles to be front-facing, and will discard back-facing triangles.

TEXTURES

The preceding section explained how a fragment shader can use the Blinn–Phong model to assign colors to fragments. But in many applications, fragment shaders select colors using data from images. That is, the fragment shader reads (or *samples*) pixel data from an image and assigns the color to the current fragment. To be sampled, the image data must be stored in objects called *textures*.

Sampling a texture is like putting up wallpaper. In both cases, blank surfaces are made more appealing by attaching decorative images. In both cases, the corners of the pattern must be carefully matched to the corners of the surface. It's also important to make sure the pattern is oriented correctly.

But textures are easier to work with than wallpaper because there's no need to do any measuring. WebGPU will stretch or shrink the texture as needed.

The goal of this section is to explain how WebGPU applications can create texture objects and sample them in a fragment shader. The first part presents the code needed to initialize a texture and pass it to the shader. The second part explains how the shader can read color data from the texture and use it to set a fragment's color. The section ends by presenting a simple application that creates a texture and samples its data.

Creating Textures and Samplers

Earlier chapters showed how applications can pass data to the GPU using buffer resources. Texture resources (or just *textures*) are essentially like buffers, but because they contain image data, GPUs store the data in dedicated texture memory.

In JavaScript, working with textures is an involved process. If the texture data is stored in an image file, at least six steps are needed:

1. Create an `ImageBitmap` from the content of an image file.
2. Create the texture by calling `device.createTexture`.
3. Write the `ImageBitmap` to the texture.
4. Create a sampler by calling `device.createSampler`.

5. Add the sampler and the texture to a bind group.

6. Access the texture and sampler in a fragment shader.

This section looks at each of these steps and then demonstrates how they can be implemented in a simple application.

Step 1: Create an ImageBitmap

Many applications create textures from image files. As I'll explain shortly, WebGPU makes it easy to create a texture from an `ImageBitmap`. In JavaScript, obtaining an `ImageBitmap` for an image file commonly requires three steps:

- Call `fetch()` with the image file path to obtain a `Promise` that resolves with a `Response`.
- Call the `blob()` method of the `Response` to obtain a `Promise` that resolves with a `Blob`.
- Call `createImageBitmap` with the `Blob` to obtain an `ImageBitmap`.

An application can attempt to access the image file by calling `fetch`. This accepts a string identifying the file path and returns a `Promise` that resolves with a `Response`. To demonstrate, the following code obtains a `Response` for the file named image.png:

```
// Obtaining a Response for a file path
let resp = await fetch("image.png");
```

The `Response` object provides many methods for accessing response data, such as `headers`, `body`, and `type`. An application can access the file's content by calling the `blob` method, which returns a `Promise` that resolves to a `Blob` object. To demonstrate, the following code obtains a `Blob` for the `Response` named `resp`:

```
// Obtaining a Blob from a Response
let blob = await resp.blob();
```

A `Blob` contains raw data and provides methods that convert the data to different forms, such as `arrayBuffer` and `stream`. JavaScript also provides `createImageBitmap`, which provides a `Promise` that returns an `ImageBitmap` if the data formatting was successful. To demonstrate, the following code calls `createImageBitmap` to obtain an `ImageBitmap` from `blob`:

```
// Convert a Blob into an ImageBitmap
let bitmap = await createImageBitmap(blob);
```

If the `ImageBitmap` was created successfully, the `copyExternalImageToTexture` method of the `GPUQueue` can be called to write the data into a texture object. But first, the application needs to create the texture object.

TABLE 6.1   Properties of the `createTexture` argument

PROPERTY	REQUIRED?	DESCRIPTION
label	N	String identifier for the texture
format	Y	Format of the texture's pixels
size	Y	The texture's dimensions
usage	Y	Identifies how the texture will be used
dimension	N	Dimensionality of the texture (1d, 2d, or 3d)
sampleCount	N	Number of samples (1 or 4)
mipLevelCount	N	Number of mipmap levels in the texture
viewFormats	N	Formats when creating a view from the texture

Step 2: Create the Texture Object

Just as empty buffer objects are created with `device.createBuffer`, empty texture objects are created with `device.createTexture`. This accepts an object with up to eight properties, and Table 6.1 lists each of them.

The `format` property identifies the structure of the texture's pixels. WebGPU supports many different types of formats, including compressed and uncompressed textures. If the texture doesn't use compression and won't be used to store depth/stencil values, the application can set `format` to any of the values in Table 6.2.

The first letter or letters identify which components are present in the pixel. If the only letter is `r`, the format represents a single-component (grayscale) pixel. After the component identifiers, the number identifies how many bits are used to store each component. For example, if a format starts with `r8`, each pixel contains an 8-bit grayscale value. If a format starts with `r16`, each pixel contains a 16-bit grayscale value.

The last part of the format identifier specifies how the numeric values are formatted:

- `uint`—unsigned integer
- `sint`—signed integer

TABLE 6.2   Texture formats (no compression or depth/stencil usage)

r8unorm	rg8uint	rgba8unorm-srbg	rg11b10ufloat
r8snorm	rg8sint	rgba8snorm	rg32uint
r8uint	r32uint	rgba8uint	rg32sint
r8sint	r32sint	rgba8sint	rg32float
r16uint	r32float	bgra8unorm	rgba16uint
r16sint	rg16uint	bgra8unorm-srbg	rgba16sint
r16float	rg16sint	rgb9e5ufloat	rgba16float
rg8unorm	rg16float	rgb10a2uint	rgba32uint
rg8snorm	rgba8unorm	rgb10a2unorm	rgba32sint

- `unorm`—unsigned normalized value (between 0 and 1)
- `snorm`—signed normalized value (between −1 and 1)
- `float`—floating-point value

Most applications I've seen set the `format` property to one of the `rgba8` formats, such as `rgba8unorm`. In this format, each pixel has 8 bits for each component (red, green, blue, and alpha), and the values are unsigned normalized (between 0 and 1).

The `size` property should be set to an array containing the texture's width, height, and depth or array layer count. If the texture will be created from an `ImageBitmap`, the width and height can be obtained by calling the `ImageBitmap`'s `width` and `height` methods.

The `usage` property of the `createTexture` method is like the `usage` property for creating buffers, and identifies how the texture can be accessed. This can be set to one or more of the flags listed in Table 6.3.

Most applications that use textures write image data to them in JavaScript and then sample the data in a fragment shader. In this case, `usage` should be set to the OR'ed combination of three flags: TEXTURE_BINDING, COPY_DST, and RENDER_ATTACHMENT. The COPY_DST is needed because the texture will be the destination of a write operation. The RENDER_ATTACHMENT flag is needed because the texture will serve as a color attachment.

The `sampleCount` property identifies how many samples can be obtained for each pixel. In general, this will be set to 1 (the default value). However, if anti-aliasing is a major priority, multisampled textures can be used. In these textures, four values are sampled for each pixel.

As a viewer moves away from a texture, the texture's resolution should decrease. One way to accomplish this is by reading fewer samples from the texture. This is referred to as level of detail (LOD). A common LOD method is to add mipmap levels to a texture, where each level's image has a lower resolution than the one preceding it. That is, the Level 0 image has the highest resolution, the Level 1 image has the next highest, and so on. The `mipLevelCount` property identifies how many mipmap levels are present in the texture.

TABLE 6.3 Texture usage flags

USAGE FLAG	DESCRIPTION
TEXTURE_BINDING	The texture can be bound for use as a sampled texture in a shader
COPY_SRC	The texture can be used as the source of a copy operation
COPY_DST	The texture can be used as the destination of a copy or write operation
RENDER_ATTACHMENT	The texture can be used as a color or depth/stencil attachment
STORAGE_BINDING	The texture can be bound as a storage texture in a shader

Step 3: Write the ImageBitmap to the Texture

When working with buffers, it is common to call `queue.writeBuffer` to copy data into the buffer. When working with textures, the `GPUQueue` provides two methods for copying data into the resource. The main difference is the source of the data to be written:

- `writeTexture`—writes an `ArrayBuffer`, `TypedArray`, or `DataView` to the texture
- `copyExternalImageToTexture`—writes an `ImageBitmap`, `HTMLVideoElement`, `VideoFrame`, `HTMLCanvasElement`, or `OffscreenCanvas` to the texture

This book is concerned with creating textures from `ImageBitmaps`, so we'll focus on `copyExternalImageToTexture`, which accepts three arguments, and all of them must be provided as objects. Table 6.4 lists each of them.

The first argument, `source`, identifies the origin of the texture data. This must be set to an object with up to three properties. Table 6.5 lists each of them.

These properties are straightforward to understand. Throughout this book, we'll set the `source` property to the `ImageBitmap` created in the first step.

The `destination` argument of `copyExternalImageToTexture` identifies the object that will receive the image data. This accepts up to six properties, and Table 6.6 lists each of them.

The last property of `copyExternalImageToTexture` is `copySize`, which identifies the dimensions of the data to be written from the source to the destination. This can accept up to three values: width, height, and the number of depth or array

TABLE 6.4   Arguments of `copyExternalImageToTexture`

ARGUMENT	REQUIRED?	DESCRIPTION
source	Y	Object identifying the source of texture data
destination	Y	Object identifying where the texture data should be written
copySize	Y	Object identifying the dimensions of the texture data

TABLE 6.5   Properties of the `copyExternalImageToTexture` source object

PROPERTY	REQUIRED?	DESCRIPTION
source	Y	The `ImageBitmap`, `HTMLVideoElement`, `VideoFrame`, `HTMLCanvasElement`, or `OffscreenCanvas` containing the data to be written
origin	N	Offset into the data source that identifies the first (upper left) location to be accessed (default is (0, 0))
flipY	N	Identifies if the source image should be flipped vertically (default is false)

TABLE 6.6   Properties of the `copyExternalImageToTexture` source object

PROPERTY	REQUIRED?	DESCRIPTION
`texture`	Y	The `GPUTexture` created with the `device.createTexture` method discussed earlier
`origin`	N	Offset into the texture that identifies the first (upper left) location to be accessed (default is (0, 0))
`aspect`	N	Identifies which aspect of the texture should be affected by the copy operation; can be `all`, `depth-only`, or `stencil-only` (default is `all`)
`mipLevel`	N	Identifies which of the texture's mip levels should be updated (default is 1)
`premultipliedAlpha`	N	Identifies if RGB channels should be multiplied by the alpha channel before rendering (default is `false`)
`colorSpace`	N	Identifies the texture's color space and encoding (default is `srgb`)

layers. These values must be provided as an array or as an object with properties named `width`, `height`, and `depthOrArrayLayers`.

Despite the large number of objects and properties, most calls to `copyExternalImageToTexture` are fairly simple. For example, if the texture data is stored in `imageBitmap` and the name of the texture object is `tex`, the following code will define an operation that writes all the pixels of `imageBitmap` into `tex`:

```
// Copy data from the bitmap into the texture
device.queue.copyExternalImageToTexture(
    { source: imageBitmap },
    { texture: tex },
    [imageBitmap.width, imageBitmap.height]
);
```

As shown, the width and height of the `ImageBitmap` can be obtained through the object's `width` and `height` properties.

Step 4: Create a Sampler

As we've seen, shaders can access data in buffers through variables with attributes such as `@location`, `@group`, and `@binding`. But to access texture data, a shader needs to use a special resource called a *sampler*. Put simply, samplers make it possible for texture shaders to read pixel data from a texture.

In JavaScript, an application can create a sampler by calling the `createSampler` method of the `GPUDevice`. This doesn't require any arguments, but it can accept an object with several optional properties. Table 6.7 lists them and provides a description of each.

TABLE 6.7   Sampler properties

PROPERTY	REQUIRED?	DESCRIPTION
label	N	Identifier for the sampler
minFilter	N	Identifies how texel data should be obtained if the sampler accesses a region smaller than one texel; possible values are nearest and linear
magFilter	N	Identifies how texel data should be obtained if the sampler accesses a region larger than one texel, possible values are nearest and linear
mipMapFilter	N	Identifies how texel data should be obtained if the sampler accesses a region between mip levels, possible values are nearest and linear
maxAnisotropy	N	Anisotropy clamp used by the sampler
lodMinClamp	N	Minimum level of detail (LOD) used when sampling a texture ranges from 0 to 32; default is 0
lodMaxClamp	N	Maximum level of detail used when sampling a texture ranges from 0 to 32; default is 32
addressModeU	N	Identifies the data to be returned when a sampler accesses a region outside the texture in the u-direction
addressModeV	N	Identifies the data to be returned when a sampler accesses a region outside the texture in the v-direction
addressModeW	N	Identifies the data to be returned when a sampler accesses a region outside the texture in the w-direction
compare	N	Creates a comparison sampler

Even though these properties are optional, they can play an important role in determining how well the application displays images. The following discussion looks at these properties and explains how they affect the rendering process.

Texture filtering

To read texel data at a specific location in a texture, fragment shaders use floating-point coordinates. If a location lies between multiple texels, the shader has two options. It can read data from the texel whose center is nearest the point, or it can compute a weighted sum of the surrounding texels. These options are represented by the two values of the minFilter, magFilter, and mipMapFilter properties:

- nearest—select data from the texel whose center is nearest
- linear—compute a weighted average of surrounding texels

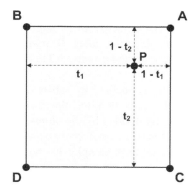

FIGURE 6.7 Bilinear interpolation.

If `minFilter` is set to `linear`, the texture sampler will read data using a process called *bilinear interpolation*. To understand how this works, suppose that the point P lies between four neighboring texels: A, B, C, and D. Figure 6.7 shows what this looks like.

To identify P's location relative to the surrounding texels, we use two values, t_1 and t_2. These are called interpolation parameters and range from 0 to 1. If t_1 and t_2 both equal 1,

P coincides with the center of D. If t_1 and t_2 both equal 0, P coincides with the center of A.

In this figure, P is closest to A. Therefore, if `minFilter` is set to `nearest`, the color of P will be set equal to that of A. But if it's set to `linear`, P's color will be computed using the following equation:

$$Color(P) = t_1 \times t_2 \times Color(A) + (1-t_1) \times t_2 \times Color(B) + t_1 \times (1-t_2)$$
$$\times Color(C) + (1-t_1) \times (1-t_2) \times Color(D)$$

The `magFilter` property identifies the filtering method to be used when texels are larger in area than fragments. If a texture contains mipmap levels, an application can customize sampling with the `mipMapFilter` property. If this is set to `nearest`, the sampler will select data from the nearest mipmap image. If it's set to `linear`, the sampler will compute a weighted average of texels in adjacent mipmaps.

Mipmap levels can be thought of as a third dimension. When bilinear filtering is combined with mipmap linear filtering, the result is called *trilinear filtering*.

Anisotropic filtering

In most applications, the fragment shader will read the same number of samples in the x and y directions. This is called *isotropic filtering* because sampling is performed the same way in each direction.

Isotropic filtering is ideal when the viewing angle is perpendicular to the texture. But if a viewer looks at a textured object from an angle, the object should appear to stretch in one direction and shrink in the other. To maintain resolution, the renderer should read more samples in the stretched direction. This directional sampling is called *anisotropic filtering.*

In code, anisotropic filtering is enabled by setting the `maxAnisotropy` property to a value between 1 and 16. This identifies the maximum ratio of the number of samples to be read in one direction divided by the number of samples to be read in the other direction. For example, if `maxAnisotropy` is set to 4, the sampler will read a maximum of four times the number of samples in one direction over the number of samples in the other.

Level of detail

As a viewer moves away from a texture, the texture's resolution should decrease. One way to accomplish this is by reading fewer samples from the texture. Another method is to take advantage of mipmapping. If the texture has mipmap levels, each level's image has a lower resolution than the one preceding it. That is, the Level 0 image has the highest resolution, the Level 1 image has the next highest, and so on.

Many sources refer to mipmap levels as *lods*, where *lod* stands for level of detail. An application can specify which lods should be used by setting values for the `lodMinClamp` and `lodMaxClamp` properties. `lodMinClamp` specifies the minimum mipmap level that should be employed, and `lodMaxClamp` specifies the maximum mipmap level. `lodMaxClamp` must be greater than or equal to `lodMinClamp`.

Accessing external coordinates

If a shader tries to read texel data beyond the texture's boundary, a question arises regarding what value should be returned. An application can configure this by assigning values to the `addressModeU`, `addressModeV`, and `addressModeW` fields. These fields can be set to one of three values:

- `clamp_to_edge`—Texels beyond the texture are set to the texels at the texture's edge
- `repeat`—In-range coordinates are repeated beyond the texture
- `mirror_repeat`—Texels beyond the texture are set to the reflections of the corresponding in-range texels

The illustrations in Figure 6.8 show what happens when a shader reads texels outside of the texture's boundaries. In each case, the coordinates run from −0.25 to 1.25.

If nearest-neighbor filtering is employed, the `clamp_to_edge` mode is automatically used. If linear filtering is configured, the address mode depends on where the point is located. If the point lies on a horizontal or vertical border, a texel from an adjacent face will be selected. If the point lies on a corner, the texel will be set to the sum of the three adjacent texels.

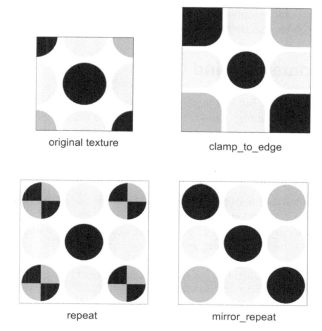

original texture

clamp_to_edge

repeat

mirror_repeat

FIGURE 6.8   Sampler addressing modes.

Comparison tests

The compare property configures a sampler to perform comparisons related to depth testing and stencil testing. When the sampler reads a value from a depth/stencil texture (the *sampled value*), it compares the value to a second value (the *reference value*), and the result of the comparison can be used in filtering operations. The nature of the test can be configured by setting compare to one of the values in Table 6.8.

TABLE 6.8   Comparison sampler values

VALUE	DESCRIPTION
never	The comparison test never passes
always	The comparison test always passes
equal	The comparison passes if the two values are equal
not-equal	The comparison passes if the two values aren't equal
less	The test passes if the reference value is less than the sampled value
less-equal	The test passes if the reference value is less than or equal to the sampled value
greater	The test passes if the reference value is greater than the sampled value
greater-equal	The test passes if the reference value is greater than or equal to the sampled value

These comparisons are important for applications that take advantage of depth testing and stencil testing. A later section of this chapter discusses these topics in more detail.

Step 5: Update the Bind Group

Chapter 5 explained how bind groups associate resources like uniform buffers with numbers that serve as *binding values*. Shaders access a resource in a bind group by providing the resource's binding value (@binding) and the group's value (@group). This is shown in the following code:

```
@group(0) @binding(0) var<uniform> exampleVariable: dataStruct;
```

Like uniform buffers, textures and samplers must be added to a bind group before they can be accessed. If the texture created by device.createTexture is named tex and the sampler created by device.createSampler is named sampler, the following code adds both to the bind group:

```
// Create a bind group for a sampler and texture
let bindGroup = device.createBindGroup({
    layout: bindGroupLayout,
    entries: [{
        binding: 0,
        resource: sampler
    },
    {
        binding: 1,
        resource: tex.createView({
          dimension: "cube",
        })
    }]
});
```

As shown, the bind group doesn't access the texture directly. Instead, it calls the texture's createView method, which provides a specific view of the texture. This accepts an object with several properties, and Table 6.9 lists them all.

All of the textures presented in this book are two-dimensional, so the only properties that will be set are the label and the dimension property, which will be set to 2d.

After creating the bind group, the application can associate it with the render pass encoder by calling the encoder's setBindGroup method. The first argument is a number that a shader can use to access the bind group's resources. For example, the following code associates the bind group with the number 0:

```
// Associate the bind group with the value of 0
renderPass.setBindGroup(0, bindGroup);
```

As a result of this code, a shader can access the group using the @group(0) attribute. The following discussion explains how fragment shaders access textures.

TABLE 6.9 View creation properties

PROPERTY	REQUIRED?	DESCRIPTION
label	N	Identifier for the view
dimension	N	Format for the view (1d, 2d, 3d, 2d-array, cube, or cube-array)
aspect	N	Aspect(s) of the texture are available (all, depth-only, or stencil-only)
format	N	Texture format (such as those listed in Table 6.1)
arrayLayerCount	N	Number of array layers in the texture
baseArrayLayer	N	Index of the first array layer to be accessed
mipLevelCount	N	Number of mipmap levels in the texture
baseMipLevel	N	Index of the first mipmap level to be accessed

Step 6: Access the Texture and Sampler in the Fragment Shader

Earlier in this chapter, I showed how a fragment shader can access data in a uniform buffer using the @group and @binding attributes. Fragment shaders can access textures and samplers using the same attributes. For example, the following code uses these attributes to declare variables for a sampler and texture.

```
@group(0) @binding(0) var sam : sampler;
@group(0) @binding(1) var tex : texture_2d<f32>;
```

This code presents two new data types that shaders can access: sampler and texture_2d. The following discussion looks at these and other data types used when accessing textures.

Data types

WGSL only provides two data types for samplers. The more common type is the sampler type, which represents a regular texture sampler. However, if a sampler is created with the compare property set to perform comparison tests, its type should be set to sampler_comparison.

In contrast, there are several data types for textures. The differences between them depend on the texture's dimensions and the nature of its data. Table 6.10 lists twelve of the available texture types.

If an application switches textures frequently, it can improve performance by using texture arrays instead of individual textures. These are represented by the types that end in _array. These arrays are easy to work with, and the only change to the sampling process is an extra argument that identifies the array index.

TABLE 6.10   Texture data types

DATA TYPE	DESCRIPTION
texture_1d<T>	One-dimensional texture
texture_2d<T>	Two-dimensional texture
texture_2d_array<T>	Array of two-dimensional textures
texture_depth_2d<T>	Two-dimensional texture containing depth
texture_depth_2d_array<T>	Array of two-dimensional textures containing depth
texture_multisampled_2d<T>	Multi-sampled two-dimensional texture
texture_depth_multisampled_2d	Multi-sampled two-dimensional texture containing depth
texture_3d<T>	Three-dimensional texture
texture_cube<T>	Cubemap texture
texture_cube_array<T>	Array of cubemap textures
texture_depth_cube<T>	Cubemap texture containing depth
texture_depth_cube_array<T>	Array of cubemap textures containing depth

Three-dimensional textures are less rarely used than two-dimensional textures, but the sampling process is essentially similar. The main difference is that, when a shader accesses a 3-D texture, it needs to provide three coordinates instead of two.

As its name implies, a texture cube (or *cubemap*) is a texture intended to cover the surfaces of a cube. It contains six separate two-dimensional textures—one for each face of a cube. The advantage of using texture cubes instead of regular textures is that you can choose the surface using the normal vector.

Texture functions

In addition to providing data types, WGSL defines several functions that access textures. Table 6.11 lists nine of these functions and provides a description of each.

Of these functions, textureSample is the most commonly used. It accepts a texture, a sampler, and the coordinates where the texture data should be read. The output depends on the nature of the texture. If the texture contains depth data, textureSample will return a 32-bit floating-point value. Otherwise, textureSample will return a vec4f.

Shaders can call textureSampleCompare if the sampler has been configured for comparison tests. In this case, the fourth argument, refValue, identifies the value to be used for the test. It returns 1.0 if the test succeeds and 0.0 if the test fails. These comparisons play a central role in depth/stencil tests, which will be discussed later in this chapter.

Like textureSample, textureLoad reads data from the texture. The difference is that textureLoad doesn't use a sampler, which means it can't take advantage of the sampler configuration discussed earlier.

TABLE 6.11   Texture functions

FUNCTION	RETURN VALUE
`textureSample(texture, sampler, coords)`	Texel data at the given location
`textureSampleBias(texture, sampler, coords, bias)`	Texel data at the given location, adding a bias for the mipmap level
`textureSampleCompare(texture, sampler, coords, refValue)`	Result of the comparison
`textureLoad(texture, coords, level)`	Texel data at the given location (no sampling)
`textureStore(texture, coords, value)`	Writes a texel value to the texture
`textureDimensions(texture)`	The number of dimensions in the texture
`textureNumLayers(texture)`	The number of elements in a texture array
`textureNumLevels(texture)`	The number of mipmap levels in a texture array
`textureNumSamples(texture)`	The number of samples per texel

The last four functions in the table are called texture query functions because they provide general information about the texture. `textureDimensions` identifies the number of dimensions, `textureNumLayers` identifies the number of elements in a texture array, `textureNumLevels` identifies the number of mipmap levels, and `textureNumSamples` identifies how many samples are present per texel.

Texture Compression

In most simple applications, every texel contains eight bits for the red component, eight bits for the green component, and eight bits for the blue component. This format is simple to work with, but textures requiring 24 bits per texel require a significant amount of time to transfer to the GPU.

Applications can dramatically reduce transfer times by using compressed textures. An application can identify a texture as compressed by setting the `format` property of the `createTexture` argument to the identifier of the compressed format. In the following code, the new texture is identified as being compressed using one of the ASTC formats.

```
// Define a texture with a compressed format
const texture = device.createTexture({
    ...
    format: "astc-5x4-unorm",
    ...
});
```

WebGPU supports three different families of texture compression methods:

- Block Compression (BCn)
- Ericsson Texture Compression (ETC/ETC2/EAC)
- Advanced Scalable Texture Compression (ASTC)

This discussion takes a brief look at each of these families. In each case, I'll explain what formats are available and how to check for device support.

Block compression (BCn)

One of the oldest texture compression methods is block compression (BCn), also known as S3 Texture Compression (S3TC). WebGPU provides format identifiers for BC1 through BC7 compression, and despite their differences, they all compress 4-by-4 blocks of pixels into 64-bit integers or 128-bit integers.

Block compression is supported by most desktop GPUs, but it's not as common on mobile GPUs. For this reason, it's important to check if the client's device supports it. An application can check for support through the features property of the GPU adapter on the target device. The following code shows how this works.

```
// Check if the device supports Block Compression (BC)
const adapter = await navigator.gpu.requestAdapter();
if (adapter) {
    if (adapter.features.has("texture-compression-bc")) {
        ...
    }
}
```

If the device supports the format, applications can set the format property in createTexture to one of the values listed in Table 6.12.

In each identifier, the first three characters identify the nature of the block compression. The next part identifies the format of the pixels to be compressed, such as rgba. After this, unorm indicates that texels are compressed into normalized unsigned integers and snorm indicates that texels are compressed into normalized signed integers.

TABLE 6.12 Block compression (BC) texture formats

bc1-rgba-unorm	bc3-rgba-unorm-srgb	bc6h-rgb-ufloat
bc1-rgba-unorm-srgb	bc4-r-unorm	bc6h-rgb-float
bc2-rgba-unorm	bc4-r-snorm	bc7-rgba-unorm
bc2-rgba-unorm-srgb	bc5-rg-unorm	bc7-rgba-unorm-srgb
bc3-rgba-unorm	bc5-rg-snorm	

TABLE 6.13   Ericsson texture compression texture formats

etc2-rgb8unorm	etc2-rgba8unorm-srgb
etc2-rgb8unorm-srgb	eac-r11unorm
etc2-rgb8a1unorm	eac-r11snorm
etc2-rgb8a1unorm-srgb	eac-rg11unorm
etc2-rgba8unorm	eac-rg11snorm

Ericsson texture compression (ETC)

Like the Block Compression method, Ericsson Texture Compression compresses textures by converting 4-by-4 blocks of pixels into smaller values (64-bit words). However, the nature of the conversion is markedly different from Block Compression.

The second version of ETC, denoted ETC2, provides better compression and can be used to compress RGBA images in addition to RGB images. ETC2 is supported by any device that supports OpenGL ES 3.0 and higher, such as modern Android mobile devices. However, this compression method isn't as common on desktop systems.

For images with fewer components per texel, Ericsson developed Ericsson Alpha Compression (EAC). This is similar to ETC2 and is also guaranteed to be available on OpenGL ES 3.x devices. An application can check for support by accessing the device's adapter, and the following code shows how this works:

```
// Check if the device supports Ericsson Texture Compression 2
(ETC2)
const adapter = await navigator.gpu.requestAdapter();
if (adapter) {
    if (adapter.features.has("texture-compression-etc2")) {
        …
    }
}
```

If ETC2 is supported, applications can use compressed textures by setting the format property of the createTexture object to one of the values in Table 6.13.

As shown, the EAC compression methods are only available for textures with one (r) or two (rg) color channels. In all other cases, it's recommended to use one of the ETC2 methods for compression.

Advanced scalable texture compression (ASTC)

Like ETC and Block Compression, Advanced Scalable Texture Compression (ASTC) is block-based, producing one value for a block of texels. ASTC isn't as widely supported

TABLE 6.14   Advanced scalable texture compression (ASTC) formats

astc-4x4-unorm	astc-8x5-unorm	astc-10x8-unorm
astc-4x4-unorm-srgb	astc-8x5-unorm-srgb	astc-10x8-unorm-srgb
astc-5x4-unorm	astc-8x6-unorm	astc-10x10-unorm
astc-5x4-unorm-srgb	astc-8x6-unorm-srgb	astc-10x10-unorm-srgb
astc-5x5-unorm	astc-8x8-unorm	astc-12x10-unorm
astc-5x5-unorm-srgb	astc-8x8-unorm-srgb	astc-12x10-unorm-srgb
astc-6x5-unorm	astc-10x5-unorm	astc-12x12-unorm
astc-6x5-unorm-srgb	astc-10x5-unorm-srgb	astc-12x12-unorm-srgb
astc-6x6-unorm	astc-10x6-unorm	
astc-6x6-unorm-srgb	astc-10x6-unorm-srgb	

as ETC2, but it generally produces better-quality compression. An application can check for ASTC support using code like the following:

```
// Check if the device supports Advanced Scalable Texture
Compression (ASTC)
const adapter = await navigator.gpu.requestAdapter();
if (adapter) {
    if (adapter.features.has("texture-compression-astc")) {
        ...
    }
}
```

One advantage of ASTC over other methods is that you can choose the size of the blocks used in the compression. Larger blocks mean greater compression but greater data loss. Smaller blocks mean lower compression and less data loss.

Table 6.14 makes this clear. The least lossy compression method processes 4-by-4 blocks, and the most lossy compression method processes 12-by-12 blocks.

The Unity Manual recommends using the BC7 compression method whenever possible. If this is unavailable, it recommends using ASTC if it's supported and ETC2/EAC if ASTC isn't supported.

EXAMPLE APPLICATION—ADDING TEXTURE

The Ch06_SimpleTexture application demonstrates how textures can be created and displayed with WebGPU. This doesn't transform any vertices or set light components. Instead, it creates a two-dimensional square and covers it with a two-dimensional texture.

Despite its simplicity, this project deserves attention because it demonstrates three important capabilities: creating ImageBitmaps from image files, creating a texture and sampler in code, and sampling the texture in a shader. This section discusses each of these capabilities and explains how they're implemented in code.

Creating an ImageBitmap from an Image File

As mentioned earlier, WebGPU makes it easy to write texture data from an ImageBitmap into a texture resource. In the Ch06_SimpleTexture application, the code obtains an ImageBitmap for an image file using three steps:

1. Calls fetch() to obtain a Response for the smiley.png file.
2. Calls the Response's blob() method to obtain a Blob.
3. Calls createImageBitmap with the Blob to obtain an ImageBitmap.

The following lines of code show how these steps are accomplished:

```
// Create ImageBitmap from image file
const response = await fetch("smiley.png");
const imageBitmap = await createImageBitmap(await response.
blob());
```

Once the ImageBitmap is available, its data can be written to a texture resource. The following discussion explains how the Ch06_SimpleTexture application creates a texture and sampler.

Creating the Texture and Sampler

After creating the ImageBitmap, the code in ch06_simpletexture.js creates an empty texture resource with the following code:

```
// Create texture object
const texture = device.createTexture({
    size: [imageBitmap.width, imageBitmap.height],
    format: "rgba8unorm",
    usage:
        GPUTextureUsage.TEXTURE_BINDING |
        GPUTextureUsage.COPY_DST |
        GPUTextureUsage.RENDER_ATTACHMENT
});
```

As shown, the code sets the texture's size, format, and usage parameters. The COPY_DST flag is needed because the texture will be written to, and the RENDER_ATTACHMENT flag is needed because the texture will serve as a color attachment.

To create the operation that writes the `ImageBitmap` to the texture, the application calls the `copyExternalImageToTexture` method of the device's queue. This is accomplished with the following code:

```
// Write data to texture
device.queue.copyExternalImageToTexture(
    { source: imageBitmap },
    { texture: texture },
    [imageBitmap.width, imageBitmap.height]
);
```

Now that the texture is created and associated with data, the application creates the sampler that will be used by the shader to read the texture's data.

```
// Create sampler
const sampler = device.createSampler({
    magFilter: "linear",
    minFilter: "linear",
});
```

By default, the sampler reads texture data using nearest-neighbor sampling. This code configures the sampler to use bilinear interpolation, which computes the sampled value by combining the values of the surrounding texels.

Before the texture and sample can be used, the application adds them to a bind group and then associates the group with the render pass encoder. To accomplish this, it executes the following code:

```
// Create the bind group
let bindGroup = device.createBindGroup({
    layout: bindGroupLayout,
    entries: [{
        binding: 0,
        resource: sampler
    },
    {
        binding: 1,
        resource: texture.createView({
            dimension: "2d",
        })
    }]
});
```

```
// Associate bind group with render pass encoder
renderPass.setBindGroup(0, bindGroup);
```

As a result of this code, a shader can access the bind group through the `@group(0)` attribute. It can access the sampler with `@binding(0)` and the texture with `@binding(1)`.

Sampling the Texture in a Shader

The goal of the fragment shader is to assign a color to each fragment in the rendering. In the Ch06_SimpleTexture application, the fragment shader obtains color values by reading data from a texture. To be precise, it uses a sampler to sample the texture's data.

The fragment shader accesses the sampler by declaring a variable of type `sampler` and accesses the texture by declaring a variable of type `texture_2d`. The following code shows what these declarations look like:

```
@group(0) @binding(0) var sam : sampler;
@group(0) @binding(1) var tex : texture_2d<f32>;
```

The `@group(0)` attribute specifies that the variable is taken from a resource in Bind Group 0. The `@binding(0)` attribute indicates that the sampler corresponds to the bind group's resource bound to the value 0. The `@binding(1)` attribute indicates that the texture corresponds to the bind group's resource bound to the value 1.

After declaring the variables, the fragment shader sets the fragment's color by calling the `textureSample` method discussed earlier. This is shown in the following code:

```
fn fragmentMain(fragData: DataStruct) -> @location(0) vec4f {
    return textureSample(tex, sam, fragData.uvPos);
}
```

The first argument of `textureSample` is the texture, the second is the sampler, and the third is the location to be sampled. This location is given in UV coordinates, which are passed to the fragment shader from the vertex shader. The UV coordinates are different than the (x, y) coordinates of the incoming vertex, and this is an important difference to understand.

In the ch06_simpletexture.js code, the vertex buffer stores four values for each vertex: (x, y) coordinates and (u, v) coordinates. The vertex shader assigns the (x, y) coordinates to each vertex, and the fragment shader uses the (u, v) coordinates to sample data from the texture.

DEPTH AND STENCIL TESTING

By default, WebGPU draws triangles in the order given by the application, without regard to their positions. This means that triangles of a far object will be drawn over triangles of a near object if the far object is drawn later. This frequently causes problems when surfaces overlap.

To resolve this, applications can take advantage of *depth testing*. The goal is to make sure that fragments with the lowest depth are drawn and fragments with greater depth are discarded.

As discussed earlier, each fragment has a depth that ranges from 0.0 (nearest) to 1.0 (farthest). At each fragment location, the application stores a minimum depth value and a corresponding fragment. If a new fragment has a lower depth value than the stored value, its depth is stored and the old fragment is discarded. This can be expressed with the following pseudocode:

```
let x = newFragment.x;
let y = newFragment.y;
let minDepthValue = depth(x, y);
if(newFragment.depth < minDepthValue) {
    depth(x, y) = newFragment.depth;
    fragment(x, y) = newFragment;
}
```

The structure that stores the minimum fragment depths at each location is called the *depth buffer*, also called the *z buffer*. In essence, it's a two-dimensional array of depth values between 0.0 and 1.0.

In addition to the depth buffer, applications can set values in a *stencil buffer*. A fragment shader can read these values, perform comparison tests, and keep or discard fragments depending on the result. In essence, stencil buffers make it possible to block out portions of the rendering area.

Stencil values don't need a lot of bits, so it's common for a buffer to serve as both the depth buffer *and* the stencil buffer. A common arrangement is to use 24 bits to store a depth value and 8 bits to store a stencil value.

For this reason, WebGPU documentation combines the topics of depth and stencil testing and refers to the combination as *depth/stencil testing*. Keep in mind that the two tests are distinct, and an application can perform depth testing, stencil testing, both, or neither.

In OpenGL, depth testing is enabled by calling `glEnable(GL_DEPTH_TEST)`. In WebGPU, the process is significantly more complicated. To implement depth/stencil testing in WebGPU, an application needs to perform five steps:

1. Create a texture to serve as the depth/stencil buffer.
2. Create and configure a comparison sampler to access the texture.
3. Configure the render pass encoder to access the depth and stencil buffers.
4. Configure the render pipeline to perform depth/stencil testing.
5. Perform the comparison test in the fragment shader.

This discussion explores each of these steps. In each case, we'll look at the objects and methods needed during the testing procedure.

Create the Depth/Stencil Texture

Before depth/stencil testing can be enabled, an application needs to create a texture to store depth and/or stencil values. This is the depth/stencil buffer, and it can be created with the same `device.createTexture` method discussed earlier in the chapter. But there are three points to keep in mind:

- The texture's content (probably) won't be set to an image, so there's (usually) no need to set the `GPUTextureUsage.COPY_DST` flag.
- The texture's size should usually be set to cover every pixel in the viewport.
- The texture's format must be set to one of the depth/stencil formats.

This last point is important. If a texture will hold depth and/or stencil values, its format can't be set to a regular texture format. Instead, the `format` property needs to be set to one of the values in Table 6.15.

At the time of this writing, the `depth32float-stencil8` format isn't supported on all compliant GPUs. Before using this, be sure to check the `features` property of the `GPUAdapter` to see if the `depth32float-stencil8` feature is supported.

As an example, the following code creates a 400-by-200 texture to serve as a depth/stencil buffer. The `format` property is set to `depth24plus-stencil8`, so the texture can store depth and stencil values.

```
// Create texture to store depth/stencil values.
const depthStencilTexture = device.createTexture({
    size: [400, 200, 1],
    usage: GPUTextureUsage.RENDER_ATTACHMENT |
        GPUTextureUsage.TEXTURE_BINDING,
    format: "depth24plus-stencil8"
});
```

TABLE 6.15 Depth/stencil texture formats

FORMAT	DESCRIPTION
stencil8	Stores 8-bit stencil values
depth16unorm	Stores depth values as 16-bit unsigned normalized integers
depth24plus	Stores integer depth values using at least 24 bits per value
depth24plus-stencil8	Stores integer depth values using at least 24 bits per value and stencil values using 8-bit values
depth32float	Stores depth values as 32-bit floating-point values
depth32float-stencil8	Stores depth values as 32-bit floating-point values and stencil values as 8-bit integers

After creating the texture, an application needs to create a *texture view* that provides access to the texture's data. This is created by calling the texture's `createView` method, as shown in the following code:

```
const depthStencilView = depthStencilTexture.createView();
```

Once this view is available, the application can configure the render pass encoder to access the texture to store depth and/or stencil values. I'll discuss this next.

Create the Comparison Sampler

As with regular textures, fragment shaders read from depth/stencil textures using samplers. But samplers used for depth/stencil testing are different than regular samplers. They're called *comparison samplers*, and applications need to make two minor changes to the configuration process.

First, the `device.createSampler` method must be called with an object whose `compare` property identifies the nature of the comparison to be performed. This is shown in the following code:

```
resource: device.createSampler({
    compare: "less",
}
```

Second, the bind group layout needs to be configured with the sampler, whose `type` property is set to `comparison`. The following code shows how this is done:

```
const bindGroupLayout = device.createBindGroupLayout({
    entries: [
        {
            binding: 0,
            visibility: GPUShaderStage.FRAGMENT,
            sampler: {
                type: "comparison",
            },
        },
    ],
});
```

As a result of this, the fragment shader will be able to access the sampler as a comparison sampler.

Configure the Render Pass Encoder

During the rendering process, the GPU relies on a special portion of memory to store the data to be displayed. This special memory is called the *framebuffer*, and it stores pixel-related data in a series of buffers. So far, the only buffer we've been creating is the color buffer, which is configured by setting the `colorAttachments` property in the `beginRenderPass` method. The following code shows how this is done:

```
// Create the render pass encoder with a color buffer
const renderPass = encoder.beginRenderPass({
    colorAttachments: [{
        view: context.getCurrentTexture().createView(),
        loadOp: "clear",
        clearValue: { … },
        storeOp: "store"
    }]
});
```

Because of this code, the color buffer will be the only buffer attached to the framebuffer. However, WebGPU makes it possible to attach a buffer that stores depth/stencil data. This is accomplished by setting `depthStencilAttachment` to an object containing up to nine properties. Table 6.16 lists these properties and provides a description of each.

The view property should be set to the texture view created from the texture serving as the depth/stencil buffer. The `depthReadOnly` property determines if the depth values are read-only and the `stencilReadOnly` property determines if the stencil values are read-only. Both properties are false by default.

If `depthLoadOp` is set to `clear`, the depth values will be initialized to `depthClearValue` before rendering starts. If `stencilLoadOp` is set to `clear`, the stencil values will be initialized to `stencilClearValue` before rendering starts.

If `depthStoreOp` is set to `store`, the depth values will be stored after the rendering. Similarly, if `stencilStoreOp` is set to `store`, the stencil values will be stored. If either property is set to `discard`, the corresponding data will be discarded.

TABLE 6.16 Configuring the depth and stencil buffers

PROPERTY	OPTIONAL?	DESCRIPTION
view	N	Texture view identifying the resource to be read from and written to
depthReadOnly	Y	Identifies if the depth buffer should be read-only
depthClearValue	Y	Identifies the initial value of each element in the depth buffer
depthLoadOp	Y	The load operation to be performed on the depth values before the rendering (load or clear)
depthStoreOp	Y	The store operation to be performed on the depth values after the rendering (store or discard)
stencilReadOnly	Y	Identifies if the stencil buffer should be read-only
stencilClearValue	Y	Identifies the initial value of each element in the stencil buffer
stencilLoadOp	Y	The load operation to be performed on the stencil values before the rendering (load or clear)
stencilStoreOp	Y	The store operation to be performed on the stencil values after the rendering (store or discard)

To demonstrate how these properties can be set, the following code calls `beginRenderPass` with the `depthStencilAttachment` property. Its view is set to the `depthStencilView` created earlier:

```
// Create the render pass encoder
const renderPassDescriptor: GPURenderPassDescriptor = {
    // Define the color attachment
    colorAttachments: [
        { ... },
    ],

    // Define the depth/stencil attachment
    depthStencilAttachment: {
        view: depthStencilView,
        depthClearValue: 1.0,
        depthLoadOp: "clear",
        depthStoreOp: "store",
        stencilClearValue: 0,
        stencilLoadOp: "clear",
        stencilStoreOp: "store"
    }
};
```

As a result of this code, the render pass will be able to access depth and stencil values in the `depthStencilView`. Before rendering, the depth values will be set to 1.0 (`depthClearValue`) and the stencil values will be set to 0 (`stencilClearValue`).

Configure the Render Pipeline

The `device.createRenderPipeline` method accepts a `depthStencil` property that configures how depth and/or stencil tests are performed. This must be set to an object with at most ten properties. Table 6.17 lists these properties and provides a description of each.

The first property, `format`, specifies the format of the depth/stencil buffer and should be set to the same format value used to create the texture. The second property, `depthCompare`, identifies the nature of the depth test. That is, it identifies how each value at (x, y) will be compared to the depth value at (x, y) in the depth buffer. This can be set to one of seven values:

- `always`—the comparison always passes
- `never`—the comparison never passes
- `less`—the comparison passes if the fragment's depth is less than the buffer's value
- `less-equal`—the comparison passes if the fragment's depth is less than or equal to the buffer's value
- `equal`—the comparison passes if the fragment's depth is equal to the buffer's value

TABLE 6.17   Configuring the depth and stencil tests

PROPERTY	OPTIONAL?	DESCRIPTION
format	N	The format of the depth/stencil buffer
depthCompare	N	Identifies the nature of the depth comparison
depthWriteEnabled	N	Specifies if the application can write to the depth buffer
depthBias	Y	Value added to each fragment before the depth test
depthBiasSlopeScale	Y	Increases bias depending on the slope of the pixel's depth value
depthBiasClamp	Y	Sets the maximum depth bias
stencilFront	Y	Configure the stencil test for front-facing primitives
stencilBack	Y	Configure the stencil test for back-facing primitives
stencilReadMask	Y	Identifies which bits of a stencil value should be accessed during read operations
stencilWriteMask	Y	Identifies which bits of a stencil value should be changed during write operations

- more-equal—the comparison passes if the fragment's depth is greater than or equal to the buffer's value
- greater—the comparison passes if the fragment's depth is greater than the buffer's value

In general, we want fragments to pass the depth test if their depth is less (closer to the viewer) than the current value in the depth buffer. For this reason, depthCompare is usually set to less.

For simple depth tests, it may be a good idea to set depthWriteEnable to false to prevent the application from changing the depth buffer. But for complex depth tests or stencil tests, this should be set to true to enable changes to the depth/stencil values.

If two objects have the same depth, the renderer may fuse their triangles together, producing unacceptable results. For this reason, many applications add a slight bias to ensure that objects have distinct depths. This is accomplished by setting the depthBias property, which assigns an initial value for the bias, and the depthBiasSlopeScale property, which is multiplied by the maximum of the horizontal or vertical slope of the depth at the given pixel. The depthBiasClamp property sets the maximum value of the bias.

Stencil tests are configured through the stencilFront and stencilBack properties, which affect front-facing and back-facing primitives, respectively. Both properties can be set to an object with four properties (all optional):

1. compare—the type of comparison used by the stencil test—accepts the same values as depthCompare

2. `passOp`—the stencil operation to be performed if the stencil test passes

3. `failOp`—the stencil operation to be performed if the stencil test fails

4. `depthFailOp`—the stencil operation to be performed if the depth test fails

The `passOp`, `failOp`, and `depthFailOp` properties identify stencil operations to be performed depending on the result of the depth and stencil tests. Each of these properties can be set to one of eight values:

- `keep`—keep the current stencil value
- `zero`—set the stencil value to 0
- `replace`—set the stencil value to the current render state stencil value
- `invert`—invert the bits of the stencil value
- `increment-wrap`—increments the current render state stencil value, sets to zero if it exceeds the maximum
- `increment-clamp`—increments the current render state stencil value, clamps to the maximum
- `decrement-wrap`—decrements the current render state stencil value, sets to the maximum if it falls below zero
- `decrement-clamp`—decrements the current render state stencil value, clamps to zero

The last two properties in the table are `stencilReadMask` and `stencilWriteMask`. These are set to values whose bits determine which stencil value bits are used in stencil operations. The bits in the `stencilReadMask` value determine which stencil bits are accessed in read operations. The bits in the `stencilWriteMask` value determine which stencil bits are changed in write operations. By default, both values are set to `0xffffffff`, which means all bits of the stencil value are used in read and write operations.

The following code demonstrates how a render pipeline can be configured to perform depth and stencil testing.

```
const shadowPipeline = device.createRenderPipeline({
    layout: device.createPipelineLayout({ … }),
    vertex: { … },
    fragment: { … },
    depthStencil: {
        format: "depth24plus-stencil8",
        depthCompare: "less",
        depthWriteEnabled: true,
        stencilFront: {
            passOp: "replace",
        }
    }
});
```

As a result of this code, the pipeline will perform depth testing and stencil testing on front-facing primitives. If the stencil test passes, the stencil value is set to the current render state stencil value.

Perform the Comparison Test

If the sampler was configured properly, the fragment shader will be able to use it for depth/stencil testing. But first, the shader needs to declare the sampler as a variable of the `sampler_comparison` data type. This is shown in the following code:

```
@group(0) @binding(0) var sampler: sampler_comparison;
```

Once this is done, the fragment shader can perform its comparison by calling `textureSampleCompare`. This accepts four parameters (at minimum):

- `texture`—the texture containing depth/stencil values used for testing
- `sampler`—the comparison sampler variable
- `coordinates`—the coordinates of the texture to be tested
- `reference`—the reference value used for testing

The `textureSampleCompare` returns an `f32` value between 0.0 and 1.0 that identifies the result of the comparison. A value of 0.0 implies that the comparison failed, and a value of 1.0 implies that the comparison succeeded. Fragment shaders can use this result to keep or discard the fragment.

SUMMARY

This chapter has explored three important operations that every graphical developer should be familiar with, and the first involves lighting. When we look at an object in the real world, we perceive its shape by seeing how its surfaces reflect light. In code, we create this effect by changing the object's color depending on its position and orientation relative to light sources. This chapter has presented two models for this: the Phong model and the Blinn–Phong model.

In many cases, we want the fragment shader to use images to assign colors to fragments. WebGPU makes this possible by providing special data structures called textures and samplers. A texture is like a buffer, but it contains image data and is stored in special memory on the GPU. Fragment shaders use samplers to extract data from textures, and this chapter presented a simple example of how this can be accomplished.

The last part of this chapter presented two types of tests that fragment shaders can perform during the rendering process. Depth tests are important to make sure that near objects are displayed instead of far objects. Stencil tests make it possible to change fragment processing by comparing stencil values to reference values. Both tests rely on data in the same texture, which needs to be specially configured for depth/stencil testing. In code, fragment shaders need special samplers called comparison samplers to perform these tests.

Advanced Features

7

At this point, you should have a solid understanding of coding graphical applications, from creating the JavaScript objects to writing the shaders. This chapter explores six capabilities that are important but not essential:

1. Debug groups—inserting messages associated with commands
2. Error handling—responding to errors and printing helpful messages
3. Viewports and scissor rectangles—defining the rendering region
4. Occlusion queries—counting how many fragments passed tests
5. Text—Displaying characters using a texture atlas
6. Animation—Drawing objects that move over time

The first two capabilities are important when you need to locate errors within complex applications. The next two capabilities make it possible to improve performance by reducing the number of objects and fragments that need to be drawn.

The last part of the chapter discusses two capabilities that I find particularly interesting. By reading textures from a texture atlas, WebGPU applications can display text with proper kerning. Applications can also use animation to render graphics whose positions and orientations change over time.

DEBUG GROUPS

When creating WebGPU objects in JavaScript, many methods accept an optional property named `label`. Labels are helpful when errors arise because the browser's message will display the label of the affected object.

As discussed in Chapter 2, the command encoder receives a series of commands and encodes them for execution on the GPU. Applications can insert labels into the command queue that can be read when errors occur. The `GPUCommandEncoder` provides two methods for this purpose:

- `pushDebugGroup(label)`—starts a debug group with the given label
- `popDebugGroup()`—ends the most-recently pushed group

The command encoder manages debug groups in a stack. This makes it possible for applications to form a hierarchy of debug groups. To demonstrate, the following code creates a command encoder and a render pass encoder that encode rendering commands. It creates a debug group for the commands encoded by the render pass encoder.

```
// Create the command encoder
const encoder = device.createCommandEncoder();

// Start the debug group
encoder.pushDebugGroup("Render Commands");

// Create the render pass encoder and define the rendering
const renderPass = encoder.beginRenderPass(…);
…
renderPass.draw(…);
renderPass.end();

// End the debug group
encoder.popDebugGroup();

// Submit the encoded commands to the GPU
device.queue.submit([encoder.finish()]);
```

As a result of this code, the rendering commands defined by the render pass encoder's draw method will be associated with the debug group labeled Render Commands. Debug groups are helpful when an application needs to add labels to different sets of commands to monitor where errors occur.

In addition to creating debug groups, an application can insert labels called *markers* in the encoder's set of commands. The command encoder provides the insertDebugMarker method for this purpose, and the following code shows how it can be used:

```
// Insert a debug marker
encoder.insertDebugMarker("Command Marker");
```

These markers are easier to use than debug groups. But they can't be nested in the way that debug groups can.

ERROR HANDLING

One frustrating aspect of graphical development is that rendering operations can fail without producing an error that halts the application. In OpenGL, the glGetError function makes it straightforward to find out if which operation produced an error.

TABLE 7.1   Detected error types

ERROR ID	DESCRIPTION
out-of-memory	Not enough memory available to perform the operation
validation	Invalid inputs to the method (wrong data type or unacceptable value)
internal	Error related to system or WebGPU implementation

WebGPU provides a similar capability through *error scopes*, which are like the try-catch blocks in JavaScript. Using error scopes requires three steps:

1. Push an error scope onto the stack.
2. Perform one or more operations that may produce an error.
3. Pop the error scope to check if the given error occurred.

For the first step, an application needs to call the pushErrorScope method of the GPUDevice. This accepts a string that identifies the type of error that should be monitored. Table 7.1 lists the three types of errors.

After an error scope has been pushed onto the stack, an application can check to see if the error occurred by calling the popErrorScope method. This returns a Promise that resolves to an object describing the first error captured in the scope. It's common to access the error object using a variable named error, as demonstrated in the following code:

```
// Respond to error if error occurred
device.popErrorScope().then((error) => {
    ...
});
```

If an error occurs, the variable will be of type GPUError, which provides a message property that identifies the nature of the error. In the following code, the application prints the error's message if an error occurred.

```
device.popErrorScope().then((error) => {

    // Check if error occurred
    if(error) {

        // Print error message
        console.log(error.message);
    }
});
```

Error scopes are helpful when an application attempts to create a rendering pipeline that may not be supported on the client's system. The following code checks to see if creating a rendering pipeline produces an internal error. If so, the application calls the createSimplerPipeline method.

```
// Monitor internal errors
device.pushErrorScope("internal");

// Attempt to create rendering pipeline
const renderPipeline = device.createRenderPipeline(…);

// Check to see if internal error occurred
device.popErrorScope().then((error) => {
    if(error) {
        console.log("Couldn't create pipeline");
        createSimplerPipeline(…);
    }
});
```

The GPUDevice is a subclass of EventTarget, so you can call its addEventListener method to keep track of events. In particular, you can handle uncaptured errors by setting the first argument to uncapturederror. This is shown in the following code:

```
// Handle errors that haven't been captured in error scopes
device.addEventListener("uncapturederror", (event) => {

    // Display the error's message in the console
    console.error("Uncaptured error: ", event.error.message);
});
```

The WebGPU specification has changed frequently in recent months. For this and other reasons, it's a good idea to employ error checking to make sure your application runs properly.

VIEWPORTS AND SCISSOR RECTANGLES

In every example application presented so far, the rendering has always occupied the entire canvas. The application identifies the canvas area when it provides the color attachments as part of creating the render pass encoder. The following code creates a view from the WebGPU context associated with the canvas:

```
// Render to the WebGPU context of the canvas
const renderPass = encoder.beginRenderPass({
    colorAttachments: [{
        view: context.getCurrentTexture().createView(),
        …
    }]
});
```

TABLE 7.2   Arguments of the setViewport method

ARGUMENTS	TYPE	DESCRIPTION
x	Integer	x-Coordinate of the upper left corner of the canvas
y	Integer	y-Coordinate of the upper left corner of the canvas
width	Integer	Width of the rendering surface
height	Integer	Height of the rendering surface
minDepth	Integer	Minimum depth value (0 by default)
maxDepth	Integer	Maximum depth value (1 by default)

If you don't want the rendering to take up the whole canvas, you can set the rendering area (called the *viewport*) by calling the setViewport method of the GPURenderPassEncoder. This accepts six values, and Table 7.2 lists them all.

An example will make this clear. Suppose you want the rendering of your application to be limited to the 100-by-100 square in the upper left of the canvas. In this case, you'd call setViewport with the upper left corner set to (0, 0) and the dimensions set to 100 and 100. The following code shows how this works:

```
// Set the boundaries of the rendering
renderPass.setViewport(0, 0, 100, 100, 0, 1);
```

In addition to customizing the viewport, applications can define regions called *scissor rectangles* that tell the renderer which fragments should be discarded. This is accomplished by calling the setScissorRect method of the GPURenderPassEncoder. This method accepts the coordinates of the upper left corner of the rectangle, followed by its width and height.

For example, suppose an application wants to discard all fragments outside the 150-by-250 rectangle whose upper left corner is at (20, 30). The following code defines a scissor rectangle for this purpose:

```
// Set the boundaries of the scissor rectangle
renderPass.setScissorRect(20, 30, 150, 250);
```

As a result of this code, any fragment outside the scissor rectangle won't be drawn. By default, the scissor rectangle has the same bounds as the viewport.

OCCLUSION QUERIES

Chapter 6 explained how applications can discard fragments using depth and stencil testing. Applications can check how many fragments passed these tests by submitting *occlusion queries*. If only a small number of fragments pass, the application may want to draw simpler objects or use simpler shaders.

An application can create and configure occlusion queries by employing six steps:

1. Create a query set and identify it when creating the render pass encoder.
2. Create a buffer to hold the query results.
3. Call the `beginOcclusionQuery` method of the render pass encoder.
4. After the rendering commands are finished, call `endOcclusionQuery`.
5. Encode a command to record queries by calling `resolveQuerySet`.
6. Destroy the query set by calling its `destroy` method.

The following discussion explores these steps. In each case, it explains what objects and methods are needed and then shows how they can be implemented in code.

Creating the Query Set

A `GPUQuerySet` object can hold multiple queries, and an application can create a set by calling the `createQuerySet` method of the `GPUDevice`. This accepts a descriptor with the properties listed in Table 7.3.

For occlusion queries, `count` must be set to an integer greater than 1, and `type` must be set to `occlusion`. For timestamp queries, `type` must be set to `timestamp`. Chapter 8 will discuss timestamp queries and show how they're used.

To demonstrate this, the following code creates a query set capable of holding four occlusion queries:

```
// Create a new query set
const querySet = device.createQuerySet({
    label: "Query Set 0",
    count: 4,
    type: "occlusion"
});
```

After creating the query set, the application needs to associate it with the render pass encoder. This is accomplished by setting the `occlusionQuerySet` property of the object used in the `beginRenderPass` method. In the following code, the render pass is configured to use the query set created earlier:

```
// Create the render pass encoder
const renderPass = encoder.beginRenderPass({
colorAttachments: [{ … }],

    // Configure the query set created earlier
    occlusionQuerySet: querySet
});
```

As a result of this code, an application can submit occlusion queries through the render pass encoder.

TABLE 7.3   Query set descriptor properties

PROPERTY	OPTIONAL?	DESCRIPTION
label	Y	String identifier for the query set
count	N	Number of queries that can be accessed
type	N	If the set contains occlusion queries (occlusion) or timestamps (queries)

Creating the Result Buffer

To store the results of the occlusion query or queries, an application needs to create a dedicated buffer. This can be done by calling the device's `createBuffer` method and setting the `usage` property to `GPUBufferUsage.QUERY_RESOLVE`. This is shown in the following code, which creates a buffer capable of holding 512 bytes.

```
// Create the buffer
const queryBuffer = device.createBuffer({
    size: 512,
    usage: GPUBufferUsage.QUERY_RESOLVE
});
```

There's no need to add this to a bind group. The command encoder has a method (`resolveQuerySet`) that tells the GPU to store the results of the occlusion query into the specified buffer.

Launching the Query

If the render pass encoder is associated with a query set, an application can encode occlusion query commands by calling its `beginOcclusionQuery` method. This accepts a value that serves as an index into the set.

For example, if the query set can hold four queries, the following code encodes an occlusion query corresponding to the third query in the set:

```
renderPass.beginOcclusionQuery(3);
```

After this is called, the application should execute further methods of the render pass encoder that perform rendering, such as `draw`, `drawIndexed`, and `drawIndirect`.

Retrieving Results

After the GPU performs the query, it needs to record the results in the query buffer. An application can encode a command for this by calling the command encoder's `resolveQuerySet` method. `resolveQuerySet` accepts five arguments, and Table 7.4 lists each of them.

TABLE 7.4 Query set creation properties

ARGUMENT	TYPE	DESCRIPTION
querySet	GPUQuerySet	Query set object associated with the render pass encoder
firstQuery	Integer	Index of the first query whose results should be accessed
queryCount	Integer	Number of queries whose results should be accessed
destination	GPUBuffer	Buffer to contain the query results
destinationOffset	Integer	Byte offset in the buffer where results should be stored

For example, the following code tells the GPU to retrieve the results of three queries in `querySet`, starting with Query 2. The results should be stored in `resultBuffer` with a byte offset of 0.

```
// Enqueue command to retrieve results
commandEncoder.resolveQuerySet(querySet, 2, 3, resultBuffer, 0);
```

When creating the buffer, it's important to add the `QUERY_RESOLVE` flag to the `usage` property. Otherwise, an error condition will be produced.

DRAWING TEXT

WebGPU doesn't provide any capabilities for drawing text, but applications can draw characters using textures. In this section, I'll present an application that creates a texture containing all characters of interest (the *texture atlas*) and displays characters by selecting rectangles from the atlas.

This section begins by explaining how texture atlases can be created. Then it presents the all-important topic of kerning, which is critical for drawing presentable text. The last part walks through the code in the Ch07_Text application.

Texture Atlases

Most computer fonts are provided in TrueType Font (TTF) format, which specifies character shapes using geometric features like line segments and Bézier curves. As a result, TTF characters can be scaled and rotated without affecting quality.

Reading TTF data is time-consuming, so many applications combine characters from a TTF font into an image and use the image as a texture atlas. For the Ch07_Text project, I downloaded the Lato Regular font from fonts.google.com and generated a

FIGURE 7.1 Texture atlas for Lato Regular.

texture atlas using Andreas Jonsson's free Bitmap Generator from http://www.angelcode.com/products/bmfont. Figure 7.1 shows what the texture atlas looks like.

Most texture atlases only include characters of a given size. In this case, the characters are meant to be printed on 32-pixel lines. Characters can be enlarged or reduced, but for acceptable results, it's a good idea to configure the sampler to use linear filtering in the horizontal and vertical directions.

In addition to generating a texture atlas, the Bitmap Generator creates a *.fnt file that provides information about the characters. In the Ch07_Text project, the file's name is lato.fnt. Each line of the file starts with a special descriptor: `info`, `common`, `page`, `chars`, `char`, or `kerning`. Table 7.5 lists these descriptors and explains the content of the corresponding line.

The Ch07_Text project is only concerned with the `common` line, the `char` lines, and the `kerning` lines. The `common` line provides geometric information about the entire font. In lato.fnt, it's given as follows:

```
common lineHeight=32 base=26 scaleW=256 scaleH=256 pages=1
    packed=0 alphaChnl=0 redChnl=0 greenChnl=0 blueChnl=0
```

The fields in this line define characteristics that apply to the entire texture and each of the font's characters. There are ten global fields in total, and Table 7.6 lists each of them.

For the example texture atlas, `lineHeight` indicates that characters are intended to be printed in 32-pixel lines. The baseline is 26 pixels below the top edge. The dimensions of the atlas are 256-by-256, and only one page is available.

TABLE 7.5 Line descriptors in a font file

LINE DESCRIPTOR	CONTENT
info	General information about the font
common	General information about the font's geometry
page	Identifies the current page
chars	Identifies the number of characters
char	Geometric information about a specific character
kerning	Information about the spacing between characters

TABLE 7.6 Global font properties

FIELD	DESCRIPTION
lineHeight	Height of each line in pixels
base	Offset of the baseline from the top edge
scaleW	Width of the entire texture
scaleH	Height of the entire texture
pages	Number of pages in the atlas
packed	Identifies if monochrome characters have been packed
alphaChnl	Content of the alpha channel
redChnl	Content of the red channel
greenChnl	Content of the green channel
blueChnl	Content of the blue channel

Most of the lines in the file start with char, which means they provide information about a single character. One char line in the Lato Regular font file is given as follows:

```
char id=112 x=30 y=67 width=14 height=19 xoffset=1 yoffset=12
xadvance=15 page=0 chnl=15
```

This line provides ten fields that identify the geometry of the character with an ID of 112. Table 7.7 lists each of these fields and explains what they represent.

The character corresponding to ASCII code 112 is p, so the char line presents the properties of that letter. Figure 7.2 depicts the dimensions of the line and the character.

The figure illustrates the difference between xoffset and xadvance. Both identify the horizontal distance from the current position. xoffset specifies the distance from the current position to where the character should be displayed. xadvance indicates the distance from the initial current position to the next current position.

TABLE 7.7 Character geometry properties

FIELD	DESCRIPTION
id	ASCII code of the character
x	x-coordinate of the character's upper left corner in the image
y	y-coordinate of the character's upper left corner in the image
width	Character width
height	Character height
xoffset	Distance from the current position to the start of the character
yoffset	Vertical offset to be applied when printing the character
xadvance	Distance from the current position to the end of the character space
page	Page containing the texture
chnl	Channel containing data (1 = blue, 2 = green, 4 = red, 8 = alpha, 15 = all)

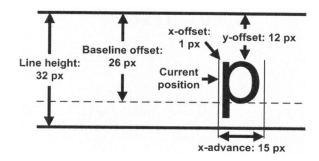

FIGURE 7.2   Character geometry.

Kerning

Simply printing out characters side-by-side isn't enough to produce a professional appearance. Different pairs of characters require different horizontal spacing, and adjusting the spacing is called *kerning*. This isn't an issue for monospaced fonts like Courier, but when a regular font is printed without proper kerning, the result looks jarring.

For this reason, the *.fnt file produced by Andreas Jonsson's Bitmap Generator contains several lines that start with `kerning`. Here's an example:

```
kerning first=111 second=120 amount=-1
```

This states that, if the first character has an ID of 111 and the second character has an ID of 120, the spacing between the characters should be reduced by 1. In other words, when the character 'o' precedes the character 'x', the space between the two should be reduced by 1 for proper kerning.

EXAMPLE APPLICATION—DISPLAYING TEXT

The Ch07_Text application demonstrates how an application can draw text on a canvas by reading rectangles from a texture atlas. Figure 7.3 shows what the resulting text looks like.

The top-level directory of the Ch07_Text application contains six files. Table 7.8 lists them and provides a description of each.

Rather than write JavaScript code that reads the font file (*.fnt), I wrote a Python script (gen_text_json.py) that converts the *.fnt file into a JSON file that defines an array containing the properties of each character. This can be easily changed to read another font by changing the FONT_NAME variable on the first line.

Ch07_Text

Hello, world!

FIGURE 7.3   The Ch07_Text application.

For example, the following text in lato_data.json shows the portion of the file that contains the properties of the character with an ID of 85 (the letter U):

```
{
    "id": 85,
    "x": 0,
    "y": 47,
    "width": 17,
    "height": 19,
    "xoffset": 1,
    "yoffset": 7,
    "xadvance": 20
    "kerning": { "38": -1, "44": -1, "46": -1, "47": -1, "65": -1 }
},
```

The kerning property identifies how spacing should be adjusted depending on the next character. For example, if "U" is followed by "A" (ID = 65), the spacing should be adjusted by -1 to set kerning properly.

The ch07_font.js file contains the main source code for the application. To describe this code, this discussion divides it into three parts:

1. Creating the vertex buffer
2. Creating the index buffer
3. Coding the vertex and fragment shaders

This section explores each of these operations and explains how they are performed in code.

TABLE 7.8   Files in the Ch07_Text directory

FILE	DESCRIPTION
index.html	Creates the web page and loads JavaScript
ch07_text.js	WebGPU code for drawing text
lato.png	Texture atlas containing Lato characters
lato.fnt	Text file containing Lato font data
lato_data.json	Lato font data in JSON format
gen_text_json.py	Python script that generates JSON file

The Vertex Buffer

From a rendering perspective, drawing a character requires two connected triangles. The topology property is set to triangle-strip, so drawing two connected triangles requires four vertices. Each vertex needs to define two coordinates in space (x and y) and the corresponding texture coordinates (u and v). Therefore, each vertex is defined by a set of four floating-point values in the vertex buffer. Each character requires four vertices, or a total of 16 floating-point values.

In ch07_text.js, forming the array of floating-point values is a complex process. The array is named vertexData, and it's created with the following code:

```
// Define vertex data
const textMsg = "Hello, world!";
let leftX = -0.9;
const topY = 0.75;
const bottomY = 0.5;
const lineHeight = 32;
const scale = (topY - bottomY)/lineHeight;

// Create vertex data array
const vertexData = new Float32Array(16 * textMsg.length);

// Read character data
const fileResponse = await fetch("./lato_data.json');
const charData = await fileResponse.json();

// Iterate through characters in message
for (let i = 0; i < textMsg.length; i++) {

    // Get index of message character
    let currentChar = charData[textMsg.charCodeAt(i) - 32];

    // Set texture coordinates
    vertexData[16 * i + 2] = currentChar.x/256.0;
    vertexData[16 * i + 3] = (currentChar.y + currentChar.
height)/256.0;
    vertexData[16 * i + 6] = currentChar.x/256.0;
    vertexData[16 * i + 7] = currentChar.y/256.0;
    vertexData[16 * i + 10] = (currentChar.x + currentChar.
width)/256.0;
    vertexData[16 * i + 11] = (currentChar.y + currentChar.
height)/256.0;
    vertexData[16 * i + 14] = (currentChar.x + currentChar.
width)/256.0;
    vertexData[16 * i + 15] = currentChar.y/256.0;

    // Set vertex coordinates
    if(i == 0) {
```

```
        vertexData[0] = leftX;
        vertexData[1] = bottomY;
        vertexData[4] = leftX;
        vertexData[5] = topY - currentChar.yoffset * scale;
    }
    else {
        vertexData[16 * i] = leftX + currentChar.xoffset *
scale;
        vertexData[16 * i + 1] = bottomY;
        vertexData[16 * i + 4] = vertexData[16*i];
        vertexData[16 * i + 5] = topY - currentChar.yoffset *
scale;
    }
    vertexData[16 * i + 8] = vertexData[16*i] + currentChar.
width * scale;
    vertexData[16 * i + 9] = bottomY;
    vertexData[16 * i + 12] = vertexData[16 * i + 8];
    vertexData[16 * i + 13] = topY - currentChar.yoffset *
scale;

    // Set kerning
    let kerning = 0;
    if('kerning' in currentChar) {

        // Get next character
        if(i != textMsg.length-1) {
            let nextId = charData[textMsg.charCodeAt(i+1)
- 32].id;

            // Apply kerning if needed
            if (nextId in currentChar.kerning) {
                kerning =
parseInt(currentChar.kerning[nextId]);
            }
        }
    }

    // Update current horizontal position
    leftX += (currentChar.xadvance + kerning) * scale;
}

// Create vertex buffer
const vertexBuffer = device.createBuffer({
    label: "Vertex Buffer 0",
    size: vertexData.byteLength,
    usage:
        GPUBufferUsage.VERTEX |
        GPUBufferUsage.COPY_DST
});
```

```
// Write data to buffer
device.queue.writeBuffer(vertexBuffer, 0, vertexData);
renderPass.setVertexBuffer(0, vertexBuffer);
```

This code starts by defining the message to be printed (Hello, world!) and the different variables used by the application. The leftX variable identifies the first x-coordinate of the rendering. Since this is set to −0.9, the first character will begin close to the left edge of the viewport.

The topY and bottomY values identify the maximum and minimum y-coordinates of the vertices in the region. As given in the font file, the characters in the Lato font are intended for 32-point lines, so lineHeight is set to 32. scale serves as a scaling factor between displayed coordinates and font dimensions, and is obtained by computing (topY − bottomY)/lineHeight.

Next, the application initializes the vertexData array. Each character requires 16 floating-point values, so the array is set to an empty Float32Array whose size is obtained by multiplying the message length by 16.

After creating the array, the application calls fetch to read character data from the lato_data.json file. If this returns properly, the application will set charData equal to the array of data objects defined in the file.

Next, the application iterates through the characters in the message. For each character, it sets 16 values in the vertexData array. It's important to note that the texture coordinates are always between 0.0 and 1.0. This explains why the x and y parameters in the JSON file need to be divided by 256 (the image's width/height) to obtain the corresponding texture coordinate.

After the sixteen values are set for the given character, the application checks if kerning is required. It performs this check by searching for the next character's ID in the current character's kerning map. If the next character's ID is present, the application sets the kerning variable equal to the required spacing adjustment.

The last portion of the loop uses kerning and the character's xadvance parameter to update the leftX variable. Once this is set, leftX will serve as the leftmost x-coordinate of the following character.

After setting all the values of vertexData, the application creates a buffer (vertexBuffer) to contain this data. Then it calls writeBuffer to encode a command that copies vertexData to vertexBuffer. The setVertexBuffer method associates the vertex buffer with the render pass encoder.

The Index Buffer

In addition to setting values in the vertex buffer, the application creates an index buffer whose values identify the order in which the vertices should be drawn. The following code shows how the index values are generated, how the index buffer is created, and how the buffer is associated with the render pass encoder.

```
// Initialize index array for atlas text
const numIndexes = ((5 * textMsg.length) % 2 == 0) ? 5 *
textMsg.length : 5 * textMsg.length + 1;
const indexData = new Uint16Array(numIndexes);
for(let i = 0; i<textMsg.length; i++) {
    indexData[5 * i] = 4 * i + 1;
    indexData[5 * i + 1] = 4 * i;
    indexData[5 * i + 2] = 4 * i + 3;
    indexData[5 * i + 3] = 4 * i + 2;
    indexData[5 * i + 4] = 0xffff;
}

// Create index buffer
const indexBuffer = device.createBuffer({
    label: "Index Buffer 0",
    size: indexData.byteLength,
    usage:
        GPUBufferUsage.INDEX |
        GPUBufferUsage.COPY_DST
});
device.queue.writeBuffer(indexBuffer, 0, indexData);
renderPass.setIndexBuffer(indexBuffer, "uint16");
```

The first line of this code deserves explanation. The `topology` property is set to `triangle-strip`, so each character requires four indices followed by the primitive restart index, which tells the renderer to restart after each character. Therefore, each character requires five index values.

Each index value is provided as a 16-bit unsigned integer, and WebGPU doesn't like transferring odd numbers of 16-bit values to the GPU. For this reason, this code begins by setting `numIndexes` to the smallest even value that will hold the index values required by the message.

An example will help make this clear. The message `Hello, world!` contains thirteen characters, which means 13 * 5 = 65 index values need to be sent to the GPU. Transferring an odd number of 16-bit values will cause an error, so `numIndexes` is set to 66 instead.

Next, the application creates a `Uint16Array` with enough space to hold `numIndexes` elements. Then it iterates through the characters of the message and sets four index values that identify vertices in the vertex buffer. After each group of four indexes, the application adds the primitive restart value, `0xffff`, which tells the renderer that the next triangle shouldn't be connected to the preceding triangle.

Once all the index values are set, the application creates the index buffer and encodes a command that writes the index data to the buffer. Then it calls `setIndexBuffer` to associate the index buffer with the render pass encoder.

Vertex and Fragment Shaders

The shader code in Ch07_Text is straightforward to understand. The vertex shader creates a structure named `DataStruct` and sets the vertex position and texture coordinates. The fragment shader receives the texture coordinates and calls `textureSample` to read the texel at the given position. The following code shows how this works:

```
// The structure that holds data for the fragment shader
struct DataStruct {
    @builtin(position) pos: vec4f,
    @location(0) uvPos: vec2f,
}
// Resources needed to access texels
@group(0) @binding(0) var sam : sampler;
@group(0) @binding(1) var tex : texture_2d<f32>;

@vertex
fn vertexMain(@location(0) coords: vec2f, @location(1)
uvCoords: vec2f) -> DataStruct {
    var outData: DataStruct;
    outData.pos = vec4f(coords, 0.0, 1.0);
    outData.uvPos = uvCoords;
    return outData;
}

@fragment
fn fragmentMain(fragData: DataStruct) -> @location(0) vec4f {
    return textureSample(tex, sam, fragData.uvPos);
}
```

When I originally wrote the code for this project, I intended to use multisampled textures to demonstrate anti-aliasing. I created the texture object with the `sampleCount` property set to 4, and I used the `texture_multisampled_2d` data type in the shader code. But I received an error every time I attempted to write data to the texture.

ANIMATION

Animation changes the position of one or more objects over time. As discussed in Chapter 5, a vertex shader can update an object's position using linear transformations (rotation, scaling, and translation). To be precise, it can transform an object's position by multiplying the object's vertices by one or more transformation matrices.

This suggests a method for animating objects in WebGPU—assign a transformation matrix to an object and update the matrix's elements over time. For example, you can rotate an object by repeatedly changing a rotation matrix. You can translate an object over time by repeatedly updating its translation matrix.

As discussed in Chapter 5, an application can transfer transformation matrices to the GPU using uniform buffers. Therefore, we can animate an object by updating the uniform buffer's content, as each new animation needs to be drawn. The example code presented in this discussion will show how this can be accomplished.

Interpolation and Animation

The hard part of implementing animation involves *continuity*. If an object is supposed to move from Point A to Point B, the application should update its position so that it appears to move continuously from A to B without sudden blinks or jerks.

Continuous animation isn't possible on a computer, but we can approximate it by making small adjustments to the object's position at short time intervals. To express this mathematically, we'll employ five terms:

- A—the starting position
- B—the ending position
- T—the total time for the object to move from A to B
- t—the current time (between 0 and T)
- x—the current position (between A and B)

It should be clear that x should equal A when t = 0, and x should equal B when t = T. This requirement leads to the following equation:

$$x = \left(\frac{T-t}{T}\right)A + \left(\frac{t}{T}\right)B$$

This procedure is called *linear interpolation* because the position of x changes linearly over time. Chapter 6 briefly explains how texture samplers can be configured to use linear interpolation to compute color data between two texels.

To see how this interpolation can be performed in JavaScript, it's important to be familiar with the `requestAnimationFrame` method. This tells the browser that the application wants to be notified when the window is redrawn. The method accepts a callback function that will be invoked just before the next repaint.

When the callback function is invoked, it receives an integer that identifies the number of milliseconds that have elapsed since `requestAnimationFrame` was called. In this manner, the application can keep track of the current time and set the interpolation properly. In the following code, the name of the callback function is newFrame, and it receives the elapsed time through an argument named t:

```
// The callback to be invoked when the window repaints
function newFrame(t) {
    ... update transformation matrices ...
    window.requestAnimationFrame(foo);
}
// Set the callback to be invoked
window.requestAnimationFrame(newFrame);
```

For animation to work properly, requestAnimationFrame needs to be called again at the end of the callback function. This tells the window to call newFrame the next time the screen is refreshed.

Example Application—Animation

The code in the Ch07_Animation project demonstrates how animation can be performed using WebGPU. It creates a red triangle and initializes its transformation matrix to an identity matrix. Then it calls requestAnimationFrame with a callback function. When the function is called, the transformation matrix is updated to translate the triangle.

The entire animation lasts four seconds, and the nature of the triangle's movement is given as follows:

- For the first two seconds, translate the triangle right until it reaches the right edge of the viewing region.
- For the next two seconds, translate the triangle left until it reaches the right edge of the viewing region.

The callback function receives the current time and subtracts it from the old time. This elapsed time is used to update the transformation matrix in the application's uniform buffer. The following code shows how the callback function is coded.

```
// Called just before the window is repainted
function newFrame(currentTime) {

    // Skip first frame
    if(oldTime == 0.0) {
        oldTime = currentTime;
        window.requestAnimationFrame(newFrame);
        return;
    }
```

```
    // Compute elapsed time in seconds
    t = (currentTime - oldTime)/1000;
    oldTime = currentTime;

    // Update total time
    totalTime += t;

    // Stop animation after four seconds
    if (totalTime > 4.0) {
        return;
    }

    // Update the uniform buffer
    motionChange = totalTime < 2.0 ? t * motionPerSec : -t *
motionPerSec;
    uniformData = mat4.translate(uniformData, [motionChange,
0.0, 0.0]);
    device.queue.writeBuffer(uniformBuffer, 0, uniformData);

    // Create the command encoder and the render pass encoder
    const encoder = device.createCommandEncoder();
    const renderPass = encoder.beginRenderPass({
        colorAttachments: [{
            view: context.getCurrentTexture().createView(),
            loadOp: "clear",
            clearValue: { r: 0.9, g: 0.9, b: 0.9, a: 1.0 },
            storeOp: "store"
        }]
    });

    // Set the vertex buffer and pipeline
    renderPass.setVertexBuffer(0, vertexBuffer);
    renderPass.setPipeline(renderPipeline);

    // Associate bind group with render pass encoder
    renderPass.setBindGroup(0, bindGroup);

    // Draw vertices
    renderPass.draw(3);
    renderPass.end();

    // Submit the render commands to the GPU
    device.queue.submit([encoder.finish()]);
    window.requestAnimationFrame(newFrame);
}
```

The callback's argument, currentTime, identifies the current time in milliseconds. The function computes the elapsed time, t, by subtracting oldTime from currentTime and dividing the difference by 1000. Then it adds the elapsed time to the total time. If this is greater than four seconds, the callback exits.

If t is less than 2.0, the triangle should move right. For this reason, motionChange is set equal to t times motionPerSec, which identifies how much the triangle should move per second. This value is used to update the transformation matrix in the uniformData array, which is written to the uniform buffer.

The command encoder needs to be rebuilt after each rendering, as does the render pass encoder. But the shader code doesn't change, so there's no need to reconstruct the shader module or the render pipeline. After the render pass encoder is created and configured, the callback function calls draw to launch the rendering operation. The callback function ends by calling requestAnimationFrame to ensure that it will be called when the window is refreshed.

SUMMARY

This chapter has covered a lot of ground. The first two sections, which discuss debug groups and error handling, are helpful when you're searching for elusive problems with an application. Similarly, occlusion queries make it possible to determine how many primitives are being displayed and how many are being discarded.

By default, WebGPU's rendering fills the entire area of its associated canvas. However, an application can configure the rendering area by configuring the viewport associated with the render pass encoder. Similarly, it can specify a specific portion of the rendering to be displayed by defining a scissor rectangle.

WebGPU doesn't provide any objects or methods for displaying text. For this reason, this chapter has explained how to create texture atlases from TrueType fonts. Once these atlases are available, an application can display characters by reading rectangles from the texture. In addition to displaying the characters, it's important to adjust the spacing with proper kerning.

The last part of the chapter discussed animation. The overall process is simple—rotate, scale, and translate objects by changing their transformation matrices over time. In practice, however, animation presents difficulties. It's crucial to understand how and when requestAnimationFrame executes callback functions and which WebGPU resources must be reconstructed each time the callback function is invoked.

Compute
Applications

8

This chapter puts aside graphical rendering and shows how WebGPU can be used to crunch numbers. Compute applications are like graphical applications in many respects, but they require different objects to manage the GPU's operations. For example, compute applications create compute pass encoders instead of render pass encoders and compute pipelines instead of render pipelines.

Compute shaders are simpler than vertex shaders and fragment shaders because they deal with basic numbers instead of vertices, textures, samplers, and fragments. But unlike vertex and fragment shaders, compute shaders are executed by *invocations* organized into *workgroups*. Understanding how to divide processing among invocations and workgroups is a major issue when coding compute applications.

The primary advantage of running compute shaders is performance. To measure this performance, WebGPU makes it possible to create timestamp queries. These queries run on the GPU and provide precise measurements of the time needed to execute commands.

When several invocations of a compute shader attempt to access a variable, race conditions can lead to undefined behavior. For this reason, WebGPU provides atomic variables, whose operations are always performed atomically. The last part of this chapter explains how to create these variables and update them in atomic functions. The chapter ends with an example project that shows how an atomic variable can be used in a compute shader to obtain the dot product of two long arrays of values.

INTRODUCING COMPUTE APPLICATIONS

The overall process of developing a compute application is like that of developing a graphical application. There are at least nine steps involved:

1. Create the GPUAdapter, GPUDevice, and GPUCommandEncoder using the same code as in a graphical application.
2. Call the command encoder's beginComputePass method to create a compute pass encoder.
3. Create one or more storage buffers and add them to one or more bind groups.
4. Write a compute shader and add it to a shader module.

DOI: 10.1201/9781003422839-8

5. Call the device's `createComputePipeline` method with the shader module.
6. Associate the compute pipeline with the compute pass encoder.
7. Associate the bind group with the compute pass encoder.
8. Call the `dispatchWorkgroups` method of the compute pass encoder.
9. Read the processed data from the buffer.

The two main objects in a compute application are the command pass encoder and the command pipeline. This section looks at both and shows how they can be created in code.

The Compute Pass Encoder

Just as a render pass encoder holds state data for graphical rendering, a compute pass encoder holds state data for general-purpose computation. An application can create a compute pass encoder by calling the `beginComputePass` method of the `GPUCommandEncoder`. This accepts an object with two optional arguments:

- `label`—optional string identifier used in debugging
- `timestampWrites`—optional array of objects that define timestamp events

The second argument is important for applications that need to measure the elapsed time of an operation. I'll explain time stamps and the `timeStampWrites` argument later in the chapter.

After creating a compute pass encoder, an application can call its methods to associate the encoder with other objects. Table 8.1 lists eight of these methods and provides a description of each.

In a graphical application, the render pass encoder creates rendering commands based on methods like `draw`, `drawIndexed`, and `drawIndirect`. In a computational application, the compute pass encoder creates compute commands based on methods like `dispatchWorkgroups` and `dispatchWorkgroupsIndirect`.

Both methods tell the GPU to perform the operations defined in the compute pipeline. The difference is that `dispatchWorkgroupsIndirect` uses indirect rendering, which tells the GPU to access rendering parameters from a buffer on the device.

The `end` method of the compute pass encoder performs the same operation as the `end` method of the render pass encoder. It completes the recording of the encoder's commands, telling the encoder that the commands can be sent to the GPU through the device's queue.

The `setPipeline` and `setBindGroup` methods are necessary to associate the encoder with the objects needed for computation. `setPipeline` associates the encoder with a compute pipeline, which identifies the nature of the computation to be performed. `setBindGroup` associates the encoder with a bind group, which provides access to the resources (data) needed by the computational task.

TABLE 8.1   Methods of the compute pass encoder

METHOD	DESCRIPTION
`dispatchWorkgroups(count)`	Performs computations defined in the compute pipeline
`dispatchWorkgroupsIndirect(buffer, offset)`	Performs computation using parameters provided in the indirect buffer
`end()`	Marks the end of the commands to be set
`setPipeline(pipeline)`	Associates a compute pipeline with the encoder
`setBindGroup(group)`	Associates a bind group with the encoder
`insertDebugMarker()`	Insert a marker in the encoder's commands
`pushDebugGroup()`	Starts a debug group with the given label
`popDebugGroup()`	Ends the most-recently pushed debug group

The Compute Pipeline

Like the render pipeline discussed in the preceding chapters, a compute pipeline defines the operations to be performed by the GPU. It can be created by calling the device's `createComputePipeline` method, which accepts a descriptor with the properties listed in Table 8.2.

Just as the render pipeline has `vertex` and `fragment` properties that provide information about vertex and fragment shaders, the compute pipeline has a `compute` property that provides information about the compute shader to be executed. This must be set to an object with the three properties listed in Table 8.3.

The `module` property must be set to a shader module, and the process of creating a shader module in a compute application is identical to that of creating one in a graphical

TABLE 8.2   Compute pipeline descriptor properties

PROPERTY	REQUIRED?	DESCRIPTION
`label`	N	Identifier for debugging
`compute`	Y	Describes the computation to be performed
`layout`	Y	Describes the arrangement of resources used in computation

TABLE 8.3   Compute module properties

PROPERTY	REQUIRED?	DESCRIPTION
`module`	Y	Shader module containing the compute shader
`entryPoint`	Y	Name of the entry point function in the compute shader
`constants`	N	Name–value pairs that can be accessed in the shader

TABLE 8.4 Shader module creation properties

PROPERTY	REQUIRED?	DESCRIPTION
label	N	Identifier for debugging
code	Y	String containing the shader code
hints	N	Map that defines compiler hints for the shader
sourceMap	N	Data used by developer tools

application. That is, the application calls the device's `createShaderModule` with an object containing the properties listed in Table 8.4.

The `layout` property required by `createComputePipeline` can be set to a GPUPipelineLayout that describes the structure of the pipeline's bind groups. For the sake of simplicity, the example code in this book sets `layout` to `auto`, which tells the pipeline to form a bind group layout by examining the shader code.

For example, the following code creates a compute pipeline that tells the GPU to execute the shader in the module named `computeModule`. The entry point in the compute shader is named `computeMain`.

```
// Creating a compute pipeline
const computePipeline = device.createComputePipeline({
    label: "Compute Pipeline 0",
    layout: "auto",
    compute: {
        module: computeModule,
        entryPoint: "computeMain"
    }
});
```

After the compute pipeline is created, it can be associated with the compute pass encoder by calling the encoder's `setPipeline` method. If the encoder's name is `computePass`, the following code creates the association:

```
// Associate the pipeline with the compute pass encoder
computePass.setPipeline(computePipeline);
```

As shown, it takes a lot less code to create a compute pipeline than a render pipeline.

BUFFER OPERATIONS

There are two major differences between the buffers used in (most) compute applications and those used in graphical applications:

1. Compute applications usually access data from storage buffers or storage textures. Uniform buffers aren't as common because of their small size.

2. After computation is finished, the application needs to retrieve the processed data from GPU memory.

In most graphical applications, buffer data moves in one direction—from the host to the GPU. But in a compute application, buffer data is transferred from the host to the GPU before computation, and from the GPU to the host after computation. This discussion focuses on storage buffers, and storage textures will be introduced in Chapter 9.

On some systems, the CPU and GPU access the same memory. On these shared memory systems, moving data to and from the GPU is simple. But on most systems, the GPU is located on a graphics card with its own separate memory. To access the GPU's memory, applications need to map and unmap buffers. Applications also need to copy data from one buffer to another. The following discussion presents both operations.

Mapping and Unmapping Buffers

A buffer is *mapped* if its data can be accessed through an `ArrayBuffer`. After creating a buffer, an application can perform mapping operations by calling three of its methods:

- `getMappedRange(offset, size)`—returns an `ArrayBuffer` containing the mapped data of the `GPUBuffer` in the specified range
- `mapAsync(mode, offset, size)`—returns a `Promise` that resolves to an `ArrayBuffer` when the buffer is successfully mapped
- `unmap()`—destroys the mapped range of the buffer, allowing it to be used for other operations

If a buffer is created with the `mappedAtCreation` property set to `true`, its mapped content can be accessed using `getMappedRange`. This makes it easy to initialize its content.

To demonstrate this, the following code creates a buffer containing 16 bytes. Then it calls `getMappedRange` to access the underlying `ArrayBuffer` and sets four floating-point values in the `ArrayBuffer`.

```
// Create buffer
const computeBuffer = device.createBuffer({
    mappedAtCreation: true,
    size: 16,
    usage: GPUBufferUsage.STORAGE
});

// Access the mapped data
const buff = computeBuffer.getMappedRange();
```

```
// Set the content of the mapped data
new Float32Array(buff).set([1.0, 2.0, 3.0, 4.0]);

// Unmap buffer
computeBuffer.unmap();
```

After the GPU completes the computation, the application will want to read the buffer containing the processed data (the results). In this case, the application can call mapAsync. If the mapping was successful, the application can read the buffer's data by calling getMappedRange and destroy the mapping by calling unmap.

For example, suppose processed data is stored in a buffer named procBuffer, which was created with the GPUBufferUsage.MAP_READ flag. The following code accesses the ArrayBuffer containing the buffer's data.

```
// Establish a mapping
await procBuffer.mapAsync(GPUMapMode.READ);

// Read the mapped data in an ArrayBuffer
const procData = procBuffer.getMappedRange();

// Access the floating-point values
const floatData = new Float32Array(procData);

// Destroy the mapping
procBuffer.unMap();
```

As shown, mapAsync requires an argument that identifies how the buffer's mapped data will be accessed. This can be set to GPUMapMode.READ or GPUMapMode.WRITE.

When coding compute applications, it's important to understand how to map and unmap a buffer. The example code in this chapter and later chapters will use similar code to read and write data to compute buffers.

Copying Buffers

If a GPU accesses memory separate from the GPU, applications can't directly map storage buffers for reading. Put another way, if a buffer's usage property includes GPUBufferUsage.STORAGE, it can't include GPUBufferUsage.MAP_READ. This means an application needs to perform four operations to read data from a storage buffer:

1. Create a mappable buffer whose usage includes GPUBufferUsage.MAP_READ.
2. Encode a command that copies the data from the storage buffer to the mappable buffer.

3. When the device is done executing its commands, map the mappable buffer to an `ArrayBuffer`.
4. Read data from the `ArrayBuffer`.

For Step 2, it's important to be familiar with the `copyBufferToBuffer` method of the `GPUCommandEncoder`. Table 8.5 lists the five arguments of this method.

Calling `copyBufferToBuffer` doesn't immediately copy the buffer's content. Instead, it encodes a command that tells the GPU to perform the copy operation. For this reason, it's important to call `copyBufferToBuffer` *after* the compute pass encoder has encoded the computational command(s), but *before* the encoder sends the commands to the GPU. The following code gives an idea of the necessary sequence of steps.

```
// Encode compute commands
computePass.dispatchWorkgroups(...);

// Complete encoding compute commands
computePass.end();

// Create mappable buffer
const mappableBuffer = device.createBuffer({ ...
    usage:
        GPUBufferUsage.COPY_DST |
        GPUBufferUsage.MAP_READ
});

// Encode command to copy data into mappable buffer
encoder.copyBufferToBuffer(...);

// Submit the commands to the GPU
device.queue.submit([encoder.finish()]);
```

As a result of this code, the mappable buffer will hold the copied data. The application can read the buffer's data by calling its `mapAsync` and `getMappedRange`

TABLE 8.5   Arguments of the `copyBufferToBuffer` method

ARGUMENT	TYPE	DESCRIPTION
source	GPUBuffer	The buffer to copy data from
sourceOffset	Integer	Byte offset into the source where copying should begin
destination	GPUBuffer	The buffer to receive data
destinationOffset	Integer	Byte offset into the destination where data should be copied
size	Integer	The number of bytes to be copied from the source buffer to the destination buffer

methods. This process will be used to read result data in every compute application presented in this book.

WORKGROUPS AND INVOCATIONS

In a graphical application, the vertex shader executes once for each vertex, and the fragment shader executes once for each fragment. But when you run a compute application, you can directly control how many times the compute shader is executed. This control is made possible through workgroups, and this section explains what they are and how they can be configured.

Introduction to Workgroups

To understand how compute shaders execute, you need to be familiar with two terms:

- an *invocation* is a single execution of a compute shader
- a *workgroup* is a collection of invocations

An application specifies the number of invocations by setting the number of workgroups and the size of each workgroup. If there are four workgroups and each workgroup contains eight invocations, the compute shader will execute thirty-two times.

Why are workgroups important? There are two reasons: memory and synchronization. Invocations in the same workgroup can access shared memory specific to that workgroup. This group-specific memory is distinct from storage buffer memory, and in theory, shaders can access workgroup data much faster than storage data. This makes workgroup memory a good place to store intermediate computation results.

Normally, there's no way to know when one invocation executes relative to another. But WebGPU provides barriers that can make it possible to synchronize invocations in a workgroup. A *workgroup barrier* forces each invocation to halt until every other invocation has finished accessing data in workgroup memory. A *storage barrier* forces each invocation to halt until every other invocation has finished accessing data in storage memory. Note that these barriers can't synchronize invocations across different workgroups.

Workgroup Analogy

Workgroups can be hard to grasp, so I'll present an analogy. Suppose a school contains multiple classrooms, and each classroom has a blackboard. Each classroom's blackboard

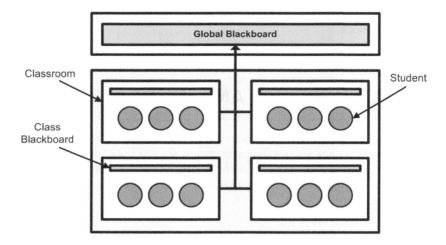

FIGURE 8.1 School of students.

can only be used by the students in that class. In addition, the school has a global black-board that every student in the school can access.

Each student has two identifiers. The Local ID identifies the student inside the classroom, and the Global ID identifies the student across the entire school. Students in different classrooms may have the same Local ID, but no two students will ever have the same Global ID.

When students enter the school, they go to the global blackboard and use their Global ID to find out what data they need to process. Then they go to their classroom and join other students in processing data with the class blackboard. Once the process-ing is finished, each student returns to the global blackboard to post his/her results. Figure 8.1 gives an idea of what this strange school looks like.

In this analogy, students are invocations, and classrooms are workgroups. The blackboard in a classroom represents the workgroup memory that every invocation in a workgroup can access. The global blackboard represents a storage buffer or storage texture that every invocation can access. Each invocation has a Local ID that identifies it within the workgroup and a Global ID that identifies it across all invocations.

When an invocation starts, it can use its Global ID to read input data from a storage resource. Then it works with other invocations in its workgroup to process data. Once the processing is finished, the invocation posts its portion of the result back to the stor-age resource. Figure 8.2 shows what this looks like.

WebGPU makes no guarantees regarding when one workgroup executes relative to another. At any time, there could be any number of workgroups executing on the GPU. The only way to be certain that a workgroup has finished is when the entire computa-tional task has finished. For this reason, it's common for applications to execute shaders multiple times to make sure the invocations are globally synchronized.

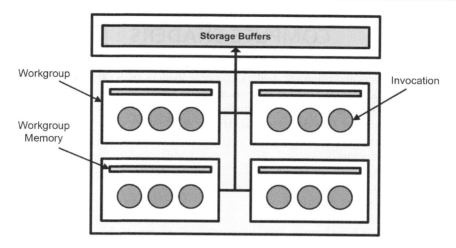

FIGURE 8.2 Invocations and workgroups.

Dispatching Workgroups

Compute applications don't call methods like `draw` or `drawIndexed`. Instead, a compute application encodes compute commands by calling the `dispatchWorkgroups` method of the compute pass encoder. This accepts 1, 2, or 3 arguments that specify how many workgroups should be created in each dimension. For example, the following code encodes a compute command to be processed by a 4-by-3 grid of workgroups:

```
computePass.dispatchWorkgroups(4, 3)
```

The value in the third dimension is 1 by default. This means the following code will create the same grid of workgroups:

```
computePass.dispatchWorkgroups(4, 3, 1)
```

Multidimensional workgroups make it convenient to process multidimensional data. As Chapter 9 will make clear, it's easier to process images with two-dimensional invocations than one-dimensional invocations.

In addition to `dispatchWorkgroups`, applications can encode compute commands by calling the `dispatchWorkgroupsIndirect` method. This accepts two arguments: a buffer containing configuration information and a byte offset into the buffer. The buffer must contain a block of three 32-bit unsigned integers that identify the number of workgroups in each dimension.

Setting the number of workgroups does not set the number of invocations to be performed. The workgroup size is determined by the compute shader, which is the subject of the following discussion.

COMPUTE SHADERS

Like vertex shaders and fragment shaders, compute shaders are written in the WebGPU Shader Language (WGSL), which was discussed at length in Chapter 4. This means compute shaders can access the same functions that operate on numbers, vectors, and matrices. But there are four characteristics that make compute shaders unique:

1. No return value
2. Different entry point attribute
3. Different built-in variables and functions
4. Access to workgroup memory

The first point is important. The return value of a vertex shader sets the location of a vertex, and the return value of a fragment shader sets the color of a fragment. But the return value of a compute shader doesn't serve any purpose. Compute shaders usually read from storage buffers and write to other storage buffers.

Entry Point Attribute

As discussed in Chapter 4, the entry point of a vertex shader must be preceded by @vertex, and the entry point of a fragment shader must be preceded by @fragment. The entry point of a compute shader must be preceded by @compute, followed by @workgroup-size, and parentheses containing 1, 2, or 3 values.

The values inside the parentheses specify the size of the workgroups used to execute the shader. For example, suppose the application created a grid of 5-by-4 workgroups with the following code:

```
computePass.dispatchWorkgroups(5, 4)
```

If each workgroup should have a 2-by-2 grid of invocations, the entry point of the compute shader should be preceded by the following attribute:

```
@compute @workgroup_size(2, 2)
```

This attribute accomplishes the same result as the following:

```
@compute @workgroup_size(2, 2, 1)
```

In both cases, the total number of invocations is $5 \times 4 \times 2 \times 2 = 80$. Keep in mind that the JavaScript code sets the *number* of workgroups, and the compute shader sets the *size* of each workgroup. The size of a workgroup is limited (256 is the maximum on my system), but the number of workgroups is unlimited.

Built-in Variables and Functions

As discussed in Chapter 4, a shader's entry point can access built-in variables using the `@builtin` attribute. For example, a vertex shader can access the index of the current vertex with `@builtin(vertex_index)` and a fragment shader can access the position of the current fragment with `@builtin(position)`.

Compute shaders can access five built-in variables that provide information related to invocations and workgroups. Table 8.6 lists each of them.

Most of these are easy to understand. `num_workgroups` identifies the number of workgroups, which equals the values given in the `dispatchWorkgroups` method. `workgroup_id` provides the unique identifier of the current workgroup, and `global_invocation_id` provides the identifier of the invocation across all invocations.

It's important to see the difference between the last two variables, `local_invocation_id` and `local_invocation_index`. The first identifies the multidimensional ID of the current invocation in the workgroup, and the second provides a one-dimensional ID of the invocation in the workgroup. The first is helpful when the invocation needs to access multidimensional data, and the second is helpful when the invocation needs to access a one-dimensional structure like a vector or array.

An example will show how these variables are used. The following entry point, `computeMain`, sets the workgroup size to 32 and accesses the `workgroup_id` and `local_invocation_id` variables in its parameter list.

```
@compute @workgroup_size(32)
fn computeMain(@builtin(workgroup_id) wg_id : vec3<u32>,
    @builtin(local_invocation_id) local_id : vec3<u32>
) { … }
```

WGSL provides two important functions that make it possible to synchronize invocations. `workgroupBarrier` makes it possible to synchronize access to workgroup memory. When an invocation reaches this function, it will halt until every other invocation in the workgroup finishes accessing workgroup memory.

TABLE 8.6 Built-in variables in a compute shader

BUILTIN VARIABLE	DATA TYPE	DESCRIPTION
num_workgroups	vec3<u32>	Number of workgroups
workgroup_id	vec3<u32>	ID of the invocation's workgroup
global_invocation_id	vec3<u32>	ID of the invocation across all invocations
local_invocation_id	vec3<u32>	ID of the invocation in the workgroup
local_invocation_index	u32	Index of the invocation among all invocations

Similarly, `storageBarrier` synchronizes access to storage buffers and storage textures. When an invocation reaches this function, it will halt until every other invocation in the workgroup finishes accessing storage data.

WGSL doesn't provide any barriers that affect invocations in different workgroups. The only way to make sure all the invocations have reached a given point is to wait for the GPU's processing to terminate. Another option is to use the atomic variables and operations described later in the chapter.

Workgroup Memory

If you want invocations to be able to access workgroup memory, you need to declare a variable in the workgroup address space. The main advantage of this memory is that, *in theory*, it should be faster to access than data in a storage buffer.

One disadvantage is that many devices don't provide a great deal of memory for workgroups. On my system, the maximum workgroup storage size is 32,768 bytes. You can check this on your system by accessing the `maxComputeWorkgroupStorageSize` limit provided by the `GPUAdapter` object.

```
// Access the maximum number of bytes in workgroup memory
const maxWorkGroupMemory =
adapter.limits.maxComputeWorkgroupStorageSize;
```

To demonstrate how workgroup memory is accessed, the following code defines a variable in the workgroup address space that contains 32 vectors of four floating-point values each:

```
var<workgroup> wg_data: array<vec4f, 32>
```

With this declaration in place, an invocation can access the workgroup's data using its local ID, as in the following code:

```
let v = wg_data[local_id]
```

Unlike memory in buffers and textures, workgroup memory can't be allocated or initialized in JavaScript. Workgroup memory is de-allocated when the compute task is complete, so it's important to transfer results to a storage buffer before the compute shader finishes.

To clearly distinguish variables intended for a single invocation, WGSL makes it possible to declare variables in the `private` address space. This is shown in the following declaration:

```
var<private> private_data: array<vec4f, 32>
```

As a result, each invocation can access `private_data`. However, because it's stored in private memory, invocations can't share data as they can in workgroup memory.

EXAMPLE APPLICATION— SIMPLE COMPUTATION

The code in the Ch08_SimpleCompute project demonstrates how compute shaders can be coded and executed. It creates eight workgroups, each containing four invocations. Each invocation performs four operations:

1. Reads a value from a storage buffer using its global ID (global_ invocation_id)
2. Multiplies the value by the workgroup ID (workgroup_ID)
3. Adds the invocation's ID inside the workgroup (local_invocation_id)
4. Writes the value back to the storage buffer

Initially, the storage buffer contains 32 values set to 1.0. When processing is finished, the code updates the page with the input vector and output vector. Figure 8.3 shows what the output looks like.

This demonstration of WebGPU's compute capability isn't particularly exciting, but it shows how compute shaders can be coded and how compute pass encoders and compute pipelines can be created.

The Compute Shader

The compute shader in the Ch08_SimpleCompute application shows how a variable declaration can access a storage buffer and how the built-in variables can be accessed. Its code is given as follows:

```
@binding(0) @group(0) var<storage, read_write> data :
array<f32, 32>;

override group_size: u32;

@compute @workgroup_size(group_size)
fn computeMain(
    @builtin(global_invocation_id) id : vec3<u32>,
    @builtin(workgroup_id) wg_id : vec3<u32>,
    @builtin(local_invocation_id) local_id : vec3<u32>)
{
    data[id.x] = f32(wg_id.x) * data[id.x] +
f32(local_id.x);
}
```

Input vector: 1,1,1,1,1,1,1,1,1,1,1,1,1,1,1,1,1,1,1,1,1,1,1,1,1,1,1,1,1,1,1,1

Output vector: 0,1,2,3,1,2,3,4,2,3,4,5,3,4,5,6,4,5,6,7,5,6,7,8,6,7,8,9,7,8,9,10

FIGURE 8.3   The Ch08_SimpleCompute application.

As shown, the shader accesses a storage buffer named `data` as an array of 32 floating-point values. Because the declaration contains the keyword `read_write`, the shader can read and write to the buffer.

The compute shader declares a variable named `group_size`. Because the declaration starts with `override`, this is an overridden variable whose value is set when the compute pipeline is created. To be precise, its value will be set to 4 because this is the value given in the constants map provided in the `createComputePipeline` method.

The name of the entry point is `computeMain`, and it accesses three built-in variables available to compute shaders. The first is `global_invocation_id`, which identifies the invocation among all other invocations, the second is `workgroup_id`, which identifies the workgroup among all the workgroups, and the third is `local_invocation_id`, which identifies the invocation among the invocations in the workgroup.

The name of the entry point is preceded by `@workgroup_size(group_size)`. `group_size` is an overridden variable that equals 4, so each workgroup will have 4 invocations. Because there are 8 workgroups, there are a total of 32 invocations. This means `global_invocation_id` will run from 0 to 31, `workgroup_id` will run from 0 to 7, and `local_invocation_id` will run from 0 to 3.

No matter what dimensions your workgroups have, the identifiers must be declared as three-dimensional vectors. For example, if a workgroup has a single dimension, its invocations will need to access IDs using the first element of the vector. This explains why the workgroup ID is accessed as `wg_id.x` and the local ID is accessed as `local_id.x`.

The Compute Pass Encoder and Pipeline

As mentioned earlier, the central data structures in a compute application are the compute pass encoder and the compute pipeline. The following code shows how these objects are created in the Ch08_SimpleCompute application.

```
// Create the compute pass encoder
const computePass = encoder.beginComputePass({
    label: "Compute Pass 0"
});
```

```
// Define the compute procedure
const computePipeline = device.createComputePipeline({
    label: "Compute Pipeline 0",
    layout: "auto",
    compute: {
        module: shaderModule,
        entryPoint: "computeMain",
        constants: {
            group_size: 4
        }
    }
});
computePass.setPipeline(computePipeline);

// Access the bind group layout
const bindGroupLayout = computePipeline.getBindGroupLayout(0);

// Create the bind group
let bindGroup = device.createBindGroup({
    layout: bindGroupLayout,
    entries: [{
        binding: 0,
        resource: { buffer: computeBuffer }
    }]
});
computePass.setBindGroup(0, bindGroup);

// Encode compute commands
computePass.dispatchWorkgroups(8);

// Complete encoding compute commands
computePass.end();
```

This code doesn't create any timestamps, so the object in the `encoder.`
`beginComputePass` method only has a label. The object in `device.create`
`ComputePipeline` has a label that describes the pipeline and a `compute` property
that identifies the shader module, the entry point, and constants to be passed to the shader.

The `constants` property can be set to an object containing name–value pairs
separated by a colon. In this case, it associates the name `group_size` with a value
of 4. The compute shader will access this value through an overridden variable named
`group_size`. This is a convenient way to set the workgroup size.

After the compute pipeline is created, the application associates it with the compute
pass encoder. It also associates the encoder with a bind group containing the application's storage buffer.

After making these associations, the application calls `dispatchWorkgroups`
to encode compute commands. Because the argument is set to 8, a total of 8 workgroups

will be created. Afterward, the application calls the compute pass encoder's end method to complete the encoding process.

Copying and Mapping Buffers

The code in the Ch08_SimpleCompute project creates a 128-byte storage buffer and fills it with values of 1.0. The following code creates the buffer:

```
// Create compute buffer
const computeBuffer = device.createBuffer({
    mappedAtCreation: true,
    size: 128,
    usage: GPUBufferUsage.STORAGE | GPUBufferUsage.COPY_SRC
});
```

It's important to understand the properties of the createBuffer method. The mappedAtCreation property is set to true because the application will access its mapped buffer immediately after the buffer's creation. The first usage flag is GPUBufferUsage.STORAGE because the application is creating a storage buffer. The second usage flag is GPUBufferUsage.COPY_SRC because the GPU will copy the buffer's data to a second buffer that the application can read from.

After the buffer is created, the application uses the following code to access its mapped content as an ArrayBuffer:

```
// Access the mapped data
const buff = computeBuffer.getMappedRange();
```

After obtaining the mapped ArrayBuffer, the application casts it to a Float32Array containing 32 floating-point values, all set to 1.0.

```
// Set the content of the mapped data
const inputVals = new Array(32);
inputVals.fill(1.0);
new Float32Array(buff).set(inputVals);
```

When the buffer's content has been set, the application closes the map by calling the buffer's unmap method:

```
computeBuffer.unmap();
```

Once the task is complete, the application doesn't read directly from computeBuffer because the GPU memory is (probably) separate from the CPU memory. Instead, it creates a second buffer named mappableBuffer to serve as a staging buffer. It creates the buffer with the following code:

```
// Create mappable buffer
const mappableBuffer = device.createBuffer({
  size: 128,
  usage: GPUBufferUsage.COPY_DST | GPUBufferUsage.MAP_READ
});
```

In this case, the first usage flag is GPUBufferUsage.COPY_DST because the application is going to copy data from the compute buffer into this buffer. The second usage flag is GPUBufferUsage.MAP_READ because the application will read the buffer's data after the copy operation is complete.

Once the buffer is created, the application calls the command encoder's copyBufferToBuffer method to encode a command that writes data from the compute buffer to the mappable buffer. This will be executed after the GPU finishes executing the command encoded with dispatchWorkgroups.

```
// Encode copy command
encoder.copyBufferToBuffer(computeBuffer, 0, mappableBuffer,
0, 128);
```

After the GPU executes the encoder's commands, the mappable buffer will hold data copied from the compute buffer. Because the buffer is mappable, the application can establish a mapping by calling mapAsync:

```
await mappableBuffer.mapAsync(GPUMapMode.READ);
```

Next, the application accesses the buffer's mapped content as an ArrayBuffer and casts it to a Float32Array.

```
const procData = mappableBuffer.getMappedRange();
const floatData = new Float32Array(procData);
```

After the application is finished with the Float32Array, it can terminate the mapping by calling the buffer's unmap method.

```
mappableBuffer.unmap();
```

This usage of storage buffers and mappable buffers is more complex than it should be. Thankfully, once you have a compute application working, it's easy to get other applications working through copy and paste.

TIME STAMPS

The goal of a compute application is to crunch numbers at high speed, so measuring time is an important priority. Normally, measuring elapsed time is simple: get the timestamp just before the task and the timestamp right after the task, and subtract the two.

Unfortunately, measuring time in a WebGPU compute application is more complex. This is because an application needs to encode query commands for the GPU and create query buffers to store the results. There are five steps involved:

1. Check if the client's system supports timestamps.
2. Create a query set.
3. Create a buffer to hold the timestamps.

4. Create the compute pass encoder with the timestamp configuration.

5. Encode a command to record timestamps.

The following discussion explores these steps. In each case, it explains what objects and methods are needed and then shows how they can be implemented in code.

Check for Timestamp Support

Before attempting to measure elapsed time, it's a good idea to make sure that the client's system supports timestamp queries. An application can check for support by accessing the `features` property of the `GPUAdapter` to see if it contains the string `timestamp-query`. The following code shows how this can be accomplished:

```
const timeSupport = adapter.features.has("timestamp-query")
```

If timestamp queries are supported, an application can specifically request a device that supports this feature. The following code uses the ternary operator to access the device, depending on whether timestamps are supported:

```
const device = timeSupport ?
    await adapter.requestDevice({
        requiredFeatures: ["timestamp-query"] }) :
    await adapter.requestDevice();
```

Once this is done, the application can be certain that the device will support timestamp queries if `timeSupport` is true.

Create the Query Set

Chapter 7 explained how applications can create a query set with the device's `createQuerySet` method. This accepts an object with two required properties:

- `count`—the number of queries to be read
- `type`—the nature of the queries to be read

For timestamp queries, `type` must be set to `timestamp`.

The Ch08_DotProduct application creates a query set with two queries: one before the computational task and one after the task. The following code shows how this is done:

```
const querySet = timeSupport ?
    device.createQuerySet({
        label: "Query Set",
        count: 2,
        type: "timestamp"
    }) : None;
```

The query set contains query results, but it can't be passed to the GPU like a buffer or texture. A special buffer needs to be created for the query set, and this will be discussed next.

Create a Buffer for Query Results

The GPU will only write query results to a buffer if the buffer has been specially configured for the purpose. When creating a query buffer for timestamps, there are two points to be aware of:

- Timestamps are provided as 64-bit integers, so the buffer's size should be set to hold the number of timestamps multiplied by the size.
- The usage property must include GPUBufferUsage.QUERY_RESOLVE.

The Ch08_DotProduct application uses the following code to create a query buffer that holds two query results:

```
// Create the query buffer
const queryBuffer = timeSupport ?
    device.createBuffer({
        size: querySet.count *
            BigInt64Array.BYTES_PER_ELEMENT,
        usage:
            GPUBufferUsage.QUERY_RESOLVE |
            GPUBufferUsage.COPY_SRC
    }) : None
```

As a result of this code, the buffer's size will always be large enough to hold the queries in the query set.

Create the Compute Pass Encoder

As mentioned earlier, an application creates the compute pass encoder by calling the command encoder's beginComputePass method. This accepts an optional timestampWrites property that can be set to an object that configures the timestamp query process. This object has three properties:

- querySet—the query set to hold the timestamp
- beginningOfPassWriteIndex—query index to record the timestamp at the start of the compute pass
- endOfPassWriteIndex—query index to record the timestamp at the end of the compute pass

In the Ch08_DotProduct application, the first timestamp should hold the time at the start of the operation, and the second timestamp should store the time at the end.

Both values should be stored in the query set named `querySet`. This can be configured with the following code:

```
const computePass = timeSupport ?
    encoder.beginComputePass({
        timestampWrites: {
            querySet,
            beginningOfPassWriteIndex: 0,
            endOfPassWriteIndex: 1
        }}) :
    encoder.beginComputePass({})
```

Once the compute pass encoder is created, it will be able to deliver timestamp queries to the device.

Encode Command to Record Timestamps

Applications encode rendering commands by calling methods like `draw` and encode compute commands by calling methods like `dispatchWorkgroups`. To tell the GPU to record timestamp queries, the application needs to call the command encoder's `resolveQuerySet` method. This requires five parameters, and Table 8.7 lists each of them.

In the Ch08_DotProduct application, queries are contained in `querySet`, the index of the first query is 0, and the number of queries is 2. The timestamp data should be written at Byte 0 of `queryBuffer`. This is configured with the following code:

```
if (timeSupport) {
    encoder.resolveQuerySet(querySet, 0, 2, queryBuffer, 0);
}
```

This should be called after the operation, whose timing should be measured. It should be called before the command that copies the data from the query buffer to a staging buffer. After the GPU executes its commands, the application can access the timestamps using the same methods that read regular data from storage buffers.

TABLE 8.7   Parameters of the `resolveQuerySet` method

PARAMETER	DATA TYPE	DESCRIPTION
querySet	GPUQuerySet	The query set to hold the timestamp
firstQuery	unsigned int	Index of the first query
queryCount	unsigned int	Number of timestamp queries to be performed
destination	GPUBuffer	The query buffer to hold the results
destinationOffset	unsigned int	Byte offset into the query buffer

ATOMIC VARIABLES AND FUNCTIONS

In a shader, hundreds or thousands of invocations may want to update a variable at the same time. For normal variables, this can result in unpredictable behavior. But if a variable is *atomic* and the invocations operate on the variable using *atomic functions*, each operation will be guaranteed to complete before another operation can start.

A variable can be made atomic if it contains integers and is stored in workgroup memory or storage buffer memory. In code, a variable is atomic if its declared type is `atomic<u32>`, `atomic<i32>`, or an array of these types. To demonstrate, the following code declares an atomic array of unsigned integers accessed in a storage buffer.

```
var<storage, read_write> counter: array<atomic<u32>>
```

As a result of this declaration, each element of the `counter` array can be updated using one of WGSL's atomic functions. Table 8.8 lists these functions and provides a description of each.

The first argument of these functions is a *pointer* to the atomic variable, not the variable itself. For this reason, the first argument is commonly preceded by the reference operator, &. To demonstrate this, the following code atomically adds the value 5 to the address of the third element of the counter array:

```
atomicAdd(&counter[2], 5)
```

TABLE 8.8   Atomic functions

FUNCTION	DESCRIPTION
`atomicStore(atom_ptr, val)`	Stores the value in the atomic object
`atomicLoad(atom_ptr, val)`	Returns the value stored in the atomic object
`atomicExchange(atom_ptr, val)`	Stores the value in the atomic object and returns its original value
`atomicAdd(atom_ptr, val)`	Adds the value to the atomic object
`atomicSub(atom_ptr, val)`	Subtracts the value from the atomic object
`atomicMax(atom_ptr, val)`	Writes the value to the atomic object if it's larger
`atomicMin(atom_ptr, val)`	Writes the value to the atomic object if it's smaller
`atomicAnd(atom_ptr, val)`	Sets the atomic object to the AND of the atomic value and the value
`atomicOr(atom_ptr, val)`	Sets the atomic object to the OR of the atomic value and the value
`atomicXor(atom_ptr, val)`	Sets the atomic object to the XOR of the atomic value and the value

There are two more points to know about atomic functions. First, they return the value of the atomic variable before the operation is performed. Second, they can be called in compute shaders and in fragment shaders, but not in vertex shaders.

EXAMPLE APPLICATION—DOT PRODUCT

The code in the Ch08_DotProduct application demonstrates how a compute shader can create and operate on atomic variables. Each invocation reads two vectors, computes their dot product, and adds the dot product to an atomic variable. After displaying the result of the dot product, the application displays the time that was needed to execute the compute command. Figure 8.4 shows what this looks like.

This section describes the application's operation in five parts:

1. Creating the storage buffers
2. Configuring the compute pipeline
3. Executing the compute shader
4. Retrieving the result
5. Measure and display elapsed time

As will be shown, atomic variables are helpful when an application needs to keep track of a running total among several invocations.

The Storage Buffers

The application passes data to the GPU in three storage buffers. The first two contain arrays of 1,024 integers. The third contains a single integer that identifies the result of the dot product. For each buffer, the application performs four operations:

- Creates a mapped buffer by calling `device.createBuffer`
- Accesses the buffer's mapped range by calling its `getMappedRange` method
- Creates an array containing the buffer's data
- Unmaps the buffer

Dot product: 179481600

Time: 1710340101589.0413 - 1710340101588.9756 = 0.065673828125

FIGURE 8.4   The Ch08_DotProduct application.

The following code shows how these operations are implemented in the ch08_dotproduct.js source file.

```javascript
// Set the number of values
const numVals = 1024;

// Create compute buffers
const aBuffer = device.createBuffer({
    mappedAtCreation: true,
    size: numVals * 4,
    usage: GPUBufferUsage.STORAGE
});
const aRange = aBuffer.getMappedRange();

// Create compute buffers
const bBuffer = device.createBuffer({
    mappedAtCreation: true,
    size: numVals * 4,
    usage: GPUBufferUsage.STORAGE
});
const bRange = bBuffer.getMappedRange();

// Create compute buffers
const resBuffer = device.createBuffer({
    mappedAtCreation: true,
    size: 4,
    usage:
        GPUBufferUsage.STORAGE |
        GPUBufferUsage.COPY_SRC
});
const resRange = resBuffer.getMappedRange();

// Create the data arrays
const aArray = new Array(numVals);
const bArray = new Array(numVals);
const res = new Array([0]);

// Initialize vectors
for (let i = 0; i < numVals; i++) {
    aArray[i] = i + 1;
    bArray[i] = numVals - i;
}

// Create arrays in buffer memory
new Uint32Array(aRange).set(aArray);
new Uint32Array(bRange).set(bArray);
new Uint32Array(resRange).set(res);
```

```
// Unmap buffers
aBuffer.unmap();
bBuffer.unmap();
resBuffer.unmap();
```

When each buffer is created, the `mappedAtCreation` property is set to `true`. This enables the application to access the buffer's mapped data by calling `getMappedRange`. The `usage` property includes `GPUBufferUsage.STORAGE` to configure the buffer as a storage buffer. The last buffer, `resBuffer`, also has the flag `GPUBufferUsage.COPY_SRC` because the application will copy data from it.

After creating the buffers, the application stores an array of unsigned 32-bit integers inside each of them. The first buffer contains 1,024 integers that increase from 1 to 1,024. The second buffer contains 1,024 integers that decrease from 1,024 to 1. The third buffer contains a single integer whose value is 0. This buffer stores the result of the dot product.

Once the buffers' data is set, the application calls `unmap` on each of them. This makes the buffers available for processing.

The Compute Pipeline

After creating and populating the buffers, the application creates the compute pass encoder and the compute pipeline. This is accomplished with the following code:

```
// Create the compute pass encoder
const computePass = encoder.beginComputePass({
    label: "Compute Pass 0"
});

// Define the compute procedure
const computePipeline = device.createComputePipeline({
    label: "Compute Pipeline 0",
    layout: "auto",
    compute: {
        module: shaderModule,
        entryPoint: "computeMain",
        constants: {
            group_size: 256
        }
    }
});
computePass.setPipeline(computePipeline);
```

```
// Access the bind group layout
const bindGroupLayout = computePipeline.getBindGroupLayout(0);

// Create the bind group
let bindGroup = device.createBindGroup({
    layout: bindGroupLayout,
    entries: [{
        binding: 0,
        resource: { buffer: aBuffer }
    },
    {
        binding: 1,
        resource: { buffer: bBuffer }
    },
    {
        binding: 2,
        resource: { buffer: resBuffer }
    }]
});
computePass.setBindGroup(0, bindGroup);
```

This is like the configuration code in the Ch08_SimpleCompute application, but there are two important differences. First, when creating the compute pipeline, the group_size constant is set to 256. On my system, this is the maximum number of invocations that can be executed in a workgroup.

The second difference involves the bind group. The bind group in the Ch08_DotProduct project references three storage buffers. aBuffer and bBuffer store the input values, and resBuffer stores the result. Because of this code, the compute shader will be able to access them using the @group(0) attribute and the appropriate @binding attribute.

The Compute Shader

The compute shader is executed by 256 invocations in a single workgroup. Each invocation reads a portion of the input data, performs a dot product, and updates the atomic variable. This is shown in the following code:

```
@binding(0) @group(0) var<storage, read> a : array<vec4u,
256>;
@binding(1) @group(0) var<storage, read> b : array<vec4u,
256>;
@binding(2) @group(0) var<storage, read_write> res :
atomic<u32>;
```

```
override group_size: u32;

@compute @workgroup_size(group_size)
fn computeMain(@builtin(global_invocation_id) id :
vec3<u32>) {

    // Compute dot product of vectors
    let prod = dot(a[id.x], b[id.x]);

    // Update result atomically
    atomicAdd(&res, prod);
}
```

The shader declares an overridden variable named group_size whose value is set to 256 when the compute pipeline is created. This variable is used by the @workgroup_size attribute to set the number of invocations in each workgroup.

Each invocation reads one vector from the first storage buffer and one vector from the second storage buffer. The index of the two vectors equals the global ID of the invocation. After reading the data, the invocation calls the dot function to obtain the dot product of the two vectors.

The last line of code calls atomicAdd to add the invocation's dot product to res. Because res is declared as an atomic<u32>, it's an atomic variable. This means multiple invocations can update its value without causing concurrency issues. It's important to note that the first argument of atomicAdd is a pointer to res (&res) and not the variable itself.

Retrieving the Result

After the invocations finish executing the compute shader, the application can access the result of the dot product. This result is stored in the storage buffer resBuffer, and the application performs five steps to obtain the result and display it on the page:

1. Create a mappable buffer whose usage includes GPUBufferUsage. MAP_READ.
2. Call copyBufferToBuffer to encode a command that copies the data from resBuffer to the mappable buffer.
3. When the copy is complete, map the mappable buffer to an ArrayBuffer.
4. Read the dot product result from the ArrayBuffer.
5. Display the result on the web page.

The following code shows how these steps are performed in the Ch08_DotProduct project.

```
// Create mappable buffer
const mappableBuffer = device.createBuffer({
  size: 4,
  usage:
      GPUBufferUsage.COPY_DST |
      GPUBufferUsage.MAP_READ
});

// Encode copy command
encoder.copyBufferToBuffer(resBuffer, 0, mappableBuffer, 0,
4);

// Submit the commands to the GPU
device.queue.submit([encoder.finish()]);

// Read data from compute buffer
await mappableBuffer.mapAsync(GPUMapMode.READ);
const procData = mappableBuffer.getMappedRange();
const resData = new Uint32Array(procData);

// Display output in page
const outputMsg = "Result: ";
document.getElementById("result").innerHTML =
outputMsg.concat(resData.toString());
```

When creating the mappable buffer, the application sets the usage property to GPUBufferUsage.COPY_DST because the buffer will receive data in a copy operation. It also sets usage to GPUBufferUsage.MAP_READ because the application will access the buffer's data by mapping it to an ArrayBuffer.

After creating the buffer, the application calls copyBufferToBuffer to encode a command that copies the content of resBuffer to mappableBuffer. Then the application submits its commands to the device's queue.

When the device finishes executing the commands, the application maps the buffer and accesses its content by calling getMappedRange. Then it casts the result to an array of unsigned integers and displays the result on the web page by accessing the label whose ID is result.

Elapsed Time

This application demonstrates how applications can measure computation time using timestamp queries. After making sure the client's device supports timestamps, the application creates a query set to store two timestamp values. Then it creates a buffer to hold the timestamp values.

To configure timestamp processing, the application creates the compute pass encoder with a `timestampWrites` object. This identifies the query set containing the query values and associates each value with the start of the compute pass or the end of the compute pass.

The application encodes timestamp query commands by calling the encoder's `resolveQuerySet` method. The following code shows how this is done:

```
// Encode command to record timestamp queries
encoder.resolveQuerySet(querySet, 0, querySet.count,
queryBuffer, 0);
```

As a result of this code, the GPU will perform the queries described in `querySet` and store the results in `queryBuffer` at Byte 0. After the command executes, the application reads the two timestamps and displays the elapsed time in the web page.

SUMMARY

While compute applications resemble graphical applications in many respects, there are interesting challenges that make them unique. One major concern involves splitting the processing among invocations and workgroups. Each invocation represents a single execution of the compute shader, and they're combined into workgroups to facilitate access to shared memory and synchronization.

Once you understand invocations and workgroups, coding a compute application is straightforward. The application needs to create a compute pass encoder instead of a render pass encoder and a compute pipeline instead of a render pipeline. For data transfer, this chapter has focused on creating storage buffers, but compute applications can also use storage textures, as Chapter 10 will make clear.

Compute shaders are simple to code, but it's important to keep track of the different built-in variables that they can use. Each invocation has a global ID, which distinguishes it from all other invocations, and a local ID, which distinguishes it from other invocations in its workgroup. These identifiers are important because they allow an invocation to access data specifically intended for it.

The next two chapters present exciting applications of WebGPU's compute capabilities. Chapter 9 uses compute applications to perform machine learning and Chapter 10 uses compute applications to process images.

Machine Learning with Neural Networks

9

In this chapter, we'll stop exploring the WebGPU API and look at an important application of compute shaders: *machine learning*. Machine learning has made a major impact on society due to its extraordinary ability to discern patterns in data. This chapter focuses on artificial neural networks (ANNs), which are one of the most effective methods of machine learning.

Most of this chapter is devoted to discussing the theory of neural networks, and the main goal is to develop a WebGPU application capable of analyzing real-world data. Before I discuss the math, I want to present the problem that this chapter's application will be designed to solve: *iris classification*.

IRIS CLASSIFICATION

A common test for neural networks involves classifying an iris based on four physical characteristics: sepal width, sepal length, petal width, and petal length. Figure 9.1 gives an idea of what an iris looks like.

The goal of this chapter is to create a neural network that accepts these four characteristics and decides which species the iris belongs to. To be specific, the network will produce three values between 0.0 and 1.0:

- the estimated probability that the iris belongs to the *setosa* species
- the estimated probability that the iris belongs to the *versicolor* species
- the estimated probability that the iris belongs to the *virginica* species

To show how this works, Figure 9.2 displays the results of six tests conducted by the Ch09_IrisNetwork application. In each case, the three values computed by the application are compared to the actual results. The application is never perfect, but in each test, the maximum computed probability corresponds to the actual classification. This means the neural network has classified the irises correctly.

DOI: 10.1201/9781003422839-9

FIGURE 9.1　Example of an iris. (Photo by David Iliff, provided under Creative Commons License 3.0.)

Ch09_Iris_Network

Actual classification: 1.000 0.000 0.000
Computed outputs:　0.996 0.004 0.000
Result: SUCCESS

Actual classification: 1.000 0.000 0.000
Computed outputs:　0.993 0.007 0.000
Result: SUCCESS

Actual classification: 0.000 0.000 1.000
Computed outputs:　0.000 0.034 0.966
Result: SUCCESS

Actual classification: 0.000 1.000 0.000
Computed outputs:　0.004 0.978 0.018
Result: SUCCESS

Actual classification: 0.000 1.000 0.000
Computed outputs:　0.010 0.989 0.001
Result: SUCCESS

Actual classification: 0.000 1.000 0.000
Computed outputs:　0.003 0.657 0.340
Result: SUCCESS

FIGURE 9.2　Iris classification results.

Though this chapter focuses on classifying flowers, classification is just one of many applications of neural networks. Another major application is *prediction*. Machine learning specialists have trained neural networks to predict weather patterns and financial movements. Of course, just because a neural network can find patterns in past data doesn't mean it can reliably predict the future.

NEURONS AND PERCEPTRONS

In my opinion, the best way to approach ANNs is to compare them with biological neurons. This section explores the basic operation of neurons and then introduces *perceptrons*, which are electrical circuits intended to behave like neurons.

Neurons

In the early 19th century, surgeons took a close look at the cells that make up nerve tissue. They referred to these nerve cells as *neurons*, and Figure 9.3 illustrates a simplified view of their structure.

A neuron receives electrical stimulation through its *dendrites*, which are shown on the left. Chemicals in the cell store the incoming electricity, and as incoming signals grow in strength, the neuron's internal voltage increases.

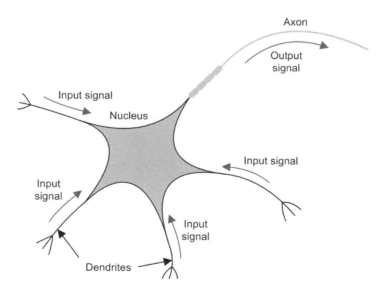

FIGURE 9.3   Simplified structure of a neuron.

When the neuron's voltage exceeds a threshold value, the neuron fires a signal through its *axon*, shown in the upper right. This output signal can stimulate other neurons, which means one neuron's firing may cause a series of other neurons to fire.

The study of neurology has advanced by leaps and bounds since the 19th century, and today, we know that neurons do much more than fire signals from one cell to another. But for this chapter, you only need to grasp two points:

1. A neuron receives multiple input signals and produces a single output. This output can serve as the input of another neuron.
2. Every neuron has a threshold, and the neuron will only produce output if its internal voltage exceeds the threshold.

If you grasp these points, you'll have no trouble understanding *perceptrons*, which are circuits whose operation resembles that of neurons.

Perceptrons

In the 1960s, a researcher named Frank Rosenblatt constructed a circuit that behaved like a neuron. He called it a *perceptron*, and Figure 9.4 gives an idea of how it works.

A perceptron receives multiple inputs and produces an output, but the inputs are provided as numeric values. In the figure, these input values are denoted x_0 through x_4.

The perceptron's threshold value and output are also given as numbers. If the sum of the input values exceeds the threshold value, the output will be 1. If the sum of the signals doesn't reach the threshold, the output will be 0.

For example, suppose x_0 is 1.5, x_1 is 0.5, x_2 is –1.0, x_3 is 0.5, and x_4 is 1.0. In this case, the sum of the values is 2.5. If the threshold value is 2.0, the perceptron will produce an output of 1 because the sum is greater than the threshold. If the threshold value is 3.0, the perceptron will produce an output of 0 because the sum falls below the threshold.

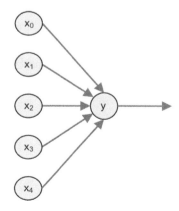

FIGURE 9.4   Approximating neural behavior with a perceptron.

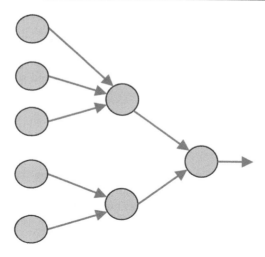

FIGURE 9.5   Connecting perceptrons.

Denoting the inputs as x_i and the output as y, a perceptron's output can be expressed with the following equation:

$$y = \begin{cases} 1 \ if \ \sum_i x_i > threshold \\ \\ 0 \ otherwise \end{cases}$$

Like neurons, perceptrons can be connected so that the output of one serves as the input of another. Figure 9.5 gives an idea of what this looks like. Perceptrons can have different numbers of input values, but each always produces one output.

Perceptrons are helpful when you're learning about the subject, but they aren't used for practical machine learning. This is because the behavior of a perceptron is *static*—its operation can't be updated. The process of updating the circuit's behavior is called *training*, and it's a major issue (maybe *the central issue*) of modern machine learning.

IMPROVING THE MODEL

After Rosenblatt demonstrated the capabilities of his perceptron, researchers updated his model in several ways. Three major improvements are:

1. Each input is multiplied by a value called a *weight*.
2. Instead of comparing the sum of inputs to a threshold, an extra input called a *bias* is added.

3. The sum of the weighted inputs (including the bias) is passed to an *activation function* that determines the output.

As a result of these changes, perceptrons come closer to being suitable for practical use. For this reason, we'll stop using the term *perceptron* and start referring to these elements as *nodes*.

Weights

In Figure 9.3, every input has equal influence in determining the output. But in real-world machine learning, some inputs have more influence than others in the decision-making process. In addition, some signals may have a negative influence on the outcome.

To reflect this, each input is multiplied by a value called a *weight*. Figure 9.6 shows what a node with weighted inputs looks like.

To compute the output, each input value is multiplied by its weight and the products are added together. Then the sum is compared to the node's threshold. The node produces an output of 1 if the sum is greater than the threshold, and a 0 otherwise.

Denoting the inputs as x_i and the weights as w_i, a node's operation can be expressed with the following equation:

$$y = \begin{cases} 1 \ if \ \sum_i w_i x_i > threshold \\ \\ 0 \ otherwise \end{cases}$$

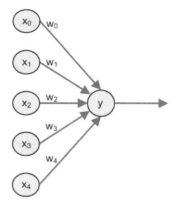

FIGURE 9.6   Nodes with weights.

An example will clarify how this works. Suppose the inputs x_i are {5.3, –2.0, 1.7, –0.3} and their weights w_i are {0.6, –0.2, 1.4, 2.3}. The sum of the weighted inputs can be computed in the following way:

$$\sum_i x_i w_i = (5.3 \cdot 0.6) + (-2.0 \cdot -0.2) + (1.7 \cdot 1.4) + (-0.3 \cdot 2.3)$$

$$= 3.18 + 0.4 + 2.38 - 0.69 = 5.27$$

The sum of the weighed inputs is 5.27, so if the node's threshold value is 5.0, it will produce an output of 1. If the threshold is 6.0, the node will produce 0.

Weights play a vital role in machine learning because they make it possible to update the neural network's operation. The process of updating these weights is called *training*, and a later section of this chapter discusses this topic.

Bias

Rather than keep track of threshold values, it's common to simplify the model by adding a constant-valued input called a *bias*. Figure 9.7 shows what this looks like.

The bias receives a weight just like every other input. For this reason, it makes sense to set the value of the bias input to 1. This is why the lowest node on the left is given as +1. In essence, the weight of the bias serves as the node's threshold value.

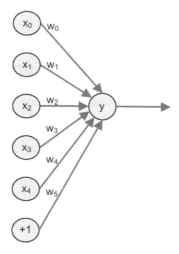

FIGURE 9.7   Adding a bias input.

ACTIVATION FUNCTIONS

The unit step function, u(x) returns 1 if x is greater than or equal to 0 and 0 if x is less than 0. Using this function, the relationship between a node's output, y, and its weighted inputs $w_i x_i$ can be expressed with the following equation:

$$y = u\left(\sum_i w_i x_i\right)$$

The unit step function is easy to understand, but in practice, data scientists use more suitable functions to produce a node's output. These are called *activation functions*. Many types of activation functions have been devised, and they all have three important characteristics:

1. *nonlinearity*—real-world machine learning problems are non-linear
2. *monotonically increasing*—if x > y, f(x) should be greater than or equal to f(y)
3. *differentiable*—the derivative of the function should exist and should be easy to compute

As given in the equation, a node's activation function accepts the weighted sum of the node's inputs and produces a single output. This section introduces three popular activation functions: the rectified linear unit (ReLU) function, the sigmoid function, and the softmax function.

The Rectified Linear Unit (ReLU) Function

In electric circuits, a rectifier accepts an input signal and transmits an output equal to the input *if the input is positive*. If the input signal isn't positive, the rectifier transmits an output of zero.

The rectified linear unit function, or ReLU, performs a similar operation. Its output equals the input if the input is positive and its output is 0 otherwise. Put another way, the ReLU function returns the maximum of the input value and 0. In code, this can be expressed as max(0, x). Figure 9.8 shows what the function's graph looks like.

The ReLU function is popular in machine learning applications, but it has one significant drawback: it's discontinuous at 0. For this reason, some data scientists prefer the exponential linear unit (ELU) function. Like ReLU, the ELU function returns the input if the input is greater than 0. Unlike ReLU, ELU returns the exponential of the input minus 1, exp(x) − 1, if the input is less than 0. This ensures that the node's output is always continuous.

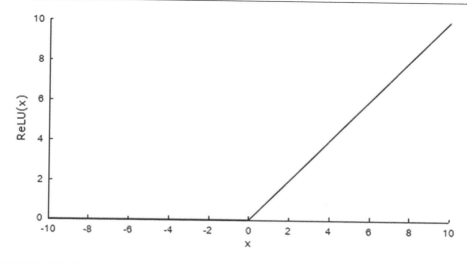

FIGURE 9.8   The rectified linear unit (ReLU) activation function.

The Logistic (Sigmoid) Function

The logistic function is used by applications that need to classify features into one of two categories. It can be expressed mathematically with the following equation:

$$\sigma(x) = \frac{1}{1 + e^{-x}}$$

Figure 9.9 shows what the graph of the logistic function looks like for values of x between −8 and 8.

The logistic function is shaped like an S, and because sigma (σ) is the Greek letter for S, it's commonly referred to as the *sigmoid function*, or $\sigma(x)$. It has three properties that make it ideal for classifying data:

1. Its output runs between 0 and 1, which means that a node's result can be interpreted as a probability.
2. $\sigma(0) = 0.5$, which implies that a data point in the center is equally likely to belong to both categories.
3. The function is symmetric around the y-axis: $\sigma(-x) = 1 - \sigma(x)$.

Some applications don't need outputs that can be interpreted as probabilities. In these cases, researchers may prefer activation functions whose output ranges beyond 0 and 1. One good alternative is the inverse tangent function, or tanh(x). The graph of this function closely resembles that of the logistic function, but its output ranges from −1 to 1.

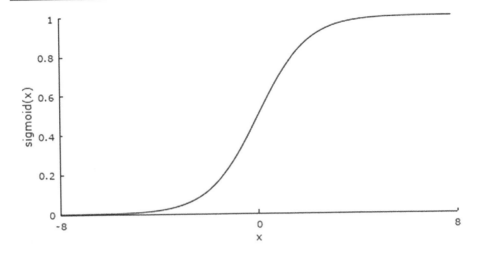

FIGURE 9.9   The logistic (sigmoid) activation function.

The Softmax Function

The logistic function makes it possible to classify features into one of two categories. But many machine learning tasks, such as the iris classification discussed in this chapter, need to classify features into one of multiple categories. For this reason, the neural network will have multiple nodes whose outputs are combined and fed into the *softmax function*.

The softmax function extends the logistic function to support multiple categories. A network needs one node for each category, and the softmax output identifies the probability that the input data belongs to the i-th category. Mathematically, the output is determined by the following equation:

$$\sigma(x_i) = \frac{e^{x_i}}{\sum_{k=1}^{N} e^{x_k}}$$

In this equation, i identifies a category and N identifies the number of categories. For the iris classification discussed in this chapter, there are three categories, so N would be set to 3.

LAYERS AND DEEP LEARNING

Individual nodes are too primitive to be useful in practice, but when combined into networks, they form sophisticated tools for machine learning. An interconnected set of nodes is called a *neural network*, and this section explores their structure.

Layers

The nodes in a neural network are organized into columns that are more commonly called *layers*. For this reason, neural networks are frequently referred to as multi-layer perceptrons, or MLPs. Every practical neural network has at least two layers and Figure 9.10 illustrates an MLP with four layers.

The first layer is the input layer and the last layer is the output layer. The layers in-between are called *hidden layers*. Layers are numbered from left to right, and the input layer is Layer 0.

A layer is *dense* or *fully-connected* if each of its nodes is connected to each node in the following layer. In Figure 9.10, every layer in the network is dense.

The nodes in a hidden layer are denoted h^x_y, where x is the index of the layer and y is the index of the node in the layer. For example, h^2_1 identifies the second node (1) in the third (2) layer.

The output of each node is computed by summing the weighted inputs and passing the sum into the activation function. For simplicity, we'll refer to a node's output using the node's name. For example, if the activation function of Node h^2_1 is ReLU, its output is obtained by passing the sum of its weighted inputs into the ReLU function. This can be expressed with the following equation:

$$h^2_1 = \mathrm{Re}\,\mathrm{LU}\left(w^1_{01}h^1_0 + w^1_{11}h^1_1 + w^1_{21}h^1_2\right)$$

As illustrated, each weight is identified by three indexes. Denoting a weight as w^x_{yz}, its position can be determined as follows:

- x identifies the layer containing the node producing the weighted signal
- y identifies the index of the node producing the signal to be weighted
- z identifies the index of the node receiving the signal

For example, w^2_{01} identifies a weight in the third layer (Layer 2). The network multiplies the weight by the signal leaving the first node (0) and entering the second node (1).

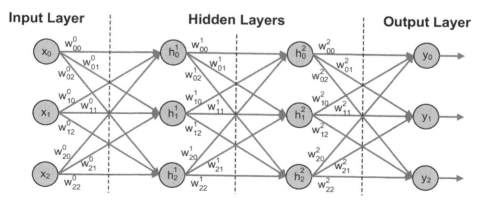

FIGURE 9.10 Four-layer multilayer perceptron.

Deep Learning

As more hidden layers are added, the network becomes more capable of sophisticated detection and classification. When an application uses a neural network with multiple hidden layers, we say that it's making use of *deep learning*.

Deep learning has proven effective in many applications. Two famous examples include Google's AlphaGo program, which uses deep learning to beat professional Go players, and self-driving cars, which use neural networks to stay on the road and avoid traffic collisions.

But there are two major drawbacks to adding more layers to a network. First, each hidden layer increases the amount of time needed to train the network. Second, each new layer increases the chances of *overfitting*, which means the network is good at classification/prediction in particular cases but it doesn't work well with general data.

TRAINING

At this point, you should have a basic understanding of nodes, weights, and activation functions. But one critical aspect of neural networks has yet to be discussed: *training*. The goal of training is to update the weights so that the output nodes produce suitable results. These results could be prediction (What will tomorrow's average temperature be?) or classification (Does this image display a cat or a dog?)

To understand training, it helps to think of a neural network as a multi-stage mathematical function involving weighted inputs. Consider the network depicted in Figure 9.11.

Denoting the activation functions as f_0, f_1, and f_2, the neural network in the illustration embodies the following mathematical relationship:

$$y(x_i) = f_2\left(w_{00}^1 f_0\left(w_{00}^0 x_0 + w_{10}^0 x_1 + w_{20}^0 x_2 + w_{30}^0 x_3\right) + w_{10}^1 f_1\left(w_{41}^0 x_4 + w_{51}^0 x_5 + w_{61}^0 x_6\right)\right)$$

The goal of training is to compute the set of weights w_i that bring $y(x_i)$ as close as possible to the observed data. The most popular method of training a neural network is called *backpropagation*, which consists of five steps:

1. Generate initial values of the weights, w_i.
2. For each batch of input vectors x_i, compute the output vectors $y(x_i)$. This is called *forward propagation*.
3. Compute the disparity between the output values $y(x_i)$ and observed results, obs_i. This is called the *loss*.
4. Use an optimization method to update the weights w_i based on the computed loss.
5. Repeat Steps 2 through 4 until the loss falls to an acceptable value.

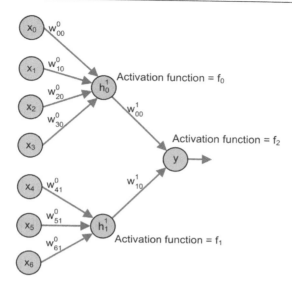

FIGURE 9.11   Example neural network.

If these steps are performed correctly, the neural network will (theoretically) produce acceptable results for real-world prediction or classification. To clarify how these steps can be performed, the following discussion presents weight initialization, loss computation, and methods of optimization.

Initializing Weights

When I started working with neural networks, weights were always initialized to 0.0. But researchers have found it better to use random values. The goal is to make sure none of the inputs are excessively magnified or reduced. This prevents weights from growing to infinity (exploding gradients problem) or shrinking to zero (vanishing gradient problem).

In the 2015 paper, *Delving Deep into Rectifiers*, Kaiming He and other researchers present a weight initialization method that takes into account the number of inputs entering a node. Each weight is assigned a value from a normal distribution whose average is zero and whose standard deviation, σ, is obtained in the following way:

$$\sigma = \sqrt{\frac{2}{fan\ in}}$$

In this equation, *fan in* refers to the number of inputs entering the node. As the number of inputs increases, the standard deviation decreases and the initialization values come closer to zero.

An example will clarify how this works. If a node has four inputs, σ will equal sqrt(2/4) = 0.707. The mean is zero, so when normally distributed weights are generated, 68% of them should lie between −0.707 and 0.707. Ninety-five percent of the generated weights should have values between −1.414 and 1.414.

JavaScript doesn't provide functions that generate normally distributed values, so the example code in this chapter initializes weights using the Box-Muller Transform. This accepts two uniformly distributed random numbers, x_1 and x_2, and generates normally distributed weights w_1 and w_2 using the following relationships:

$$w_1 = \sqrt{-2\ln(x_1)}\cos(2\pi x_2)\sigma$$
$$w_2 = \sqrt{-2\ln(x_1)}\sin(2\pi x_2)\sigma$$

In these equations, σ is the standard deviation computed from the He weight initialization method. The following code shows how the Ch09_IrisNetwork initializes its weights and stores them inside a buffer named `weightBuffer`.

```
const weightData = new Array(numWeights);
for (let i = 0; i < numWeights; i+= 2) {
    let x1 = Math.random();
    let x2 = Math.random();
    weightData[i] = Math.sqrt(-2.0 * Math.log(x1)) *
Math.cos(2 * Math.PI * x2) * sigma;
    weightData[i + 1] = Math.sqrt(-2.0 * Math.log(x1)) *
Math.sin(2 * Math.PI * x2) * sigma;
}
const weightRange = weightBuffer.getMappedRange();
new Float32Array(weightRange).set(weightData);
weightBuffer.unmap();
```

Note that bias weights are always initialized to zero. This ensures that regular input signals are given priority in determining the output.

Computing Loss

During training, an application needs to measure how well the neural network is operating. To make this determination, it computes the disparity between the values of the network's output nodes and the observed values. This disparity is called the *loss*, and the method of computing the loss depends on many factors, including the nature of the neural network's output.

When training starts, all the weights have random values, so the output will likely be far away from the desired values (high loss). As training progresses, the weights will be updated to bring the network's output in line with observed values. When the network's output is acceptable, training stops (low loss). Loss is always greater than or equal to 0, and the lower the loss value, the better the training.

If a neural network is trained to make predictions, the loss will usually be found by computing the mean-square error, or MSE. If a neural network is trained to classify features, the loss is found by computing negative log-likelihood. This discussion presents both methods.

Prediction and mean-square error (MSE)

Suppose you're training a neural network to predict three values: the daily average temperature, the daily average barometric pressure, and the daily average precipitation. In this case, the network will have three output nodes—one for each predicted value. We'll collectively call these values y_i (y_0 is the predicted temperature, y_1 is the predicted pressure, and y_2 is the predicted precipitation).

During training, the application will compare y_i with observed values from past days. To see how well training is working, the application measures the disparity between the predicted values and the observed values.

A common way to measure this disparity (loss) involves computing the mean-square error, or MSE. This subtracts each prediction value (y_i) from each observed value (obs_i), squares the result, and adds the squared differences together. If there are N prediction values, the MSE computes the loss with the following equation:

$$loss = \frac{1}{N} \sum_{i=0}^{N-1} \left(obs_i - y(x_i)\right)^2$$

An explanation will make this clear. Suppose yesterday's average temperature was 14.5°C, the average barometric pressure was 760.8 mm Hg, and the average precipitation was 682.0 mm. This forms the vector [14.5, 760.8, 682.0]. Now suppose the output of the neural network is [12.8, 772.4, 689.4]. The loss can be computed in the following way:

$$
\begin{aligned}
loss &= \frac{1}{N} \sum_{i=0}^{N-1} \left(obs_i - y(x_i)\right)^2 \\
&= \frac{1}{3}\left[(14.5-12.8)^2 + (760.8-772.4)^2 + (682.0-689.4)^2\right] \\
&= \frac{1}{3}(2.89 + 134.56 + 54.76) \\
&= 64.07
\end{aligned}
$$

Because this method adds the squares of differences, the result is always greater than or equal to zero. For this reason, the MSE is an acceptable method of computing loss in machine learning.

Classification and maximum likelihood

Now let's consider neural networks that are intended to classify features instead of making predictions. For example, suppose the goal of a neural network is to determine if the animal in an image is a cat, dog, or horse (and it's always one of these three).

In this case, the output layer of the network will have three nodes, and each will produce a *probability* related to the corresponding category. y_0 is the computed probability that the animal in the image is a cat, y_1 is the computed probability that the animal in the image is a dog, and y_2 is the computed probability that the animal in the image is a horse. Because we're dealing with probabilities, each value will lie between 0.0 and 1.0 and the sum should always be close to 1.0.

Ideally, the neural network will produce an output of 1.0 for the correct category and an output of 0.0 for the incorrect categories. In practice, this never happens.

If there are only two categories involved, the most common activation function is the logistic function discussed earlier. For more than two categories, the softmax function is used instead.

To compute classification loss, neural networks use the *cross-entropy method*, also called *log-likelihood*. If the observed values are obs_i and the predicted values are $y(x_i)$, the loss is computed in the following way:

$$loss = -\sum_{i=0}^{N} obs_i \cdot \log\big(y(x_i)\big)$$

At first, it may seem that this will produce negative values for the loss. But it's important to remember that all of the values are *probabilities*, which means they range from 0.0 to 1.0. The logarithm of a probability is always negative or zero, so this loss will always be positive or zero.

An example will clarify how this works. Suppose that the network produces three probabilities: the probability that the iris belongs to the setosa species, the probability that it belongs to the versicolor species, and the probability that it belongs to the virginica species. If we know in advance that an iris belongs to the versicolor species, the observed values obs_i are [0.0, 1.0, 0.0].

Of course, the neural network won't produce these perfect values, so let's assume it produces a probability vector of [0.09, 0.76, 0.15]. The loss can be computed in the following way.

$$loss = -\big[0.0 \cdot \log(0.09) + 1.0 \cdot \log(0.76) + 0.0 \cdot \log(0.15)\big]$$
$$= -\log(0.76) = 0.2744$$

As shown, only one of the terms in the loss will be non-zero. It doesn't matter what probability the network assigns to the wrong classes. The only probability that matters is the one assigned to the correct class.

Optimization

Computing loss is important, but to improve the network's operation, we need a way to update its weights in a manner that reduces the loss. This procedure is called *optimization*, and researchers have devised several algorithms for this purpose. This section presents five methods that are frequently employed:

- gradient descent—simple but slow, ignores past gradients, may result in oscillation
- momentum—faster than graduate descent because it uses past gradients
- AdaGrad—applies a different learning rate to each weight
- RMSProp—like AdaGrad, but avoids learning rate decay
- Adam—like RMSProp, but adds momentum

Technically, the second through fifth methods are just variations of the gradient descent algorithm. But like many sources, this book treats them as distinct methods.

Gradient descent optimization

The gradient descent method is the oldest optimization algorithm used in machine learning, and if you look through textbooks, you're likely to encounter it frequently. But despite its popularity, few experts recommend it over the alternatives.

Gradient descent optimization relies on a crucial mathematical fact: a function decreases fastest at Point P in the direction determined by the *negative gradient* at Point P. Before proceeding further, I need to explain what a gradient is and how it can be computed.

If you're familiar with calculus, you know that the derivative of a function at a point equals the function's slope at that point. In other words, if f(x) is differentiable, its derivative with respect to x is denoted f'(x) and the slope at point a is denoted f'(a). Figure 9.12 shows what this looks like.

A function that depends on multiple variables will have multiple derivatives. For example, if f(x, y) is differentiable, it has a derivative with respect to x and a derivative

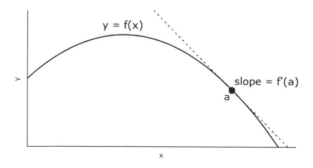

FIGURE 9.12 Derivative and slope.

with respect to y. These are *partial derivatives*, and they're denoted with the following notation:

$$\text{Partial derivative of } f(x, y) \text{ with respect to } x : \frac{\partial f}{\partial x}$$

$$\text{Partial derivative of } f(x, y) \text{ with respect to } y : \frac{\partial f}{\partial y}$$

To show what partial derivatives look like, Figure 9.13 depicts the relationship $f(x, y) = 16 - 4x^2 - 2y^2$. At point (1, 2), the partial derivative with respect to x is −8 and the partial derivative with respect to y is −8.

A vector is a quantity with a magnitude and a direction, and it can be defined as an array of components that identify the vector's magnitude in each direction. Graphically, you can think of a vector as an arrow in space, and if a vector points two units in the positive x-direction and three units in the negative y-direction, it can be represented as [2, −3].

The gradient descent algorithm is concerned with a special type of vector called a *gradient*. A function's gradient is a vector whose components equal the function's partial derivatives. The gradient of f is denoted ∇f, and if the function has three variables, its gradient will have three components. This can be expressed with the following equation:

$$\nabla f(x, y, z) = \left[\frac{\partial f}{\partial x}, \frac{\partial f}{\partial y}, \frac{\partial f}{\partial z} \right]$$

If the function has two variables, its gradient vector will have two components. In Figure 9.13, the gradient at (1, 2) is the vector [−8, −8]. This is represented by the black arrow extending from the point (1, 2).

Suppose that the function in the figure represents a mountain. If you attempt to climb this mountain, you'll find that the gradient identifies the steepest direction of

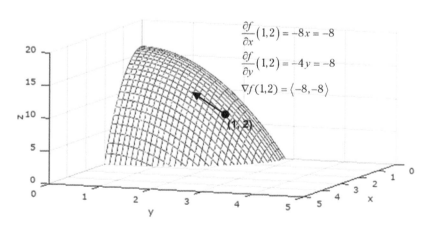

FIGURE 9.13 Partial derivatives.

climbing. This isn't a coincidence. A function's gradient *always* points in the direction of steepest ascent. Similarly, the opposite vector always identifies the steepest direction for *descent*.

Now that you understand the significance of the gradient, you're ready to tackle the gradient descent algorithm. This computes the gradient of the loss and updates the model's variables until the gradient of the loss approaches zero. To express this mathematically, I need to introduce some notation:

- The set of trainable variables (weights) is denoted θ. The values of the weights at Step t is denoted θ_t.
- The loss, which is a function of the model's variables, is denoted $J(\theta)$. The gradient of the loss is $\nabla J(\theta)$. This is a *vector* containing the partial derivatives of the loss with respect to each weight. If there are N weights, $\nabla J(\theta)$ will contain N partial derivatives.
- The learning rate, denoted η, is a single value that affects how much θ_j will be updated from step to step.

With this notation in mind, each step of the gradient descent optimization method can be expressed with the following equation:

$$\theta_t = \theta_{t-1} - \eta \nabla J(\theta)$$

To make sense of this, it helps to look at a simple example. Suppose the old value of weight w_0 is 0.4 and the partial derivative of the loss with respect to w_0 is −0.5. The loss increases as w_0 *decreases*, so we want to *increase* the next value of w_0. The first element of θ_{t-1} is 0.4, so this equation sets the first element of θ_t (the next value of w_0) to $0.4 - \eta(-0.5)$ or $0.4 + 0.5\eta$. It performs a similar operation for the other weights in θ_t.

Now suppose the partial derivative of the loss with respect to w_0 is zero. In this case, the loss doesn't depend on w_0 at all, so the equation leaves the value of w_0 unchanged.

As training continues, the elements of $\nabla J(\theta)$ should approach a minimum, which means that each new set of variables should be approximately equal to the previous set. At this point, optimization is finished because it has (theoretically) found a set of weights that produce minimum loss. This condition is called *convergence*.

The value of η is chosen by the developer, and selecting this value is a major decision. If η is too large, the algorithm will progress quickly, but it may step around the minimum and never reach a final value.

If η is too small, the algorithm will move more precisely, but it will take a great deal of time. In addition, the optimizer may stop at a *local minimum* instead of a *global minimum*. Figure 9.14 illustrates the difference.

In addition to the difficulty of finding a global minimum, the gradient descent method has three significant shortcomings:

- It's generally slow to converge to a minimum value.
- It can only optimize differentiable functions.
- It can oscillate between values and never reach a minimum.

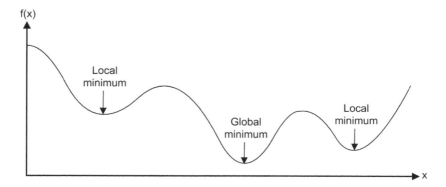

FIGURE 9.14 Local and global minima.

This last issue deserves explanation. If the learning rate is large, the algorithm may jump back and forth between a pair of points and never reach a minimum. This jumping is called *oscillation*, and it's a source of frequent frustration. Applications can reduce the likelihood of oscillation by reducing the learning rate, but then training takes more time.

While gradient descent optimization is still commonly used, researchers have developed several alternatives to make up for its shortcomings. The following discussion presents four of them: momentum, AdaGrad, RMSProp, and Adam optimization.

Momentum optimization

The momentum method has a lot in common with gradient descent optimization, but it usually converges faster with a reduced likelihood of oscillation. It accomplishes this by weighting the update from the preceding step and using it to compute the update for the current step. The following equations show how this works:

$$v_t = \alpha v_{t-1} - \eta \nabla J(\theta)$$

The weight α is called the *momentum*, and its value indicates how much the preceding step should influence the current step. It's always set to a value between 0 and 1, and if it's set to 0, the result is the basic gradient descent method. Applications commonly set α equal to 0.9.

It's important to see how the momentum affects the convergence rate. If the optimizer moves quickly toward a minimum, v will be significant and the optimizer will approach the minimum even faster. If the optimizer is stuck between two values, v will decrease the amount by which the variables are updated and the optimizer will slow its approach.

Adaptive gradient (AdaGrad) optimization

The gradient descent algorithm and the momentum algorithm apply the same learning rate to each weight being trained. But this may not be suitable for all cases—weight w_i may need a different learning rate than w_j.

The AdaGrad optimization method takes this into account. It forms a matrix G containing squares of past gradients and then divides the learning rate by the square root of G, adding a small value (ϵ) to ensure that the denominator is never zero. The following equation shows what this looks like:

$$\theta_t = \theta_{t-1} - \frac{\eta}{\sqrt{G} + \epsilon} \nabla J(\theta)$$

The diagonal elements of the G matrix contain squares of the loss gradient with respect to each weight. As a result, the learning rate changes from variable to variable and from step to step. But because G always increases from step to step, the new learning rates always decrease in magnitude. As training continues, their values will eventually reach zero, bringing training to a halt.

Root-Mean-Square propagation (RMSProp) optimization

Like AdaGrad optimization, the RMSProp method uses preceding loss gradients to compute a separate learning rate for each weight. The main difference is that, instead of factoring in every preceding loss gradient, RMSProp essentially *forgets* past values. As a result, the computed learning rates don't always drop to 0.

Instead of storing loss gradient values as diagonal elements of a G matrix, RMSProp updates a vector named v_t, where t is the step index. The values of this vector are partially determined by two factors:

- the square of the latest loss gradient, $[\nabla J(\theta)]^2$
- the preceding value of v, given as v_{t-1}

The following equation shows how RMSProp takes these values into account:

$$v_t = \beta v_{t-1} + (1 - \beta)\left[\nabla J(\theta)\right]^2$$
$$\theta_t = \theta_{t-1} - \frac{\eta}{\sqrt{v_t} + \epsilon} \nabla J(\theta)$$

In this equation, β is called the *forgetting factor* because it determines how much the past update affects the current update. As β decreases, the optimization step is more determined by the current loss than the previous updates.

Adaptive momentum (Adam) optimization

Like the RMSProp method, the Adam (Adaptive Moment Estimation) algorithm computes a separate learning rate for each weight. And like the momentum algorithm, the current update step is partly determined by the result of the preceding update step.

To compute weight-specific learning rates, the Adam method computes a vector v_t that serves the same purpose as the v_t vector in RMSProp. The following equation shows how this is obtained:

$$v_t = \beta_2 v_{t-1} + (1 - \beta_2)[\nabla J(\theta)]^2$$

In addition to computing v_t, the Adam method keeps track of momentum by computing another vector named m_t. As shown in the following equation, this is partly determined by the preceding m_t vector and partly by the loss.

$$m_t = \beta_1 m_{t-1} + (1 - \beta_1)\nabla J(\theta)$$

After computing v_t and v_t, the Adam method performs bias correction, which divides v_t by $1 - \beta_2^t$ and m_t by $1 - \beta_1^t$. Then these scaled values are used to change the learning weight, as shown in the following equation:

$$\hat{v}_t = \frac{v_t}{1 - (\beta_2)^t}$$

$$\hat{m}_t = \frac{m_t}{1 - (\beta_1)^t}$$

$$\theta_t = \theta_{t-1} - \frac{\eta \hat{m}_t}{\sqrt{\hat{v}_t} + \epsilon}\nabla J(\theta)$$

Because Adam optimization incorporates momentum into the update, it converges quickly and avoids oscillation. It computes separate learning rates for the network's weights, and these rates don't necessarily decay to zero.

Batching and Mini-Batching

When training a neural network, one major issue involves how often the weights should be updated. On one extreme, an application can compute the losses for all the input vectors and then use the average loss to update the weights. This is called *batching*. On the other extreme, the application can update the weights after computing the loss for each individual input vector.

The example code in this chapter relies on *mini-batching*, which serves as a compromise between these two extremes. This splits the training set into groups and then updates the weights after computing the average loss of each group of vectors.

An example will clarify how mini-batching works. In the Ch09_IrisNetwork application, there are a total of 150 vectors containing iris dimensions and associated classifications. The application uses 144 vectors for training and the remaining 6 to test the trained neural network. At the start of the chapter, Figure 9.2 shows example results of the six tests.

During training, the application splits the 144 training vectors into nine mini-batches of 16 vectors each. In each group, the 16 vectors are processed in parallel and a separate loss gradient vector is computed for each mini-batch. The average loss gradient vector is used to update the weights.

EXAMPLE APPLICATION—CLASSIFYING IRISES

The Ch09_IrisNetwork application demonstrates how a basic neural network can be implemented with a WebGPU compute shader. The application feeds iris measurements into a dense neural network that produces three values as output: the probability that the iris belongs to the setosa species, the probability that it belongs to the versicolor species, and the probability that it belongs to the virginica species. Figure 9.15 illustrates the network's structure.

As shown, the network has two hidden layers with four nodes each and an output layer with three nodes. Each of the eleven nodes receives five weighted inputs: four coming from inputs and nodes and one coming from the bias, denoted as +1. Therefore, the network has a total of 11 * 4 = 44 regular weights and 11 bias weights.

The activation function of the nodes in the hidden layers is ReLU, which means each hidden node will output the maximum of zero or the sum of its weighted inputs. The activation function of the nodes in the last layer is *softmax*, so the output nodes will produce probabilities corresponding to the iris's estimated classification.

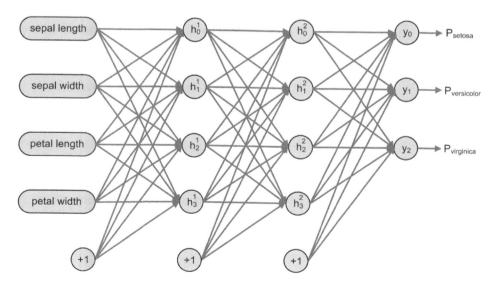

FIGURE 9.15   Neural network structure for iris classification.

TABLE 9.1 Storage buffers

BUFFER	DESCRIPTION
train_data	Contains iris characteristics used during training
train_results	Contains iris classifications used during training
weights	Weights applied to node-node connections
bias_weights	Weights applied to bias-node connections
test_data	Contains iris characteristics used during testing
test_results	Stores the neural network's classification outputs

The code in Ch09_IrisNetwork creates the neural network and provides it with data. This data is stored in six storage buffers. Table 9.1 lists and describes each of them.

After defining the storage buffers, the shader declares 12 overridden variables. Table 9.2 lists each of them and the values provided by the application.

After declaring these variables, the shader defines variables in workgroup memory. Table 9.3 lists each of these variables and describes its content.

To explain how the compute shader works, this discussion splits its operation into two parts: training and testing.

TABLE 9.2 Overridden variables in the training compute shader

VARIABLE	VALUE	DESCRIPTION
group_size	64	Number of invocations per group
batch_size	16	Number of training vectors processed per iteration
num_train_points	144	Number of training vectors (each vector contains sepal length, sepal width, petal length, and petal width)
num_test_points	6	Number of test vectors (each vector contains sepal length, sepal width, petal length, and petal width)
num_inputs	4	Number of inputs into the network's first layer (excluding bias)
l1_size	4	Number of nodes in the first layer
l2_size	4	Number of nodes in the second layer
l3_size	3	Number of nodes in the output layer
num_weights	44	Number of weights for node-node connections
num_bias	11	Number of weights for bias-node connections
num_epochs	150	Number of times the training process cycles through all the training vectors
eta	0.001	Learning rate used during optimization

TABLE 9.3 Workgroup variables

WORKGROUP VARIABLE	DESCRIPTION
layer1	Stores the output of each node in Layer 1
layer2	Stores the output of each node in Layer 2
layer3	Stores the output of each node in Layer 3
J	Stores the loss gradients for the network weights
J_bias	Stores the loss gradients for the bias weights

Training the Network

Most of the code in the compute shader is used to train the network, which involves updating the weights until the network produces acceptable output values. Training is a lengthy process that requires two execution loops. The outer loop executes once for each *epoch*. An epoch is a training procedure that uses each vector of the training data. The compute shader executes 150 epochs, so it cycles through all the training data 150 times.

The inner loop iterates nine times for each epoch. This is because the training data consists of 144 vectors and the compute shader accesses 16 vectors in parallel. Therefore, it needs to execute 144/16 = 9 iterations per epoch.

Processing layers with mini-batches

The compute shader divides training vectors into 16 mini-batches during the training process. Each mini-batch has four invocations, and each invocation uses its global ID to compute a batch_id that runs from 0 to 15 and a node_id that runs from 0 to 3. The invocation uses its batch_id to read training data and uses its node_id to determine which nodes of the network it's responsible for processing.

The following code shows how the network's nodes are processed by the shader's invocations. Because the network has three layers, the code is split into three parts.

```
// First layer
sum = 0.0;
for (i = 0; i < num_inputs; i++) {
    sum += train_data[train_id + i] * weights[weight_addr +
i];
}
sum += bias_weights[bias_addr];
layer1[l1_id + node_id] = max(0.0, sum);
weight_addr += l1_size * num_inputs;
bias_addr += num_inputs;
workgroupBarrier();
```

```
// Second layer
sum = 0.0;
for (i = 0; i < l1_size; i++) {
    sum += layer1[l1_id + i] * weights[weight_addr + i];
}
sum += bias_weights[bias_addr];
layer2[l2_id + node_id] = max(0.0, sum);
weight_addr += l2_size * l1_size;
bias_addr += l2_size;
workgroupBarrier();

// Third layer
if(node_id < l3_size) {
    sum = 0.0;
    for (i = 0; i < l2_size; i++) {
        sum += layer2[l2_id + i] * weights[weight_addr + i];
    }
    sum += bias_weights[bias_addr];
    layer3[l3_id + node_id] = sum;
}
workgroupBarrier();
```

When the shader starts, each invocation reads a vector containing four measurements from the `train_data` buffer. Then, during the Layer 1 processing, it multiplies each input by a weight from the `weights` buffer. Then it adds the weighted inputs together and adds the bias weight. If the sum is greater than zero, the sum will be stored in workgroup memory. Otherwise, zero will be stored in workgroup memory.

The processing for Layer 2 and Layer 3 are similar. In each case, an invocation performs a node's processing based on its `node_id`. It reads inputs from the preceding layer, multiplies them by weights, and adds the bias weight.

After each stage, the shader executes `workgroupBarrier`, which forces the invocations to halt until each invocation has finished accessing workgroup memory. This synchronization is a major priority because the computation of one layer needs to finish before the next layer can start.

Computing the loss gradient—Part 1

The nodes in Layer 3 use softmax for their activation function instead of ReLU, so these nodes don't compare the sum of their weighted inputs to zero. Instead, the compute shader executes the following code:

```
// Compute the softmax outputs
d = exp(layer3[l3_id]) + exp(layer3[l3_id+1]) +
exp(layer3[l3_id+2]);
```

```
sm1 = exp(layer3[13_id])/d;
sm2 = exp(layer3[13_id+1])/d;
sm3 = exp(layer3[13_id+2])/d;

// Compute loss gradients for output nodes
var res = train_results[iter * batch_size + batch_id];
layer3[13_id]   = sm1 - res[0];
layer3[13_id+1] = sm2 - res[1];
layer3[13_id+2] = sm3 - res[2];
```

The first part of this code should look familiar because it obtains the softmax of the Layer 3 values. But the second part of the code may be confusing. It reads the correct classification values for the training vector in the `train_results` buffer. Then it subtracts each result from the corresponding softmax output.

To see why the compute shader does this, you need to understand how gradients are computed for cross-entropy loss. This is a complex subject, so I'll work through the theory step-by-step.

The neural network's output is a vector p_i containing three values:

- p_0 is the probability that the iris belongs to the setosa species
- p_1 is the probability that the iris belongs to the versicolor species
- p_2 is the probability that the iris belongs to the virginica species

If the correct probabilities are contained in the vector obs_i, the cross-entropy loss for a training sample is computed with the following equation:

$$J = -\sum_{i=0}^{2} obs_i \cdot \log(p_i)$$

To compute the gradient of this loss, the compute shader needs to find the derivative of the logarithm of cross-entropy loss. The derivative of $\log(x)$ is $1/x$, so the partial derivative can be obtained using the Chain Rule. If y_i is the sum of weighted inputs entering an output node, the derivative of the loss with respect to y_i is given as follows:

$$\frac{\partial J}{\partial y_j} = -\sum_{i=0}^{2} obs_i \cdot \frac{\partial}{\partial y_j} \log(p_i)$$

$$= -\sum_{i=0}^{2} obs_i \cdot \frac{\partial \log(p_i)}{\partial p_i} \frac{\partial p_i}{\partial y_j}$$

$$= -\sum_{i=0}^{2} obs_i \cdot \frac{1}{y_i} \frac{\partial p_i}{\partial y_j}$$

The probabilities p_i are computed using the softmax function, so to find the gradient of the loss, the first step is to compute the derivative of the softmax with respect to its input, y_i. We'll use the Quotient Rule, which states that the derivative of $f(x)/g(x) = [f'(x)g(x) - f(x)g'(x)]/g(x)^2$. The following expression shows how it's used with the softmax function.

$$\frac{\partial p_i}{\partial y_j} = \frac{\partial}{\partial y_j} \left\{ \frac{e^{y_i}}{\Sigma_k e^{y_k}} \right\}$$

$$= \frac{\left(\dfrac{\partial}{\partial y_j} e^{y_i}\right) \Sigma_k e^{y_k} - e^{y_i} \left(\dfrac{\partial}{\partial y_j} \Sigma_k e^{y_k}\right)}{\left(\Sigma_k e^{y_k}\right)^2}$$

The derivative of $\exp(y_j)$ with respect to y_j is $\exp(y_j)$, so the derivative of the summation is always $\exp(y_j)$. However, the derivative of $\exp(y_i)$ with respect to y_j depends on whether $i = j$. If $i = j$, the softmax derivative is given as follows:

$$\frac{\partial p_i}{\partial y_j} = \frac{e^{y_i} \Sigma_k e^{y_k} - e^{y_i} e^{y_j}}{\left(\Sigma_k e^{y_k}\right)^2}$$

$$= \frac{e^{y_i} \left(\Sigma_k e^{y_k} - e^{y_j}\right)}{\left(\Sigma_k e^{y_k}\right)^2}$$

$$= \frac{e^{y_i}}{\Sigma_k e^{y_k}} \left(\frac{\Sigma_k e^{y_k} - e^{y_j}}{\Sigma_k e^{y_k}}\right)$$

$$= p_i \left(1 - p_i\right)$$

If i doesn't equal j, the derivative of $\exp(y_i)$ with respect to y_j equals 0. In this case, the softmax derivative is computed in the following way:

$$\frac{\partial p_i}{\partial y_j} = \frac{0 - e^{y_i} e^{y_j}}{\left(\Sigma_k e^{y_k}\right)^2}$$

$$= \frac{-e^{y_i}}{\Sigma_k e^{y_k}} \frac{e^{y_j}}{\Sigma_k e^{y_k}}$$

$$= -p_i \cdot p_j$$

As shown, the derivative's value depends on whether $i = j$. To form a single expression that takes both conditions into account, we use the Kronecker delta, δ_{ij}, which is defined in the following way:

$$\delta_{ij} = \begin{cases} 0 \; if \; i \neq j \\ 1 \; if \; i = j \end{cases}$$

Using this value, we can tie together both expressions for the softmax derivative into a single equation:

$$\frac{\partial p_i}{\partial y_j} = p_i \left(\delta_{ij} - p_j \right)$$

Replacing this in the expression for the loss gradient, we obtain the following result:

$$\frac{\partial J}{\partial y_j} = -\sum_{i=0}^{2} obs_i \frac{1}{p_i} \frac{\partial p_i}{\partial y_j} = -\sum_{i=0}^{2} obs_i \frac{1}{p_i} \left[p_i \left(\delta_{ij} - p_j \right) \right]$$

$$= -\sum_{i=0}^{2} obs_i \left(\delta_{ij} - p_j \right)$$

$$= -obs_j \left(1 - p_j \right) + \sum_{i \neq j} obs_i p_j$$

$$= -obs_j + obs_j p_j + \sum_{i \neq j} obs_i p_j$$

$$= p_j \left(obs_j + \sum_{i \neq j} obs_i \right) - obs_j$$

$$= p_j - obs_j$$

The last line is obtained by setting the sum of obs_i to 1. This can be done because obs_i contains the known probabilities of the iris's species—one of the three values will always be 1 while the others are 0. This explains why the compute shader subtracts the correct values from the softmax outputs.

Computing the loss gradient—Part 2

Finding the derivative of cross-entropy loss with respect to y_j (the softmax input) is an important step, but to obtain the final loss gradient, the compute shader needs to go further. The goal is to obtain a vector containing the partial derivative of loss with respect to each weight w_i. Using the Chain Rule, we can form an expression for this with the following equation:

$$\frac{\partial J}{\partial w_i} = \frac{\partial J}{\partial y_j} \frac{\partial y_j}{\partial w_i}$$

Now the goal is to find the second term, which is the partial derivative of the softmax input (y_j) with respect to each weight (w_i). To see how this can be accomplished for the example network, consider the diagram shown in Figure 9.16.

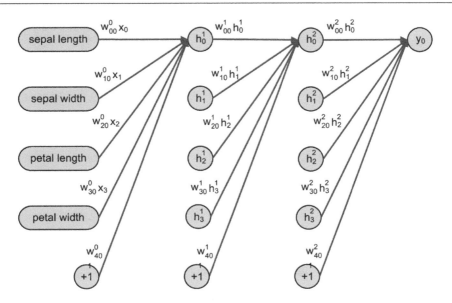

FIGURE 9.16   Relating softmax input to weights.

This diagram illustrates the inputs, signals, and weights that affect the top-most output node, y_0. As discussed earlier, each weight is denoted $w_{yz}{}^x$, and its indices can be interpreted in the following way:

- x identifies the layer containing the node producing the weighted signal
- y identifies the index of the node producing the signal to be weighted
- z identifies the index of the node receiving the signal

Suppose we want to know the partial derivative of y_0 with respect to $w^2{}_{00}$. This is simple to compute when you see the equation:

$$y_0 = w^2_{00}h^2_0 + w^2_{10}h^2_1 + w^2_{20}h^2_2 + w^2_{30}h^2_3 + w^2_{40}$$

$$\frac{\partial y_0}{\partial w^2_{00}} = h^2_0$$

As shown, the partial derivative of y_0 with respect to $w^2{}_{00}$ is just the signal multiplied by the weight ($h^2{}_0$ in this case). But what about the partial derivative of y_0 with respect to $w^1{}_{00}$?

The hidden nodes use ReLU as their activation function, so it's important to see how its derivative is obtained. If x is greater than 0, ReLU(x) returns x and its derivative is 1. If x is less than or equal to 0, ReLU returns 0 and its derivative is 0. This is shown in the following equation, which derives the partial derivative of y_0 with respect to w^1_{00}.

$$y_0 = w^2_{00} h^2_0 + w^2_{10} h^2_1 + w^2_{20} h^2_2 + w^2_{30} h^2_3 + w^2_{40}$$

$$\frac{\partial y_0}{\partial w^1_{00}} = \frac{\partial}{\partial w^1_{00}} \left[w^2_{00} h^2_0 + w^2_{10} h^2_1 + w^2_{20} h^2_2 + w^2_{30} h^2_3 + w^2_{40} \right]$$

$$= \frac{\partial}{\partial w^1_{00}} \left(w^2_{00} h^2_0 \right) = w^2_{00} \frac{\partial}{\partial w^1_{00}} h^2_0$$

$$w^2_{00} \frac{\partial}{\partial w^1_{00}} h^2_0 = w^2_{00} \frac{\partial}{\partial w^1_{00}} \left[\mathrm{Re\,LU} \left(w^1_{00} h^1_0 + w^1_{10} h^1_1 + w^1_{20} h^1_2 + w^1_{30} h^1_3 + w^1_{40} \right) \right]$$

$$\frac{\partial y_0}{\partial w^1_{00}} = \begin{cases} 0 \ \text{if } h^2_0 \leq 0 \\ w^2_{00} h^1_0 \ \text{if } h^2_0 > 0 \end{cases}$$

We can obtain further derivatives using a similar method. For example, the following equation presents the partial derivative of y_0 with respect to w^0_{00}.

$$\frac{\partial y_0}{\partial w^0_{00}} = \begin{cases} 0 \ \text{if } h^2_0 \leq 0 \ or \ h^1_0 \leq 0 \\ w^2_{00} w^1_{00} x_0 \ \text{if } h^2_0 > 0 \ and \ h^1_0 > 0 \end{cases}$$

Loss gradients are easier to compute for the weights nearest the output nodes. For this reason, the compute shader obtains loss gradients by executing a series of loops that proceed from Layer 3 to Layer 1. The loss gradients for the node-node weights are stored in the J variable in workgroup memory. The gradients for the bias-node weights are stored in the J_bias variable.

After computing the loss gradients, the compute shader updates the network's weights and biases with the following code:

```
// Update weights and biases
if (id.x == 0) {

    // Iterate through weights
    for (i = 0; i < num_weights; i++) {
        sum = 0.0;
        for (j = 0; j < batch_size; j++) {
            sum += J[j * num_weights + i];
        }
        weights[i] -= eta * sum;
    }
}
```

```
    // Iterate through biases
    for (i = 0; i < num_bias; i++) {
        sum = 0.0;
        for (j = 0; j < batch_size; j++) {
            sum += J_bias[j * num_bias + i];
        }
        bias_weights[i] -= eta * sum;
    }
}
storageBarrier();
```

The learning rate, eta, is set to 0.001, so the weights don't change significantly from one iteration to the next. But after enough training iterations, the shader sets the weights to values suitable for proper iris classification.

Testing the Network

After the last training iteration, the compute shader attempts to classify the irises whose characteristics are stored in the `test_data` buffer. For each input vector, the compute shader produces three values: the probability that the iris belongs to the setosa species, the probability that it belongs to the versicolor species, and the probability that it belongs to the virginica species.

To perform the test, the shader processes each node of the network. The following code shows how this is done:

```
// Iterate through test points
for (var test: u32 = 0; test < num_test_points; test++) {

    var test_addr = test * num_inputs;

    // First layer
    if (batch_id == 0) {
        sum = 0.0;
        for (i = 0; i < num_inputs; i++) {
            sum += test_data[test_addr + i] * weights[node_id
* num_inputs + i];
        }
        sum += bias_weights[node_id];
        layer1[node_id] = max(0.0, sum);
    }
    workgroupBarrier();
```

```
    // Second layer
    weight_addr = l1_size * num_inputs;
    bias_addr = l1_size;
    if (batch_id == 0) {
        sum = 0.0;
        for (i = 0; i < l1_size; i++) {
            sum += layer1[i] * weights[weight_addr + node_id
* l1_size + i];
        }
        sum += bias_weights[bias_addr + node_id];
        layer2[node_id] = max(0.0, sum);
    }
    workgroupBarrier();

    // Third layer
    weight_addr += l2_size * l1_size;
    bias_addr += l2_size;
    if((batch_id == 0) && (node_id < l3_size)) {
        sum = 0.0;
        for (i = 0; i < l2_size; i++) {
            sum += layer2[i] * weights[weight_addr + node_id
* l2_size + i];
        }
        sum += bias_weights[bias_addr + node_id];
        layer3[node_id] = sum;
    }
    workgroupBarrier();

    // Update test result buffer
    if(id.x == 0) {
        d = exp(layer3[0]) + exp(layer3[1]) + exp(layer3[2]);
        test_results[test * 3] = exp(layer3[0])/d;
        test_results[test * 3 + 1] = exp(layer3[1])/d;
        test_results[test * 3 + 2] = exp(layer3[2])/d;
    }
    storageBarrier();
}
```

As shown, the nodes in Layer 1 read the test input data, multiply the weights, and add the bias weight to the sum. The nodes in Layer 2 receive the weighted outputs of the Layer 1 nodes and the nodes in Layer 3 receive the weighted outputs of the Layer 2 nodes. The final probabilities are computed by taking the softmax of the Layer 3 values.

SUMMARY

The importance of machine learning in modern data processing can't be overstated, and its importance grows with each passing day. This chapter has shown how WebGPU makes it possible to harness this power in a web application. While iris classification may not seem impressive, the methodology presented in this chapter can be applied to other tasks.

Neural networks are the most popular implementation of machine learning. A neural network consists of nodes arranged in layers. Each node receives multiple weighted inputs, adds them together, and passes the sum into an activation function. As discussed in this chapter, the most popular activation functions are the ReLU, logistic, and softmax functions.

The main difficulty in working with neural networks involves updating the weights so that the nodes in the final layer produce suitable outputs. This is called *training*, and it's not easy to understand or code. But once a neural network has been fully trained, it can perform classification and prediction tasks that many will find astounding.

Image and Video Processing

10

In the last two chapters, compute shaders have operated on raw data in storage buffers. This is fine for crunching numbers, but compute shaders can also access special textures called *storage textures*. This makes it possible for compute shaders to process images at high speed.

This chapter begins by explaining what storage textures are, how they're created, and how they can be accessed in compute shaders. To demonstrate, I'll walk through the development of an application that performs image filtering in a compute shader.

The next part of the chapter focuses on video processing. I'll explain how to create video elements in HTML and how the WebCodecs API makes it possible to access video frames. Then I'll explain how to create textures from video frames and process them using WebGPU.

STORAGE TEXTURES

Chapter 6 introduced the topic of textures and demonstrated how they can be created and displayed. WebGPU supports several different texture formats, and fragment shaders read texel data from them using samplers.

At a low level, storage textures are exactly like regular textures. The fundamental difference is that shaders can write to storage textures. At the time of this writing, storage textures are write-only. The specification indicates support for read-write storage textures, but this isn't currently available in browsers.

From a coding perspective, storage textures are different than regular textures in three main ways:

- When calling `createTexture`, the usage flag must include `GPUTextureUsage.STORAGE_BINDING` to identify the texture as a storage texture.
- In the compute shader, the storage texture must be declared with a suitable storage texture type.
- In the compute shader, the storage texture can be written to by calling `textureStore`.

DOI: 10.1201/9781003422839-10

TABLE 10.1 Storage texture types

STORAGE TEXTURE TYPE	DESCRIPTION
texture_storage_1d	One-dimensional storage texture
texture_storage_2d	Two-dimensional storage texture
texture_storage_2d_array	Array of two-dimensional storage textures
texture_storage_3d	Three-dimensional storage texture

TABLE 10.2 Storage texture formats

rgba8unorm	rgba16float	rg32float
rgba8snorm	r32uint	rgba32uint
rgba8uint	r32sint	rgba32sint
rgba8sint	r32float	rgba32float
rgba16uint	rg32uint	bgra8unorm
rgba16sint	rg32sint	

For the second point, the general declaration of a storage texture is given as follows:

```
@group(…) @binding(…) var name: storage_type<format, access>;
```

The group and binding attributes were introduced in Chapter 4. The storage _ type portion can be replaced by one of the types listed in Table 10.1.

Storage textures don't support depth/stencil value access or multisampling. In addition, the format portion of the declaration can only be set to a limited number of texture formats. Table 10.2 lists the different formats supported for storage textures.

Each of these texture formats has one (r), two (rg), or four (rgba/bgra) color channels. Compression isn't supported for storage textures.

The last part of the declaration identifies how the texture will be accessed in the shader. According to the specification, this can be set to read, write, or read-write. At the time of this writing, every storage texture must have this value set to write.

To demonstrate, the following code declares a variable named tex that represents a two-dimensional write-only storage texture. Each texel contains four channels given as 8-bit unsigned normalized integers.

```
// Declare a storage texture
@binding(0) @group(0) var tex: texture_storage_2d<rgba8unorm,
write>
```

After the storage texture has been declared, a shader can write to it by calling textureStore. This accepts a texture variable, the location where the value should be written, and the value to be written. As an example, the following code writes a four-element vector to the location (3, 3).

```
// Write texture data
textureStore(tex, vec2u(3, 3), vec4f(1.0, 1.0, 1.0, 1.0));
```

It's worth noting that `textureStore` doesn't accept a sampler. Also, the second argument must be given as a vector of unsigned integers.

IMAGE FILTERING

Professional image editing tools, such as Adobe Photoshop and the GNU Image Manipulation Program (GIMP), make it possible to add effects to images like blurring, sharpening, and embossing. These effects are accomplished using image filters. This section explains how image filters work and how they can be implemented with WebGPU.

The fundamental operation is the two-dimensional dot product, which accepts two matrices and returns the sum of the products of their corresponding elements. For example, suppose A and B are two matrices given as follows:

$$A = \begin{vmatrix} a_{00} & a_{01} & a_{02} \\ a_{10} & a_{11} & a_{12} \\ a_{20} & a_{21} & a_{22} \end{vmatrix} \qquad B = \begin{vmatrix} b_{00} & b_{01} & b_{02} \\ b_{10} & b_{11} & b_{12} \\ b_{20} & b_{21} & b_{22} \end{vmatrix}$$

The two-dimensional dot product of A and B can be computed with the following equation:

$$A \cdot B = a_{00}b_{00} + a_{01}b_{01} + a_{02}b_{02} + a_{10}b_{10} + a_{11}b_{11} + a_{12}b_{12} + a_{20}b_{20} + a_{21}b_{21} + a_{22}b_{22}$$

Image filtering treats an image as a matrix of values, and computes a two-dimensional dot product for each of its pixels. In essence, the goal is to intensify or diminish the differences between adjacent pixels.

The second matrix is called the filter's *kernel*, and its elements determine what effect the filter will have. To demonstrate this, I'll show how image filtering can reduce the noise in the image illustrated in Figure 10.1.

You can think of noise as unwanted variation between nearby pixels. One way to reduce this variation is to replace each pixel with the average of it and its surrounding pixels. To express this mathematically, we'll denote the image as a matrix called M. Then Mij is the pixel at Row I and Column J. The color of the filtered pixel can be computed in the following way:

$$M_{ij, filtered} = \frac{1}{9} \left(\begin{array}{l} M_{i-1,j-1} + M_{i,j-1} + M_{i+1,j-1} + M_{i-1,j} + M_{i,j} \\ + M_{i+1,j} + M_{i-1,j+1} + M_{i,j+1} + M_{i+1,j+1} \end{array} \right)$$

FIGURE 10.1 Image before filtering. (Photo by 663highland, Provided under Creative Commons License 2.5.)

This operation can also be performed by taking the dot product of these nine image pixels with a kernel matrix, K_{box}, whose elements are given as follows:

$$K_{box} = \frac{\begin{vmatrix} 1 & 1 & 1 \\ 1 & 1 & 1 \\ 1 & 1 & 1 \end{vmatrix}}{9} \qquad M_{ij,filtered} = K_{box} \cdot M_{ij}$$

To fully filter an image, this dot product must be performed for each pixel. Once this is done, the filtered image will have the same size as the original. Because the elements of the kernel add to 1, the filtered result will also have the same average brightness. Figure 10.2 shows what the filtered image looks like.

This filter, called a *box filter* or *mean filter*, has removed much of the noise in the original image by averaging neighboring pixels. But it has also removed a significant amount of detail. The following discussion introduces the Gaussian blur, which does a better job.

Gaussian Blur

When it comes to removing noise, the Gaussian blur generally gives better results than the box filter. The term *Gaussian* refers to a special function that produces the commonly encountered bell curve. Figure 10.3 shows what the Gaussian function looks like in two dimensions.

FIGURE 10.2   Image filtered with box filter.

To implement Gaussian filtering in code, we need to approximate its values in a 3-by-3 matrix. One possible kernel is given as follows:

$$K_{gaussian} = \frac{\begin{vmatrix} 1 & 2 & 1 \\ 2 & 4 & 2 \\ 1 & 2 & 1 \end{vmatrix}}{16}$$

Filtering with this kernel produces a blurring effect like that of the box filter, but it gives priority to the central pixel and the immediately adjacent pixels. This means

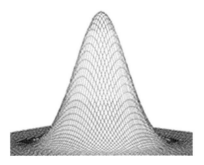

FIGURE 10.3   Two-dimensional Gaussian function.

FIGURE 10.4   Effect of Gaussian blur.

that the filtered image keeps more of the differences between one pixel and the next. Figure 10.4 shows what the result looks like.

The Gaussian blur serves as a compromise between the noisy image and the deep blurring produced by the box filter. The kernel used in this filter is only one possible implementation of the Gaussian blur.

Image Sharpening

Just as the box filter and Gaussian blur reduce differences between pixels, a sharpening filter emphasizes differences. It accomplishes this by subtracting nearby pixels from the central pixel. An example kernel is shown here:

$$K_{sharpen} = \begin{vmatrix} -1 & -1 & -1 \\ -1 & 9 & -1 \\ -1 & -1 & -1 \end{vmatrix}$$

If the central pixel has the same value as those around it, the filtered pixel will be equal to that of the original. But if the central pixel is much greater than its neighbors, the filtered value will be large. This is shown in Figure 10.5, which displays an image before and after sharpening.

A sharpening filter magnifies noise along with other details. The following discussion explains how this filter can be implemented using WebGPU.

FIGURE 10.5   Effect of image sharpening.

EXAMPLE APPLICATION—IMAGE SHARPENING

The Ch10_SharpenImage application demonstrates how compute shaders can use storage textures for image filtering. It filters an input image using a sharpening kernel and then displays the result in the page. Its operation can be split into three main steps:

1. The application creates a texture from an image file and an empty storage texture.
2. The compute shader reads texels from the texture and writes grayscale values to the storage texture.
3. The vertex and fragment shaders display the content of the storage texture as though it was a regular texture.

The last point is important to understand. At a low level, storage textures are identical to regular textures. The only difference is that storage textures are specially configured so that shaders can modify their content.

Creating Textures

The code in ch10_sharpenimage.js starts by creating the fundamental objects needed for WebGPU operation (adapter, device, encoder, and so on). Then it creates two textures.

The first texture serves as the input for the compute shader and holds the content of the smiley.png image. The following code shows how it's created.

```
// Create ImageBitmap from image file
const response = await fetch("tower.png");
const imageBitmap = await createImageBitmap(await
response.blob());

// Create texture to hold input image
const imageTexture = device.createTexture({
    size: [imageBitmap.width, imageBitmap.height, 1],
    format: "rgba8unorm",
    usage:
        GPUTextureUsage.TEXTURE_BINDING |
        GPUTextureUsage.COPY_DST |
        GPUTextureUsage.RENDER_ATTACHMENT
});

// Write data to input texture
device.queue.copyExternalImageToTexture(
    { source: imageBitmap },
    { texture: imageTexture },
    [imageBitmap.width, imageBitmap.height]
);
```

This code is similar to that of the ch06_simpletexture code presented in Chapter 6. The texture has the rgba8unorm format, which means each texel stores red, green, blue, and alpha components as 8-bit unsigned normalized integers. The usage property includes RENDER_ATTACHMENT, which means it can be displayed in a rendering application. usage doesn't include GPUTextureUsage.STORAGE_BINDING, so its content is read-only.

Some WebGPU implementations don't support read-write textures, so the application needs to create a second texture to hold the filtered texels. This texture will be written to, so it needs to be created as a *storage texture*. The following code shows how this works:

```
// Create texture to hold storage image
const storageTexture = device.createTexture({
    size: [imageBitmap.width, imageBitmap.height],
    format: "rgba8unorm",
    usage:
        GPUTextureUsage.TEXTURE_BINDING |
        GPUTextureUsage.COPY_DST |
        GPUTextureUsage.STORAGE_BINDING
});
```

The output texture will have the same size as the input texture, so the dimensions are set to `imageBitmap.width` and `imageBitmap.height`. The `STORAGE_BINDING` flag indicates that it will serve as a storage texture, which means shaders can access it as a variable with the `texture_storage_2d` type.

Create the Compute Pipeline

After creating the textures, the application creates three more objects: the shader module for the compute shader, the compute pass encoder, and the compute pipeline. The following code creates these objects and forms the association between them:

```
// Create the shader module
const computeModule = device.createShaderModule({
    label: "Shader module 0",
    code: computeCode
});

// Create the compute pass encoder
const computePass = encoder.beginComputePass({
    label: "Compute Pass 0"
});

// Define the compute procedure
const computePipeline = device.createComputePipeline({
    label: "Compute Pipeline 0",
    layout: "auto",
    compute: {
        module: computeModule,
        entryPoint: "computeMain",
        constants: {
            group_size_x: 16,
            group_size_y: 16
        }
    }
});
computePass.setPipeline(computePipeline);
```

This code creates the `computeModule` from the content of the `computeCode` string. Then the shader module is used to initialize the compute pipeline. In addition to setting the shader module and entry point, `createComputePipeline` provides two constants (`image_width` and `image_height`), which can be accessed by the compute shader as overridden variables. The last line of this code associates the pipeline with the compute pass encoder.

Next, the application defines the data for the compute operation by creating a bind group that contains the two textures. The following code shows how this is accomplished:

```
// Create the bind group
let computeBindGroup = device.createBindGroup({
    layout: computeBindGroupLayout,
    entries: [
    {
        binding: 0,
        resource: imageTexture.createView({
            dimension: "2d",
        })
    },
    {
        binding: 1,
        resource: storageTexture.createView({
            dimension: "2d",
        })
    }]
});
computePass.setBindGroup(0, computeBindGroup);
```

After the bind group is created, the last line associates it with the compute pass encoder and binds it to the value 0. As a result, shaders can access its resources by setting the @group attribute to 0 and the @binding attribute to the resource's binding value.

After associating the compute pass encoder with its instructions (compute pipeline) and data (bind group), the application encodes the computation commands with the following code:

```
// Encode compute commands
computePass.dispatchWorkgroups(40, 40);

// Complete encoding compute commands
computePass.end();
```

The argument of dispatchWorkgroups tells the compute shader to process the data using a 40-by-40 grid of work groups. Each work group contains a 16-by-16 grid of invocations, so there are a total of 640-by-640 invocations. As a result, each invocation can process one pixel of the input image using its global ID.

The Compute Shader

The compute shader is quite simple. Each invocation calls textureLoad to load a texel from the input image. Then it converts the RGB values to grayscale and calls textureStore to write the grayscale to the texture storage.

```
@group(0) @binding(0) var in_tex : texture_2d<f32>;
@group(0) @binding(1) var out_tex :
texture_storage_2d<rgba8unorm, write>;

override group_size_x: u32;
override group_size_y: u32;

@compute @workgroup_size(group_size_x, group_size_y)
fn computeMain(
    @builtin(global_invocation_id) global_id: vec3<u32>) {

    var x = global_id.x;
    var y = global_id.y;
    var k = array<f32, 9>(-1.0, -1.0, -1.0, -1.0, 9.0, -1.0,
-1.0, -1.0, -1.0);

    // Load the texel at the given position
    var texel: vec4f =
        k[0] * textureLoad(in_tex, vec2(x-1, y-1), 0) +
        k[1] * textureLoad(in_tex, vec2(x,   y-1), 0) +
        k[2] * textureLoad(in_tex, vec2(x+1, y-1), 0) +
        k[3] * textureLoad(in_tex, vec2(x-1, y),   0) +
        k[4] * textureLoad(in_tex, vec2(x,   y),   0) +
        k[5] * textureLoad(in_tex, vec2(x+1, y),   0) +
        k[6] * textureLoad(in_tex, vec2(x-1, y+1), 0) +
        k[7] * textureLoad(in_tex, vec2(x,   y+1), 0) +
        k[8] * textureLoad(in_tex, vec2(x+1, y+1), 0);

    // Store result to the storage texture
    textureStore(out_tex, vec2(x, y), texel);
}
```

In this code, k contains the elements of the image-sharpening kernel. Each invocation multiplies the elements of k by the 3-by-3 block of texels located by its global ID. Then the sum is written to the output texture using the textureStore method.

While fragment shaders read texels using `textureSample`, this compute shader reads texel data using `textureLoad`. Unlike `textureSample`, `textureLoad` requires integer coordinates and doesn't use a sampler. Another important difference between the two functions is that compute shaders can't call `textureSample`.

Displaying the Texture

After the compute shader completes, the application creates a render pipeline to display the storage texture in the canvas. This code resembles that from Chapter 6, but there's one interesting point: the vertex/fragment shaders access the texture as a `texture_2d` instead of `texture_storage_2d`. This clarifies the point that there's no fundamental difference between storage textures and regular textures.

VIDEO PROCESSING

One of the most fascinating capabilities of WebGPU is its ability to read frames of a video source and process them as textures. This makes it possible to perform the same operations on video as those performed on regular images. The general process of processing video with WebGPU consists of four steps:

1. Create, configure, and play an `HTMLVideoElement`.
2. Create a `VideoFrame` for each frame.
3. Create a texture from each `VideoFrame`.
4. Process the texture in a shader.

This section explores these steps and shows how they can be performed in code. A later section presents an application that processes frames received from a *.webm file.

Video Elements

HTML5 makes it possible to insert `<video>` elements in web pages. In JavaScript, these elements are accessed as `HTMLVideoElements`, and applications can create them by calling `document.createElement` with the argument set to `video`. `HTMLVideoElement` plays a central role in this discussion, so it's a good idea to be familiar with its inheritance hierarchy. This is illustrated in Figure 10.6.

`HTMLVideoElement` and `HTMLAudioElement` (to be discussed in Chapter 12) both inherit from `HTMLMediaElement`, which provides most of the properties and methods we'll need to configure video for WebGPU processing. After an application creates one of these objects, it can configure its behavior through its properties. Table 10.3 lists seven important properties of an `HTMLVideoElement` and its ancestors.

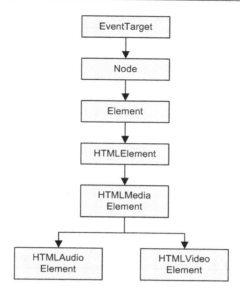

FIGURE 10.6 HTMLVideoElement inheritance hierarchy.

Most of these properties are straightforward to understand. The following code creates an HTMLVideoElement and sets its source to a file named example.webm.

```
// Create video element
const video = document.createElement("video");

// Set source to URL string in local directory
video.src = "example.webm"
```

Google's WebM format (*.webm) is one of the three main video formats supported for HTMLVideoElements. The others are MP4 (*.mp4) and Ogg video (*.ogv). At the time of this writing, *.ogv files aren't supported by Safari browsers.

TABLE 10.3 Important properties of HTMLVideoElement and ancestors

PROPERTY	TYPE	DESCRIPTION
loop	boolean	Indicates if playback should resume after the end
autoplay	boolean	Indicates if playback should begin as soon as enough content is available
muted	boolean	Indicates if audio is muted
defaultPlaybackRate	double	Playback speed (relative to 1.0)
disableRemotePlayback	boolean	Enables/disables remote playback
src	URL	Location of the media to be played
volume	double	The volume of the playback (0.0 to 1.0)

TABLE 10.4   Methods of `HTMLVideoElement`

METHOD	DESCRIPTION
`canPlayType(type)`	Identifies if the given MIME type can be played
`captureStream()`	Returns a MediaStream for the element's content
`load()`	Resets the media to its start position
`fastSeek(time)`	Seeks to the given time position in the media
`pause()`	Pauses playback of the media
`play()`	Plays the media from the current position
`setSinkId(id)`	Identifies the device to be used for audio playback
`requestVideoFrameCallback(callback)`	Identifies a callback to be invoked when a new frame is available

After an application creates an `HTMLVideoElement` and sets its source, it can call its methods. Table 10.4 lists eight of the methods available.

When HTML5 was first released, developers couldn't respond to every video frame. Instead, applications called the `requestAnimationFrame` method with a callback function. As a result, the callback would be invoked with every refresh of the browser (usually about 60 times a second).

Today, browsers support `requestVideoFrameCallback`. Like `request AnimationFrame`, this accepts a callback function. But unlike `request AnimationFrame`, it invokes the callback depending on the *video's* frame rate, not the *display's* refresh rate. To be precise, it uses the lesser of the frame rate and the refresh rate to determine when the callback is invoked. In other words, `request VideoFrameCallback` will never outpace the browser.

For example, if a video provides 30 frames per second and the browser refreshes 60 times a second, `requestVideoFrameCallback` will invoke the callback 30 times a second. However, if the video's frame rate is 100 frames per second, `requestVideoFrameCallback` will invoke the callback 60 times a second because the browser's refresh rate is lower.

The following code shows how this works. If the browser supports `request VideoFrameCallback`, the application calls `requestVideoFrameCallback` to configure a callback to be invoked when new frames are received. If this isn't supported, the application will call `requestAnimationFrame`.

```
// Set foo to be called when a new frame is available
if ("requestVideoFrameCallback" in HTMLVideoElement.prototype) {
    video.requestVideoFrameCallback(foo);
} else {
    requestAnimationFrame(foo);
}
```

By default, the callback will only be invoked once. Therefore, if an application needs to access a series of frames, the callback should call `requestVideoFrameCallback` or `requestAnimationFrame` when it's done processing.

Obtaining a Video Frame

The new WebCodecs specification provides a standard set of mechanisms for encoding/decoding video and audio. It provides several useful interfaces, including `VideoFrame`, which obtains a video frame from an `HTMLVideoElement`.

An example will demonstrate how `VideoFrame` works. If `video` is an `HTMLVideoElement`, the following code will retrieve a `VideoFrame` corresponding to the current frame.

```
// Access frame of HTMLVideoElement
let frame = new VideoFrame(video);
```

After obtaining a `VideoFrame`, an application can obtain information about its content through its properties. Table 10.5 lists these properties, which are all read-only.

By accessing the `format` and `colorspace` properties, an application can determine how different types of video should be processed. The following code performs additional processing if the frame's format is Planar YUV 4:2:2 (I422):

```
// Access frame of HTMLVideoElement
let frame = new VideoFrame(video);

// Check the frame's format
if(frame.format == "I422") {
    ...
}
```

TABLE 10.5 `VideoFrame` properties

PROPERTY	TYPE	DESCRIPTION
format	string	Format of the video's pixels (I420, I420A, I422, I444, NV12, RGBA, RGBX, BGRA, or BGRX)
codedWidth	integer	Width of the video frame in pixels
codedHeight	integer	Height of the video frame in pixels
codedRect	DOMRectReadOnly	Rectangle containing the frame's width and height
visibleRect	DOMRectReadOnly	Rectangle containing visible dimensions
displayWidth	integer	Width after aspect ratio adjustment
displayHeight	integer	Height after aspect ratio adjustment
duration	integer	Time length of the video in microseconds
timestamp	integer	Timestamp of the video in microseconds
colorspace	VideoColorSpace	Properties of the video's color space

TABLE 10.6   VideoFrame methods

METHOD	DESCRIPTION
allocationSize()	Returns the number of bytes needed to store the video frame's data
clone()	Returns a new VideoFrame containing the same data as the original
close()	Releases the reference to the media source
copyTo(destination)	Copies the frame's content to an ArrayBuffer, TypedArray, or DataView

In addition to checking the frame's properties, applications can call the VideoFrame's methods to obtain information and access the frame's data. Table 10.6 lists these methods and provides a description of each.

The copyTo method is particularly interesting. In general, video frames must be converted to a format like RGBA or BGRA before processing. But if the video is in a different format and the color conversion takes too much time, copyTo enables an application to process the frame's raw data.

Creating a Texture

Once the VideoFrame is available, an application can create a texture from it by calling the device's importExternalTexture method with an object that describes the texture. Table 10.7 lists the properties of this object.

Interestingly, importExternalTexture returns a GPUExternalTexture instead of a GPUTexture. This doesn't provide any methods and its only property is label. For this reason, applications usually call importExternalTexture inside a bind group definition. The following code shows how this is done:

```
// Access frame of HTMLVideoElement
let frame = new VideoFrame(video);

// Create bind group containing texture
const bindGroup = device.createBindGroup({
    layout: ...,
    entries: [
        ...
        {
            binding: ...,

            // Create texture from video frame
            resource: device.importExternalTexture({
                source: frame,
            }),
        }
    ]
});
```

TABLE 10.7   Properties of the `importExternalTexture` argument

PROPERTY	REQUIRED?	DESCRIPTION
label	N	Identifier for the new texture
source	Y	The `VideoFrame` or `HTMLVideoElement` that provides the source content
colorSpace	N	Color space of the new texture (`srgb` or `display-p3`)

As a result of this code, a shader can access the texture as a regular `texture_2d` variable. Then it can process it as needed.

A new bind group needs to be created for each new frame. Because the bind group changes from frame to frame, the render pass encoder also needs to be re-created for each frame. The following section shows how this works in a practical application.

EXAMPLE APPLICATION—VIDEO CONVERSION

The Ch10_VideoProc application demonstrates how WebGPU can access video frames, process them in a shader, and display the frames in a canvas. It converts color video to grayscale, and its operation can be divided into four steps:

1. Create video element and play video.
2. Set callback function for video frames.
3. Create a texture for each frame.
4. Perform grayscale conversion in the fragment shader.

In the last step, the fragment shader reads the content of each pixel and returns the grayscale value.

The Video Element

The application starts by creating a video element, configuring its properties, and playing the video. This is shown in the following code:

```
// Create video element
const video = document.createElement("video");

// Configure video
video.loop = true;
video.autoplay = true;
video.muted = true;
video.src = "example.webm";
```

```
// Play video
await video.play();
```

The application calls play, but this doesn't display the video's content in the web page. This is because the video element doesn't exist in the page. But it produces frames like a regular video, and because the loop property is set to true, it produces frames indefinitely.

The Callback Function

The application needs to respond when the HTMLVideoElement produces new frames. Many browsers support the element's requestVideoFrameCallback method, but some don't. If this method isn't supported, the application should call requestAnimationFrame, which responds when the browser refreshes.

The Ch10_VideoProc application checks for requestVideoFrameCallback support and calls it if it's available. The following code shows how this is done:

```
// Set callback for the next frame
if ("requestVideoFrameCallback" in HTMLVideoElement.prototype)
{
    video.requestVideoFrameCallback(newframe);
} else {
    requestAnimationFrame(newframe);
}
```

The requestVideoFrameCallback and requestAnimationFrame methods both accept the name of the function to be called when the corresponding event occurs. In this code, the callback function is newframe.

Creating the Texture

When the callback function executes, it accesses the HTMLVideoElement and converts its current frame into a VideoFrame. This is done with the following code:

```
// Access new frame
const videoFrame = new VideoFrame(video);
```

Next, the callback function creates the bind group that provides the frame to the GPU as a texture. This is accomplished by calling the device.importExternal Texture method, as shown in the following code:

```
// Create the bind group
let bindGroup = device.createBindGroup({
    layout: bindGroupLayout,
    entries: [
    {
        binding: 0,
        resource: sampler
    },
    {
        binding: 1,
        resource: device.importExternalTexture({
            source: videoFrame,
        })
    }]
});
```

After creating the bind group, the application creates a command encoder and a render pass encoder. It associates the render pass encoder with the bind group, the vertex buffer, and the render pipeline. Then it calls the draw method to encode the rendering operation.

After submitting the commands to the GPU, the callback function closes the VideoFrame. Then it calls requestVideoFrameCallback or requestAnimationFrame to reset the callback function.

Processing the Texture

Each rendering operation creates a rectangular region in which to draw the texture. The fragment shader sets the color of each shader using the following code:

```
@group(0) @binding(0) var sam : sampler;
@group(0) @binding(1) var tex : texture_external;

@vertex
fn vertexMain(@location(0) coords: vec2f, @location(1)
uvCoords: vec2f) -> DataStruct {
    var outData: DataStruct;
    outData.pos = vec4f(coords, 0.0, 1.0);
    outData.uvPos = uvCoords;
    return outData;
}

@fragment
fn fragmentMain(fragData: DataStruct) -> @location(0) vec4f {
```

```
    // Read clamped texel value
    var texel = textureSampleBaseClampToEdge(tex, sam,
fragData.uvPos);

    // Convert to grayscale
    var gray = 0.299 * texel.r + 0.587 * texel.g + 0.114 *
texel.b;

    // Return grayscale texel
    return vec4f(gray, gray, gray, 1.0);
}
```

It's important to see that the texture's data type is `texture_external`. This can only be used if the texture was created with the `device.importExternalTexture` method.

The fragment shader computes the `gray` value by weighting the red, green, and blue components of the current fragment. Then it returns a vector in which the red, green, and blue components are all set to `gray`.

SUMMARY

WebGPU is known primarily for graphical rendering, but it's also capable of processing images and video at high speed. WebGPU images are represented by textures, and the only type of texture that can be modified in a shader is a *storage texture*. The first application discussed in this chapter showed how a compute shader can read from one texture, perform filtering, and write to another texture.

An application needs to perform two steps to obtain textures from video. The first step is to create a `VideoFrame` object for each frame and the second step is to call `device.importExternalTexture` for each `VideoFrame`. Once the texture is added to a bind group, a shader can access it as a variable of the `texture_external` type. The second application in this chapter demonstrated how these steps can be performed.

Matrix
Operations

11

Chapter 4 presented the matrix data types and functions provided by the WebGPU Shading Language (WGSL). These matrix functions can be called in all types of shaders, but they only operate on matrices whose dimensions equal 2, 3, or 4. To process larger matrices, you'll need to code your own functions. The goal of this chapter is to show how this can be done.

The first part of this chapter focuses on two particularly common matrix operations: matrix transposition and matrix multiplication. The remainder of the chapter discusses matrix decomposition. If a matrix is large and complex, mathematicians can factorize it into matrices that are easier to analyze, and then perform operations on the two factors. This is conceptually similar to factoring an integer into its divisors or factoring a polynomial into its roots.

To be specific, the chapter focuses on a popular method of matrix factorization called QR decomposition. The last part of this chapter explains the theory behind QR decomposition and shows how it can be implemented with WebGPU.

MATRIX TRANSPOSITION

Taking the transpose of a matrix is one of the simplest operations in linear algebra. This section presents a brief overview of matrices, including the notation for rows and columns, and then shows how large matrices can be transposed using a compute shader.

Overview of Matrices

Graphically, a matrix is represented as a grid of numbers inside vertical bars. Figure 11.1 depicts a typical matrix, and the notation used for its rows and columns.

In code, matrices are frequently represented by two-dimensional arrays. The two dimensions identify the number of rows and the number of columns in the matrix. If a matrix has m rows and n columns, it's referred to as an m-by-n matrix. If the number of rows equals the number of columns, it's a *square matrix*.

The numbers that make up a matrix are called *elements*, and each element is identified by its row and column. In Figure 11.1, the element c_{ij} belongs to the ith row and the

DOI: 10.1201/9781003422839-11

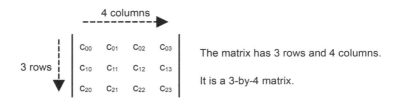

FIGURE 11.1 Notation for matrix rows and columns.

jth column. If i equals j, then the element lies on an imaginary line called the matrix's *diagonal*, which runs from the upper-left to the lower-right.

Computing the Transpose

The process of transposing a matrix is simple: reflect each element across the diagonal so that each element c_{ij} becomes c_{ji}. After a transpose, rows become columns and columns become rows. This is shown in Figure 11.2, in which Column 2 of the matrix becomes Row 2. In text, we use ^{T} to denote a transposed matrix. That is, C^T is the transpose of the matrix C.

The Ch11_Transpose application demonstrates how in-place transposition can be performed. It splits the matrix into 4-by-4 blocks and then assigns each invocation a block on or above the diagonal.

Figure 11.3 shows what this looks like for a 32-by-32 matrix, which has been divided into an 8-by-8 grid of blocks. Each invocation is assigned a block on or above the diagonal. Because there are 8 blocks per row and column, the total number of required invocations is $8(8 + 1)/2 = 36$.

Each invocation has two `mat4x4f` variables named `src_mat` and `dst_mat`. While executing the compute shader, an invocation performs eight steps:

1. It determines the row and column of its assigned block.
2. It reads values from its block into the `src_mat` matrix.
3. It calls the WGSL's `transpose` function to take the transpose of `src_mat`.

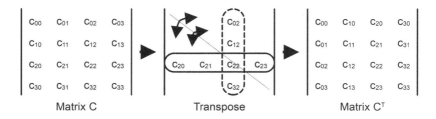

FIGURE 11.2 Matrix transposition.

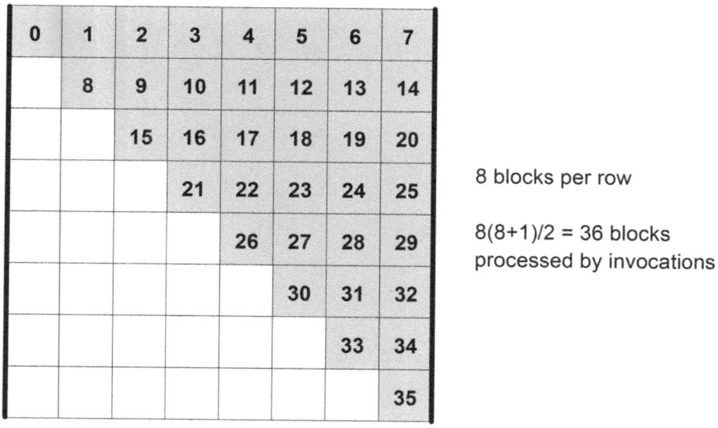

0	1	2	3	4	5	6	7
	8	9	10	11	12	13	14
		15	16	17	18	19	20
			21	22	23	24	25
				26	27	28	29
					30	31	32
						33	34
							35

8 blocks per row

8(8+1)/2 = 36 blocks
processed by invocations

FIGURE 11.3   Invocations and the transpose function.

4. If it's on the diagonal, the invocation stores `src_mat` in the original block's location. Then its processing is complete.
5. If it's not on the diagonal, the invocation reads values from the opposite block into the `dst_mat` matrix.
6. It calls WGSL's `transpose` function to take the transpose of `dst_mat`.
7. It stores `dst_mat` in the location of the original block.
8. It stores `src_mat` in the location of the opposite block.

The following code presents the compute shader that performs these steps. Keep in mind that an invocation's processing depends on whether its block is located on the diagonal or not.

```
override block_dim: u32;
override group_size: u32;

@binding(0) @group(0) var<storage, read_write> matrix :
array<vec4f>;

@compute @workgroup_size(group_size)
fn computeMain(@builtin(global_invocation_id) gid : vec3<u32>)
{

    /* Matrix variables */
    var src_mat: mat4x4f;
    var dst_mat: mat4x4f;
```

```
/* Determine the row and column of the block */
var tmp = block_dim;
var col = gid.x;
var row = u32(0);
while (col >= tmp) {
    col -= tmp;
    tmp--;
    row++;
}
col += row;

/* Read source block into source matrix */
src_mat = mat4x4f(
    matrix[4 * row * block_dim + col],
    matrix[(4 * row + 1) * block_dim + col],
    matrix[(4 * row + 2) * block_dim + col],
    matrix[(4 * row + 3) * block_dim + col]);

/* Take the transpose of source matrix */
src_mat = transpose(src_mat);

/* Block on matrix diagonal */
if (row == col) {
    matrix[4 * row * block_dim + col] = src_mat[0];
    matrix[(4 * row + 1) * block_dim + col] = src_mat[1];
    matrix[(4 * row + 2) * block_dim + col] = src_mat[2];
    matrix[(4 * row + 3) * block_dim + col] = src_mat[3];
}
/* Block off matrix diagonal */
else {

    /* Read destination block into destination matrix */
    dst_mat = mat4x4f(
        matrix[4 * col * block_dim + row],
        matrix[(4 * col + 1) * block_dim + row],
        matrix[(4 * col + 2) * block_dim + row],
        matrix[(4 * col + 3) * block_dim + row]);

    /* Take the transpose of source matrix */
    dst_mat = transpose(dst_mat);

    /* Write transposed destination matrix to source
block */
    matrix[4 * row * block_dim + col] = dst_mat[0];
    matrix[(4 * row + 1) * block_dim + col] = dst_mat[1];
    matrix[(4 * row + 2) * block_dim + col] = dst_mat[2];
    matrix[(4 * row + 3) * block_dim + col] = dst_mat[3];
```

```
          /* Write transposed source matrix to destination
block */
          matrix[4 * col * block_dim + row] = src_mat[0];
          matrix[(4 * col + 1) * block_dim + row] = src_mat[1];
          matrix[(4 * col + 2) * block_dim + row] = src_mat[2];
          matrix[(4 * col + 3) * block_dim + row] = src_mat[3];
    }
}
```

After the computation is finished, the application copies the matrix data into a mappable buffer and reads its data. Then it checks to see if the matrix transposition was performed properly and prints the result in the web page.

MATRIX MULTIPLICATION

Matrix multiplication is a time-intensive operation, so it's a popular metric for measuring computational performance. If a supercomputer needs to perform linear algebra at a large scale, it's likely that a great deal of its time is spent multiplying matrices.

Chapter 4 explained the fundamentals of matrix-matrix multiplication. As a quick review, suppose we want to multiply matrices A and B to obtain C. Each element of C, c_{ij}, is obtained by taking the dot product of the ith row of A and the jth row of B.

Many algorithms have been devised to multiply matrices, and the Strassen algorithm is particularly impressive. But the code in the Ch11_MatrixMult project takes a simpler approach. It computes A * B by taking the transpose of B and finding the dot products of the rows of A and the rows of B^T. This requires executing two compute shaders: one to obtain the transpose of B and one to multiply the rows of A and the rows of B.

Figure 11.4 shows what this look like. Because B is transposed, the elements in A and B can both be accessed row by row.

The Ch11_MatrixMult application multiplies two 16-by-16 matrices (A and B) and stores the result in C. To accomplish this, it launches two compute shaders: one that transposes B and one that multiplies the A and B matrices together. The code for the

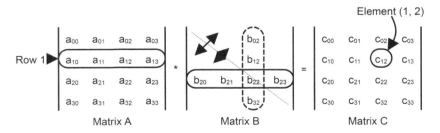

FIGURE 11.4   Matrix multiplication after transposition.

transpose is the same as the code presented earlier. The code for the compute shader that performs multiplication is given as follows:

```
override vectors_per_row: u32;
override group_size_x: u32;
override group_size_y: u32;

@binding(0) @group(0) var<storage, read_write> aMat :
array<vec4f>;
@binding(1) @group(0) var<storage, read_write> bMat :
array<vec4f>;
@binding(2) @group(0) var<storage, read_write> cMat :
array<f32>;

@compute @workgroup_size(group_size_x, group_size_y)
fn computeMain(@builtin(global_invocation_id) gid : vec3<u32>)
{

    var sum = 0.0;
    let a_row = gid.x * vectors_per_row;
    let b_row = gid.y * vectors_per_row;

    // Multiply row of A by row of B^T
    for (var i: u32 = 0; i < vectors_per_row; i++) {
        sum += dot(aMat[a_row + i], bMat[b_row + i]);
    }

    // Store the result to C
    cMat[a_row * 4 + gid.y] = sum;
}
```

Each invocation is responsible for setting a value in the C matrix. To compute this value, it reads vectors from the A and B matrices and adds their dot products together. Once all the dot products have been computed, the invocation stores the sum in the C matrix at the location given by its global ID.

While matrix multiplication is an important part of many matrix operations, this chapter is particularly concerned with matrix factorization using QR decomposition. The factorization methodology discussed in this chapter relies on the Householder transformation, which will be discussed next.

THE HOUSEHOLDER TRANSFORMATION

Most discussions of vector math include addition, subtraction, and multiplication, but *vector reflection* is also important in many applications. The concept is simple: given an input vector and a vector perpendicular to a surface, find the reflection of the input vector across the surface.

The procedure for computing this is called the *Householder transformation*, and this section shows how it can be implemented in WebGPU. But first, it's important to be familiar with vector projection.

Vector Projection

A vector projection is the portion of one vector that points in the same direction as a second vector. In Figure 11.5, vector b is split into two components: a component called p, which points in the same direction as a, and q, which points in a direction orthogonal to a. It should be clear that b = p + q.

In this diagram, p is the vector projection of b on a. If θ is the angle between a and b and lbl is the length of b, the length of p equals lbl cos θ. The direction of p is given by a's unit vector. This is obtained by dividing a by its length, denoted as lal. The following equation shows the result:

$$p = |b| \cos(\theta) \frac{a}{|a|}$$

This would be easy to compute it weren't for the cosine. Thankfully, a relationship exists between the cosine of the angle between two vectors and their dot product. The proof is lengthy, but the result is given as follows:

$$\cos(\theta) = \frac{a \cdot b}{|a||b|}$$

By placing this into the previous equation, we can arrive at a better equation for computing p:

$$p = |b| \frac{a \cdot b}{|a||b|} \frac{a}{|a|} = \frac{a \cdot b}{|a|} \frac{a}{|a|} = \frac{a \cdot b}{|a|^2} a$$

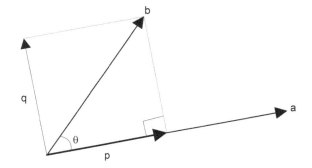

FIGURE 11.5   Vector projection.

In general, the vector projection of vector b on a vector a is expressed with the term $proj_a$ b. $proj_a$ b has the same direction as a, and b – $proj_a$ b is orthogonal to a.

Vector Reflection

Many algorithms in linear algebra require vector reflection, and the reason for this will become clear shortly. Figure 11.6 illustrates a simple example. We start with two vectors: x and u. u is perpendicular to M (which stands for mirror). The goal is to find x′, the vector obtained by reflecting x in M. In this two-dimensional case, M is simply a line. But it's a plane in three dimensions and a hyperplane in four or more dimensions.

To find x′ in terms of x and u, we need to take vector projections. Figure 11.7 shows how this works. x is split into p and q, where p is the vector projection of x on u and q is orthogonal to p. Similarly, x′ is split into p′ and q′, where p′ is the vector projection of x′ on u and q′ is orthogonal to p′.

This figure clarifies the relationships between p and p′ and q and q′. Because x′ equals the sum of p′ and q′, we can compute it in the following manner:

$$x' = p' + q' = \left(-proj_u x\right) + \left(x - proj_u x\right)$$

$$x' = x - 2\, proj_u x$$

$$x' = x - 2u \frac{u \cdot x}{|u|^2}$$

This final equation gives us a clear relationship between x′, x, and u. This equation helps us compute the QR decomposition of a matrix, but before we discuss the decomposition algorithm, I need to introduce the outer product and show how it can be used to form Householder matrices.

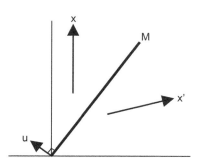

FIGURE 11.6 Vector reflection.

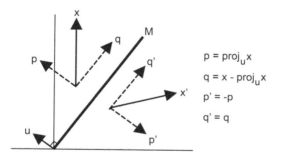

$p = \mathrm{proj}_u x$

$q = x - \mathrm{proj}_u x$

$p' = -p$

$q' = q$

FIGURE 11.7 Vector reflection in terms of vector projection.

Outer Products and Householder Matrices

A vector can be thought of as a matrix with a single row or a single column. Mathematicians commonly treat vectors as matrices with a single column, and such vectors are called *column vectors*. In contrast, transposed column vectors are considered matrices with a single row, or *row vectors*.

With this matrix interpretation of vectors, we can arrive at a new interpretation of the dot product. Instead of multiplying vectors, the dot product can be thought of as multiplying a 1-by-n matrix and an n-by-1 matrix. The result is a 1-by-1 matrix, or a scalar. With this interpretation, we can refer to the dot product using matrix terminology: $a^T b$ instead of $a \cdot b$. The following equation makes this clearer:

$$a \cdot b = a^T b = \begin{vmatrix} a_0 & a_1 & a_2 & a_3 \end{vmatrix} \begin{vmatrix} b_0 \\ b_1 \\ b_2 \\ b_3 \end{vmatrix} = a_0 b_0 + a_1 b_1 + a_2 b_2 + a_3 b_3$$

Using this notation, we can arrive at a new type of product called the *outer product*. Instead of multiplying a row vector by a column vector, this product reverses the operation and computes ab^T instead of $a^T b$. Despite the similar appearance, the outer product is significantly different from the dot product. The dot product multiplies a 1-by-n matrix by an n-by-1 matrix and produces a 1-by-1 matrix. The outer product multiplies an n-by-1 matrix by a 1-by-n matrix and produces an n-by-n matrix. This is shown in the following equation:

$$ab^T = \begin{vmatrix} a_0 \\ a_1 \\ a_2 \\ a_3 \end{vmatrix} \begin{vmatrix} b_0 & b_1 & b_2 & b_3 \end{vmatrix} = \begin{vmatrix} a_0 b_0 & a_0 b_1 & a_0 b_2 & a_0 b_3 \\ a_1 b_0 & a_1 b_1 & a_1 b_2 & a_1 b_3 \\ a_2 b_0 & a_2 b_1 & a_2 b_2 & a_2 b_3 \\ a_3 b_0 & a_3 b_1 & a_3 b_2 & a_3 b_3 \end{vmatrix}$$

We can use this vector-as-matrix interpretation to manipulate the equation for vector reflection. If we replace u • x with $u^T x$, the new relationship will be given as follows:

$$x' = x - 2u\frac{u \cdot x}{|u|^2} = x - 2\frac{u\left(u^T x\right)}{|u|^2}$$

As mentioned earlier, matrix multiplication is associative, so A(BC) = (AB)C. We can use this relationship to change $u(u^T x)$ in the reflection equation to $(uu^T)x$. This provides the following relationship:

$$x' = x - 2\frac{u\left(u^T x\right)}{|u|^2} = x - 2\frac{\left(uu^T\right)x}{|u|^2} = x - 2\frac{uu^T}{|u|^2}x$$

Instead of finding x′ with a dot product, we now need to compute an outer product, which is more difficult. But there is a good reason to do this. If we factor the vector x out of the equation, we can arrive at the following relationship:

$$x' = \left(I - 2\frac{uu^T}{|u|^2}\right)x = Px$$

It should be clear that the term inside the parentheses is a matrix. This matrix is commonly denoted by P, and when P pre-multiplies a vector x, the result is the reflection of x through the hyper-plane perpendicular to u. This procedure was conceived by Alston Householder, so u is called the Householder vector and P is called the Householder matrix. The reflection operation represented by P is called the Householder transformation.

When a vector is reflected twice, the result will be the vector itself. That is, P(Px) = x for all x. P is its own inverse, and this property is called *involution*.

One more point about the Householder transformation needs to be addressed. The preceding discussion explained how to find x′ given x and u, but what if you start with x and x′ and want to find a vector with u's direction? The answer is simple: u = x − x′. Figure 11.8 presents this graphically, using the same x and x′ vectors from earlier figures.

This result may not be immediately obvious, but remember that x and x′ are symmetrical about M, and that u is perpendicular to M. The u vector in Figure 11.9 has a

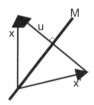

FIGURE 11.8 Finding the reflection vector.

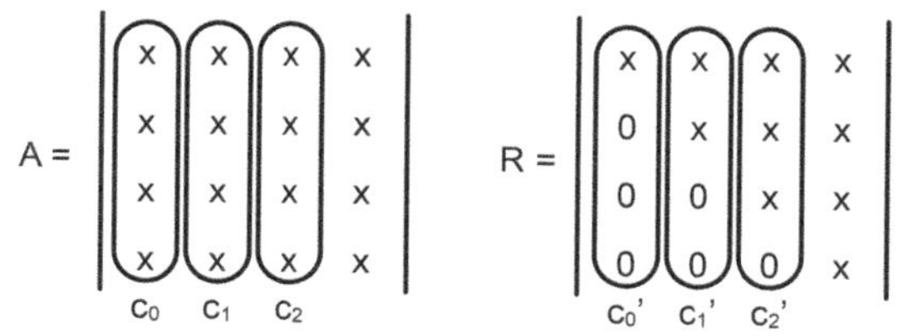

FIGURE 11.9   Finding the reflection vectors.

different length than the u vector in previous figures, but this isn't a concern—the only requirement we have for u is that its direction be perpendicular to M. Also, the length of u is divided out as part of the Householder transformation.

Vector Reflection in WebGPU

Implementing vector reflection in code is a straightforward process, consisting of three main steps:

1. Multiply u by -sqrt(2)/|u|
2. Compute the matrix uu^T
3. Add the identity matrix I to the result

The compute shader in the Ch11_Reflection project shows how this can be accomplished in WebGPU. The two input vectors are x_vec, which equals [1.0, 2.0, 3.0, 4.0], and u_vec, which equals [0.0, 5.0, 0.0, 0.0]. Because u_vec is perpendicular to the x-z-w hyperplane, the reflection of x_vec can be determined by inspection: [1.0, -2.0, 3.0, 4.0].

```
@binding(0) @group(0) var<storage, read> x_vec : vec4f;
@binding(1) @group(0) var<storage, read_write> u_vec : vec4f;
@binding(2) @group(0) var<storage, read_write> x_prime_vec :
vec4f;

override group_size: u32;

@compute @workgroup_size(group_size)
fn computeMain() {

    var p_mat: array<vec4f, 4>;

    /* Multiply u by sqrt(2)/|u| */
    u_vec *= sqrt(2)/length(u_vec);
```

```
/* Compute Householder matrix */
p_mat[0] = vec4f(1.0, 0.0, 0.0, 0.0) - (u_vec * u_vec.x);
p_mat[1] = vec4f(0.0, 1.0, 0.0, 0.0) - (u_vec * u_vec.y);
p_mat[2] = vec4f(0.0, 0.0, 1.0, 0.0) - (u_vec * u_vec.z);
p_mat[3] = vec4f(0.0, 0.0, 0.0, 1.0) - (u_vec * u_vec.w);

/* Transform x to obtain x_prime */
x_prime_vec.x = dot(p_mat[0], x_vec);
x_prime_vec.y = dot(p_mat[1], x_vec);
x_prime_vec.z = dot(p_mat[2], x_vec);
x_prime_vec.w = dot(p_mat[3], x_vec);
}
```

If you're only interested in finding the reflection of a vector, you don't have to worry about the outer product and its matrix operations. It's easier to compute x′ with the following equation:

$$x' = x - 2u\frac{u \cdot x}{|u|^2}$$

However, many applications of the Householder transformation require finding both a vector's reflection and the Householder matrix corresponding to the reflection. One such application is the QR decomposition.

QR DECOMPOSITION

In linear algebra, a common task involves factoring a complex matrix into simpler matrices that are easier to analyze. This is helpful when solving linear systems, computing determinants, or obtaining eigenvalues. One popular method of factoring a matrix is called QR decomposition. This operates on a square matrix A and produces two matrices: an orthogonal matrix Q and an upper triangular matrix R. A matrix is upper triangular if every element below the main diagonal equals zero.

Before I explain how to compute Q, let's focus our attention on R. Figure 11.9 presents the goal: to transform the columns of A (c_0 through c_{k-1}) into columns of R (c_0' through c_{k-1}'), where k identifies the number of columns in A.

Computer scientists have come up with many ways to convert a square matrix like A into an upper triangular matrix like R. One of the most efficient methods relies on Householder transformations. This method computes the u_k vectors needed to transform the columns of A into columns of R. Once the Householder vectors are obtained, this method computes their corresponding Householder matrices and multiplies them together. This combined matrix is Q. The steps for finding Q and R can be given as follows:

1. Find u_0, the vector that reflects c_0 into c_0'.
2. Transform each column of A with the u_0 reflection.
3. Find u_1, the vector that reflects c_1 into c_1'.
4. Transform each column of A with the u_1 reflection.
5. Construct the Householder matrix P_k for each u_k vector.
6. Repeat steps 3–5 for columns up to $k-1$.
7. Multiply the Householder matrices to form Q.

The rest of this section elaborates on these steps, and we'll walk through a QR decomposition of a 4-by-4 matrix. Then we'll look at how to implement QR decomposition in WebGPU.

Finding the Householder Vectors and R

We've seen how to find a Householder vector u given a vector x and its reflection x'. We can use this method to determine the u_k vectors that transform the columns c_k in Figure 11.9 to their reflections c_k'. But first, we need to obtain the non-zero elements in each c_k'. This isn't difficult so long as you remember that, because x' is the reflection of x, both vectors must have the same length.

An example shows how this works. The matrix A has three rows and three columns. We want to find two Householder vectors, u_0 and u_1, such that, when used to reflect the first two columns of A, A will become upper triangular.

$$A = \begin{vmatrix} 13 & -17 & -10 \\ 4 & 18 & -32 \\ -16 & -8 & -24 \end{vmatrix}$$

We'll start with the left-most column vector, which we'll call c_0. We want the reflection, c_0', to have one non-zero element on top and two zero elements below. To make sure that c_0 and c_0' have the same length, we'll set the non-zero element of c_0' equal to the length of c_0. Then we can find u_0 by subtracting c_0' from c_0. This is given as follows:

$$c_0' = \begin{vmatrix} |c_0| \\ 0 \\ 0 \end{vmatrix} = \begin{vmatrix} 21 \\ 0 \\ 0 \end{vmatrix}$$

$$u_0 = c_0 - c_0' = \begin{vmatrix} 13 \\ 4 \\ -16 \end{vmatrix} - \begin{vmatrix} 21 \\ 0 \\ 0 \end{vmatrix} = \begin{vmatrix} -8 \\ 4 \\ -16 \end{vmatrix}$$

Now that we have u_0, we need to transform each column of A according to the reflection corresponding to u_0. We can perform these reflections using an equation presented earlier:

$$c'_k = c_k - 2u_0 \frac{u_0 \cdot c_k}{|u_0|^2}$$

This transformation gives us a new A matrix. As desired, the first column has two zeros beneath the non-zero element.

$$A = \begin{vmatrix} 21 & -1 & 6 \\ 0 & 10 & -40 \\ 0 & 24 & 8 \end{vmatrix}$$

Now we want to transform the second column, c_1, so that its bottom element equals zero. We can do this by setting the first element of the reflection, c'_1, equal to the first element of c_1. Then, to make sure $|c'_1| = |c_1|$, we need to set the second element of c'_1 equal to the length of the subvector containing the lower two elements of c_1.

$$c'_1 = \begin{vmatrix} -1 \\ \sqrt{10^2 + 24^2} \\ 0 \end{vmatrix} = \begin{vmatrix} -1 \\ 26 \\ 0 \end{vmatrix}$$

$$u_1 = c_1 - c'_1 = \begin{vmatrix} -1 \\ 10 \\ 24 \end{vmatrix} - \begin{vmatrix} -1 \\ 26 \\ 0 \end{vmatrix} = \begin{vmatrix} 0 \\ -16 \\ 24 \end{vmatrix}$$

Again, we need to transform each column of A according to the new reflection identified by u_1. This gives us the following matrix:

$$A = \begin{vmatrix} 21 & -1 & 6 \\ 0 & 26 & -8 \\ 0 & 0 & -40 \end{vmatrix} = R$$

It's important to note that transforming c_0 with the reflection corresponding to u_1 leaves c_0 unchanged. This is because the dot product of c_0 and u_1 is zero. When this dot product equals zero, the reflection produces the original vector. This means we don't have to transform columns that have already been transformed—once we compute a Householder vector u_k, we only have to find reflections for columns c_k and higher.

After this last set of reflections, A is upper triangular. This transformed version of A is the R matrix generated by the QR decomposition. Next, we'll see how to use the Householder vectors u_k to create the Q matrix.

Finding Householder Vectors and Q

Now that we've computed the Householder vectors u_k that transform A into R, we need to find the matrix Q that serves as the inverse of this transformation. That is, we want to find Q such that $Q^{-1}A = R$, or $A = QR$.

The previous section explained how to create a Householder matrix P from a Householder vector u. The relationship is given by:

$$P = I - 2\frac{uu^T}{|u|^2}$$

As discussed earlier, uu^T is an outer product that generates a square matrix. If u contains k elements, P has k rows and k columns.

In our example, we obtained R by transforming the column vectors of A with u_0's reflection first and u_1's reflection second. Therefore, R equals P_1P_0A. Because every Householder transformation is its own inverse, we can set Q equal to P_0P_1. The following equation shows how Q is computed for our example:

$$Q = P_0P_1 = \left(I - 2\frac{u_0u_0^T}{|u_0|^2}\right)\left(I - 2\frac{u_1u_1^T}{|u_1|^2}\right)$$

$$Q = \left(I - \frac{2}{336}\begin{vmatrix} 64 & -32 & 128 \\ -32 & 16 & -64 \\ 128 & -64 & 256 \end{vmatrix}\right)\left(I - \frac{2}{832}\begin{vmatrix} 0 & 0 & 0 \\ 0 & 256 & -384 \\ 0 & -384 & 576 \end{vmatrix}\right)$$

$$Q = \begin{vmatrix} 0.61905 & 0.19048 & -0.76190 \\ 0.19048 & 0.90476 & 0.38095 \\ -0.76190 & 0.38095 & -0.52381 \end{vmatrix} \cdot \begin{vmatrix} 1.0 & 0.0 & 0.0 \\ 0.0 & 0.38462 & 0.92308 \\ 0.0 & 0.92308 & -0.38462 \end{vmatrix}$$

$$Q = \begin{vmatrix} 0.61905 & -0.63004 & 0.46886 \\ 0.19048 & 0.69963 & 0.68864 \\ -0.76190 & -0.33700 & -0.55311 \end{vmatrix}$$

If you multiply this Q matrix by the R matrix computed earlier, the product will be the original A matrix. This is because $QR = (P_0P_1)(P_1P_0A) = A$.

EXAMPLE APPLICATION— MATRIX FACTORIZATION

The Ch11_Factorization project uses QR decomposition to factorize a 32-by-32 matrix. The application generates one invocation for each column of the matrix. All of the invocations belong to the same workgroup, so we can use `storageBarrier` and `workgroupBarrier` to synchronize their access to storage and workgroup memory.

The QR decomposition code is complicated, but the main difficulty isn't computing R. The main problem involves storing and multiplying the Householder matrices needed to form Q. For large matrices, we can't store each P_k separately. Instead, we need to initialize the Q matrix and update it as each new P_k is obtained.

For this reason, the discussion of the QR decomposition code is divided into two parts. In the first part, we'll look at how to transform the first column of A and use it to initialize Q. In the second part, we'll examine how to transform the second through kth columns of A and update Q with each new Householder matrix.

Transforming the First Column and Initializing Q

The compute shader in the Ch11_QR project computes the first Householder vector, u_0, needed to transform the first column into a column of an upper triangular matrix. Then it creates the Householder matrix, P_0, from u_0 and sets it equal to Q. The following code shows how this works:

```
@binding(0) @group(0) var<storage, read_write> a_mat :
array<f32>;
@binding(1) @group(0) var<storage, read_write> q_mat :
array<f32>;
@binding(2) @group(0) var<storage, read_write> r_mat :
array<f32>;
@binding(3) @group(0) var<storage, read_write> check_mat :
array<f32>;

override num_cols: u32;

var<workgroup> u_vec: array<f32, num_cols>;
var<workgroup> dot: f32;
var<workgroup> u_length_squared: f32;

@compute @workgroup_size(num_cols)
fn computeMain(@builtin(global_invocation_id) gid : vec3<u32>)
{

    /* Variable declarations */
    var vec_length = 0.0;
    var prod: f32;
    var i: u32;
    var j: u32;

    /* Load first column into workgroup memory */
    u_vec[gid.x] = a_mat[gid.x * num_cols];
    workgroupBarrier();
```

```
/* Find length of first column and u vector */
if (gid.x == 0) {
    for (i = 1; i < num_cols; i++) {
        vec_length += u_vec[i] * u_vec[i];
    }
    u_length_squared = vec_length;
    vec_length = sqrt(vec_length + u_vec[0] * u_vec[0]);
    a_mat[0] = vec_length;
    u_vec[0] -= vec_length;
    u_length_squared += u_vec[0] * u_vec[0];

}
else {
    a_mat[gid.x * num_cols] = 0.0;
}
storageBarrier();

/* Transform further columns of A */
for (i = 1; i < num_cols; i++) {
    dot = 0.0;
    if(gid.x == 0) {
        for (j = 0; j < num_cols; j++) {
            dot += a_mat[j * num_cols + i] * u_vec[j];
        }
    }
    workgroupBarrier();
    a_mat[gid.x * num_cols + i] -= 2 * u_vec[gid.x] *
dot/u_length_squared;
}

/* Update Q matrix */
for (i = 0; i < num_cols; i++) {
    q_mat[gid.x * num_cols + i] = -2 * u_vec[i] *
u_vec[gid.x]/u_length_squared;
}
q_mat[gid.x * num_cols + gid.x] += 1;
storageBarrier();
```

It's important to see how this code obtains and uses the first Householder vector, u_0. First, it loads the first column of A into workgroup memory. Then it computes the length of the vector and subtracts this length from the column's first element. This sets the workgroup memory vector equal to u_0, and once this is obtained, the shader uses it to transform each succeeding column of A using the following equation:

$$c_k' = c_k - 2u_0 \frac{u_0 \cdot c_k}{|u_0|^2}$$

After updating A, the kernel forms the Householder matrix P_0 from the Householder vector u_0 using the following equation:

$$P_0 = I - 2\frac{u_0 u_0^T}{|u_0|^2}$$

Once the kernel obtains P_0, it places its elements in the Q matrix. As the rest of the kernel executes, Q will multiply further Householder matrices to arrive at its final value.

Transforming Successive Columns and Updating Q

The next part of the compute shader in Ch11_QR loops through the remaining columns of A and computes the Householder vectors needed to transform A into an upper triangular matrix. As each Householder vector is computed, the kernel finds the corresponding Householder matrix, P_0, and uses this to update Q.

```
/* Loop through other columns */
for (var col: u32 = 1; col < num_cols-1; col++) {

    /* Load new column into memory */
    u_vec[gid.x] = a_mat[gid.x * num_cols + col];
    workgroupBarrier();

    /* Find length of A column and u vector */
    if(gid.x == col) {
        vec_length = 0.0;
        for (i = col + 1; i < num_cols; i++) {
            vec_length += u_vec[i] * u_vec[i];
        }
        u_length_squared = vec_length;
        vec_length = sqrt(vec_length + u_vec[col] *
u_vec[col]);
        u_vec[col] -= vec_length;
        u_length_squared += u_vec[col] * u_vec[col];
        a_mat[col * num_cols + col] = vec_length;
    }
    else if(gid.x > col) {
        a_mat[gid.x * num_cols + col] = 0.0;
    }
    storageBarrier();

    /* Transform further columns of A */
    for (i = col+1; i < num_cols; i++) {
        if(gid.x == 0) {
            dot = 0.0;
```

```
        for (j = 0; j < num_cols; j++) {
            dot += a_mat[j * num_cols + i] * u_vec[j];
        }
    }
    workgroupBarrier();

    if(gid.x >= col) {
        a_mat[gid.x * num_cols + i] -= 2 * u_vec[gid.x] *
dot/u_length_squared;
    }
    storageBarrier();
}

/* Update P matrix */
if (gid.x >= col) {
    for (i = col; i < num_cols; i++) {
        r_mat[gid.x * num_cols + i] = -2 * u_vec[i] *
u_vec[gid.x]/u_length_squared;
    }
    r_mat[gid.x * num_cols + gid.x] += 1;
}
storageBarrier();

/* Check operation by computing q_mat * r_mat */
for (i = col; i < num_cols; i++) {
    prod = 0.0;
    for (j = col; j < num_cols; j++) {
        prod += q_mat[gid.x * num_cols + j] * r_mat[j *
num_cols + i];
    }
    check_mat[gid.x * num_cols + i] = prod;
}
storageBarrier();

/* Place the content of check_mat in q_mat */
for (i = col; i < num_cols; i++) {
    q_mat[gid.x * num_cols + i] = check_mat[gid.x *
num_cols + i];
    }
    storageBarrier();
}
```

This code iterates through the columns of A and performs most of the same tasks as in the preceding code. The important difference is how Q is updated. In theory, Q is obtained with the following equation:

$$Q = P_0 P_1 P_2 \cdots P_{k-2} P_{k-1}$$

In practice, however, we can't store k–1 Householder matrices in computer memory. The compute shader creates three matrices (q_mat, p_mat, and prod_mat) and updates q_mat using three steps:

1. When the kernel computes a new u_k, it sets p_mat equal to the corresponding P_k matrix.
2. The kernel computes the product of q_mat and p_mat, and places the result in prod_mat.
3. The kernel moves the elements of prod_mat to q_mat, and prepares for another multiplication.

With so much data transferred to and from global memory, this procedure is not particularly fast. However, because there are only three matrices involved, this process is more memory-efficient than algorithms that require k–1 Householder matrices.

Once the kernel finishes the last transformation of the columns of A, the result will be the upper triangular matrix R. After the final multiplication of Householder matrices, the resulting transformation matrix will be Q. To test the decomposition, the host application multiplies Q and R and compares the result to the original values in A.

SUMMARY

Matrix operations require a lot of number crunching and data manipulation, but very little decision making. For this reason, these operations are ideal for implementation with WebGPU.

This chapter has proceeded from simple matrix operations to complex. Matrix transposition doesn't really perform any math, but simply rearranges a matrix's elements. The example code in this chapter demonstrates how the transpose can be performed efficiently by dividing the matrix into blocks and assigning each block to an invocation.

Matrix multiplication relies on the dot product of rows and columns. More specifically, each row of the first matrix multiplies each column of the second, and the result of each dot product is a scalar. If the first matrix has dimensions n-by-k and the second has dimensions k-by-p, the product will have dimensions n-by-p. Vectors can be thought of as matrices—a row vector has dimensions 1-by-n and a column vector has dimensions n-by-1.

The Householder transformation reflects a vector across a region perpendicular to another vector. This transformation can be performed using a dot product or an outer product. Dot products are easier to compute, but when you need to combine multiple reflections, you need to use the matrices associated with the outer products.

The QR decomposition relies on Householder transformations to reflect the columns of a matrix so that they become upper triangular. We can combine these transformations by multiplying Householder matrices to obtain the Q matrix. Once the input matrix has been transformed into upper triangular form, it becomes the R matrix. We can test the accuracy of the decomposition by checking whether A = QR.

Filtering Audio with the Fast Fourier Transform (FFT)

12

This chapter explains how to filter audio using compute shaders. To be specific, we'll look at two applications that both perform the same five operations:

1. Read audio content from a Waveform Audio File Format (WAV) file.
2. Use the Fourier Transform to obtain the frequencies of the audio content.
3. Filter the audio by removing high-frequency components.
4. Use the Inverse Fourier Transform to convert the frequencies back to a time signal.
5. Format the filtered time signal as WAV data that can be played in the browser.

Most of this chapter is concerned with Steps 2 and 4, which convert data between the time and frequency domains. This conversion requires complex mathematics, and the ultimate goal is to implement the Fast Fourier Transform (FFT) in a compute shader. But first, I'll explain how the Discrete Fourier Transform (DFT) works. The DFT is relatively simple to understand, and as we'll see, the FFT is just an accelerated algorithm of the DFT.

The FFT has many more applications than just audio processing. Cell phones, X-ray scanners, radar receivers, and biometric scanning systems all rely on the FFT to extract frequency information from time-varying signals.

Before I can discuss audio filtering, I need to explain how to read audio data from a file. Therefore, the first section of this chapter discusses the Web Audio API, whose objects and methods make it straightforward to extract audio from files.

THE WEB AUDIO API

Chapter 10 explained how JavaScript can process video by creating frames from `HTMLVideoElements`. Applications can also access `HTMLAudioElements` associated

DOI: 10.1201/9781003422839-12

with <audio> elements. An HTMLAudioElement provides methods for playing audio, but it doesn't provide access to the underlying audio data. If you want to filter the content of an audio file, obtaining an HTMLAudioElement won't be sufficient.

For this reason, the example code in this chapter relies on the Web Audio API, which makes it possible to access audio data at a low level. This API provides a wide range of capabilities, but for this chapter, we'll only use it to read audio samples from a file. This section explains how this can be accomplished and then shows how the data can be played in a web page.

Reading Audio Data from a File

The Web Audio API supports the same types of audio files supported by HTMLAudioElements. Opus files (*.opus) and Advanced Audio Coding (*.aac) files provide excellent performance with minimal loss. However, this chapter focuses on the Waveform Audio File Format (*.wav) due to its simplicity and universal support. If you look in the Ch12_DFT and Ch12_FFT projects, you'll find a file named noisy.wav that contains audio samples to be processed.

To read audio data in noisy.wav, three steps are needed:

1. Call fetch to read the content of noisy.wav into an ArrayBuffer.
2. Create an AudioContext and call its decodeAudioData method to convert the ArrayBuffer into an AudioBuffer.
3. Access the audio data through the properties of the AudioBuffer.

The two applications in this chapter, Ch12_DFT and Ch12_FFT, employ these steps to remove noise from the audio data in noisy.wav. The only difference between them is that the code in Ch12_DFT processes the data using the DFT and the code in Ch12_FFT processes the data using the FFT.

Obtaining the ArrayBuffer

As discussed in Chapter 6, fetch accepts a string and provides a Promise that resolves with a Response object. If noisy.wav is in the current directory, the following code will create a Response:

```
// Obtain the response for the URL
const resp = await fetch("noisy.wav");
```

This Response has an arrayBuffer method that provides a Promise that resolves with an ArrayBuffer containing the response body. The following code shows how this can be obtained:

```
// Obtain an ArrayBuffer from the response
const arrayBuff = await resp.arrayBuffer();
```

This `ArrayBuffer` contains the content of noisy.wav, but more steps are needed to access the audio data. To decode the `ArrayBuffer`'s data, the application needs to create an `AudioContext`.

AudioContext

An `AudioContext` is the primary object for managing and processing web audio. If the browser supports the Web Audio API, applications can create a context by accessing the window object. On Safari browsers, the object's name is `webkitAudioContext`. On other browsers, it's called `AudioContext`. Therefore, we can create a context with the following code:

```
// Create an audio context
const AudioContext =
    window.AudioContext || window.webkitAudioContext;
const ctx = new AudioContext(...);
```

The `AudioContext` constructor accepts an optional object that can be used to configure the context's audio processing. Table 12.1 lists the properties that can be set.

Digital audio data is a sequence of numbers that represent sound amplitude over time. We refer to these numbers as *samples*, and the first property, `sampleRate`, identifies how many samples are taken per second. If the sample rate is R, the time between samples is 1/R seconds. A higher sampling rate means greater sound quality, but more memory is needed for storage and more time is needed to transfer audio data.

Latency is the delay between the time when the application initiates audio playback and the time when audio starts playing. Lower latency means more responsive playback but greater power consumption. Applications can configure an application's latency by setting `latencyHint` to a double or one of the following values:

* `interactive`—selects the lowest possible latency that doesn't cause glitches (low latency—default)
* `balanced`—selects balance between latency and power consumption (medium latency)
* `playback`—minimizes power consumption (high latency)

TABLE 12.1 `AudioContext` creation properties (optional)

PROPERTY	TYPE	DESCRIPTION
sampleRate	double	Number of samples per second
latencyHint	double	Delay in audio playback
sinkId	integer	Identifies the device to play audio

An application can determine what media devices are present on the client's system by calling the enumerateDevice method of the MediaDevices object. This provides a Promise that resolves to an array of MediaDeviceInfo objects that identify the devices. An application can select a specific device by setting sinkId to the deviceId property of one of the MediaDeviceInfo objects. If this isn't set, the browser will choose a default device.

In this chapter, we'll configure the audio context to send low-latency audio to the default device. Most consumer audio, such as the content of a compact disc (CD), is sampled at 44,100 samples per second, so we'll set sampleRate to 44100.0. The following code demonstrates how this can be accomplished:

```
// Create context with a sample rate of 44,100 samples/sec
const AudioContext =
    window.AudioContext || window.webkitAudioContext;
const ctx = new AudioContext( { sampleRate: 44100.0 } );
```

AudioContext inherits from BaseAudioContext, which provides a particularly important method named decodeAudioData. This accepts the ArrayBuffer containing the audio file's data and returns a Promise that resolves to an AudioBuffer containing the audio data. It also accepts two optional functions: one to be invoked if decoding succeeds and one to be invoked if decoding fails.

To demonstrate, the following code calls decodeAudioData to access the audio data in the ArrayBuffer named arrayBuff. If the operation succeeds, the decodeSuccess function will be called.

```
// Process audio buffer
function decodeSuccess(buffer) {
...
}

// Obtain audio data
const audioBuff =
    await ctx.decodeAudioData(arrayBuff, decodeSuccess);
```

As shown, decodeSuccess receives an argument named buffer. This is an instance of AudioBuffer, which will be discussed next.

AudioBuffer

An AudioBuffer contains audio samples and provides information about the audio signal. It plays a central role in this chapter, so it's a good idea to be familiar with its properties and methods. Table 12.2 lists the properties of AudioBuffer and provides a description of each. All of them are read-only.

When dealing with audio, a *channel* refers to a stream directed to a specific output. If an audio file is intended to be played in stereo (two outputs), it will have two channels.

TABLE 12.2 AudioBuffer properties (read-only)

PROPERTY	TYPE	DESCRIPTION
numberOfChannels	integer	Number of audio streams in the buffer
duration	double	Total time needed to play the audio
length	integer	Number of samples
sampleRate	double	Rate at which audio data was recorded

If it's intended for surround sound, it will have six channels. To simplify analysis, the audio discussed in this chapter has a single channel.

It's important to understand the difference between *duration* and *length*. Duration identifies the time it takes to play the entire audio. This is given in seconds, and for noisy.wav, the duration property is 2.97. The length property identifies the number of samples in the data. For noisy.wav, this is 131,072, or 2^{17}.

The last property, sampleRate, returns the sample rate of the AudioContext. Our application created the AudioContext with the sample rate set to 44,100, so the buffer's sampleRate property will equal 44100.0. The audio duration can be computed by dividing the length by sample rate: 131,072/44,100, which is about 2.97 seconds.

The methods of AudioBuffer make it possible to access and transfer the buffer's audio data. Table 12.3 lists these methods and provides a description of each.

These methods are easy to understand. An application can read audio data from a buffer channel by calling copyFromChannel and write data to a channel by calling copyToChannel. In each case, the data is provided in a Float32Array whose values lie between –1.0 and 1.0.

Playing Audio Data

In the Ch12_DFT and Ch12_FFT projects, the web page has two buttons. The first button, labeled **Play Noisy Audio**, has an ID of noisy and plays the content of noisy.wav. The second button, labeled **Play Filtered Audio**, has an id of filtered and plays the audio data processed by the compute shader.

TABLE 12.3 AudioBuffer methods

METHOD	DESCRIPTION
copyFromChannel (...)	Copies sample data from a channel to a Float32Array
copyToChannel (...)	Copies sample data from a Float32Array to a channel
getChannelData (...)	Returns a Float32Array containing the channel's sample data

Writing code for the first button is easy. The application creates an `HTMLAudioElement` by calling the `Audio` constructor and then configures the button's event handling to play and pause the audio. The following code shows how this works:

```
// Play noisy audio
var noisyAudio = new Audio("noisy.wav");
const noisyButton = document.getElementById("noisy");
noisyButton.onclick = function() {
    if (noisyAudio.duration > 0 && !noisyAudio.paused) {
        noisyAudio.pause();
        noisyButton.innerHTML = "Play Noisy Audio";
    } else {
        noisyAudio.play();
        noisyButton.innerHTML = "Pause Noisy Audio";
    }
}
```

When the second button is pressed, it plays the audio data processed by the compute shader. The following code shows how this button is configured:

```
// Play filtered audio
var filteredAudio = new Audio();
const filteredButton = document.getElementById("filtered");
filteredButton.onclick = function() {
    if (filteredAudio.duration > 0 && !filteredAudio.paused) {
        filteredAudio.pause();
        filteredButton.innerHTML = "Play Filtered Audio";
    } else {
        filteredAudio.play();
        filteredButton.innerHTML = "Pause Filtered Audio";
    }
}
filteredButton.disabled = true;
```

Unlike the `noisyAudio` element, the `filteredAudio` element doesn't have a data source. To define the source, the application creates a URL representing a `Blob` that can be accessed as WAV audio. The Web Audio API doesn't provide any capabilities for this, so the application performs the steps manually:

1. Create an `ArrayBuffer` and a `DataView`.
2. Write audio data to the `DataView` in the WAV format.
3. Create a `Blob` from the `ArrayBuffer`.
4. Obtain a URL for the `Blob`.
5. Make the URL the source of the `HTMLAudioElement`.

Once the last step is performed, the application sets the disabled property of the second button to false, allowing users to play the processed audio. The following discussion explains how these steps are accomplished.

Defining the WAV data

For the simple audio in this chapter, WAV data consists of 44 bytes of metadata followed by audio samples. Each sample occupies two bytes, so if the audio consists of one channel containing N samples, the WAV data will occupy 44 + 2 * N bytes. The following code creates a suitable `ArrayBuffer` to hold the WAV data:

```
// Create an ArrayBuffer to hold WAV data
const len = 44 + 2 * N;
const buffer = new ArrayBuffer(len);
```

A `DataView` makes it easy to insert numbers into an `ArrayBuffer`. It provides several methods like `setUint16` and `setFloat32`, and they all accept three arguments: a byte offset, the value to be written, and whether the value should be written in little-endian format. The WAV format expects little-endian values, so the last argument will always be set to true.

For example, the following code creates a `DataView` for the `ArrayBuffer` and writes an unsigned 16-bit value at an offset of 64:

```
// Write an integer to the DataView at an offset of 64
view = new DataView(buffer);
view.setUint16(64, val, true);
```

The structure of WAV data is based on Microsoft's Resource Interchange File Format (RIFF). According to this format, data is provided in a series of *chunks* that begin with a chunk identifier and the chunk length. The WAV data discussed in this chapter has three chunks:

- RIFF chunk—identifies the overall file as a RIFF file.
- Format chunk—defines the format of the audio data.
- Data chunk—contains the audio data.

Table 12.4 lists the fields that define these chunks. After the last field, the WAV data needs to provide the audio samples as 2-byte integers.

The WAV data in this chapter consists of a single channel, so setting these fields is fairly simple. If the length of the file is given by `len`, the sample rate is given as `sampleRate`, and the number of samples is `numSamples`, the following code will set the initial WAV data:

```
// Define RIFF chunk
view.setUint32(0, 0x46464952, true);
view.setUint32(4, len - 8, true);
view.setUint32(8, 0x45564157, true);
```

```
// Define Format chunk
view.setUint32(12, 0x20746d66, true);
view.setUint32(16, 16, true);
view.setUint16(20, 1, true);
view.setUint16(22, 1, true);
view.setUint32(24, sampleRate, true);
view.setUint32(28, sampleRate * 2, true);
view.setUint16(32, 2, true);
view.setUint16(34, 16, true);

// Define Data chunk
view.setUint32(36, 0x61746164, true);
view.setUint32(40, numSamples * 2, true);
```

TABLE 12.4 WAV audio structure

FIELD	BYTE COUNT	DESCRIPTION
Chunk identifier	4	Start of the RIFF chunk (0x46464952)
Chunk length	4	Length of the file in bytes (minus 8)
WAV identifier	4	WAV identifier (0x45564157)
Chunk identifier	4	Start of Format chunk (0x20746d66)
Chunk length	4	Number of bytes in chunk (16)
Sample format	2	Format of audio samples (1 for PCM)
Number of channels	2	Number of audio channels (1)
Sample rate	4	Number of samples/second
Byte rate	4	Number of bytes/second
Block align	2	Number of bytes/sample across all channels
Bits per sample	2	Number of bits contained in each sample
Chunk identifier	4	Start of Data chunk (0x61746164)
Chunk length	4	Number of bytes in chunk

For this chapter, the audio samples need to be encoded using 16-bit Pulse Coded Modulation, or PCM. But as discussed earlier, the `AudioBuffer` samples are provided as 32-bit floating-point values between −1.0 and 1.0. The following code performs the conversion and adds the 16-bit values to the `DataView`:

```
// Add 16-bit PCM values to DataView
var offset = 44;
for (let i = 0; i < numSamples; i++) {
    samples[i] *= 32768;
    if(samples[i] > 32767) {
        samples[i] = 32767;
    }
```

```
    if (samples[i] < -32768) {
        samples[i] = -32768;
    }
    view.setUint16(offset, samples[i], true);
    offset += 2;
}
```

WAV files don't have footers or supplemental metadata. Once the audio samples are added to the `DataView`, the underlying `ArrayBuffer` can be accessed as a WAV container.

Setting the audio source

Before we can play the samples in the `ArrayBuffer`, we need to create a `Blob`. This can be accomplished by calling the `Blob` constructor, which accepts the `ArrayBuffer` and the data's MIME (Multipurpose Internet Mail Extensions) type. The following code shows how this works:

```
// Create a Blob containing WAV audio data
const audioBlob = new Blob([buffer], {type: "audio/wav"});
```

Next, we can create a URL for this `Blob` by calling the `createObjectURL` method of the `URL` object. This is demonstrated with the following code:

```
// Create a URL for the Blob
const audioURL = URL.createObjectURL(audioBlob);
```

Once this is done, the application can set the URL as the source of an `HTMLAudioElement`. In the Ch12_DFT and Ch12_FFT projects, this is accomplished with the following code:

```
// Set the audio to be played by the second button
filteredAudio.src = audioURL;
filteredButton.disabled = false;
```

Once this code executes, the web page will be able to play the filtered audio when the user clicks the second button.

OVERVIEW OF AUDIO PROCESSING

At this point, you should have a good understanding of how audio data can be accessed and played in a web page. In this section, we'll start looking at how the data can be filtered using compute shaders.

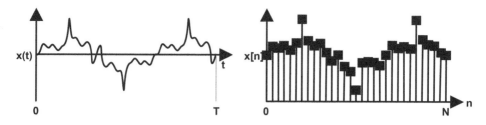

FIGURE 12.1   Time-domain signals: continuous and discrete.

As mentioned earlier, the duration of our audio signal, denoted as T, is 2.97 seconds long. If the audio had been recorded perfectly, we'd have an infinite number of sounds during those 2.97 seconds—one sound for each instant. We'll denote this infinite collection of sounds by x(t), where t denotes time in seconds from t = 0.0 to t = 2.97. For example, the exact sound at t = 1.546 seconds is given by x(1.546).

In the real world, there are no perfect recordings. Our audio was recorded at 44,100 samples per second, so the digital data contains (44,100 samples/second) * (2.97 seconds), which is approximately 131,072 samples. We'll call this sequence of samples x[n], where the square brackets imply a finite number of values. In this case, n identifies the *sample index* instead of the time. That is, x[463] denotes the sound corresponding to the 463rd sample. The time between samples, measured in seconds, is denoted as Δt.

Figure 12.1 illustrates the difference between ideally sampled x(t) and computer-sampled x[n]. The data contained in x(t) and x[n] are both related to time, so we'll call x(t) a time-domain *signal* and x[n] a time-domain *sequence*.

Returning to audio filtering, it should be clear that you can't remove the high-pitched noise by manipulating x[n] directly. If you change values of x[n], you'll diminish the song and noise equally. Similarly, if you amplify values of x[n], you'll increase both the song and the noise.

To understand how to remove noise from digital audio, you need to think of the content in terms of frequency. A signal's frequency tells you how often it changes, or *oscillates*, in a second. For example, the highest string of a bass guitar vibrates nearly 98 times a second, so its frequency is about 98 Hz.

In the real world, frequencies of most sounds are spread across a range. For example, the vocal chords of the average human male vibrate between 85 and 180 Hz while the vocal chords of the average human female vibrate between 165 and 255 Hz.

We'll use the word *component* to identify the strength of a signal at a particular frequency, and we'll denote this as X(f). If a signal oscillates twelve-and-a-half times a second, its frequency component at 12.5 Hz, X(12.5), will be greater than X(f) at any other frequency.

To clarify this, Figure 12.2 illustrates the frequency components of the audio content of noisy.wav. The high peaks at the beginning and end represent the music while the hill in the center represents the high-pitched noise. The goal of this chapter is to remove the noise without affecting the music.

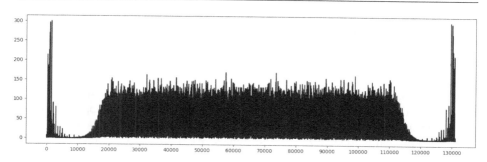

FIGURE 12.2   Frequency components of noisy.wav.

For those interested, the music in noisy.wav is taken from Paul Pitman's rendition of Beethoven's *Moonlight Sonata*, which is available at musopen.org through a Creative Commons 1.0 License (Thanks, Paul!). I added high-frequency noise using the open-source Audacity tool.

Because the audio content has a finite number of samples, we can only compute a finite number of frequency components. We'll use X[k] to identify the finite set of components, in contrast with the infinite set X(f). Here, k is an integer that identifies the kth frequency component, so X[26] returns the strength of the 26th frequency component. The frequency interval between samples, measured in Hertz, is denoted as Δf.

We can't remove noise from audio by changing x[n], but we can remove noise by changing X[k]. To do this, find the frequency components corresponding to the noise and either diminish them or set them to zero.

Two questions remain to be answered. First, how do we convert the x[n] sequence to the X[k] sequence? Second, once we've modified X[k], how do we convert it back to a form like x[n]? The answer to both questions involves the Fourier Transform. This converts time-domain data to frequency-domain data, and the inverse operation converts frequency-domain data to time-domain data. Therefore, removing the noise from a song requires three steps:

1. Use the Fourier Transform to convert x[n] to X[k].
2. Modify the frequency components of X[k].
3. Use the Inverse Fourier Transform to convert the modified X[k] to a new x[n].

This process doesn't just apply to music. This type of analysis, called *frequency analysis*, is also used to find patterns in images, detect radar signatures from aircraft, and extract communication data from wireless signals. The next section explores the mathematics behind the Fourier Transform and will show how to implement the algorithm in WebGPU.

Before proceeding further, I need to mention that professionals don't filter signals simply by removing or diminishing frequency components. Instead, engineers have devised several types of sophisticated filters, such as Butterworth and Bessel filters, that produce a more gradual noise-reduction effect. There is a great deal of literature on this topic, and I strongly recommend not using the code in this chapter for professional audio processing.

THE DISCRETE FOURIER TRANSFORM (DFT)

In 1822, the physicist Joseph Fourier published *The Analytic Theory of Heat*, which presented a method of decomposing complex mathematical relationships into a sum of trigonometric functions. Over the centuries, this method has been applied to many more applications than the analysis of heat, and though Fourier focused on continuous functions, our goal is to analyze discrete signals. We'll refer to these discrete signals as *sequences*, and the procedure that implements Fourier's method on sequences is the *Discrete Fourier Transform*.

The DFT and the FFT both accomplish the same operation. That is, they convert time-domain sequences, such as the one depicted on the right-hand side of Figure 12.1, into frequency-domain sequences, such as that shown in Figure 12.2. The FFT is faster but the DFT is easier to understand, so we'll start with the DFT. This section presents the mathematical theory behind the DFT, works through an example of its computation, and then shows how it can be implemented in WebGPU.

But before we proceed, let's review the notation presented in the previous section.

- x(t)—the input signal, contains infinite values, t identifies time in seconds.
- T—the period (or duration) of the input signal, measured in seconds.
- x[n]—the input sequence, contains N values, n identifies the sample index.
- Δt—the time interval between x[n] values, measured in seconds.
- X(f)—the frequency response, contains infinite values, f identifies frequency in Hertz.
- X[k] —the frequency sequence, contains N values, k identifies the frequency index.
- Δf—the frequency interval between X[k] values, measured in Hertz.

DFT Theory

As discussed in Chapter 4, the dot product multiplies components of two vectors and adds the products together. The result tells us how similar the two vectors are. A large dot product implies that the vectors point in similar directions and a negative dot product implies that the vectors point in opposite directions.

The dot product is the fundamental operation of the DFT. If you take the dot product of x[n] and a vector representing a given frequency, you'll see how similar x[n] is to that frequency. More precisely, the result will tell you how often x[n] *oscillates* at that frequency. We'll denote this second vector by $w_k[n]$, so the equation for X[k] is given as follows:

$$X[k] = x[n] \cdot w_k[n]$$

The DFT consists of N such dot products, and each produces a different value of X[k]. That is, the first dot product gives us X[0], the second gives us X[1], and so on.

Two questions arise. First, the DFT only computes components for N frequencies, so what frequencies should we be interested in? Second, how do we compute $w_k[n]$, the vector that represents a single frequency? Once we have answers to these questions, we'll be able to compute the series of dot products that make up the DFT. The following discussions will provide these answers.

Frequencies of interest

The goal of the DFT is to compute X[k] for a finite number of frequencies. It would be nice if we could select an arbitrary set of frequencies, but the DFT algorithm makes the selection for us. The values of the DFT frequencies depend on the signal's period, T, and the number of samples, N.

The first frequency of interest, called the *fundamental frequency* or f_1, has a value of 1/T. This represents a single oscillation over the course of the signal, so if a signal oscillates once during its period, f_1 will be significant. In the case of our song, $T = 2.97$ seconds, so the fundamental frequency equals $1/2.97 = 0.336$ Hz. This is below the human hearing range, but the DFT computes the frequency component at f_1 as $X[1] = x[n] • w_1[n]$.

Further frequencies of interest, f_k, can be obtained by multiplying the fundamental frequency by k. This is given mathematically by the following equation:

$$f_k = kf_1 = \frac{k}{T}$$

Just as f_k identifies the frequency corresponding to k oscillations in a period, f_0 identifies the frequency corresponding to no oscillations at all. This represents a frequency of 0 Hz. If a signal's value is constant over the course of its period, then it doesn't oscillate at all. In this case, X[0] will be significant and components at higher frequencies will equal 0.

For general signals, our highest frequency of interest is f_{N-1}, where N is the number of samples in x[n]. This gives us N frequencies of interest: f_0 through f_{N-1}. However, in some instances, we'll only need to compute components of frequencies up to $f_{N/2}$. The rationale for this will have to wait until after we examine the full DFT algorithm.

Single-frequency vectors

For each frequency component of x[n], the DFT computes the dot product of x[n] and a vector that represents a single frequency. The values in these single-frequency vectors are given as *sinusoids*—the complex sums of a cosine and sine. The values of continuous sinusoids depend on frequency and time, so we'll denote them by $w_f(t)$, where f is the frequency corresponding to the sinusoid. Mathematically, $w_f(t)$ is given as:

$$w_f(t) = \cos(2\pi ft) - i\sin(2\pi ft)$$

The i in this equation represents $\sqrt{-1}$. Because $w_f(t)$ is the sum of a number multiplied by i and a regular number, $w_f(t)$ is a *complex number*. Complex numbers tend to make people nervous, so let's briefly review the basic theory:

- Each complex number, z, has a real part, denoted as Re(z), and an imaginary part, denoted as Im(z). If $z = a + bi$, Re(z) = a and Im(z) = b.

- The conjugate of a complex number, denoted as z^*, can be obtained by negating the imaginary part. If $z = a + bi$, $z^* = a - bi$.
- The modulus or magnitude of a complex number, denoted as $|z|$, can be obtained by adding the squares of the real and imaginary parts. If $z = a + bi$, $|z| = \text{sqrt}(a^2 + b^2)$.
- Complex numbers can be added by adding the real parts and imaginary parts separately. If $z1 = a + bi$ and $z2 = c + di$, $z1 + z2 = (a + c) + (b + d)i$.
- Complex numbers can be multiplied in the following manner: if $z1 = a + bi$ and $z2 = c + di$, $z1 * z2 = (ac - bd) + (ad + bc)i$.

The real part of $w_f(t)$ is $\cos(2\pi ft)$ and the imaginary part is $-\sin(2\pi ft)$. Figure 12.3 depicts these terms graphically. Note that the graphs of the cosine and negative sine both oscillate once from $t = 0$ to $t = T$. Therefore, these graphs present $w_f(t)$ where $f = f_1$. If you set f equal to f_2, the graphs oscillate twice, and if you set f equal to f_k, the graphs oscillate k times during the course of the period.

This function is helpful when you perform a continuous Fourier transform, but the DFT requires that we select a finite number of values from $w_f(t)$. For this reason, we need to rework the expression for $w_f(t)$ so that it depends only on n and k. We know that our frequencies of interest, $f_k = k/T$, and we know that $n = \Delta t$. This gives us the following relationship:

$$w_f(t) = \cos\left(\frac{2\pi k(n\Delta t)}{T}\right) - i\sin\left(\frac{2\pi k(n\Delta t)}{T}\right)$$

One last step. We can relate the period of the signal, T, to the total number of samples, N, by noting that $T = N\Delta t$. Replacing this in the equation, we arrive at a final expression:

$$w_k[n] = \cos\left(\frac{2\pi nk}{N}\right) - i\sin\left(\frac{2\pi nk}{N}\right)$$

$$\cos(2\pi f_1 t) = \cos\left(\frac{2\pi t}{T}\right) \qquad\qquad -i\sin(2\pi f_1 t) = -i\sin\left(\frac{2\pi t}{T}\right)$$

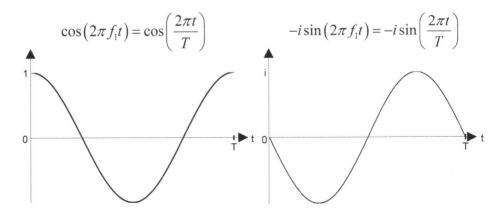

FIGURE 12.3 Continuous sinusoid at the fundamental frequency.

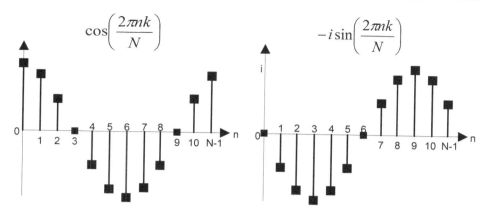

FIGURE 12.4 Discrete sinusoid at the fundamental frequency.

This gives us a vector with N values, and Figure 12.4 depicts $w_k[n]$ from $n = 0$ to N–1. As with Figure 12.3, this discrete sinusoid corresponds to the signal's fundamental frequency, given by $k = 1$.

Note that neither the cosine nor the sine returns to its starting value. Instead, they proceed from 0 to N–1. This is important to remember when computing these vectors in code. Now that we've arrived at the $w_k[n]$ vector, we can discuss the full DFT algorithm.

The DFT and IDFT equations

The DFT computes the X[k] vector by taking the dot product of x[n] and $w_k[n]$ as k runs from 0 to N–1. This is commonly expressed using the DFT equation:

$$X[k] = x[n] \cdot w_k[n] = \sum_{n=0}^{N-1} x[n] \left(\cos\left(\frac{2\pi nk}{N}\right) - i \sin\left(\frac{2\pi nk}{N}\right) \right)$$

The relationship between X[k] and x[n] can also be expressed using matrix-vector multiplication. That is, if we make $w_k[n]$ the rows of a matrix as k runs from 0 to N–1, the resulting matrix-vector product, $Wx = X$, can be expressed as follows:

$$\begin{vmatrix} w_0[0] & w_0[1] & w_0[2] & \cdots & w_0[N-1] \\ w_1[0] & w_1[1] & w_1[2] & \cdots & w_1[N-1] \\ w_2[0] & w_2[1] & w_2[2] & \cdots & w_2[N-1] \\ \vdots & \vdots & \vdots & & \vdots \\ w_{N-1}[0] & w_{N-1}[1] & w_{N-1}[2] & \cdots & w_{N-1}[N-1] \end{vmatrix} \begin{vmatrix} x[0] \\ x[1] \\ x[2] \\ \vdots \\ x[N-1] \end{vmatrix} = \begin{vmatrix} X[0] \\ X[1] \\ X[2] \\ \vdots \\ X[N-1] \end{vmatrix}$$

This matrix, denoted as W, is called the *DFT matrix*. If scaled properly, W is both unitary and symmetric, which means that its inverse, W^{-1}, equals its conjugate, W^*. We obtain the conjugate of a matrix by reversing the sign of every imaginary term. For the DFT, this means converting the negative imaginary sine in $w_k[n]$ into a positive imaginary sine.

This inverse matrix is important because it can be used to compute the inverse DFT, or IDFT. The IDFT transforms frequency-domain data to time-domain data, and can be expressed in matrix-vector form as $x = W^{-1}X$. The IDFT equation is given as follows:

$$x[n] = X[k] \cdot w_k^*[n] = \frac{1}{N}\sum_{k=0}^{N-1} X[k]\left(\cos\left(\frac{2\pi nk}{N}\right) - i\sin\left(\frac{2\pi nk}{N}\right)\right)$$

The $w_k^*[n]$ term identifies the conjugate of $w_k[n]$, in which $-i\sin(x)$ is replaced with $+i\sin(x)$. The only other difference between this and the DFT equation is the scaling factor $1/N$. This is necessary to ensure that, once $x[n]$ is transformed into $X[k]$, the inverse transformation will produce the original $x[n]$. Alternatively, both the DFT equation and IDFT equation can be scaled by $1/\sqrt{n}$.

EXAMPLE APPLICATION—FILTERING AUDIO WITH THE DFT

At this point, you should be moderately comfortable with the DFT and IDFT. This section explores the code in the Ch12_DFT application, which uses the DFT and IDFT to remove noise from audio. To be precise, the project performs five operations:

1. Read audio data from noisy.wav using the Web Audio API.
2. Use the DFT to convert the time-domain sequence $x[n]$ to the frequency-domain sequence $X[k]$.
3. Set the frequency components in the noise ranges to 0.
4. Use the IDFT to convert the modified frequency-domain sequence $X[k]$ to the time-domain sequence $x[n]$.
5. Play the filtered audio data when the user presses the button in the page.

The first section in this chapter explained how Steps 1 and 5 can be accomplished. This section focuses on Steps 2, 3, and 4.

Implementing the DFT and IDFT

The compute shader in the Ch12_DFT application performs the DFT or IDFT depending on a variable named `factor`. The compute shader is defined in the string named `dftShader`, and its code is given as follows:

```
// Real part of time-domain sequence
@binding(0) @group(0) var<storage, read_write> xn_real :
array<vec4f>;

// Imaginary part of time-domain sequence
@binding(1) @group(0) var<storage, read_write> xn_imag :
array<vec4f>;

// Real part of frequency-domain sequence
@binding(2) @group(0) var<storage, read_write> xk_real :
array<vec4f>;

// Imaginary part of frequency-domain sequence
@binding(3) @group(0) var<storage, read_write> xk_imag :
array<vec4f>;

// Whether to perform the DFT or IDFT @binding(4) @group(0)
var<storage, read_write> factor : f32;

override group_size: u32;
override filter_start: u32;
override filter_end: u32;

@compute @workgroup_size(group_size)
fn computeMain(@builtin(global_invocation_id) gid : vec3<u32>,
    @builtin(num_workgroups) num_groups : vec3<u32>) {

    let N = group_size * num_groups.x;
    let two_pi_k_over_N = (-1.0 * 2.0 * 3.14159 *
f32(gid.x))/f32(N);
    let num_vectors = N/4;
    var real_sum = 0.0;
    var imag_sum = 0.0;
    var real_val: vec4f;
    var imag_val: vec4f;

    // Iterate through input vectors
    for (var i: u32 = 0; i < num_vectors; i++) {

        // Form vectors of wk values
        var arg = vec4f(two_pi_k_over_N * f32(4 * i),
                        two_pi_k_over_N * f32(4 * i + 1),
                        two_pi_k_over_N * f32(4 * i + 2),
                        two_pi_k_over_N * f32(4 * i + 3));

        var w_real = cos(arg);
        var w_imag = sin(arg);
```

```
        // Process input vector
        if (factor == -1.0) {
            real_val = xn_real[i];
            imag_val = xn_imag[i];
        } else {
            real_val = xk_real[i];
            imag_val = xk_imag[i];
        }
        real_sum += dot(real_val, w_real) - dot(imag_val,
w_imag);
        imag_sum -= dot(real_val, w_imag) + dot(imag_val,
w_real);
    }

    // Store results to memory
    if (factor == -1.0) {

        // Apply filter
        if((gid.x > filter_start) && (gid.x < filter_end)) {
            xk_real[gid.x/4][gid.x % 4] = 0.0;
            xk_imag[gid.x/4][gid.x % 4] = 0.0;
        } else {
            xk_real[gid.x/4][gid.x % 4] = real_sum;
            xk_imag[gid.x/4][gid.x % 4] = imag_sum;
        }
    } else {
        xn_real[gid.x/4][gid.x % 4] = real_sum/f32(N);
        xn_imag[gid.x/4][gid.x % 4] = imag_sum/f32(N);
    }
}
```

As shown, the shader receives five storage buffers:

1. xn_real—real part of the time-domain sequence x[n]
2. xn_imag—imaginary part of the time-domain sequence x[n]
3. xk_real—real part of the frequency-domain sequence X[k]
4. xk_imag—imaginary part of the frequency-domain sequence X[k]
5. format—value that determines whether the DFT or IDFT is performed

If format is set to -1, the compute shader will perform the DFT and convert the data in xn_real and xn_imag into the sequences xk_real and xk_imag. If format is set to 1, the compute shader will perform the IDFT, and convert the data in xk_real and xk_imag into the sequences xn_real and xn_imag.

Before reading the input data, each invocation determines the total number of samples, N, by multiplying the work group size by the number of work groups. Because the data has 131,072 samples, the application creates 512 work groups with 256 invocations each (N = 512 * 256 = 131,072).

After computing N, each invocation computes a value named two_pi_k_over_N by multiplying 2π by its global ID and dividing the product by N. With each iteration, an invocation creates a vector containing four such values. Then it computes the sine and cosine of this vector.

Next, each invocation reads data from a location determined by its global ID. If the DFT is being performed, invocations will read data from xn_real and xn_imag. If the IDFT is being performed, invocations will read data from xk_real and xk_imag. As each input vector is read, the invocation multiplies it by the sine and cosine vectors computed earlier. Each product is added to two values, real_sum and imag_sum.

When the loop is complete, the invocation stores real_sum and imag_sum to the appropriate locations in the output buffers. If the DFT is being performed, invocations store their results to xk_real and xk_imag. If the IDFT is being performed, invocations store their results to xn_real and xn_imag.

Audio Filtering

Audio data has no imaginary values (xn_imag = 0.0 for all n), so the magnitude of frequency components repeat after N/2. In noise.wav, the frequency components representing noise extend from approximately 11,000 to 120,072. In code, the start of the noise range is filter_start and the end of the range is filter_end. This is illustrated in Figure 12.5.

At the end of the DFT, each invocation checks its global ID to see if it falls between filter_start and filter_end. If so, it sets its frequency component to 0.0. This has the effect of removing noise without significantly changing the original music.

The code in the Ch12_DFT project is straightforward to understand, but it takes a great deal of time to execute. By taking advantage of the DFT properties, researchers have devised an algorithm that obtains the same output with fewer operations. This algorithm is called the FFT, and is the topic of the next section.

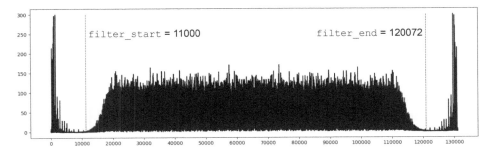

FIGURE 12.5   Frequency noise range of noisy.wav.

THE FAST FOURIER TRANSFORM (FFT)

Performance is always a concern for software developers, but if you're a radar analyst on an aircraft or a sonar analyst on a submarine, performance is a matter of life or death. If you detect your adversary before your adversary detects you, you get to shoot first.

For this and other reasons, mathematicians have spent decades finding ways to accelerate frequency analysis. At the time of this writing, the most popular method is the Cooley-Tukey FFT. Researchers have devised variations on this algorithm since its publication in 1965, but its high speed and computational simplicity have made it the reigning champion.

The goal of this section is to present this algorithm and show how it can be coded in WebGPU. This presentation will rely on intuition instead of mathematical rigor, and will start with an examination of three important properties of the DFT.

Three Properties of the DFT

The FFT isn't easy to understand, and in my opinion, mathematical derivations tend to make the algorithm more confusing. For this reason, I prefer to approach the subject by presenting three properties of the DFT that can be employed to accelerate its operation. In order of increasing complexity, these three properties are:

- Superposition—If two sequences are added together, the frequency components of the sum will be the sum of the individual frequency components.
- Shifting—If a sequence is shifted to the right, the resulting frequency components will equal the original frequency components multiplied by a sinusoid.
- Stretching—If a signal is stretched from N to 2N by placing a zero after every original sample, the new frequency components $X[0]$ through $X[N-1]$ will equal the old frequency components $X[0]$ through $X[N-1]$. Further, the components $X[N]$ through $X[2N-1]$ will equal the components $X[0]$ through $X[N-1]$.

These properties may not seem interesting by themselves, but once you fully grasp them, it's straightforward to combine them in such a way as to convert the DFT to the FFT.

The superposition property

The superposition property of the Fourier transform is one of the most fundamental concepts in signal processing. Thankfully, it's easy to understand. The frequency components of the sum of two sequences equal the sum of the individual frequency components of the sequences. That is, if z[n] = x[n] + y[n], then Z[k] = X[k] + Y[k]. Using the DFT equation, this is easy to prove:

$$z[n] = x[n] + y[n]$$

$$Z[k] = \sum_{n=0}^{N-1} z[n] \left(\cos\left(\frac{2\pi nk}{N}\right) - i \sin\left(\frac{2\pi nk}{N}\right) \right)$$

$$= \sum_{n=0}^{N-1} (x[n] + y[n]) \left(\cos\left(\frac{2\pi nk}{N}\right) - i \sin\left(\frac{2\pi nk}{N}\right) \right)$$

$$= \sum_{n=0}^{N-1} x[n] \left(\cos\left(\frac{2\pi nk}{N}\right) - i \sin\left(\frac{2\pi nk}{N}\right) \right) + \sum_{n=0}^{N-1} y[n] \left(\cos\left(\frac{2\pi nk}{N}\right) - i \sin\left(\frac{2\pi nk}{N}\right) \right)$$

$$= X[k] + Y[k]$$

It can be proved in a similar manner that a scaled sequence produces scaled frequency components. That is, if the DFT transforms x[n] to X[k] and c is a scalar, then cx[n] will be transformed to cX[k].

The shifting property

If a sequence is shifted, or delayed, in time, the real and imaginary parts of the frequency components will be multiplied by a sinusoid. To be precise, if $x'[n] = x[n - n_0]$, then $X'[k] = X[k](\cos(2\pi n_0 k/N) - i\sin(2\pi n_0 k/N))$ as k runs from 0 to N–1. This relationship can be derived in the following way:

$$X'[k] = \sum_{n-n_0=0}^{N-1} x[n - n_0] \left(\cos\left(\frac{2\pi nk}{N}\right) - i \sin\left(\frac{2\pi nk}{N}\right) \right)$$

$$= \sum_{n=0}^{N-1} x[n - n_0] e^{\frac{-i2\pi nk}{N}}$$

$$= \sum_{n-n_0=0}^{N-1} x[n - n_0] e^{\frac{-i2\pi(n-n_0)k}{N}} e^{\frac{-i2\pi n_0 k}{N}}$$

$$= X[k] e^{\frac{-i2\pi n_0 k}{N}}$$

$$= X\left[= X[k] e^{\frac{-i2\pi n_0 k}{N}} k \right] \left(\cos\left(\frac{2\pi n_0 k}{N}\right) - i \sin\left(\frac{2\pi n_0 k}{N}\right) \right)$$

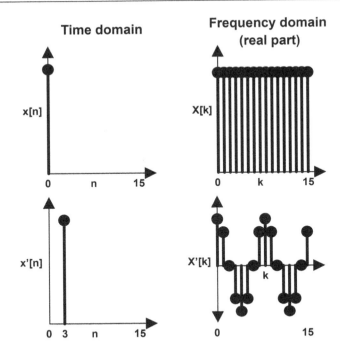

FIGURE 12.6   Frequency analysis of a shifted sequence.

Figure 12.6 depicts the relationship between X[k] and X'[k] graphically. The graphs on the right present only the real part of the frequency components corresponding to x[n] and x[n–3]. In the lower right, the real part of X'[k] equals the real part of X[k] multiplied by $\cos(3\pi k/16)$.

Shifting a sequence changes the real and imaginary parts of its frequency components, but the overall frequency response remains unchanged. This overall response is called the *magnitude*, which is obtained by taking the square root of the squares of the real and imaginary parts. This should make sense. If you delay pressing a key on a piano, the real and imaginary parts of the frequency components may change, but the overall frequency content of the signal stays the same.

The stretching property

The term stretching refers to the process of placing a zero after every sample of x[n], thereby doubling the size of the signal from N to 2N. I can't think of a practical reason why anyone would want to do this, but this operation is important from a theoretical perspective: when you stretch a signal, the frequency components of the result have interesting properties.

For example, if we stretch x[n] to x'[n], the new lower-frequency components, X'[0] through X'[N–1], will equal the old components, X[0] through X[N–1]. Further, the

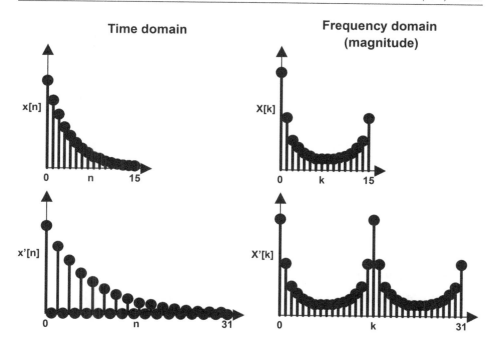

FIGURE 12.7   Frequency analysis of a stretched sequence.

upper frequency components, X′[N] through X′[2N–1], have the same values as X′[0] through X′[N–1]. Figure 12.7 presents this graphically.

In this figure, x[n] is an exponentially decaying sequence with 16 samples and x′[n] is a stretched version with 32 samples. The frequency components of x′[n] are exactly similar to those of x[n] for k = 0 to k = 15. Also, the frequency components of x′[n] from k = 16 to k = 31 are exactly equal to those from k = 0 to k = 15. This means that if we stretch a sequence, we don't need to compute the frequency components of the stretched sequence.

To get an intuitive feel for this, look closely at the graph of x′[n] and picture sines and cosines oscillating at frequencies f_k and f_{N+k}. You may notice that the sinusoids at both frequencies intercept the non-zero x[n] elements in the same places. This means the dot product of x[n] and $w_k[n]$ equals the dot product of x[n] and $w_{N+k}[n]$, and therefore, the frequency component X[k] equals the component X[N+k] for stretched sequences.

Constructing the Fast Fourier Transform

The merge sort algorithm compares elements two at a time, merges the 2-element sorts into 4-element sorts, merges the 4-element sorts into 8-element sorts, and continues until the entire set is sorted. The FFT algorithm is fundamentally similar. It computes the frequency components of two samples at a time, merges this for four elements, then eight elements, and so on. In this manner, it computes X[k] using a number of operations proportional to N $\log_2$N, where N is the number of samples in x[n]. This is a great improvement over the DFT, which requires a number of operations on the order of N^2.

To show how the FFT algorithm works, this discussion will walk through the frequency transformation of the 4-element sequence [12.5, 6.0, –9.5, 2.0]. Here are the main steps:

1. Explain how to compute the FFT of a 2-element sequence.
2. Derive the FFT merge process, which converts a pair of 2-element FFTs into a 4-element FFT.
3. Show how this merge process can be extended to transform larger sequences.

After this derivation, we'll examine how the FFT's mathematical theory can be implemented with a WebGPU compute shader.

The 2-element FFT

The Cooley-Tukey FFT can be used to process any sequence whose size is a power of 2, and that includes sequences with only two elements. For these sequences, the FFT performs the same operation as the DFT. There are only two frequency components, X[0] and X[1], and they can be computed as follows:

$$X[0] = \sum_{n=0}^{1} x[n]\left(\cos\left(\frac{2\pi(0)k}{2}\right) - i\sin\left(\frac{2\pi(0)k}{2}\right)\right) = \sum_{n=0}^{1} x[n](1 - 0i) = x[0] + x[1]$$

$$X[1] = \sum_{n=0}^{1} x[n]\left(\cos\left(\frac{2\pi(1)k}{2}\right) - i\sin\left(\frac{2\pi(1)k}{2}\right)\right) = \sum_{n=0}^{1} x[n](\pi k) = x[0] - x[1]$$

It doesn't get much easier than this. The first frequency component equals the sum of x[0] and x[1] and the second frequency component equals the difference between them. For example, if x[n] = [12.5, –9.5], X[0] = 12.5 + (–9.5) = 3.0 and X[1] = 12.5 – (–9.5) = 22.0.

Mathematicians depict this operation using figures called *butterfly diagrams*. Figure 12.8 presents the butterfly diagram corresponding to our simple example.

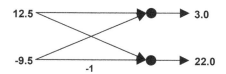

FIGURE 12.8 Butterfly diagram of a 2-element FFT.

The circles are called *nodes*, and each node returns the sum of its inputs. Both inputs arrive at the first node unchanged, so this node returns their sum, 3.0. But the −1 at the bottom of the diagram negates the lower input entering the second node, so this node returns the sum of 12.5 and −(−9.5), or 22.0.

The 4-element FFT

After the 2-element operations are performed, the rest of the FFT consists of merging the results into larger and larger sequences. This can be complicated. I'll work through a simple 4-element merge and then describe the general procedure.

Let's take the example sequence from the previous stage [12.5, −9.5], and stretch it so that the resulting sequence equals [12.5, 0, −9.5, 0]. We'll call this x[n]. Because of the stretching property, we know that X[k] equals [3.0, 22.0, 3.0, 22.0].

Let's take another sequence [6.0, 2.0], and find its frequency components: [8.0, 4.0]. We'll stretch this sequence to produce [6.0, 0, 2.0, 0]. If we call this y[n], the stretching property tells us that Y[k] equals [8.0, 4.0, 8.0, 4.0]. So far, so good.

Next, let's shift y[n] one place to the right, producing [0, 6.0, 0, 2.0]. We'll call this y′[n]. Because of the shifting property, we know that Y′[k] equals Y[k] multiplied by a sinusoid. That is, $Y′[k] = Y[k](\cos(2\pi k/4) + i \sin(2\pi k/4))$. The elements of Y′[k] can be computed as follows:

$$Y'[k] = Y[k]\left(\cos\left(\frac{2\pi k}{4} \right) - i \sin\left(\frac{2\pi k}{4} \right) \right)$$

$$Y'[0] = Y[0]\left(\cos\left(\frac{2\pi (0)}{4} \right) - i \sin\left(\frac{2\pi (0)}{4} \right) \right) = 8.0(1.0 - 0.0i) = 8.0$$

$$Y'[1] = Y[1]\left(\cos\left(\frac{2\pi (1)}{4} \right) - i \sin\left(\frac{2\pi (1)}{4} \right) \right) = 4.0(0.0 - 1.0i) = -4.0i$$

$$Y'[2] = Y[2]\left(\cos\left(\frac{2\pi (2)}{4} \right) - i \sin\left(\frac{2\pi (2)}{4} \right) \right) = 8.0(-1.0 - 0.0i) = -8.0$$

$$Y'[3] = Y[3]\left(\cos\left(\frac{2\pi (3)}{4} \right) - i \sin\left(\frac{2\pi (3)}{4} \right) \right) = 4.0(0.0 + 1.0i) = 4.0i$$

By these equations, Y′[k] equals [8.0, −4.0i, −8.0, 4.0i]. This equals [8.0, 4.0, 8.0, 4.0] multiplied by the corresponding elements of [1, −i, −1, i].

Because of the superposition property, we know that the frequency components of a sum of sequences equal the sum of the individual frequency components. That is, if we add x[n] and y′[n] to form z[n], Z[k] = X[k] + Y′[k]. In this example, adding x[n] and y′[n] gives us z[n] = [12.5, 6.0, −9.5, 2.0]. Adding X[k] and Y′[k], we get Z[k] = [3.0, 22.0, 3.0, 22.0] + [8.0, i4.0, −8.0, −i4.0] = [11.0, 22.0 + i4.0, −5.0, 22.0 − i4.0].

This may seem complicated, but by stretching, shifting, and adding, we can compute the Fourier transform of [12.5, 6.0, −9.5, 2.0] without performing a full DFT. The general rules for computing a four-element FFT are as follows:

1. Compute the 2-element FFT of the first and third elements and the 2-element FFT of the second and fourth elements.
2. Obtain the frequency components of the stretched sequences by repeating the original frequency components.
3. Multiply the frequency components of the second sequence by a sinusoid. This corresponds to shifting the sequence.
4. Add the frequency components of the first sequence to those of the second sequence.

This merge process is the heart of the FFT, and when I first encountered the algorithm, I had to work through several examples before this process made sense. I also found it helpful to trace through butterfly diagrams. Figure 12.9 presents the diagram corresponding to our full 4-element example.

There are two important points to note. First, the input elements are split into even/odd pairs before the processing starts. That is, this FFT processes elements x[0], x[2], x[1], and x[3] in that order. If there were eight input elements, they would be processed as follows: x[0], x[4], x[2], x[6], x[1], x[5], x[3], x[7].

This rearranging is called *bit reversal* because the bits that make up an element's index must be reversed to obtain the element's position. For example, if you reverse the bits of the index 3, 0x011, you get 0x110, or 6. This means x[3] takes the position that x[6] would normally take in an 8-element FFT. Similarly, x[6] takes the position that x[3] would normally take.

It's also important to notice the w_k terms on the right side of the diagram. These identify the elements of the sinusoid used to multiply a shifted sequence. For a

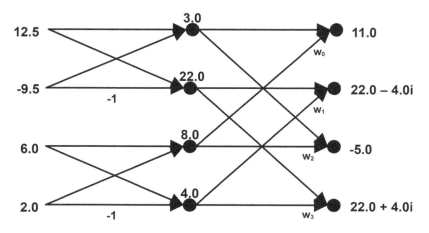

FIGURE 12.9   Butterfly diagram of a 4-element FFT.

four-element FFT, the w_k terms equal $\cos(2\pi k/4) - i \sin(2\pi k/4)$ as k runs from 0 to 3, or [1, −i, −1, i]. These w_k elements scale values on the nearby lines. For example, the upward arrow from the node equaling 4.0 is multiplied by w_1, or −i. Therefore, the final node returns 22 − 4i. In an 8-element FFT, w_k equals $\cos(2\pi k/8) - i \sin(2\pi k/8)$ as k runs from 0 to 7.

The process used to merge 2-element FFTs into a 4-element FFT can be further extended to compute FFTs of any size, so long as the size is a power of 2. In each case, the input elements are stretched, shifted, and added to form 2-element FFTs, then 4-element FFTs, and so on until the entire N-element FFT is computed. Next, we'll look at how to code this algorithm in a compute shader.

EXAMPLE APPLICATION: FILTERING AUDIO WITH THE FFT

If a sequence contains N complex values, the FFT requires $\log_2 N$ stages to compute its frequency components. The first stage computes 2-element FFTs, the second stage merges the results to form 4-element FFTs, and this merging continues all the way up to the final stage, which computes the N-element FFT. In general, Stage k performs N/2k FFTs, each of whose size is 2k.

If the FFT computation is partitioned among D invocations, and D is a power of 2 less than N, then each invocation computes the first $\log_2(N/D)$ stages of the FFT. In the final stages ($\log_2 N - \log_2(N/D) = \log_2 D$), the invocations need to synchronize their processing.

An example will make this clear. Suppose x[n] contains 64 elements (6 stages) and you want to compute its FFT with 4 invocations. Each invocation will process the first $\log_2(64/4) = 4$ stages on its own. Then, after the fourth stage is complete, the invocations need to synchronize their processing to compute the fifth and sixth stages. Figure 12.10 depicts this relationship graphically.

In theory, invocations can access workgroup memory faster than storage buffers. Therefore, it's a good idea to use workgroup memory when possible. The Ch12_FFT

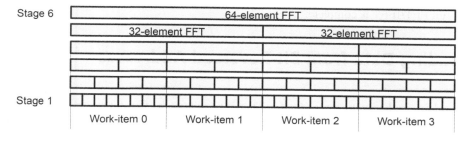

FIGURE 12.10 A 64-element FFT with four invocations.

application allocates the maximum amount of workgroup memory and uses it to store intermediate results. It's assumed that the size of workgroup memory is a power of 2.

On my system, the maximum size of workgroup memory is 16,384 bytes. Each pair of real and imaginary values occupies 8 bytes, so the largest FFT/IFFT result that can be stored in workgroup memory is 16,384/8 = 2,048. Each group needs to perform a 2,048-point FFT/IFFT, so `pts_per_group` is set to 2048. Each group contains 256 invocations, so the largest FFT/IFFT that can be performed by an invocation in workgroup memory is 2048/256 = 8. For this reason, `pts_per_inv` is set to 8.

The Ch12_FFT application defines two compute shaders. The first, `fftInit`, performs the FFT and IFFT up to the size of workgroup memory. The second, `fftStage`, performs stages of the FFT and IFFT that are too large to fit in workgroup memory. Combining the two shaders, the full audio filtering process consists of five steps:

1. The `fftInit` shader performs FFT stages up to the size of workgroup memory.
2. The `fftStage` shader is called repeatedly to perform FFT stages up to the total number of samples.
3. The `fftInit` shader is called to perform an IFFT. Before it starts processing, it sets frequencies in the desired ranges to 0.
4. After setting frequencies to 0, the `fftInit` shader performs the IFFT stages up to the size of workgroup memory.
5. The `fftStage` shader is called repeatedly to perform IFFT stages up to the total number of samples.

In the `fftInit` shader, each invocation performs four steps:

1. Computes bit-reversed addresses and loads input data from storage buffers.
2. Performs 4-point FFTs/IFFTs and stores the results in workgroup memory.
3. Performs successive stages independently (up to `pts_per_inv`).
4. Performs successive stages with other invocations in the workgroup (up to `pts_per_group`).

This discussion explores these steps and presents the corresponding code. Keep in mind that, after `fftInit`, the `fftStage` shader must be executed repeatedly until the full FFT/IFFT is complete.

Loading Data from Bit-Reversed Addresses

In the `fftInit` shader, each invocation uses its global ID to obtain an address (`g_addr`) in the input storage buffer. Then it computes the four bit-reversed addresses corresponding to `g_addr`, `g_addr+1`, `g_addr+2`, and `g_addr+3`, and stores them in a vector named `bitrev`. The following code shows how this is done.

```
var index = vec4u(g_addr, g_addr+1, g_addr+2, g_addr+3);
var mask_left: u32 = N/2;
var mask_left_vec = vec4u(mask_left, mask_left, mask_left,
mask_left);
var mask_right: u32 = 1;
var mask_right_vec = vec4u(mask_right, mask_right, mask_right,
mask_right);
var shift_pos = u32(log2(f32(N))) - 1;
var shift_vec = vec4u(shift_pos, shift_pos, shift_pos,
shift_pos);
var bitrev = (index << shift_vec) & mask_left_vec;
bitrev |= (index >> shift_vec) & mask_right_vec;

// Bit-reverse addresses
while(shift_pos > 1) {
    shift_pos -= 2;
    mask_left >>= 1;
    mask_left_vec = vec4u(mask_left, mask_left, mask_left,
mask_left);
    mask_right <<= 1;
    mask_right_vec = vec4u(mask_right, mask_right, mask_right,
mask_right);
    shift_vec = vec4u(shift_pos, shift_pos, shift_pos,
shift_pos);
    bitrev |= (index << shift_vec) & mask_left_vec;
    bitrev |= (index >> shift_vec) & mask_right_vec;
}
```

Now that the addresses have been obtained, the invocation loads input values corresponding to each element of bitrev. The source of the input is determined by the value of factor. If factor equals -1, the FFT will be performed and the invocation will read time-domain data from xn_real and xn_imag. If factor equals 1, the IFFT is being performed and the invocation will read frequency-domain data from xk_real and xk_imag. The following code shows how this is done:

```
// Load global data
// Load storage data
if (factor == -1.0) {
    x1 = vec2f(xn_real[bitrev.x], xn_imag[bitrev.x]);
    x2 = vec2f(xn_real[bitrev.y], xn_imag[bitrev.y]);
    x3 = vec2f(xn_real[bitrev.z], xn_imag[bitrev.z]);
    x4 = vec2f(xn_real[bitrev.w], xn_imag[bitrev.w]);
} else {
```

```
    if(((bitrev.x > first_filter_start) && (bitrev.x <
first_filter_end)) ||
        ((bitrev.x > second_filter_start) && (bitrev.x <
second_filter_end))) {
        x1 = vec2f(0.0, 0.0);
    } else {
        x1 = vec2f(xk_real[bitrev.x], xk_imag[bitrev.x]);
    }
    if(((bitrev.y > first_filter_start) && (bitrev.y <
first_filter_end)) ||
        ((bitrev.y > second_filter_start) && (bitrev.y <
second_filter_end))) {
        x2 = vec2f(0.0, 0.0);
    } else {
        x2 = vec2f(xk_real[bitrev.y], xk_imag[bitrev.y]);
    }
    if(((bitrev.z > first_filter_start) && (bitrev.z <
first_filter_end)) ||
        ((bitrev.z > second_filter_start) && (bitrev.z <
second_filter_end))) {
        x3 = vec2f(0.0, 0.0);
    } else {
        x3 = vec2f(xk_real[bitrev.z], xk_imag[bitrev.z]);
    }
    if(((bitrev.w > first_filter_start) && (bitrev.w <
first_filter_end)) ||
        ((bitrev.w > second_filter_start) && (bitrev.w <
second_filter_end))) {
        x4 = vec2f(0.0, 0.0);
    } else {
        x4 = vec2f(xk_real[bitrev.w], xk_imag[bitrev.w]);
    }
}
```

The real/imaginary input values are stored in 2-element vectors named x1, x2, x3, and x4. If the IFFT is being performed, the input frequency values will be set to 0 if they fall within the noise ranges discussed earlier in the chapter.

Perform 4-Point FFTs/IFFTs

4-point FFTs and IFFTs are easy to compute because there's no need to calculate sine and cosine values. In essence, the operation consists of addition and subtraction. The following code shows how the FFT/IFFT of x1, x2, x3, and x4 is computed:

```
// Perform 4-pt FFT
sum12 = x1 + x2;
diff12 = x1 - x2;
sum34 = x3 + x4;
diff34 = vec2f(x4.y - x3.y, x3.x - x4.x) * factor;

// Store results to workgroup memory
wg_mem[wg_addr] = sum12 + sum34;
wg_mem[wg_addr + 1] = diff12 + diff34;
wg_mem[wg_addr + 2] = sum12 - sum34;
wg_mem[wg_addr + 3] = diff12 - diff34;
```

The FFT/IFFT results are stored in `wg_mem`, which stands for *workgroup memory*. The address, `wg_addr`, is computed using the invocation's local ID, which identifies it among other items in the workgroup. The following code shows how the address is obtained:

```
var wg_addr = local_id * pts_per_inv;
```

In this code, `pts_per_inv` identifies how many points (real-imaginary pairs) are to be processed independently by each invocation.

Perform Independent FFTs/IFFTs

After the 4-point FFTs/IFFTs are computed and stored in workgroup memory, the next step is for each invocation to perform as many independent operations as possible. For example, if `pts_per_inv` is 64, each invocation will perform FFT/IFFT stages up to the 64-point FFT/IFFT. The following code shows how this is done:

```
// Iterate through further stages
for(N2 = 4; N2 < pts_per_inv; N2 <<= 1) {

    // Reset local memory address
    wg_addr = local_id * pts_per_inv;

    // Trig constant
    k = -3.14159/f32(N2);

    // Iterate through FFT/IFFT operations
    for (var fft_index: u32 = 0; fft_index < pts_per_inv;
    fft_index += 2*N2) {
        var first_val = wg_mem[wg_addr];
```

```
            wg_mem[wg_addr] += wg_mem[wg_addr + N2];
            wg_mem[wg_addr + N2] = first_val - wg_mem[wg_addr +
N2];

            // Iterate through FFT/IFFT points
            for (i = 1; i < N2; i++) {
                c = cos(k * f32(i));
                s = sin(k * f32(i)) * factor;
                wk = vec2f(
                    c * wg_mem[wg_addr + N2 + i].x +
                    s * wg_mem[wg_addr + N2 + i].y,
                    c * wg_mem[wg_addr + N2 + i].y -
                    s * wg_mem[wg_addr + N2 + i].x);
                wg_mem[wg_addr + N2 + i] = wg_mem[wg_addr + i] -
wk;
                wg_mem[wg_addr + i] += wk;
            }
            wg_addr += 2*N2;
        }
    }
    workgroupBarrier();
```

In this code, N2 is half the size of the FFT/IFFT currently being performed. Because it starts at 4, the first operation performed by the loop is an 8-point FFT/IFFT. It's important to note that the invocation may need to perform many of these operations, and the index of the operation is given by fft_index.

For each FFT/IFFT, the invocation performs a sum and difference to compute the first result and the middle result. Then it computes sines and cosines and multiplies them by the suitable values in workgroup memory. Each FFT/IFFT is performed in-place, which means the invocation overwrites the old values with the computed values after each stage.

After an invocation has performed its independent operations, it will wait for other invocations in the workgroup to complete their processing. This is the result of the workgroupBarrier function.

Perform FFTs/IFFTs with Other Workgroup Invocations

After each invocation obtains the largest FFT/IFFT that it can compute independently, it needs to coordinate processing with other invocations in the workgroup. The following code shows how successive FFT/IFFT stages are performed:

```
// Iterate through further stages
var stage: u32 = 2;
var start: u32;
for(N2 = pts_per_inv; N2 < pts_per_group; N2 <<= 1) {
    start = (local_id + (local_id/stage)*stage) *
(pts_per_inv/2);
        var angle = start % (N2*2);
        k = -3.14159/f32(N2);

        // Iterate through FFT/IFFT points
        for (i = start; i < start + pts_per_inv/2; i++) {
            c = cos(k * f32(angle));
            s = sin(k * f32(angle)) * factor;
            wk = vec2f(
                c * wg_mem[N2 + i].x + s * wg_mem[N2 + i].y,
                c * wg_mem[N2 + i].y - s * wg_mem[N2 + i].x);
            wg_mem[N2 + i] = wg_mem[i] - wk;
            wg_mem[i] += wk;
            angle++;
        }
        stage <<= 1;
        workgroupBarrier();
}
```

As before, `N2` is half the size of the FFT/IFFT being performed. This value is needed to compute the sine/cosine values that multiply values in `wg_mem`. After each operation is complete, the `workgroupBarrier` function forces every invocation to wait until all other invocations in the workgroup are finished.

Once the loop is complete, the workgroup memory contains the largest FFT/IFFT result that it can hold. The last part of the shader stores the values of the result to the storage buffers, as shown in the following code:

```
// Store vectors in storage buffers
g_addr = global_id.x * pts_per_inv;
wg_addr = local_id * pts_per_inv;
for (i = 0; i < pts_per_inv; i++) {

    if (factor == -1.0) {
        xk_real[g_addr + i] = wg_mem[wg_addr + i].x;
        xk_imag[g_addr + i] = wg_mem[wg_addr + i].y;
    } else {
        xn_real[g_addr + i] = wg_mem[wg_addr + i].x/f32(N);
        xn_imag[g_addr + i] = wg_mem[wg_addr + i].y/f32(N);
    }
}
```

The output storage depends on the value of factor. If factor is -1.0, the result will be stored in the frequency-domain buffers, xk_real and xk_imag. If factor is 1.0, the result will be scaled by 1/N and stored in the time-domain buffers, xn_real and xn_imag.

If the size of the FFT/IFFT is less than or equal to the size of workgroup memory, no further processing is needed. But in the Ch12_FFT project, the audio data contains 131,072 samples, so further processing is required.

Perform FFTs/IFFTs with All Other Invocations

The size of the FFT/IFFT exceeds the size of workgroup memory, so the Ch12_FFT application performs further operations by executing the compute shader in the fftStageShader string. In this shader, each invocation reads two points from the real/imaginary output buffers, processes them, and writes the processed data back to the output buffers. This is shown in the following code:

```
@compute @workgroup_size(group_size)
fn fft_stage(@builtin(global_invocation_id) global_id :
vec3<u32>,
    @builtin(num_workgroups) num_groups : vec3<u32>,
    @builtin(workgroup_id) group_id : vec3<u32>,
    @builtin(local_invocation_index) local_id : u32) {

    var points_per_inv = pts_per_group/group_size;
    var addr = (global_id.x + (group_id.x/stage)*stage) *
(pts_per_group/2) +
        local_id * (points_per_inv/2);
    var N = pts_per_group*(stage/2);
    var angle = addr % (N*2);
    var k = -3.14159/f32(N);
    var c: f32; var s: f32;
    var x1: vec2f; var x2: vec2f; var wk: vec2f;

    for(var i: u32 = 0; i < addr + points_per_inv/2; i++) {

        // Compute trig values
        c = cos(k * f32(angle));
        s = sin(k * f32(angle)) * factor;

        // Read data from buffer
        if (factor == -1.0) {
            x1 = vec2f(xk_real[i], xk_imag[i]);
            x2 = vec2f(xk_real[i + N], xk_imag[i + N]);
        } else {
```

```
        x1 = vec2f(xn_real[i], xn_imag[i]);
        x2 = vec2f(xn_real[i + N], xn_imag[i + N]);
    }

    // Compute scaled value
    wk = vec2f(c * x2.x + s * x2.y, c * x2.y - s * x2.x);

    // Write data to buffer
    if (factor == -1.0) {
        xk_real[i] = x1.x + wk.x;
        xk_imag[i] = x1.y + wk.y;
        xk_real[i + N] = x1.x - wk.x;
        xk_imag[i + N] = x1.y - wk.y;
    } else {
        xn_real[i] = (x1.x + wk.x);
        xn_imag[i] = (x1.y + wk.y);
        xn_real[i + N] = (x1.x - wk.x);
        xn_imag[i + N] = (x1.y - wk.y);
    }
    angle++;
    }
}
```

After the last IFFT execution of `fftStageShader`, the final results are stored in the `xn_real` and `xn_imag` buffers. The content of the `xn_real` buffer is copied into a mappable buffer and converted into the WAV format.

SUMMARY

Of all the mathematical algorithms discussed in this book, the FFT is my favorite. No other algorithm combines mathematical beauty with hard, practical utility. It is the fundamental algorithm of signal processing, and the better you understand it, the faster your analysis routines will execute.

The first part of this chapter discussed audio processing in general, focusing on how to remove noise from a song using digital remastering. The goal is to sample a continuous time-domain signal, x(t), to produce a time-domain sequence, x[n]. The DFT transforms x[n] into a sequence containing frequency components, X[k], and you can remove noise by setting unwanted frequencies to zero. The inverse DFT transforms the frequency components back into a time-domain signal.

The rest of the chapter explored the mathematics behind these transformations, and began with a discussion of the internals of the DFT. This simple algorithm consists of a series of dot products involving x[n] and sinusoids of various frequencies. The first frequency of interest corresponds to a single oscillation over the course of the signal's period, and further frequencies are multiples of this. If a signal is real-valued, the DFT only needs to compute components for frequencies f_0 through $f_{N/2}$. The remaining components can be determined through symmetry.

By combining three properties of the DFT (superposition, shifting, and stretching), we can derive a better algorithm for extracting frequency data: the FFT. This computes the DFTs of element pairs, merges the results into 4-element FFTs, then 8-element FFTs, and so on. If a digital sequence contains N elements, the FFT requires $\log_2 N$ stages.

Appendix A
Node and TypeScript

Many of the applications presented in this book can be run by opening index.html in a browser. But in other chapters, the applications need to access external files. For example, the projects in Chapters 5 and 6 rely on the wgpu-matrix library, and the projects in Chapters 10 and 12 require media files. Applications can access these files in JavaScript by calling `fetch`, but many browsers will produce an error due to cross-origin restrictions.

To avoid these errors, you can access these pages in a local HTTP server. A simple way to launch this server is to run the http-server utility in the directory containing index. html. Then the WebGPU application can be executed by opening http://localhost:8080/index.html in a browser.

http-server is a free HTTP server that makes it easy to run and test WebGPU applications. It's also one of the many utilities provided by the Node.js ecosystem. Node.js (usually shortened to *Node*) is extremely popular in web development, and the npm package manager makes it easy to install packages that facilitate software development.

This appendix begins by discussing npm, and then explores two utilities that can be accessed through Node. After a brief discussion of http-server, it explores the features of the TypeScript programming language. TypeScript has gained a wide following because it adds strong typing and error-checking to web development.

This appendix ends by describing how WebGPU applications can be coded in TypeScript and compiled into JavaScript. As we'll see, the main difficulty isn't writing the code, but providing the compiler with declarations of WebGPU's objects.

THE NODE PACKAGE MANAGER (npm)

At the time of this writing, the Node ecosystem is 14 years old and provides over 2.2 million packages for software development. Most of the packages are completely free, so if you're building a complex application, you'll probably find multiple packages that will help you.

To take advantage of these capabilities, the first step is to install Node.js. The main page is https://nodejs.org, and after clicking the Download link, you can download the installer or binary by clicking the link for your operating system and processor type (probably 64-bit). This discussion assumes you're running version 21 of Node or higher.

TABLE A.1   npm commands and abbreviations (abridged)

COMMAND NAME	ABBREVIATION	DESCRIPTION
install	i	Installs a package
update	up	Updates an installed package
uninstall	un	Uninstalls a package
list	ls	Lists installed packages
init	--	Creates a new package.json
start	--	Runs the command given in package.json
stop	--	Halts the running command

After you've downloaded and installed Node, you should be able to use the package manager on a command line. Every npm command starts with npm *cmd* where *cmd* identifies the command or the command's abbreviation. Table A.1 lists seven helpful commands to know.

Packages are installed by running npm install (or npm i) followed by the package name(s). For example, you can install the wgpu-matrix package with the following command:

```
npm install --global wgpu-matrix
```

You can install multiple packages with one command, and for this book, I recommend installing the http-server and typescript packages with the following command:

```
npm install --global http-server typescript
```

The npm list command makes it easy to verify that your packages have been installed correctly. If you run npm ls, you'll see a list of your installed packages and their versions.

THE HYPERTEXT TRANSFER PROTOCOL (HTTP) SERVER

Once you've installed the http-server package, you can run a basic HTTP server on your development system. This is important when you need to test an application that needs to access local files.

You can launch the HTTP server with the following command:

```
http-server [path] [options]
```

If the http-server command is entered without flags, the server will serve the files in the current directory. Then you can access the server by opening a browser and visiting http://localhost:8080.

The `path` parameter tells the server to serve files in the given directory. You can also configure the server by following the command with options. The `--port N` option tells the server to listen to Port N during its operation. The `--silent` option tells the server to suppress log messages. You can learn more about the http-server package by visiting its main page at https://www.npmjs.com/package/http-server.

An example will clarify how http-server can be used. If you want to run the Ch06_SimpleTexture project, you can't just open index.html in a browser. But you can launch the server in the project's directory by opening a command prompt in the Ch06_SimpleTexture top-level folder and running `http-server`. Then you can launch the application by opening a browser and visiting http://localhost:8080/index.html.

GETTING STARTED WITH TypeScript

When a JavaScript codebase becomes large enough to require multiple developers, errors may occur due to misinterpreted data types. If one developer assumes `foo` is an array of integers and it turns out to be a string, the code is likely to fail. To make matters worse, another developer might redeclare `foo` to be a function, which is likely to confuse everyone.

The problem is that JavaScript is a *weakly typed* language. Developers don't have to specify the types of their variables, so the interpreter won't care if x is used as a number in one portion of code and used as a string elsewhere.

While some developers appreciate this freedom, others appreciate the error-checking provided by *strongly typed* languages like Python or C++. In a strongly typed language, the data type of every variable needs to be clearly identified. This allows developers to be more confident of how their data structures are being used. It also makes it easier for development environments to manage and refactor variables.

For this reason, Anders Hejlsberg at Microsoft developed TypeScript, a strongly typed language that can be easily converted to JavaScript. The proper term for this conversion is *transpilation* because both languages occupy the same level of abstraction. But this appendix will employ the term *compilation*, which is more commonly used.

This section explains how to install and use the TypeScript compiler. Later sections present its data types, classes, interfaces, and declaration files.

Installing and Using the Compiler

At the time of this writing, the only TypeScript compiler is provided by Microsoft, and you can install it through npm. If you have Node installed, you can install the compiler with the following command:

```
npm install --global typescript
```

After installation, you should be able to access the TypeScript compiler. Its name is tsc and you can check its version by running the following command:

```
tsc -v
```

tsc accepts a wide range of command-line arguments, but there's usually no need to learn them. Most developers set compiler options in a file named tsconfig.json. If tsc is executed in a directory containing tsconfig.json, it will read the file's settings and use them to constrain its operation.

As its suffix implies, tsconfig.json defines a JSON object. Four important fields of the object are:

1. files—names of files to be compiled
2. include—patterns identifying files to be included in the compilation
3. exclude—patterns identifying files to be excluded from the compilation
4. compilerOptions—an object whose fields constrain the compilation process

An example will clarify how these fields can be set. Consider the following JSON:

```
{
    // Identify files to be compiled
    "files": [ "src/app/app.ts" ],

    // Identify files to be included in compilation

    "include": [ "src/utils/*.ts" ],

    // Configure the compiler's behavior
    "compilerOptions": {
        "noEmitOnError": true
    }
}
```

This tells tsc to compile app.ts in the src/app folder and every TypeScript file (*.ts) in the src/utils directory. The noEmitOnError flag tells the compiler not to produce JavaScript files if any errors are found. noEmitOnError is one of several options that tell the compiler how to operate. The following discussion explores many of these options and explains how they can be used.

Compiler Options

Table A.2 lists 14 of the parameters that can be set in the compilerOptions field of tsconfig.json.

TABLE A.2   Compiler options (abridged)

FLAG	DESCRIPTION
target	Desired ECMAScript version (es3, es5, es6/es2015, es2016, es2017, es2018, es2019, es2020, es2021, es2022, esnext)
rootDir	Root directory of input files
listFiles	Print file names processed by the compiler
outDir	Directory to contain compiled results
outFile	File to contain concatenated results
noLib	Don't include the main library, lib.d.ts, in the compilation process
lib	Type definitions accessed by the compiler
types	Packages providing type definitions
alwaysStrict	Specifies whether strict mode should be enabled
noEmitOnError	Don't generate output if any errors were encountered
noImplicitThis	Raise an error on this expressions with implied any type
noUnusedLocals	Report errors on unused locals
noUnusedParameters	Report errors on unused parameters
noImplicitAny	Print a warning for every variable that isn't explicitly declared

By default, the compiler generates JavaScript according to the ECMAScript 5 (ES5) standard. But the `target` option makes it possible to generate code in other standards. For example, the following object tells the compiler to compile TypeScript files to ES2021:

```
{
    "compilerOptions": {
        "target": "es2021",
    }
}
```

By default, the TypeScript compiler places JavaScript code in a *.js file in the same directory with the same name of the TypeScript file. That is, if src/a.ts and src/b.ts need to be compiled, the compiler will place the resulting code in src/a.js and src/b.js. The `outDir` option tells the compiler to store the results in another directory. If `outFile` is set, the compiler will concatenate its results and store the code in the given file.

To do its job properly, the compiler needs to know about the data types used in the TypeScript code. Data types can be provided in declaration files (*.d.ts), which will be discussed in a later section. The most important declaration file is the main library, lib.d.ts, which declares basic types like `Array`, `Number`, and `String`. If noLib is set in tsconfig.json, the compiler won't be able to access these types.

The compiler can access high-level libraries besides the main library, such as type definitions for the document object model (DOM) and advanced versions of ECMAScript. This becomes very important if TypeScript code includes features like

`Promises` and `TypedArrays`. To enable access, the `lib` flag can be set in the following way:

```
"compilerOptions": {
    ...
    "lib": [ "dom", "esnext" ],
    ...
}
```

As a later section explains, you can install additional libraries that declare types for different platforms and toolsets. This is particularly important because WebGPU's types aren't defined in any of TypeScript's built-in libraries. To alert the compiler, these libraries need to be identified with the `types` flag in tsconfig.json.

If `alwaysStrict` is set to `true`, browsers will run the script in strict mode. This mode treats mistakes as errors and prevents the creation of accidental global variables. It also throws an error if a JavaScript object contains duplicate properties.

EXAMPLE APPLICATION— INTRODUCTION TO TypeScript

Before delving into the technical details of TypeScript, it's a good idea to build a simple project. The AppA_HelloTS project contains three files needed to build the hello_ts application:

- appa_hello.ts—TypeScript code to be compiled to JavaScript (appa_hello.js)
- tsconfig.json—Configures the compilation process
- index.html—Web page that imports the compiled code

Once you understand how to build and run this application, you'll have no trouble working with more complex TypeScript projects.

Compiler Configuration

The TypeScript compiler reads configuration settings from tsconfig.json. Its content is given as follows:

```
{
    "files": [ "appa_hello.ts" ],
    "compilerOptions": {
        "target": "es2021",
        "removeComments": true,
        "alwaysStrict": true,
```

```
    "noEmitOnError": true,
    "noUnusedLocals": true,
    "noUnusedParameters": true
  }
}
```

This tells the compiler that the only file to compile is appa_hello.ts, which is located in the current directory. When it performs the compilation, the compiler should generate JavaScript according to the ECMAScript 2021 specification. Because always-Strict is set, the generated code will execute in strict mode.

The noEmitOnError field tells the compiler not to generate JavaScript if an error occurs. Because noUnusedLocals and noUnusedParameters are set to true, the compiler will check for unused declarations.

Source Code

The code in hello.ts file isn't particularly impressive, but it demonstrates an important feature of TypeScript. Its content is given as follows:

```
class HelloTS {
    public printMessage() {
        document.write("Hello TypeScript!");
    }
}

let hello: HelloTS = new HelloTS();
hello.printMessage();
```

This defines a TypeScript class named HelloTS which has a method named printMessage. If you're not familiar with classes and methods, don't be concerned. A later section in this appendix discusses classes in detail.

To build this code, go to the project's directory and enter tsc on the command line. The compiler will convert the TypeScript to JavaScript and place the resulting code in appa_hello.js. If you open index.html in a browser, the web page will display Hello TypeScript!

FUNDAMENTAL DATA TYPES OF TypeScript

TypeScript allows you to set a variable's type in its declaration. This is an optional feature, and the type specifications disappear when the code is compiled into JavaScript. But they provide one major advantage: *type-checking*. If a TypeScript variable of one type is set to a value of another type, the compiler will flag an error.

An example will make this clear. In the following code, the first line sets x equal to a number and the second line sets it equal to a string:

```
var x = 5;
x = "Hello";
```

This is acceptable in JavaScript and TypeScript, but TypeScript makes it possible to specifically identify x as a number. Consider this code:

```
var x: number;
x = "Hello";
```

The first line specifies that x is a number. When the code is compiled, the compiler recognizes that the second line is setting x equal to a string, and it will report an error.

Type-checking serves three main purposes:

- Early error discovery—The compiler reports errors at compile-time so that you don't have to figure them out at run-time.
- Tooling—Editors can analyze text better when variables have types. This affects features like code completion, error-checking, and syntax coloring.
- Readability—When a variable has a type, it's easier to understand the purpose it serves.

Setting a variable's type involves following the variable's name with a colon and the desired type. A general declaration has the following form:

```
var <name>: <type>;
```

If the variable needs to be initialized, the declaration's form can be given as follows:

```
var <name>: <type> = <value>;
```

When an untyped variable is initialized, the compiler automatically sets the variable's type to that of the value. In other words, if a variable is initialized to a value, there's no need to define its type.

A variable's type can be set to a custom type or a predefined TypeScript type. A later section discusses custom types, which include classes and interfaces. This section focuses on TypeScript's built-in types, which include boolean, number, string, array, tuple, Object, any, undefined, and null.

The Boolean Type

Of TypeScript's predefined types, boolean is the easiest to use and understand. A boolean variable can be set to one of two values: true or false. As an example, the following code declares a `boolean` variable named check and initializes its value to `true`:

```
const check: boolean = true;
```

A `boolean` variable can be set equal to any operation that returns a `boolean` value. These operations include comparison operations (>, <, >=, <=, ==, !==, and ===) and logical operations (&&, ||, and !). The following examples demonstrate how `boolean` variables can be declared and initialized:

- `const x: boolean = 5 > 3;`
- `const y: boolean = "a" !== "b";`
- `const z: boolean = ((3 < 5) && ("a" != "b"));`

JavaScript provides two operators for testing equality: == and ===. The difference is that x == y returns `true` if x and y have the same value and x === y returns true if x and y have the same value and the same type.

The Number Type

In TypeScript, integers and floating-point values belong to the `number` type, regardless of their sign or size. This is shown in the following examples, which declare and initialize three `number` values:

```
let three: number = 3;
let pi: number = 3.14159;
let avogadro: number = 6.022e-23;
```

As in JavaScript, every number in TypeScript is considered to be a floating-point value. There are no integer types or integer-specific operations. Numbers are stored as 64-bit double-precision values in accordance with the IEEE-754 standard. Values can be given using fixed-point notation (0.01) or exponential notation (6.02e-23).

TypeScript supports literal values in different bases. That is, TypeScript recognizes hexadecimal (0x10), octal (0o20), and binary (0b10000), in addition to decimal.

TypeScript provides special number values that can be used in code. Five of them are given as follows:

- `Number.MAX_VALUE`—the largest possible number value (about 1.7977e+308)
- `Number.MIN_VALUE`—the smallest possible number value (equals 5.0e−324)
- `Number.POSITIVE_INFINITY`—positive infinity (returned when a positive value is too large to be stored)

- `Number.NEGATIVE_INFINITY`—negative infinity (returned when a negative value is too large to be stored)
- `Number.NaN`—not a number (returned when an operation returns an impossible value, such as performing a mathematical operation on a string)

TypeScript supports the same kinds of operations on numbers as JavaScript. These include mathematical operations and operations that convert (and format) numbers to strings.

The String Type

Strings make it possible to store and operate on text. A string variable can be initialized by setting it equal to one or more characters surrounded by quotes—double quotes or single quotes. This is shown in the following examples:

```
let single_char: string = "D";
let large: string = 'Single or double, it does not matter';
```

A string stores its characters in order and each has an index, starting with 0. This is important to understand when using the many methods available for string handling.

The Array Type

An array is an ordered collection of elements of the same type. When declaring an array in TypeScript, the declaration must identify the type of the array's elements. There are two ways to declare an array:

```
let arr1: element_type[];
let arr2: Array<element_type>;
```

An array can be initialized by setting it equal to a comma-separated list of elements surrounded by square brackets. The following code shows how arrays can be declared and initialized:

```
const num_array: number[] = [5, 7, 9];
const str_array: string[] = ["p", "q", "r"];
```

After an array is declared, its elements can be accessed as `array[index]`, where *index* is the position of the element in the array. The first element has Index 0 and the second has Index 1. If the array has N elements, the last element has Index N–1. This is shown in the following code:

```
let x: number = num_array[1];     // x = 7
let c: string = str_array[2];     // c = "r"
```

An array's length can be obtained by accessing its `length` property. If you attempt to read an element beyond the array's length, the compiler won't return an error. But when you execute the compiled code, the misread value will be undefined.

The Tuple Type

Tuples are like arrays but their elements can have different types. In a tuple declaration, each element's type must be provided in order. The following code declares and initializes two tuples:

```
const t1: [boolean, number] = [true, 6];
const t2: [number, number, string] = [17, 5.25, "green"];
```

As with arrays, an element of a tuple can be accessed by its index, which starts with 0 for the first element. This is shown with the following code:

```
const x: boolean = t1[0];      // x = true
const y: number = t2[1];       // y = 5.25
```

A tuple may seem suitable for storing data elements that are related to one another. But as I'll explain shortly, classes are better suited for this. Tuples are particularly helpful when a function needs to return a single data structure that contains multiple values of different types.

The Object Type

Like a tuple, a variable of the `Object` type contains values that can have different types. But there are at least three crucial differences between the two:

- Each value of an `Object` has an associated string called a *key* that serves as an identifier for the value.
- The order of values in an object isn't important. `Object` values are accessed by key, but not by a numeric index.
- When initializing an object, key-value pairs are surrounded by curly braces instead of square brackets.

The following code shows how `Objects` can be declared and initialized:

```
let count = {first: "one", second: "two"};
let house = {num: 31, street: "Main", forSale: true};
```

As shown, the keys of an object aren't surrounded in quotes, though they can be. If an object's value is surrounded by quotes, it will be interpreted as a string. Otherwise, it will be interpreted as another type.

The Any, Undefined, and Null Types

If a variable's type is unknown, it can be assigned to the any type. This tells the compiler not to be concerned with type-checking the variable. Using this type isn't recommended, but it may be necessary when accessing data structures in third-party JavaScript code.

If noImplicitAny isn't set to true, the TypeScript compiler will assign untyped variables to the any type. But in JavaScript, variables without values are considered undefined. In TypeScript, every value needs a type, and an undefined value has a type of undefined.

As with undefined, any type of variable can be set equal to the null value. This indicates that the variable doesn't contain data. However, if a variable is assigned to the null type, it can only be set to the value of null.

It's important to understand the difference between undefined and null. If a variable is declared but uninitialized, JavaScript will consider it undefined. If a variable is set to null, it is defined and its value is null.

TypeScript CLASSES

In the early days of software development, the only structures available for storing data were variables, strings, and arrays. But as applications grew in complexity, developers encapsulated data and related operations into structures called *objects*. An object's content is determined by its *class*. In essence, a class serves as the blueprint by which objects are created.

For example, suppose an application creates software representations of cars. A good way to organize the data is to define a Car class that contains car-related data. This data might include the car's make, model, type of engine, and year of manufacture. The Car's class might also identify operations performed by the car, including driving, parking, and moving in reverse.

In TypeScript, a class's variables are referred to as *properties* and its routines are called *methods*. Collectively, a class's properties and methods are referred to as *members*.

At minimum, a TypeScript class definition consists of the word class followed by the class name and the body in curly braces. As an example, the following Car class has four properties and three methods:

```
class Car {

    // Properties
    make: string;
    model: string;
    engineType: string;
    year: number;
```

```
// Methods
park() { ... };
driveForward() { ... };
driveReverse() { ... };
}
```

After this class is defined, a `Car` object can be created by calling the constructor with the new keyword. This is shown in the following TypeScript code:

```
let myCar = new Car();
```

JavaScript also supports creating objects with the new keyword, but there are many differences between JavaScript objects and TypeScript objects. One major difference is that TypeScript objects aren't *mutable*, which means they can't be given new properties or methods.

To see what this means, suppose we want to add a new property called numDoors. After myCar is created, the following assignment is acceptable in JavaScript:

```
myCar.numDoors = 2;
```

But in TypeScript, this causes an error: *Property 'numDoors' does not exist on type 'Car'.* If you want to add a new property, you need to define a new class. But you don't have to copy and paste code from the original class. TypeScript makes it possible to create subclasses that extend existing classes. These subclasses receive (or *inherit*) members from the original class and can define properties and methods of their own.

For example, Class A can be declared as a subclass of Class B by following its name with `extends B`. The following code shows how this works:

```
class A extends B {
    ...
}
```

As a more practical example, suppose we want to define a new class, `SportsCar`, that inherits the members of the `Car` class. In addition to accessing the properties and methods of `Car`, `SportsCar` should have an additional property called maxSpeed. The `SportsCar` class could be defined in the following way:

```
class SportsCar extends Car {
    maxSpeed: number;
}
```

With this definition, a property of a `SportsCar` instance can be accessed through dot notation, which consists of the instance name, a dot, and the name of the property.

When coding with TypeScript classes, there are three features to be familiar with. The remainder of this section discusses class constructors, method overriding, and the `this` and `super` keywords.

Class Constructors

A TypeScript class can contain a special routine that will be called when applications create new instances of the class. This is called a *constructor* and it's commonly used to set an object's properties when it's created. There are four aspects of constructors that every TypeScript developer should know:

1. Every constructor must be named `constructor`.
2. Each class can have only one constructor. If no constructor is defined in code, a constructor with no arguments (a *no-arg constructor*) will be created.
3. Constructors are public, so the `private` or `protected` modifiers can't be used.
4. A constructor can be invoked by calling `new class_name` followed by the constructor's parameter list.

An example will demonstrate how constructors are used. A preceding discussion introduced the `Car` class and its properties. The class definition didn't contain a constructor, so a new instance can be created by calling `new Car()`. Then the `Car`'s properties can be set individually with code such as the following:

```
let carInstance = new Car();
carInstance.make = "Honda";
carInstance.model = "Civic";
carInstance.engineType = "240hp,turbocharged";
carInstance.year = 2006;
```

By adding a constructor to the `Car` class, we can simplify the process of creating and initializing `Car` instances. The following code presents a simple example of how a simple constructor can be coded:

```
class Car {

    make: string;
    model: string;
    engineType: string;
    year: number;

    constructor(make: string, model: string,
                engineType: string, year: number) {
        this.make = make;
        this.model = model;
        this.engineType = engineType;
        this.year = year;
    }
    ...
}
```

With this code in place, a `Car` object can be created and initialized with the following code:

```
let carInstance =
    new Car("Honda", "Civic", "240hp,turbocharged", 2006);
```

In real-world applications, class constructors do more than just initialize properties of a new object. They can also perform other tasks such as obtaining data about the environment, initializing server connections, and so on.

If a constructor's parameter has an access modifier (`public`, `protected`, or `private`), the corresponding property doesn't need to be declared in the class. This is useful to know, but can be hard to grasp at first. Let's look at an example.

In the preceding `Car` definition, the `make`, `model`, `engineType`, and `year` properties were declared in the class and initialized in the constructor. By adding access modifiers to the constructor's parameters, the following definition accomplishes the same result with much less code.

```
class Car {
    constructor(public make: string, public model: string,
        public engineType: string, public year: number) {}
}
```

Method Overriding

Earlier, I explained how TypeScript makes it possible for one class (the *subclass*) to inherit properties and methods from another class (the *superclass*). A subclass can add methods that aren't in the superclass and it can redefine methods coded in the superclass.

For example, if a superclass contains a method called `addConstant`, the subclass can implement its own `addConstant` method with different code. When an instance of the subclass is created, a call to `addConstant` will invoke the subclass's method.

The process of reimplementing a method in a subclass is called *overriding*. To override a method, the subclass's method must have the same parameter list and return value as the superclass's method.

A subclass can also override properties. That is, if a superclass initializes `arg` to a value of 6, a subclass can initialize its value to 19. But the property must have the same type in the superclass and subclass. That is, if the superclass declares `arg` as a number, the subclass must make sure `arg` is a number. Otherwise, the compiler will return the error: *Types of property 'arg' are incompatible.*

Important Keywords: This and Super

Within a class definition, the keywords `this` and `super` have special meanings. This discussion explains what these keywords mean and demonstrates how they can be used.

The this keyword

It's common for a class's method to access other members of the class. This is particularly true for constructors that initialize properties. But if a property's name is `prop`, methods in the class definition can't access it as `prop`. Dot notation requires that properties be accessed through instances of a class. In a class definition, the instance can be obtained using the `this` keyword. Therefore, if `prop` is a property, it must be accessed as `this.prop`.

If `this` is omitted, the compiler will return an error. For example, if `this.prop` is replaced with `prop`, the compiler will respond with *Cannot find name "prop."*

The super keyword

Like `this`, the `super` keyword can be used to access methods of a class instance. But `super` provides access to an instance of the class's superclass. That is, if Class B is a subclass of Class A, `super` makes it possible for the definition of B to call methods of A.

In a subclass's constructor, it's common to invoke the superclass's constructor before performing class-specific operations. This is made possible by `super()`, which calls the superclass's constructor. If the superclass's constructor accepts arguments, those arguments should be provided in `super()`.

The `super` keyword can be used to access a superclass's methods if they're public or protected. But it can't access the superclass's properties. For example, suppose Class B is a subclass of Class A and its `num` property overrides the `num` property set in Class A. The class definition of B can't access the superclass's property with `super.num`. The `super` keyword is only available for accessing methods.

TypeScript INTERFACES

Just as a class can extend another class, a class can *implement* an interface. When a class implements an interface, it doesn't inherit anything. Instead, it receives an obligation to declare the interface's properties and provide code for its methods. For example, a class that implements the `SoccerPlayer` interface must redeclare `jerseyNum` and provide code for the `passBall`, `receiveBall`, and `blockOpponent` methods.

In addition to uninitialized properties and empty methods, there's one crucial difference between classes and interfaces: *interfaces can't be instantiated.* That is, there's no way to create an object from an interface—you can't create an instance of `AddSubtractConstant` with new `AddSubtractConstant()` and you can't create a `SoccerPlayer` instance with new `SoccerPlayer()`.

This raises a question: if interfaces can't be instantiated, what are they good for? Why would you define an interface when you can define a class instead?

To answer this question, I'd like to present an example. Suppose you've written an application whose behavior can be customized. You want to tell third-party developers what methods are needed, but you don't want to show them your underlying code. In this case, it's easier to provide an interface, which lists methods and their signatures but doesn't provide any code. Then, if a developer defines a class that implements the interface, the application knows that it can invoke the required methods.

Put another way, an interface defines a *contract*. A class that implements an interface must provide code for a specific set of methods. If a function or method receives an object from an implementing class, it knows that specific methods can be called. This allows the interface name to be used as a type.

When dealing with classes and interfaces, there are three rules to keep in mind:

1. A class can only inherit from one other class, but it can implement any number of interfaces.
2. When a class declares properties from an interface, each property must have the same accessibility modifiers.
3. When a class implements the methods of an interface, the methods must be instance methods, not static methods.

There's one point that's interesting but not particularly important. If a class contains only uninitialized properties, the compiler will allow the class to serve as an interface. The TypeScript handbook refers to this as *type compatibility*, which means the compiler identifies types according to their members.

DECLARATION FILES

If you try to compile regular WebGPU code with `tsc`, the compiler will produce several errors because it doesn't know anything about WebGPU's data types. Here are some examples of the errors you might encounter:

- *error TS2339: Property 'getContext' does not exist on type 'HTMLElement'*
- *error TS2339: Property 'gpu' does not exist on type 'Navigator'*
- *error TS2304: Cannot find name 'GPUBufferUsage'*

To resolve these issues, we need to provide the compiler with information about these new types. TypeScript files that declare types but don't contain code are called *declaration files*, and they all have the suffix *.d.ts. Declaration files make it possible for TypeScript code to access untyped JavaScript code.

We can tell the compiler where to find a project's declaration files by identifying their names and locations in the `files` array of tsconfig.json. Once this is done, the declared types can be used as easily as TypeScript's built-in files.

In many cases, a declaration file will need to import declarations from another file. To identify the second file, the declaration file needs to use a *triple-slash directive*, which contains an XML tag preceded by three slashes. As an example, the following directive tells the compiler that the declaration file requires mytypes.d.ts:

```
/// <reference path="mytypes.d.ts" />
```

Many declaration files are freely available on the Internet. One particularly helpful resource is DefinitelyTyped, which is located at https://github.com/DefinitelyTyped/

DefinitelyTyped. The types directory of this repository contains hundreds of declaration files that can be accessed in TypeScript.

Rather than copy declaration files manually, you can install declaration files through npm. The following command installs the @webgpu/types package, which provides a declaration file for WebGPU development.

```
npm install -D @webgpu/types
```

When the installation is finished, the node_modules directory will contain a file named index.d.ts in the @webgpu/types/dist folder. This contains declarations for many of the data structures used in WebGPU applications. As an example, the following code declares an interface for GPUShaderModule, which represents WebGPU's GPUShaderModule object:

```
// Represents a WebGPU shader module
interface GPUShaderModule extends GPUObjectBase {
    readonly __brand: "GPUShaderModule";
    getCompilationInfo(): Promise<GPUCompilationInfo>;
}
```

As another example, the following code declares a variable named GPUShaderStage, which represents the different types of shader stages.

```
// Represents a WebGPU shader stage
declare var GPUShaderStage: {
    prototype: GPUShaderStage;
    readonly VERTEX: GPUFlagsConstant;
    readonly FRAGMENT: GPUFlagsConstant;
    readonly COMPUTE: GPUFlagsConstant;
};
```

The declarations in the @webgpu/types package cover most of the WebGPU API, but many applications may still need additional declarations to satisfy the compiler.

EXAMPLE APPLICATION—
WebGPU IN TypeScript

The files in the AppA_Triangle project show how a simple WebGPU application can be coded in TypeScript. The project contains three files—appa_triangle.ts, tsconfig.json, and index.html—and they serve the same purposes as the corresponding files in the AppA_HelloTS project.

However, the tsconfig.json file is a little more interesting. Its content is given as follows:

```
{
    "files": [ "appa_triangle.ts" ],
    "compilerOptions": {
        "target": "es2021",
        "lib": [ "dom", "esnext" ],
        "types": [ "@webgpu/types" ],
        "removeComments": true,
        "alwaysStrict": true,
        "noEmitOnError": true,
        "noUnusedLocals": true,
        "noUnusedParameters": true
    }
}
```

In this case, the lib field is set to an array containing dom and esnext. The first element tells the compiler to access declarations in the DOM library, which include definitions of types like HTMLElement and Navigator. The second element tells the compiler to access the ECMAScript Next library, which declares types related to advanced features of JavaScript. If the compiler throws an error related to fundamental JavaScript types, make sure the lib flag is set correctly.

In addition, the types flag is set to an array containing @webgpu/types. This tells the compiler to access the declaration files provided by the @webgpu/types package. This can be installed by executing the following command in the AppA_Triangle directory:

```
npm install -D @webgpu/types
```

After this is installed, the application can be compiled by invoking tsc. Once the appa_triangle.js file is available, you can launch the application by opening index.html in a browser.

The code in appa_triangle.ts is nearly identical to the code in ch04_multitriangle. js source file discussed in Chapter 4. One interesting difference involves accessing elements in the web page. In JavaScript, the following code can be used to access the canvas and its context:

```
const canvas = document.getElementById("canvas_example");
const context: GPUCanvasContext = canvas.getContext("webgpu");
```

But this causes a problem in TypeScript because the compiler thinks canvas is an HTMLElement, which doesn't provide a getContext method. For this reason, this code will produce an error: *Property 'getContext' does not exist on type 'HTMLElement'*.

To fix this, the code needs to explicitly identify that canvas is an `HTMLCanvas Element`, not an `HTMLElement`. This can be accomplished with the following code:

```
const canvas = document.getElementById("canvas_example") as
HTMLCanvasElement;
```

Besides this change, minor changes are needed to the structures used to create the render pipeline. Otherwise, the compiler is satisfied with the types used in appa_triangle.js.

SUMMARY

This appendix has discussed three capabilities that aren't essential to WebGPU development, but can dramatically improve the coding process:

- Node.js—framework that provides access to free software tools
- http-server—utility that launches a basic HTTP server, making it possible to run applications without triggering CORS errors
- typescript— package that provides tsc, which compiles TypeScript code into JavaScript

The http-server utility is helpful when you need to test applications that access local files. For many applications, if you open index.html in a browser, you may see an error like *Access to script at from origin 'null' has been blocked by CORS policy.* But if you install http-server and run it inside the directory containing index.html, you can access the application without error by opening a browser to http://localhost:8080/index.html.

Most of this appendix focuses on TypeScript, a strongly typed language that can be compiled to JavaScript. Configuring the compilation process is complex, but given the language's popularity, it's clear that many developers consider type safety worth the inconvenience.

The last part of this appendix explained how WebGPU applications can be coded in TypeScript. The code is essentially similar to JavaScript, but it needs to specify the type of each object in the application. In addition, tsconfig.json needs to identify which libraries and declaration files should be accessed by the compiler.

Appendix B
WebAssembly, Emscripten, and Google Dawn

Most of this book has focused on coding applications in JavaScript, but WebGPU's capabilities can be accessed in other languages. If you'd like to develop WebGPU applications in Rust, you can use wgpu (https://wgpu.rs). If you prefer coding in C++, you can use Google Dawn (https://dawn.googlesource.com/dawn). Both frameworks are very exciting, and this appendix focuses on Google Dawn.

In my experience, most graphical applications that demand performance (games and design tools) are coded in C++. With Dawn, you can compile C++ code into a WebGPU browser application without rewriting the codebase in JavaScript. Unfortunately, the build process is rather complex.

To the best of my knowledge, no browser supports C++ code directly. Instead, the code needs to be linked to the Google Dawn libraries and compiled into a WebAssembly module (*.wasm). Then the *.wasm file can be accessed in JavaScript using the WebAssembly API.

This appendix explores this process in two parts. It starts by explaining how to compile basic C++ applications into WebAssembly modules and access them in JavaScript. Then it explains how to build the Dawn development tools and use them in a WebAssembly project.

WebAssembly AND Emscripten

The source code of the Google Dawn project is written in C++, so before it can be used in a WebGPU application, it needs to be converted into a form that can be accessed in a web page. This appendix discusses the process of compiling the code it into a WebAssembly module file (*.wasm). Then its functions can be invoked inside JavaScript using the WebAssembly object.

The most popular tools for compiling C++ into WebAssembly are provided as part of the Emscripten package. This section explains how to install Emscripten and use its utilities to convert C++ files (*.cpp) to WebAseembly modules (*.wasm). It also shows how to access these modules in JavaScript and invoke their functions.

329

Installing Emscripten

Emscripten is a software development kit (SDK) whose tools can compile source code into WebAssembly modules. It's free and open-source, and it requires Python 3.6 or later to be installed on the development system. If you don't already have Python, you can find many online resources that explain how to install it on your computer.

The recommended way to install Emscripten is through Git. To download the basic environment, open a terminal and execute the following command:

```
git clone https://github.com/emscripten-core/emsdk.git
```

Once this finishes, you'll have a new folder named emsdk in your current directory. To get the latest version, enter the following commands:

```
// Change to the Emscripten SDK directory
cd emsdk

// Pull the latest changes from the repository
git pull
```

At this point, you have the most recent Emscripten files on your development system. Now you'll need to install and activate the latest tools. The directions depend on your operating system, and for Windows systems, the update commands are as follows:

```
// Install the most recent tools
emsdk.bat install latest

// Activate Emscripten and set environment variables
emsdk.bat activate latest --permanent
emsdk_env.bat
```

For operating systems besides Windows, the installation procedure requires the emsdk executable. For these systems, the installation and activation commands are given as follows:

```
// Install the most recent tools
./emsdk install latest

// Activate Emscripten for the current user
./emsdk activate latest

// Set PATH and other environment variables
source ./emsdk_env.sh
```

At this point, the Emscripten SDK and its tools should be available for use. The following discussion explains how to perform real-world computation.

TABLE B.1   Emscripten tools

TOOL	DESCRIPTION
emcc	Compiles C to WebAssembly
em++	Compiles C++ to WebAssembly
emar	Combines (archives) object files
emmake	Executes build instructions from a makefile
emrun	Opens HTML pages in a local web server
emsize	Shows the size of each section in the WebAssembly module
emstrip	Removes non-essential elements from the WebAssembly module

Compiling to WebAssembly

If you look in the $EMSDK/upstream/emscripten directory, you'll find several batch files and scripts. Many have names similar to the utilities you'd find in the popular GNU toolchain (emcc instead of gcc, emmake instead of make, and so on). These batch files and scripts perform WebAssembly build operations or assist with the build process. Table B.1 lists seven of them and provides a description of each.

In this appendix, we'll be primarily interested in two of these tools: em++ and emmake. To start, I'll explain how to use em++, which compiles C++ source code into a WebAssembly module. This works like the g++ utility provided in the GNU toolchain, and the following command tells Emscripten to compile example.cpp into example.wasm:

```
em++ example.cpp -o example.wasm
```

In this command, the -o flag identifies the name of the target file (WebAssembly module) that should be built. When this executes, em++ will compile example.cpp into example.wasm. Table B.2 lists the -o flag and other flags accepted by the em++ utility.

TABLE B.2   Important flags of the em++ utility

FLAG	DESCRIPTION
-o <target>	Identifies the name of the file to be built
-v	Turns on verbose mode
-c	Create an object file (*.o) but don't link into an executable
--no-entry	The main function isn't required
-flto	Enables link-time optimization (LTO)
--emrun	Makes output accessible through the emrun utility
-gN	Controls debug level (0—no debug, 3—keep all debug info)
-ON	Controls optimization (0—no optimization, 3—max optimization)
-std=version	Sets the version of C++ to be used by the compiler
-DMACRO	Defines a macro used during compilation
-s OPTION[=VALUE]	Assigns values to options during compilation

In a normal C/C++ application, a `main` function is required to serve as the application's starting function, or *entry point*. The `--no-entry` flag tells Emscripten not to look for a `main` function. None of the modules discussed in this appendix have `main` functions, so `--no-entry` will always be set.

To demonstrate how these flags can be used, the following command tells em++ to print information as it compiles (verbose mode) and reduce the size of the resulting file (optimize) as best as it can:

```
em++ -v -O3 example.cpp -o example.wasm --no-entry
```

Optimization is important in WebAssembly deployment. To see what I mean, suppose that example.cpp contains the following code:

```
#include <iostream>
int main() {
    std::cout << "Hello World!" << std::endl;
    return 0;
}
```

The source code only occupies 87 bytes, but after compilation, the unoptimized example.wasm contains 166,714 bytes. This is because the compiler inserts a lot of the C++ standard library into the module. If the -O3 flag is set, the size of the module falls to 148,825 bytes.

The -D and -s flags play crucial roles in the build process. The -D flag makes it possible to define a symbol that will be recognized by the compiler. For example, if the -DNDEBUG flag is included in the build command, the NDEBUG symbol will be defined. As a result, assertions will be disabled.

The -s flag makes it possible to associate a name with a value. In WebAssembly builds, this is required to associate the EXPORTED_FUNCTIONS name with an array of function names preceded by underlines. For example, the following build command makes the foo function an exported function:

```
em++ -DNDEBUG example.cpp -o example.wasm --no-entry -s
"EXPORTED_FUNCTIONS=['_foo']"
```

The following discussion shows how build commands like this are used in practice.

Accessing WebAssembly in JavaScript

At the time of this writing, all major browsers support WebAssembly. As a result, JavaScript code can access a WebAssembly object whose methods make it possible to load and execute WebAssembly modules. The most important method to know is `instantiateStreaming`, which accepts two objects:

1. A `Response` containing the content of the WebAssembly module (*.wasm).
2. An optional `import` object containing data needed by the module.

The `instantiateStreaming` method returns a `Promise` that resolves to a `ResultSet` containing two properties:

- `module`—a `WebAssembly.Module` containing the compiled code
- `instance`—a `WebAssembly.Instance` object that provides exported functions

To obtain the input `Response`, many applications call `fetch`, which was discussed in Chapter 6. This provides a `Promise` that resolves to a `Response`, and the following code shows how it can be used:

```
// Obtain Response containing file content
let resp = await fetch("example.wasm");
```

Once the `Response` is available and the `imports` object has been created, the application can access the WebAssembly results by calling `instantiateStreaming`:

```
// Obtain the ResultSet containing the module and instance
let wasm = await WebAssembly.instantiateStreaming(resp);
```

This `wasm` object has two properties named `module` and `instance`. The `instance` property is important because it provides access to exported functions through its `exports` property. For example, if the *.wasm file exports a function named `func`, the following code show how it can be invoked in JavaScript:

```
// Invoke the exported function
wasm.instance.exports.func();
```

Now let's look at a simple example. Suppose source.cpp contains the following function definition:

```
extern "C" {
    int foo() {
        return 123;
    }
}
```

At the start of the file, the `extern "C"` prevents the compiler from mangling the function's name. The following command compiles source.cpp with full optimization, no entry point, and assertions disabled. The result is a module named source.wasm whose list of exported functions contains `foo`:

```
em++ -DNDEBUG -O3 source.cpp -o source.wasm --no-entry -s
"EXPORTED_FUNCTIONS=['_foo']"
```

If the build completes successfully, the `foo` function can be called from JavaScript. This requires three steps:

1. Create a `Response` for the source.wasm file.
2. Instantiate the module from the `Response`.
3. Invoke the function through the `exports` property of the resulting instance.

The following code shows how these steps can be accomplished:

```
// Obtain Response containing file content
let resp = await fetch("source.wasm");

// Obtain the ResultSet containing the module and instance
let wasm = await WebAssembly.instantiateStreaming(resp);

// Print the return value of the exported function
console.log(wasm.instance.exports.foo());
```

If these operations complete successfully, the console will display `123`, the return value of the `foo` function in source.cpp.

Makefiles

Rather than enter a lengthy command every time you want to run a build, it's more efficient to use the emmake utility. This invokes the make utility, which must be installed on the development system. On Linux and macOS, this is installed by default. Windows users can install make by installing Cygwin or the Minimalist GNU for Windows (MinGW).

When emmake runs, it looks for a makefile (usually named Makefile) in the current directory. If it exists, emmake reads its commands and executes them. Makefiles provide many advantages over entering commands on the command line:

- A command only needs to be typed once—inside the makefile.
- Build commands can be modified and extended in the makefile instead of retyping the entire command.
- Makefiles can build different types of applications in different languages and environments, and can perform non-build operations like installing and archiving.
- Makefiles can be organized in a hierarchy in which a master makefile contains all the build commands and dependent makefiles specify which commands should be run.

Makefiles differ widely depending on the writer and purpose, but most consist of four types of statements:

1. Dependency lines—lines that identify a file to be created (*target*) and the files needed for its creation (*dependencies*).
2. Shell lines—contain the commands that build a target from its dependencies.

3. Variable declarations—text substitution statements that function like #define directives in C/C++.
4. Comments—lines that start with # and provide additional information.

This subsection describes each of these statements. Then I'll present the App0B_SimpleWASM project, which shows how makefiles can be used to build WebAssembly modules.

Dependency lines

Before performing a build, emmake looks for two pieces of information: the name of the file to be built and the names of the files needed to build it. The file to be built is called the *target* and the files needed to build the target are called *dependencies*.

A makefile provides this information with dependency lines. A dependency line contains the target name, a colon, and names of dependencies separated by spaces. Its basic syntax is given by

```
target: dependency1 dependency2 …
```

For example, if you want emmake to build an application called app.wasm using source files src1.c, src2.c, and src3.c, the dependency line is

```
app.wasm: src1.c src2.c src3.c
```

If the target file already exists, emmake checks to see when the target and dependency files were last modified. If any of the dependencies is more recent than the target, emmake rebuilds the target. Otherwise, it takes no action.

When emmake is called with no arguments, it processes the first dependency line in the makefile. But if it's called with the name of a target, such as in the command emmake target_name, emmake will search for a dependency line whose target is target_name.

Target and dependency files can be of any type: source code or object code, text or binary. All that matters is that make knows what to build and what files it needs to build it. But dependency lines don't specify how the target should be built. For this, you need to add shell lines.

Shell lines

Shell lines tell emmake what steps to perform when building the target identified in the preceding dependency line. Shell lines contain the same type of commands as those you'd enter on a command line. In a makefile, shell lines follow dependency lines and each shell line *must start with a tab*. The general syntax is given as follows:

```
target: dependency1 dependency2 ...
    command1
    command2
    . . .
```

The combination of a dependency line and its shell lines is called a *rule*. A complete rule tells emmake what target to build, what files are needed, and what commands must be processed to build the target.

For example, the previous section explained how to use em++ to compile source. cpp into source.wasm. This operation can be expressed with the following rule:

```
source.wasm: source.cpp
    em++ -DNDEBUG -O3 source.cpp -o
source.wasm --no-entry -s "EXPORTED_FUNCTIONS=['_foo']"
```

This rule is grammatically fine, but it can be simplified using variables. I'll discuss this next.

Variables and comments

Variables and comments make it easier to modify and read makefiles. A variable is an identifier that represents text, and these identifiers commonly consist of capital letters. Each variable declaration has the form X=Y, and wherever emmake encounters $(X) in the makefile, it replaces the reference with its corresponding text, Y.

An example will help make this clear. Suppose a makefile contains the following rules:

```
long_file_name.wasm: long_file_name.cpp
    em++ long_file_name.cpp -o long_file_name.wasm

other_file_name.wasm: other_file_name.cpp
    em++ other_file_name.cpp -o other_file_name.wasm
```

You can make this more readable by replacing each occurrence of long_file_ name with $(LONG) and each occurrence of other_file_name with $(OTHER). This is done using variables, as shown in the following rewritten rules:

```
LONG=long_file_name
OTHER=other_file_name

$(LONG).wasm: $(LONG).cpp
    em++ $(LONG).cpp -o $(LONG).wasm

$(OTHER).wasm: $(OTHER).cpp
    em++ $(OTHER).cpp -o $(OTHER).wasm
```

Using variables does more than just increase readability. If the name of a file changes, you don't have to modify each occurrence of its name. Just change the variable declaration, and the modification will propagate throughout the file.

Makefile comments are even simpler to understand than variables. Each comment starts with a # and the comment continues until the end of the line. This works like the comment marker // in C++. The following lines show how comments work:

```
PROJ=source      # Name of the source file and module
CPPFLAGS=-O3 -DNDEBUG --no-entry -s
"EXPORTED_FUNCTIONS=['_foo']"

# Build the WebAssembly module
$(PROJ).wasm: $(PROJ).cpp
        em++ $(CPPFLAGS) $(PROJ).cpp -o $(PROJ).wasm
```

Variables and comments have made the build procedure must easier to read. But we can simplify the makefile further using automatic variables.

Automatic variables

When you write a shell line, you can use predefined variables whose content depends on the target and dependencies. Table B.3 lists each of these variables and the information they hold.

Of these variables, $@ and $^ are particularly helpful because they make it unnecessary to rewrite names of targets and dependency files. To see what I mean, consider the following makefile rule:

```
foo.wasm: foo.cpp bar.cpp
       em++ foo.cpp bar.cpp -o foo
```

Using automatic variables, this can be updated in the following way:

```
foo.wasm: foo.cpp bar.cpp
       em++ $^ -o $@
```

This change is harder to read but easier to type, copy, and paste. This construction is used throughout the makefiles in this appendix.

The text representation of an automatic variable is recomputed for each rule, so the value of $@ changes from rule to rule. Also, automatic variables can only be used in the shell lines, not in the dependency lines that precede them.

TABLE B.3 Makefile automatic variables

AUTOMATIC VARIABLE	DESCRIPTION
$@	The name of the rule's target
$%	Name of the target, which is a member of an archive
$^	Names of all dependencies, separated by spaces
$<	The name of the first dependency
$?	Names of all dependencies newer than the target
$+	Names of all dependencies with duplicates in proper order

EXAMPLE PROJECT—SIMPLE WebAssembly

The code in the AppB_SimpleWASM project demonstrates how a simple C++ source file can be compiled into a WebAssembly module. The content of the Makefile is given as follows:

```
PROJ=simplewasm

CPP=em++

EXPORTED_FUNC=foo

CPPFLAGS=-DNDEBUG -O3 --no-entry -s
"EXPORTED_FUNCTIONS=['_${EXPORTED_FUNC}']"

$(PROJ).wasm: $(PROJ).cpp
        $(CPP) $(CPPFLAGS) -o $@ $^

.PHONY: clean

clean:
        rm $(PROJ).wasm
```

If you call emmake make in the directory containing this file, the emmake utility will analyze the content of Makefile and execute the following command:

```
em++ -DNDEBUG -O3 --no-entry -s "EXPORTED_FUNCTIONS=['_foo']" -o
simplewasm.wasm simplewasm.cpp
```

This tells em++ to compile simplewasm.cpp into simplewasm.wasm. The --no-entry flag tells the compiler not to look for a main function and the -O3 flag tells the compiler to optimize the result as well as it can. The -s "EXPORTED_FUNCTIONS=['_foo']" flag tells the compiler that the function named foo will be exported.

The code in simplewasm.cpp is very simple, and the function foo simply returns an integer. The content of the source file is given as follows:

```
extern "C" {
    int foo() {
        return 123;
    }
}
```

After the code in simplewasm.cpp is compiled into simplewasm.wasm, the code in appb_simplewasm.js creates a Response from the module and then reads its content by calling `WebAssembly.instantiateStreaming`. Then it calls the exported function by accessing the `instance` object. The following code shows how this is done:

```
// Create top-level asynchronous function
async function runExample() {

    // Obtain Response containing file content
    let resp = await fetch("simplewasm.wasm");

    // Obtain the ResultSet containing the module and instance
    let wasm = await WebAssembly.instantiateStreaming(resp);

    // Print the return value of the exported function
    console.log(wasm.instance.exports.foo());
}

// Run example function
runExample();
```

If you try opening index.html in a browser, you'll probably get a CORS error because of the attempt to access a local file. You can resolve this by launching http-server in the AppB_SimpleWASM directory and opening a browser to http://localhost:8080/index.html.

EMSCRIPTEN AND GOOGLE DAWN

At this point, you should be familiar with how to compile a C++ source file into a WebAssembly module and how to access the module in JavaScript. The goal of this section is to go beyond trivial C++ functions and develop applications that perform WebGPU rendering in a browser's canvas.

But there's a problem. WebAssembly doesn't have any capabilities for accessing web pages and their elements. A WebAssembly module can import JavaScript methods and call them in C++, but this is difficult to configure. Thankfully, Emscripten provides functions that take of this for us.

If you look in Emscripten's installation directory, you'll find a series of include files in the $EMSDK/upstream/emscripten/system/include/emscripten folder. Three of them are particularly important for this discussion:

- emscripten.h—functions that interface JavaScript and the environment
- html5.h—functions that handle events in the user interface
- html5_webgpu.h—functions that interface WebGPU

In addition, there are two header files in the $EMSDK/upstream/emscripten/ system/include/webgpu folder that play significant roles in this discussion:

- webgpu.h—functions that perform WebGPU operations
- webgpu_cpp.h—C++ functions that wrap around the functions in webgpu.h

The webgpu.h header was generated by the Google Dawn project, whose goal is to enable developers to compile WebGPU applications for multiple environments. Using Dawn, you can generate WebGPU implementations for native applications or smartphones. The webgpu.h file in the $EMSDK directory was specifically generated to enable WebGPU code to run in applications based on Emscripten.

The rest of this appendix focuses on the classes and functions declared in webgpu_cpp.h, which serves as a C++ wrapper for webgpu.h. Most of the discussion explains how to write code that relies on webgpu_cpp.h. Afterward, I'll explain how to compile this code to JavaScript and WebAssembly.

To be more specific, I'm going to explain how to draw a simple orange triangle in a canvas, just as in the Ch04_OrangeTriangle project. The development process requires six steps:

1. Access the client's device.
2. Create the vertex buffer and specify its layout.
3. Configure the render pipeline.
4. Create a surface and swapchain.
5. Acquire a command encoder and render pass encoder.
6. Define rendering commands and submit them to the queue.

Most of these data structures should look familiar, although the surface and swapchain may seem foreign. Once you understand how this code works, you'll be able to integrate existing C++ code into WebGPU applications and port your WebGPU applications to run on different platforms.

Accessing the Device

As in a regular WebGPU application, the first step is to access the client's device. This requires three steps:

1. Create an instance of the Instance class.
2. Obtain an adapter, which represents the WebGPU implementation.
3. Acquire the device associated with the adapter.

The first step is the simplest. Dawn provides a central class named Instance, which serves as the primary entry class of the API. Instance provides two important functions named RequestAdapter and CreateSurface. As its name implies,

TABLE B.4 Properties of `RequestAdapterOptions`

FIELD	DATA TYPE	DESCRIPTION
nextInChain	ChainedStruct*	Points to specialized classes
compatibleSurface	Surface	The desired surface used for rendering
powerPreference	PowerPreference	The desired power setting
backendType	BackendType	The graphical toolset used to perform rendering
forceFallbackAdapter	bool	Indicates that only a fallback adapter should be returned
compatibilityMode	bool	Indicates that the adapter needs to run in compatibility mode

`RequestAdapter` provides access to a WebGPU adapter, and its signature is given as follows:

```
void RequestAdapter(RequestAdapterOptions const *options,
RequestAdapterCallback callback, void *userdata)
```

The first argument sets criteria for the desired adapter, the second defines a function to be called if the adapter becomes available, and the last argument sets data to be associated with the adapter. The `RequestAdapterOptions` struct has six fields, and Table B.4 lists each of them.

The first two fields of the structure relate to surfaces. In Dawn, a `Surface` represents a generic window that can be used for rendering. Later, I'll explain how Dawn makes it possible to access an `HTMLCanvasElement` as a surface.

The `powerPreference` field specifies the desired power setting for the adapter. This must be set to one of the three fields of the `PowerPreference` enumerated type: `LowPower`, `HighPerformance`, or `Undefined`.

Dawn can access several different toolsets for rendering. An application can set the desired toolset through the `backendType` field, which can be set to a field of the `BackendType` enumerated type. Available values include `WebGPU`, `D3D11`, `D3D12`, `Metal`, `Vulkan`, `OpenGL`, and `OpenGL ES`. In this discussion, the default value is `WebGPU`.

Some systems support software implementations of WebGPU that don't use a physical device. In WebGPU, these software devices are represented by *fallback adapters*. An application can specify that a fallback adapter should be provided by setting the `forceFallbackAdapter` field to true.

The second argument of `RequestAdapter` identifies a function to be called when the request for an adapter succeeds or fails. This callback function must return void and accept the four parameters listed in Table B.5.

The second parameter, `adapter`, is the most important because it represents the adapter being requested. But there's an important point to be aware of. The provided structure is a `WGPUAdapter`, which is the C structure defined in webgpu.h. To convert this into an object of the C++ `Adapter` class, the application needs to call the `Acquire` function.

TABLE B.5 Parameters of the `RequestAdapter` callback

PARAMETER	DATA TYPE	DESCRIPTION
status	WGPURequestAdapterStatus	The status of the adapter request
adapter	WGPUAdapter	The requested adapter
message	char*	Message that identifies request result
userdata	void*	Associated user data

The following code demonstrates how an application can request an adapter. It calls the `RequestAdapter` function of the Instance using default settings and specifies that the `adapterCallback` function should be called when the request is complete.

```
// Request default adapter
instance.RequestAdapter(nullptr, adapterCallback, nullptr);

// Function called when request completes
void adapterCallback(WGPURequestAdapterStatus status,
    WGPUAdapter cAdapter, const char* message, void* data) {
    if (status == WGPURequestAdapterStatus_Success) {

        // Convert the C type adapter to the C++ class
        wgpu::Adapter adapter = wgpu::Adapter::Acquire(cAdapter);
    }
    ...
}
```

Looking at this code, it's important to see that the `cAdapter` provided by the function is a C structure. To be accessible in C++, it needs to be converted into an instance of the `Adapter` class, and this is accomplished by calling the `Acquire` function. Applications need to call `Acquire` to convert all such C structures.

After the `Adapter` instance has been acquired, an application can obtain information about the system by calling its functions. Table B.6 lists each of them.

TABLE B.6 Functions of the `Adapter` class

FUNCTION	DESCRIPTION
EnumerateFeatures(FeatureName *feats)	Accesses the GPU's supported features
HasFeature(FeatureName feat)	Identifies if the given feature is supported
GetLimits(SupportedLimits* limits)	Provides maximum values for supported capabilities
GetProperties(AdapterProperties* props)	Identifies properties of the target device
RequestDevice(DeviceDescriptor* desc, RequestDeviceCallback func, void* userdata)	Requests access to device

Chapter 2 explained how to access a device's features and limits in JavaScript. The Adapter functions work in essentially the same way. FeatureName and SupportedLimits are both enumerated types whose values correspond to the feature names and limit names discussed in Chapter 2.

For example, the value corresponding to the support of half-precision floating-point values is FeatureName::ShaderF16. The following code demonstrates how an application can use the Adapter to check for the feature's support:

```
// Acquire adapter
wgpu::Adapter adapter = wgpu::Adapter::Acquire(cAdapter);

// Check for feature availability
if(adapter.HasFeature(wgpu::FeatureName::ShaderF16)) {
    ...
} else {
    ...
}
```

The GetProperties function in the table is like the GPUAdapter's requestAdapterInfo method in JavaScript. It provides a pointer to an AdapterProperties struct whose fields provide information about the vendor, device, and adapter. The driverDescription field contains a text description of the device's driver and the adapterType field identifies the nature of the processor (DiscreteGPU, IntegratedGPU, or CPU).

The RequestDevice function is essentially similar to the RequestAdapter function discussed earlier. The first argument is a DeviceDescriptor that identifies criteria for the target device, and Table B.7 lists its fields.

TABLE B.7   Properties of DeviceDescriptor

FIELD	DATA TYPE	DESCRIPTION
nextInChain	ChainedStruct*	Points to specialized classes
label	char*	Desired label for the device
requiredFeaturesCount	size_t	Desired number of supported features
requiredFeatures	FeatureName*	Desired supported features
requiredLimits	RequiredLimits*	Desired capability limits
defaultQueue	QueueDescriptor	Indicates that only a fallback adapter should be returned
deviceLostCallback	DeviceLostCallback	The callback function to be invoked if the connection to the device is lost
deviceLostUserdata	void*	Data to be provided to the callback if the device connection is broken

TABLE B.8   Parameters of the `RequestDevice` Callback

PARAMETER	DATA TYPE	DESCRIPTION
status	WGPURequestDeviceStatus	The status of the device request
adapter	WGPUDevice	The requested device
message	char*	Message that identifies request result
userdata	void*	Associated user data

The second argument of `RequestDevice` identifies a function to be invoked when the request operation is finished. This callback function must return void and it requires the four parameters listed in Table B.8.

As given in the table, the device object provided by the callback is a `WGPUDevice`, which is a C structure. To make the device accessible in C++ code, the `Acquire` function needs to be called. The following code shows how this works:

```
// Request device
adapter.RequestDevice(nullptr, deviceCallback, nullptr);

// Function called when request completes
void deviceCallback(WGPURequestDeviceStatus status,
    WGPUDevice cDevice, const char* message, void* data) {

    if (status == WGPURequestDeviceStatus_Success) {

        // Convert the C type device to the C++ class
        wgpu::Device device = wgpu::Device::Acquire(cDevice);
    }
    ...
}
```

After acquiring the device, the application can call its functions. Like the `GPUDevice` discussed in Chapter 2, most of these functions create instances of other classes, such as `CreateCommandEncoder` and `CreateBindGroup`. The `GetQueue` function is particularly important because it provides access to the device's queue. The following discussion explains how the `CreateBuffer` function makes it possible to create a vertex buffer.

Vertex Buffer and Layout

To set the triangle's vertices, the application needs to define the vertex coordinates and create a vertex buffer to hold them. The classes and functions that accomplish this are very similar to those discussed in previous chapters.

In code, vertex buffers are represented by instances of the `Buffer` class. To create a `Buffer`, an application needs to call the device's `CreateBuffer` function. This

TABLE B.9   Fields of the `BufferDescriptor` structure

FIELD	DATA TYPE	DESCRIPTION
nextInChain	ChainedStruct*	Points to specialized classes
label	char*	Desired label for the device
usage	BufferUsage	Methods of accessing the buffer
size	uint64_t	Amount of data that can be stored
mappedAtCreation	bool	Identifies if the buffer is mapped to memory when created

accepts a `BufferDescriptor` structure whose fields identify the buffer's properties. Table B.9 lists the different fields that can be set.

The `usage` field is particularly important because it identifies how the buffer can be accessed. This is set to the `BufferUsage` enumerated type, whose possible values are `MapRead`, `MapWrite`, `CopySrc`, `CopyDst`, `Index`, `Vertex`, `Uniform`, `Storage`, `Indirect`, and `QueryResolve`.

For vertex buffers, usage should include the `BufferUsage::Vertex` flag. This is shown in the following code, which creates a `BufferDescriptor`, sets its fields, and uses it to create a `Buffer`.

```
// Create a buffer descriptor and buffer
wgpu::BufferDescriptor buffDesc {
    .usage = wgpu::BufferUsage::Vertex |
wgpu::BufferUsage::CopyDst,
    .size = 24
};
wgpu::Buffer vertexBuffer = device.CreateBuffer(&buffDesc);
```

For the AppB_DawnTriangle project, the application needs to store six floating-point values (two coordinates for each vertex) in the vertex buffer. The array of data can be defined with the following code:

```
// Define vertex data to be stored in the vertex buffer
const float vertexData[6] = { 0.0, 0.5, -0.5, -0.5, 0.5, -0.5 };
```

To write this data to the vertex buffer, the application needs to call the `WriteBuffer` function of the device's queue. This accepts the four arguments listed in Table B.10.

TABLE B.10   Arguments of the `WriteBuffer` function

ARGUMENT	DATA TYPE	DESCRIPTION
buffer	Buffer&	The buffer to receive data
bufferOffset	uint64_t	Byte offset into the buffer for writing data
data	void*	The data to be written to the buffer
size	size_t	The number of bytes to be written

TABLE B.11   Fields of the `VertexBufferLayout` structure

FIELD	DATA TYPE	DESCRIPTION
arrayStride	uint64_t	Number of bytes between each set of attributes
stepMode	VertexStepMode	Indicates if the vertex buffer should be indexed by vertex or by instance
attributeCount	size_t	Number of attributes passed to the vertex shader for each vertex
attributes	VertexAttribute*	Describes each attribute passed to the vertex shader

To demonstrate, the following code accesses the device's queue and calls `WriteBuffer` to encode a command that writes `vertexData` into `vertexBuffer`:

```
// Encode command to write data to buffer
device.GetQueue().WriteBuffer(vertexBuffer, 0, vertexData,
sizeof(vertexData));
```

After creating the vertex buffer, an application needs to define the layout of the data being passed to the vertex shader. This is accomplished by creating a `VertexBufferLayout` structure. Table B.11 lists the fields of this structure and provides a description of each.

In the AppB_DawnTriangle project, the application passes two coordinates to each vertex to sets its location. Each coordinate is given as a floating-point value that occupies four bytes, so `arrayStride` should be set to 8 and `attributeCount` should be set to 1.

To identify the composition of each attribute, the application needs to set the attributes field to an array of `VertexAttribute` structures. Each `VertexAttribute` has three fields, and Table B.12 lists each of them.

The `format` field identifies the number and type of the values that make up the attribute. This must be set to one of the values in the `VertexFormat` enumerated type, which include `Uint8x2`, `Sint32x3`, and `Unorm16x4`. In this example, each attribute contains two 32-bit floating-point values, so format should be set to `Float32x2`.

The `offset` field identifies how many bytes separate the attribute from the start of the element. In this example, each element only has one attribute, so offset will be 0. Similarly, because there's only one attribute per element, `shaderLocation` will be set to 0.

TABLE B.12   Fields of the `VertexAttribute` structure

FIELD	DATA TYPE	DESCRIPTION
format	VertexFormat	The attribute's format
offset	uint64_t	The offset of the attribute in the element
shaderLocation	uint64_t	The location to be associated with the attribute

The following code shows how a `VertexAttribute` structure can be defined in code:

```
// Define the content of the vertex attribute
wgpu::VertexAttribute attr {
    .format = wgpu::VertexFormat::Float32x2,
    .offset = 0,
    .shaderLocation = 0
};
```

Once this is set, the `VertexBufferLayout` structure can be defined with the following code:

```
// Set the layout of the vertex buffer
wgpu::VertexBufferLayout vertLayout {
    .arrayStride = 8,
    .attributeCount = 1,
    .attributes = &attr
};
```

After creating the vertex buffer, setting its data, and defining its layout, the application needs to associate the buffer with the render pass encoder. It also needs to add the layout to the configuration of the render pipeline. These objects will be discussed in the next section.

Creating the Render Pipeline

The render pipeline identifies the sequence of steps to be performed during the render process. For this reason, it's one of the most complex data structures in WebGPU. It can be created by calling the device's `CreateRenderPipeline` function, which accepts a `RenderPipelineDescriptor` structure. Table B.13 lists the fields of this structure and provides a description of each.

Rather than explore each of these fields, this discussion will focus on three crucial topics: defining the pipeline layout, configuring the shader module, and defining the primitive state.

Defining the pipeline layout

In JavaScript, we've set the `layout` argument of `createRenderPipeline` to `auto`, which tells WebGPU to analyze the shader code and automatically create a pipeline layout. But in Dawn, this isn't a possibility. The `layout` field of the `RenderPipelineDescriptor` must be set to a `PipelineLayout`, which can be created by calling the device's `CreatePipelineLayout` function.

`CreatePipelineLayout` accepts a `PipelineLayoutDescriptor`, which describes the relationship between bound resources and the shaders. This structure has four fields and Table B.14 lists each of them.

TABLE B.13   Fields of the `RenderPipelineDescriptor` structure

FIELD	DATA TYPE	DESCRIPTION
nextInChain	ChainedStruct*	Points to specialized classes
label	char*	Desired label for the device
layout	PipelineLayout	Describe the bind groups used by the pipeline
vertex	VertexState	Sets the operation of the vertex shader
primitive	PrimitiveState	Configures how vertices are assembled into primitives
depthStencil	DepthStencilState*	Defines behavior of the depth/stencil buffer
multisample	MultisampleState	Configures multisampling
fragment	FragmentState*	Sets the operation of the fragment shader

As discussed in Chapter 5, a bind group layout describes the resources in a bind group. To set the `bindGroupLayouts` field, an application needs to provide a `BindGroupLayout` for each bind group. An application can create a `BindGroupLayout` by calling the device's `CreateBindGroupLayout` function with a `BindGroupLayoutDescriptor`. Table B.15 lists four of the fields that can be set.

Each entry in a bind group layout corresponds to a resource, such as a texture or uniform buffer, in a bind group. To describe the bind group layout in code, the application needs to set the `entries` field to an array of `BindGroupLayoutEntry` structures. This structure has seven fields and Table B.16 lists each of them.

The `binding` field identifies the integer to which the entry's corresponding resource is bound. To identify the types of shaders that can access the resource, the `visibility` field must be set to one or more of the values of the `ShaderStage` enumerated type: `Vertex`, `Fragment`, or `Compute`.

The remaining fields of the structure identify the properties of the bound resource. For example, suppose a uniform buffer is intended to be accessed by a vertex shader. If the buffer is bound to 0 in the bind group, the following code will create the

TABLE B.14   Fields of the `PipelineLayoutDescriptor` structure

FIELD	DATA TYPE	DESCRIPTION
nextInChain	ChainedStruct*	Points to specialized classes
label	char*	Desired label for the device
bindGroupLayoutCount	size_t	Number of bind group layouts in the pipeline
bindGroupLayouts	BindGroupLayout*	The bind group layouts used by the pipeline

TABLE B.15   Fields of the `BindGroupLayoutDescriptor` structure

FIELD	DATA TYPE	DESCRIPTION
nextInChain	ChainedStruct*	Points to specialized classes
label	char*	Desired label for the device
entryCount	size_t	Number of entries
entries	BindGroupLayoutEntry*	Entries corresponding to resources in the bind group

TABLE B.16   Fields of the `BindGroupLayoutEntry` structure

FIELD	DATA TYPE	DESCRIPTION
nextInChain	ChainedStruct*	Points to specialized classes
binding	uint32_t	Binding number for the resource
visibility	ShaderStage	The shader(s) that can access the resource
buffer	BufferBindingLayout	Describes the bound buffer resource
sampler	SamplerBindingLayout	Describes the bound sampler resource
texture	TextureBindingLayout	Describes the bound texture resource
storageTexture	StorageTextureBindingLayout	Describes the bound storage texture resource

`BindGroupLayoutEntry` that describes the entry corresponding to the uniform buffer in the bind group layout:

```
// Define the buffer binding layout
wgpu::BufferBindingLayout uniformBufferLayout {
    type = BufferBindingType:: Uniform
};

// Define a bind group layout entry for a uniform buffer
wgpu::BindGroupLayoutEntry uniformBufferEntry {
    .binding = 0,
    .visibility = ShaderStage.Vertex,
    .buffer = uniformBufferLayout
};
```

In the AppB_DawnTriangle project, the only resource created by the application is a vertex buffer. This doesn't need to be added to a bind group, so there's no need to create any `BindGroupLayout` or `BindGroupLayoutEntry` objects. However, the pipeline still needs a `PipelineLayout`, which is created with the following code:

```
// Create pipeline layout
wgpu::PipelineLayoutDescriptor plDesc {
    .bindGroupLayoutCount = 0,
    .bindGroupLayouts = nullptr
};
wgpu::PipelineLayout pipelineLayout =
device.CreatePipelineLayout(&plDesc);
```

After creating this layout, the application can set it equal to the `layout` field of the `RenderPipelineDescriptor`.

Shader modules and shader states

The `RenderPipelineDescriptor` has two fields related to shaders. The `vertex` field needs to be set to a `VertexState` structure and the `fragment` field needs to be set to a `FragmentState` structure. Both structures need to access a `ShaderModule` that contains the shader code.

To create the `ShaderModule`, an application needs to call the device's `CreateShaderModule` function, which accepts a `ShaderModuleDescriptor`. The only fields of this descriptor are `nextInChain` and `label`.

Here's where coding gets tricky. In addition to supporting multiple rendering frameworks, Dawn supports multiple shader languages. For this reason, it has a `ShaderModuleSPIRVDescriptor` structure for shaders coded with SPIR-V and a `ShaderModuleWGSLDescriptor` structure for shaders coded with WGSL. Both structures have a field named `code` that should be set to the shader code.

If the shaders are written in WGSL, the `ShaderModule`'s `nextInChain` field should be set to a `ShaderModuleWGSLDescriptor` reference. If the WGSL shader code is contained in `shaderCode`, the following code will create the `ShaderModule`:

```
// Create shader module
wgpu::ShaderModuleWGSLDescriptor wgslDesc{};
wgslDesc.code = shaderCode;
wgpu::ShaderModuleDescriptor shaderDesc {
    .nextInChain = &wgslDesc
};
wgpu::ShaderModule shaderModule =
device.CreateShaderModule(&shaderDesc);
```

Once the shader module is created, the application can define the `VertexState` that must be assigned to the `vertex` field of the pipeline descriptor. Table B.17 lists the seven fields of this structure:

Chapter 4 introduced the topic of constants, which make it possible for applications to pass key-value pairs to shaders. Dawn provides a similar capability through the `constants` field of the `VertexState`, which can be set to one or more

TABLE B.17   Fields of the `VertexState` structure

FIELD	DATA TYPE	DESCRIPTION
nextInChain	ChainedStruct*	Points to specialized classes
module	ShaderModule	Contains shader code
entryPoint	char const*	Entry point of the vertex shader
constantCount	size_t	Number of constants passed to the vertex shader
constants	ConstantEntry*	Key-value pairs to be passed to the vertex shader
bufferCount	size_t	Number of vertex buffers
buffers	VertexBufferLayout*	Layouts of the vertex buffers

ConstantEntry structures. Each ConstantEntry has a key field and a value field, which can be accessed in the vertex shader through overridden variables.

The last two fields in the table relate to buffers. The bufferCount field identifies how many vertex buffers are available, and the buffers field identifies the layout of each buffer. Keep in mind that buffers must be set to the buffer layouts, not the buffers themselves.

The code in the AppB_DawnTriangle project doesn't use constants and only has one buffer, so the VertexState structure is created with the following code:

```
// Create vertex state
wgpu::VertexState vertexState {
    .module = shaderModule,
    .entryPoint = "vertexMain",
    .bufferCount = 1,
    .buffers = &vertLayout
};
```

Just as the VertexState defines the operation of the vertex shader, the FragmentState structure defines the operation of the fragment shader. Table B.18 lists the fields of this structure.

TABLE B.18   Fields of the `FragmentState` structure

FIELD	DATA TYPE	DESCRIPTION
nextInChain	ChainedStruct*	Points to specialized classes
module	ShaderModule	Contains the shader code
entryPoint	char const*	Entry point of the fragment shader
constantCount	size_t	Number of constants passed to the fragment shader
constants	ConstantEntry*	Key-value pairs to be passed to the fragment shader
targetCount	size_t	Number of vertex buffers
targets	ColorTargetState*	Layouts of the vertex buffers

Most of the `FragmentState` fields are identical to those in the `VertexState` structure, but the `targetCount` and targets fields are new. The `targets` field must be set to one or more `ColorTargetState` structures that configure the colors produced by the fragment shader.

The `ColorTargetState` structure has a `format` field that must be set to one of the texture formats presented in Chapter 6. The following code configures the fragment shader to produce colors containing blue, green, red, and alpha components as 8-bit unsigned normalized values.

```
// Define the color state
wgpu::ColorTargetState colorTargetState {
    .format = wgpu::TextureFormat::BGRA8Unorm
};
```

After creating this, the code in the AppB_DawnTriangle creates the FragmentState structure with the following code:

```
// Create fragment state
wgpu::FragmentState fragmentState {
    .module = shaderModule,
    .entryPoint = "fragmentMain",
    .targetCount = 1,
    .targets = &colorTargetState
};
```

After creating the `VertexState` and `FragmentState`, the application assigns the structures to the vertex and fragment fields of the `PipelineDescriptor`.

Assembling primitives

By default, Dawn creates one triangle from the first three vertices, another triangle from the next three vertices, and so on. This method of assembly corresponds to the *triangle list*, and it's one of the many features that can be configured by setting the `primitive` field of the `PipelineDescriptor` to a `PrimitiveState` structure. Table B.19 lists the five fields of this structure.

The `topology` field tells the renderer how to form shapes from vertices. This can be set to any value of the `PrimititveTopology` type, which includes `PointList`, `LineList`, `LineStrip`, `TriangleList`, and `TriangleStrip`.

An earlier chapter explained how an application can improve performance by discarding (or *culling*) triangles. With Dawn, configuring the culling process requires two steps. First, the `frontFace` field needs to identify the vertex orientation of triangles considered to be front-facing. This can be set to `FrontFace::CW` and `FrontFace::CCW`. By default, triangles with vertices oriented in a counter-clockwise fashion are considered facing the front.

The `cullMode` identifies which triangles should be discarded from rendering. This must be set to a value of the `CullMode` type, which includes `None`, `Front`, and `Back`. By default, the renderer doesn't discard any triangles.

TABLE B.19 Fields of the `PrimitiveState` structure

FIELD	DATA TYPE	DESCRIPTION
nextInChain	ChainedStruct*	Points to specialized classes
topology	PrimitiveTopology	Sets the type of primitive to be assembled
stripIndexFormat	IndexFormat	The data type of the vertex indices
frontFace	FrontFace	The orientation of triangles considered to be front-facing
cullMode	CullMode	Identifies which triangles should be discarded

The code in the AppB_DawnTriangle sets the renderer to assemble triangle strips and leaves the rest of the fields to their default values. The following code shows how this works:

```
// Set the primitive state
wgpu::PrimitiveState primitiveState {
    .topology = wgpu::PrimitiveTopology::TriangleStrip
};
```

After creating this structure, the AppB_DawnTriangle application assigns it to the `primitive` field of the `PipelineDescriptor`. The following discussion looks at this important structure.

Creating the pipeline

The AppB_DawnTriangle project doesn't use multisampling or a depth/stencil buffer. Therefore, the only fields that need to be set of the `PipelineDescriptor` are `layout`, `vertex`, `shader`, and `primitive`. The following code shows how these fields are set using the structures created earlier.

```
// Create the render pipeline
wgpu::RenderPipelineDescriptor pipelineDescriptor{
    .layout = pipelineLayout,
    .vertex = vertexState,
    .primitive = primitiveState,
    .fragment = &fragmentState
};
pipeline = device.CreateRenderPipeline(&pipelineDescriptor);
```

Once the pipeline descriptor is created, the application can associate it with a render pass encoder. But before the render pass encoder can be created, the application needs to define the surface and swapchain for rendering.

Surface and Swapchain

If you're writing WebGPU code to run in a browser, you don't need to be concerned about low-level rendering details. However, Dawn's rendering isn't limited to browsers. For this reason, Dawn applications need to precisely define how and where rendering will be performed.

To define the rendering procedure at a low level, an application needs to create a `Surface`, which identifies the abstract region for rendering. It also needs to create a `Swapchain`, which controls how rendering is performed. This discussion explains how to create both data structures.

Creating a surface

Dawn provides a `Surface` class to represent the rendering region. To create a `Surface`, applications need to call the `createSurface` function of the `Instance` object. This accepts a `SurfaceDescriptor`, which has two fields: `nextInChain` and `label`.

The AppB_DawnTriangle application runs in a browser and uses an HTML canvas as its rendering surface. For this reason, it needs to set the `nextInChain` field of the `SurfaceDescriptor` to point to a `SurfaceDescriptorFrom` `CanvasHTMLSelector`. This has a `selector` field that identifies the canvas to serve as the rendering surface.

The following code demonstrates how the `Surface` and `SurfaceDescriptor` `FromCanvasHTMLSelector` classes work together to identify the HTML canvas. In this case, the element's ID in the web page is canvas.

```
// Create the rendering surface
wgpu::SurfaceDescriptorFromCanvasHTMLSelector canvasDesc{};
canvasDesc.selector = "#canvas";
wgpu::SurfaceDescriptor surfDesc {
    .nextInChain = &canvasDesc
};
wgpu::Surface surface = instance.CreateSurface(&surfDesc);
```

Once an application has created a `Surface` for rendering, it can create a `Swapchain` that configures the rendering process. I'll discuss this next.

Creating a Swapchain

In the early days of computer graphics, applications drew graphics by writing values to a special memory region called the *framebuffer*. Once the writing was finished, the framebuffer's graphics would be displayed.

As computers became more capable, double-buffering became possible. This improved performance by allowing an application to write to one buffer while a second buffer's content was displayed. When the writing was finished, the buffers would be swapped.

TABLE B.20   Fields of the `SwapChainDescriptor` structure

FIELD	DATA TYPE	DESCRIPTION
nextInChain	ChainedStruct*	Points to specialized classes
label	char const*	Text identifier
usage	TextureUsage	How the swapchain data will be used
format	TextureFormat	Format of the swapchain's color data
width	uint32_t	Width of the rendering area
height	uint32_t	Height of the rendering area
presentMode	PresentMode	How quickly attachments are displayed

In modern computers, the framebuffer has several rendering areas called *attachments*, and they're managed by a central object called a *swapchain*. Unlike regular WebGPU, Dawn requires that you create a `Swapchain` object that defines how framebuffers should be processed. To create this, an application needs to call the device's `CreateSwapChain` function with a `Surface` and a `SwapChainDescriptor`.

The `SwapChainDescriptor` sets the properties of the swapchain's operation. Table B.20 lists each of its fields.

The `usage` field identifies how the swapchain will be used and is similar to WebGPU's usage field when creating a texture. This is set to a value of the `TextureUsage` type, which includes `CopySrc`, `CopyDst`, `TextureBinding`, `StorageBinding`, and `RenderAttachment`. Most applications will set usage to `TextureUsage::RenderAttachment`.

The `format` field identifies the structure of the swapchain's color data. In JavaScript, this will usually be set to the preferred format of the HTML canvas. But with Dawn, this needs to be set manually, and the two most popular choices are `TextureFormat::BGRA8Unorm` and `TextureFormat::RGBA8Unorm`. The `width` and `height` fields also need to be set manually, without being able to access the canvas element.

If the renderer sends images to be displayed faster than the refresh rate, multiple buffers may be displayed at once. This is called *screen tearing*. To prevent this from happening, the display can provide a signal that tells the renderer when it's ready to display a new image. This is called vertical synchronization and the signal is commonly called *v-sync*. The `presentMode` field identifies how the renderer responds to synchronization signals. This is set to a value of the `PresentMode` type, which includes `Immediate`, `Fifo`, and `Mailbox`.

If `presentMode` is set to `PresentMode::Immediate`, the renderer won't wait for synchronization signals—it provides images as soon as they become available. This provides the fastest rendering results, but because multiple images may be sent to the display at once, screen tearing is likely to occur.

If `presentMode` is set to `PresentMode::Fifo`, images will be stored in a first-in, first-out (FIFO) data structure. With each v-sync signal, the images shift position and the first image is dispatched for display. Figure B.1 gives an idea of what this looks like if four images are available.

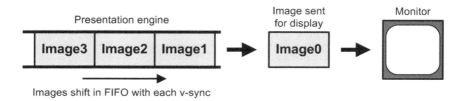

FIGURE B.1   Presenting images in FIFO mode.

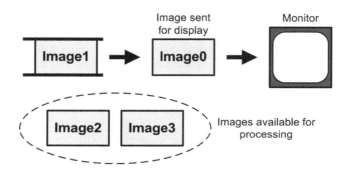

FIGURE B.2   Presenting images in Mailbox mode.

FIFO mode doesn't display images as quickly as immediate mode, but it guarantees that only one image will be displayed at a time. From what I've seen, FIFO mode is much more popular than Immediate mode.

If `presentMode` is set to `PresentMode::Mailbox`, images won't be stored in a FIFO. Instead, the swapchain will only provide an image when a v-sync signal is received. As a result, other images can be accessed by the application. Figure B.2 shows what this looks like.

In general, if performance without tearing is a chief concern, Mailbox mode should be preferred to FIFO mode. However, it's likely that the extra images rendered through Mailbox mode may be discarded. Therefore, if power consumption is a major concern, FIFO mode should be selected.

In the AppB_DawnTriangle code, the swapchain is configured to present images to the surface created from the HTML canvas. Each color should use the `BGRA8Unorm` format, the rendering area should be 400-by-400 pixels, and the presentation mode should be set to FIFO mode. This is accomplished with the following code.

```
// Create the swapchain
wgpu::SwapChainDescriptor swapDesc {
    .usage = wgpu::TextureUsage::RenderAttachment,
    .format = wgpu::TextureFormat::BGRA8Unorm,
    .width = 400,
```

```
    .height = 400,
    .presentMode = wgpu::PresentMode::Fifo,
};
wgpu::SwapChain swapChain = device.CreateSwapChain(surface,
&swapDesc);
```

After creating the `SwapChain`, the application can call its two functions, `GetCurrentTextureView` and `Present`. `GetCurrentTextureView` returns a texture view that can be used to create the render pass attachment.

Encoders and Commands

At this point, we've created most of the descriptors and state objects that Dawn needs to launch the rendering process. But three more steps are necessary:

1. Create and configure a command encoder.
2. Create and configure a render pass encoder.
3. Submit commands to the device's queue.

This section explains how these steps can be performed in a Dawn application.

Creating the command encoder

As discussed in Chapter 2, a command encoder stores commands intended for the GPU and provides them in a command buffer. To create a command encoder in Dawn, an application needs to call the device's `CreateCommandEncoder` function. This accepts a `CommandEncoderDescriptor`, but because this object only has two fields (`nextInChain` and `label`), the descriptor is optional.

As a result, the code in AppB_DawnTriangle can create the command encoder without any arguments:

```
wgpu::CommandEncoder encoder = device.CreateCommandEncoder();
```

After creating the `CommandEncoder`, an application can call its functions. Table B.21 lists 11 of them and provides a description of each.

Of these functions, only two are necessary in rendering applications. The `BeginRenderPass` function provides a render pass encoder that can be used to define the rendering process. The `Finish` function is needed to end the encoding.

Creating the render pass encoder

In Dawn, the render pass encoder is represented by the `RenderPassEncoder` class, and an application can create an instance by calling the `BeginRenderPass` function of the `CommandEncoder`. This requires a `RenderPassDescriptor` that defines properties of the rendering to be performed. Table B.22 lists the fields of this structure.

TABLE B.21   Functions of the `CommandEncoder` class

FUNCTION	DESCRIPTION
`BeginRenderPass(RenderPassDescriptor const* desc)`	Starts encoding commands for a render pass
`BeginComputePass(ComputePassDescriptor const* descriptor)`	Starts encoding commands for a compute pass
`ClearBuffer(Buffer& buff, uint64_t offset, uint64_t size)`	Clears the content of the given buffer
`CopyBufferToBuffer(Buffer& src, uint64_t sourceOffset, Buffer& destination, uint64_t destinationOffset, uint64_t size)`	Copies the content of one buffer to another
`CopyBufferToTexture(ImageCopyBuffer *src, ImageCopyTexture* dst, Extent3D const* copySize`	Copies the content of a buffer to a texture
`CopyTextureToBuffer(ImageCopyTexture *src, ImageCopyBuffer *dst, Extent3D const* copySize)`	Copies the content of a texture to a buffer
`CopyTextureToTexture(ImageCopyTexture *src, ImageCopyTexture *dst, Extent3D const* copySize)`	Copies the content of one texture to another
`Finish(CommandBufferDescriptor *desc)`	Ends the encoder's command recording
`InsertDebugMarker(char const* label)`	Add message to be displayed during debugging
`SetLabel(char const *label)`	Set label for the encoder to be displayed during debugging
`WriteTimestamp(QuerySet& set, uint32_t index)`	Add timestamp query to query set

TABLE B.22   Fields of the `RenderPassDescriptor` structure

FIELD	DATA TYPE	DESCRIPTION
`nextInChain`	`ChainedStruct*`	Points to specialized classes
`label`	`char const*`	Text identifier
`colorAttachmentCount`	`size_t`	Number of color attachments
`colorAttachments`	`RenderPassColorAttachment*`	Color attachments
`depthStencil Attachment`	`RenderPassDepth StencilAttachment*`	Depth/stencil attachments
`occlusionQuerySet`	`QuerySet`	Container of occlusion queries
`timestampWrites`	`RenderPassTimestampWrites*`	Timestamp configuration

TABLE B.23   Fields of the `RenderPassColorAttachment` structure

FIELD	DATA TYPE	DESCRIPTION
nextInChain	ChainedStruct*	Points to specialized classes
view	TextureView	Resource accessed by the color attachment
resolveTarget	TextureView	Subresource affected by the color attachment if multisampling is enabled
loadOp	LoadOp	How the view's initial color should be set
storeOp	StoreOp	Identifies if the view's color should be stored after the render pass
clearValue	Color	Color to serve as the view's initial color

Most of these fields are optional, but every rendering application needs to identify the color attachment(s) that serves as the basis for rendering. This requires creating one or more `RenderPassColorAttachment` structures, and Table B.23 lists each of its fields.

The most important field is `view`, which identifies the texture that serves as the target of the rendering process. If a `SwapChain` has been created, this field can be assigned to the result of the `SwapChain`'s `GetCurrentTextureView` function.

The `loadOp` field identifies how the view's initial content should be set. If `loadOp` is set to `LoadOp::Load`, the view will retain its existing data. If it's set to `LoadOp::Clear`, the view's content will be set to the `Color` given by the `clearValue` field. In Dawn, `Color` is a structure with four fields of type `double`: r, g, b, and a.

The `storeOp` field specifies if the view's data should be stored when rendering is complete. If this is set to `StoreOp::Store`, the view's content will be stored after rendering. If it's set to `StoreOp::Discard`, the view's data will be discarded.

In the AppB_DawnTriangle project, the rendering is associated to the canvas through the `SwapChain` created earlier. This association is created by setting the `view` field to the `SwapChain`'s current texture view.

The initial content of the canvas should be set to light gray. To accomplish this, the `loadOp` field must be set to `LoadOp::Clear` and the `clearValue` field must be set to a `Color` structure whose components are (0.9, 0.9, 0.9, 1.0). The following code shows how this can be done:

```
// Define render pass color attachment
wgpu::RenderPassColorAttachment attachment {
    .view = swapChain.GetCurrentTextureView(),
    .loadOp = wgpu::LoadOp::Clear,
    .storeOp = wgpu::StoreOp::Store,
    .clearValue = {
        .r = 0.9,
        .g = 0.9,
        .b = 0.9,
        .a = 1.0 }
};
```

Once the `RenderPassColorAttachment` is created, the application can set the `colorAttachmentCount` and `colorAttachments` fields of a `RenderPassDescriptor`. Then it can obtain a render pass encoder by calling the `BeginRenderPass` function of the `CommandEncoder`. The following code shows how this can be done:

```
// Create render pass encoder
wgpu::RenderPassDescriptor renderDesc {
    .colorAttachmentCount = 1,
    .colorAttachments = &attachment
};
wgpu::RenderPassEncoder renderPass =
encoder.BeginRenderPass(&renderDesc);
```

After obtaining a `RenderPassEncoder`, an application can configure the rendering process by calling its functions. This discussion focuses on the functions that associate the encoder with other rendering objects and functions that launch the drawing process. Table B.24 lists the functions that associate the encoder with objects.

TABLE B.24   `RenderPassEncoder` functions that associate objects

FUNCTION	DESCRIPTION
`SetBindGroup(uint32_t index, BindGroup& group, size_t dynamicOffsetCount, uint32_t* dynamicOffsets)`	Associate the bind group with the encoder at the given index
`SetBlendConstant(Color* color)`	Associate the encoder with the color used for blending
`SetIndexBuffer(Buffer& buffer, IndexFormat format, uint64_t offset, uint64_t size)`	Set the buffer containing index values to be used during rendering
`SetLabel(char* label)`	Associate the label with the encoder to be displayed during debugging
`SetPipeline(RenderPipeline& pipeline)`	Set the render pipeline to be used during the render process
`SetScissorRect(uint32_t x, uint32_t y, uint32_t width, uint32_t height)`	Select a rectangular region to be displayed in the rendering
`SetStencilReference(uint32_t reference)`	Sets reference value to be used during stencil tests
`SetVertexBuffer(uint32_t slot, Buffer& buffer, uint64_t offset, uint64_t size)`	Associate the encoder with a buffer containing vertex data
`SetViewport(float x, float y, float width, float height, float minDepth, float maxDepth)`	Define the viewport used for rendering

TABLE B.25   `RenderPassEncoder` functions for drawing

FUNCTION	DESCRIPTION

`Draw(uint32_t vCount, uint32_t iCount,`
`uint32_t firstVertex, uint32_t`
`firstInstance)`
	Draws vertices based on their order in the vertex buffer

`DrawIndexed(uint32_t iCount, uint32_t`
`instanceCount, uint32_t firstIndex,`
`int32_t baseVertex, uint32_t firstInstance)`
	Draws vertices in the order given by the values in the index buffer

`DrawIndirect(Buffer const& indirectBuffer,` `uint64_t indirectOffset)`	Draws vertices in order based on parameters in an indirect buffer
`DrawIndexedIndirect(Buffer const&` `indirectBuffer, uint64_t indirectOffset)`	Draws vertices according to index based on parameters in an indirect buffer
`End()`	Complete recording of rendering commands

Most of these functions have been discussed in preceding chapters, and are straightforward to use and understand. The code in the AppB_DawnTriangle project uses two of these functions: `SetPipeline` and `SetVertexBuffer`. This is shown in the following code:

```
// Create associations for the render pass encoder
renderPass.SetPipeline(pipeline);
renderPass.SetVertexBuffer(0, vertexBuffer);
```

After creating and configuring the render pass encoder, the application calls its functions that perform drawing operations. Table B.25 lists the functions involved.

The AppB_DawnTriangle project doesn't use an index buffer or an indirect buffer, so it calls `Draw`. This tells the renderer to access attributes in the order in which they're stored in the vertex buffer. Then the application calls the `End` function to complete the encoding of rendering commands.

```
// Launch draw operation
renderPass.Draw(3);
renderPass.End();
```

At this point, the render pass encoder has completed encoding the rendering commands. To send these commands to the GPU, the application needs to perform two steps:

1. Obtain the `CommandBuffer` by calling the `CommandEncoder`'s `Finish` function.
2. Submit the commands to the device by calling the `Queue`'s `Submit` function with the `CommandBuffer`.

The following code shows how this works. The application accesses the Queue by calling the device's GetQueue function and then passes it the CommandBuffer.

```
// Send the rendering commands to the GPU
wgpu::CommandBuffer commands = encoder.Finish();
device.GetQueue().Submit(1, &commands);
```

Unlike the submit method in JavaScript, Dawn's Submit function can accept multiple command buffers. The first argument identifies the number of command buffers and the second argument points to them.

EXAMPLE PROJECT—DRAWING AN ORANGE TRIANGLE

This section has discussed the code in the AppB_Triangle project at length, so you should have a solid understanding of the code in the dawn_triangle.cpp source file.

However, the Makefile in the AppB_DawnTriangle project is different from the Makefile in the AppB_SimpleWasm project. Its content is given as follows:

```
PROJ=dawn_triangle

CPP=em++

CPPFLAGS=-sUSE_WEBGPU=1 -std=c++17

$(PROJ).js: $(PROJ).cpp
        $(CPP) $(CPPFLAGS) -o $@ $^

.PHONY: clean

clean:
        rm $(PROJ).js $(PROJ).wasm
```

While the preceding Makefile told Emscripten to create a WebAssembly module (*.wasm), this Makefile tells Emscripten to compile the C++ code into a JavaScript file (*.js). This is important to understand. If you run the build with emmake make, you'll see that Emscripten produces two files: a JavaScript file and a WebAssembly module.

If you look at the JavaScript file, you'll see that its content is practically unreadable. So you may wonder how you're supposed to access WebAssembly and launch the rendering application. As it happens, the JavaScript code will handle this for you. That is, it will load WebAssembly and execute its main function when the code is invoked.

The good news is that you don't have to export functions or call WebAssembly methods in JavaScript. The bad news is that you lose control of executing your code.

SUMMARY

At the time I write this, WebAssembly hasn't made a major impact on web development. Professional developers argue over JavaScript frameworks and laugh at the idea of using anything besides JavaScript. Despite this, WebAssembly development provides two major advantages: improved performance and the ability to compile high-level languages to WebAssembly.

The first part of this appendix showed how Emscripten makes it possible to compile C++ code to WebAssembly. This discussion introduced the em++ compiler and its many flags, as well as the emmake tool. This section also explained how to write Makefiles capable of telling Emscripten how C++ code should be compiled.

The rest of the appendix focused on Dawn, Google's unofficial implementation of WebGPU. Dawn makes it possible to run WebGPU on multiple platforms, and this appendix has focused on running WebGPU in Emscripten. More precisely, this appendix explained how to code a C++ application that uses Dawn to render an orange triangle in an HTML canvas.

While drawing a triangle may not seem interesting, the potential advantages of combining Dawn and WebAssembly are very exciting. Developers of high-performance graphical applications, such as computer-aided drafting (CAD) and games, will be able to run their code in a browser without significant loss of performance and without needing to learn a new language.

Index

Note: Page numbers in **bold** and *italics* refer to tables and figures, respectively.